C000264751

Atlas symbols

Scale 1:250,000 or 3.95 miles to 1 inch (2.5km to 1cm) Some islands are shown at smaller scales and Ireland at 1:1,000,000 scale.

Motoring information

M4	Motorway with number	Restricted primary route junctions	Narrow primary/other A/B road with passing places (Scotland)	Railway line, in tunnel	Safety camera site (fixed location) with speed limit in mph
Toll	Toll motorway with toll station	Primary route service area	Road under construction	Railway station and level crossing	Section of road with two or more fixed safety cameras, with speed limit in mph
	Motorway junction with and without number	BATH Primary route destination	Road tunnel	Tourist railway	Average speed (SPECS™) camera system with speed limit in mph
	Restricted motorway junctions	A1123 Other A road single/dual carriageway	Road toll, steep gradient (arrows point downhill)	City, town, village or other built-up area	Fixed safety camera site with variable speed limit
	Motorway service area	B2070 B road single/dual carriageway	Distance in miles between symbols	Airport, heliport, international freight terminal	Height in metres
	Motorway and junction under construction	Minor road more than 4 metres wide, less than 4 metres wide	Park and Ride (at least 6 days per week)	24-hour Accident & Emergency hospital	Mountain pass
	Primary route single/dual carriageway	Roundabout	Vehicle ferry	Crematorium	National boundary
	Primary route junction with and without number	Interchange/junction	Fast vehicle ferry or catamaran	Sandy beach	County, administrative boundary

Touring information   To avoid disappointment, check opening times before visiting.

Scenic route	Museum or art gallery	Aquarium	Steam railway centre	National Trust for Scotland property
Tourist Information Centre	Industrial interest	National Nature Reserve (England, Scotland, Wales)	Cave	English Heritage site
Tourist Information Centre (seasonal)	Aqueduct or viaduct	Local nature reserve	Windmill, monument	Historic Scotland site
Visitor or heritage centre	Garden	Wildlife Trust reserve	Golf course (AA listed)	Cadw (Welsh heritage) site
Picnic site	Arboretum	RSPB	County cricket ground	Other place of interest
Caravan site (AA inspected)	Vineyard	Forest drive	Rugby Union national stadium	Boxed symbols indicate attractions within urban areas
Camping site (AA inspected)	Country park	National trail	International athletics stadium	World Heritage Site (UNESCO)
Caravan & camping site (AA inspected)	Agricultural showground	Viewpoint	Horse racing, show jumping	National Park
Abbey, cathedral or priory	Theme park	Hill-fort	Motor-racing circuit	National Scenic Area (Scotland)
Ruined abbey, cathedral or priory	Farm or animal centre	Roman antiquity	Air show venue	Forest Park
Castle	Zoological or wildlife collection	Prehistoric monument	Ski slope (natural, artificial)	Heritage coast
Historic house or building	Bird collection	Battle site with year	National Trust property	Major shopping centre

34th edition June 2014

© AA Media Limited 2014

Revised version of the atlas formerly known as *AA Big Road Atlas*. Original edition printed 1981.

Cartography:
All cartography in this atlas edited, designed and produced by the Mapping Services Department of AA Publishing (A05188).

This atlas contains Ordnance Survey data © Crown copyright and database right 2014 and Royal Mail data © Royal Mail copyright and database right 2014.

This is based upon Crown Copyright and is reproduced with the permission of Land & Property Services under delegated authority from the Controller of Her Majesty's Stationery Office, © Crown copyright and database right 2014. PMLPA No. 100497.

© Ordnance Survey Ireland/Government of Ireland Copyright Permit No. MP0000314.

Ireland's National Mapping Agency

Publisher's notes:
Published by AA Publishing (a trading name of AA Media Limited, whose registered office is Fanum House, Basing View, Basingstoke, Hampshire RG21 4EA, UK. Registered number 06112600).
All rights reserved. No part of this publication may be reproduced, stored in a retrieval system, or transmitted in any form or by any means – electronic, mechanical, photocopying, recording or otherwise – unless the permission of the publisher has been given beforehand.

A CIP catalogue record for this book is available from The British Library.

Disclaimer:
The contents of this atlas are believed to be correct at the time of the latest revision, it will not include any subsequent amended, new or temporary information including diversions and traffic control or enforcement systems. The publishers cannot be held responsible or liable for any loss or damage occasioned to any person acting or refraining from action as a result of any use or reliance on material in this atlas, nor for any errors, omissions or changes in such material. This does not affect your statutory rights.

The publishers would welcome information to correct any errors or omissions and to keep this atlas up to date. Please write to the Atlas Editor, AA Publishing, The Automobile Association, Fanum House, Basing View, Basingstoke, Hampshire RG21 4EA, UK. E-mail: *roadatlasfeedback@theaa.com*

Acknowledgements:
AA Publishing would like to thank the following for their assistance in producing this atlas:
RoadPilot® Information on fixed speed camera locations provided by and © 2014 RoadPilot® Driving Technology.
Crematoria data provided by the Cremation Society of Great Britain. Cadw, English Heritage, Forestry Commission, Historic Scotland, Johnsons, National Trust and National Trust for Scotland, RSPB, The Wildlife Trust, Scottish Natural Heritage, Natural England, The Countryside Council for Wales (road maps).

Printer:
Printed in Britain by Wyndeham Peterborough Ltd.

Map pages & route planner

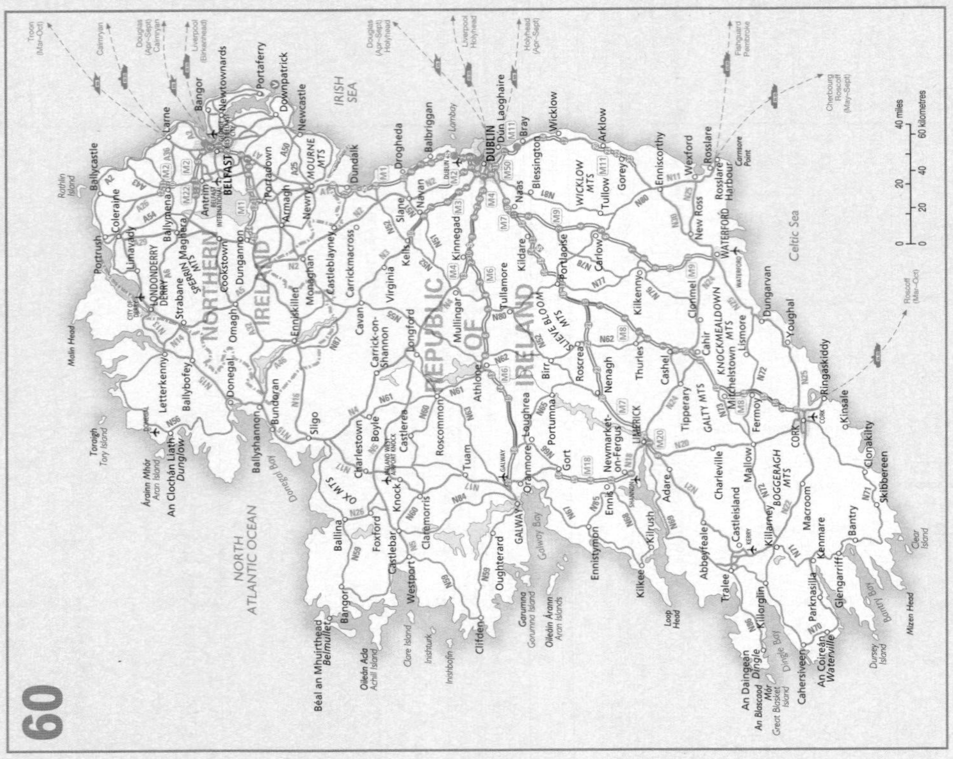

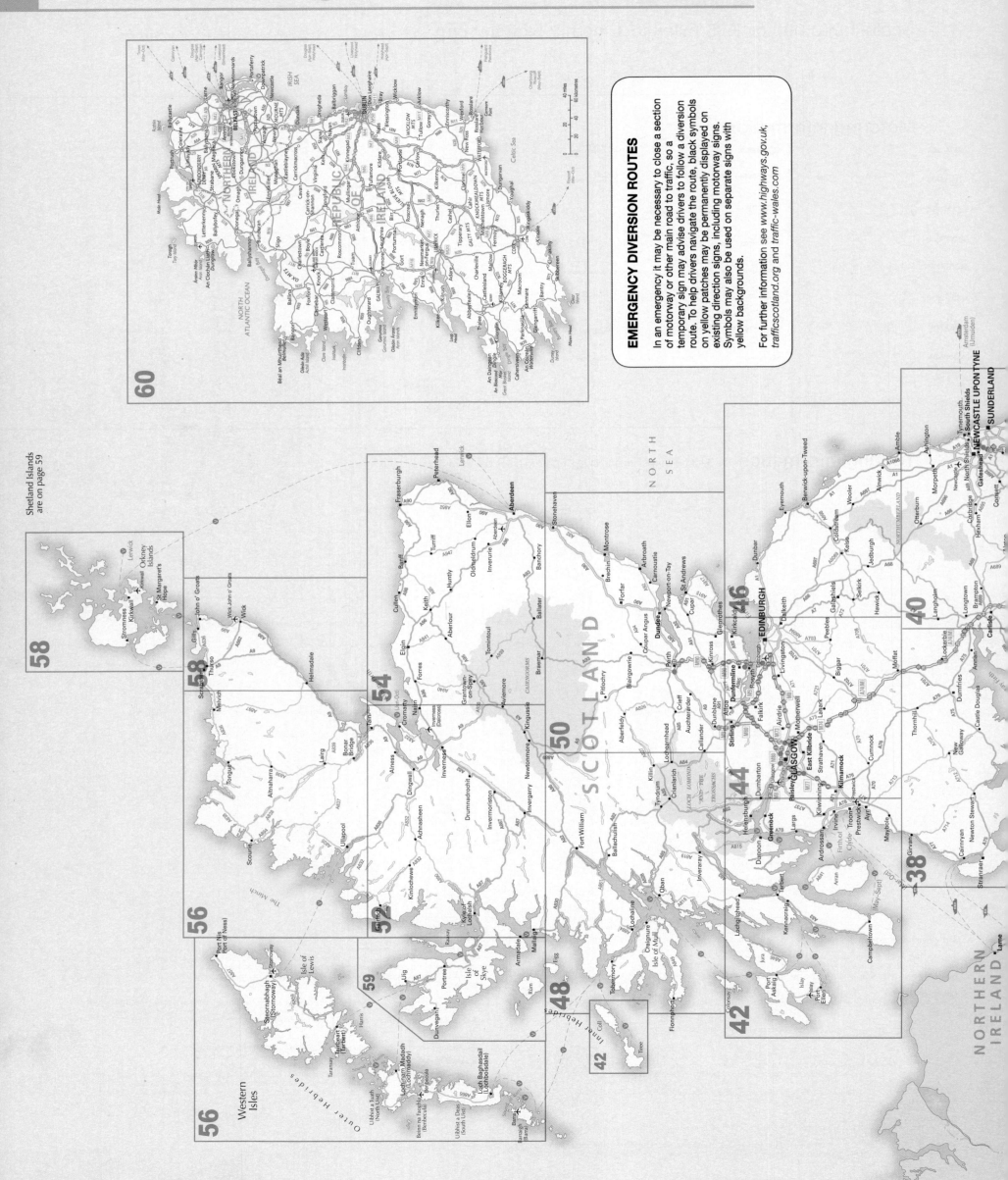

Shetland Islands are on page 59

EMERGENCY DIVERSION ROUTES

In an emergency it may be necessary to close a section of motorway or other main road to traffic, so a temporary sign may advise drivers to follow a diversion route. To help drivers navigate the route, black symbols on yellow patches may be permanently displayed on existing direction signs, including motorway signs. Symbols may also be used on separate signs with yellow backgrounds.

For further information see www.highways.gov.uk, trafficscotland.org and traffic-wales.com

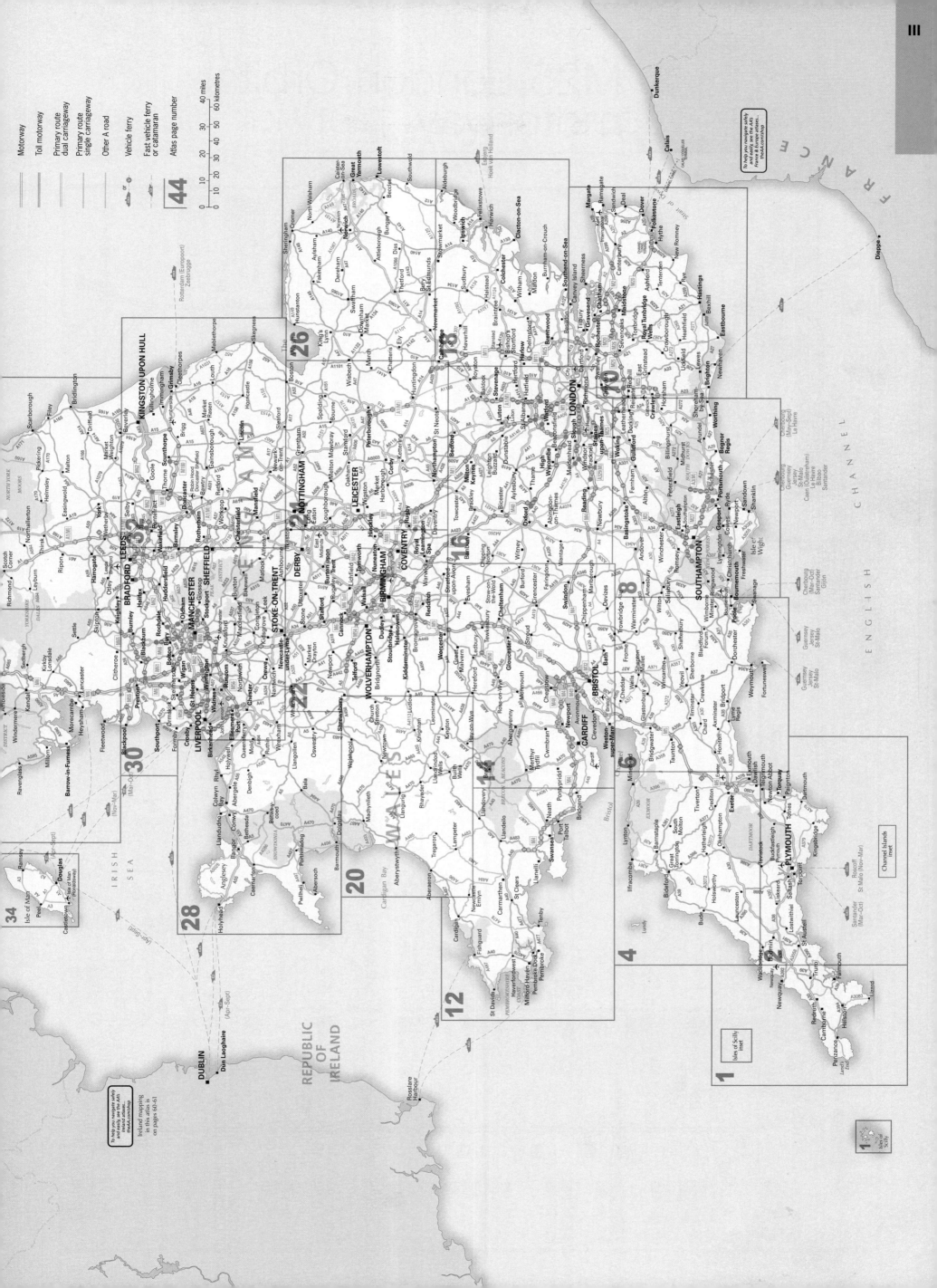

Motorway

Toll motorway

Primary route
dual carriageway

Primary route
single carriageway

Other A road

Vehicle ferry

Fast vehicle ferry
or catamaran

44 Atlas page number

0   10   20   30   40 miles
0 10 20 30 40 50 60 kilometres

To help you navigate safely
and easily, see the AA's
France & Europe atlases...
theAA.com/shop

To help you navigate safely
and easily, see the AA's
Ireland atlases...
theAA.com/shop

Ireland mapping
in this atlas is
on pages 60-61

Isle of Scilly
inset

Channel Islands
inset

M25 London Orbital motorway

Refer also to atlas pages 9–10 and 17–18

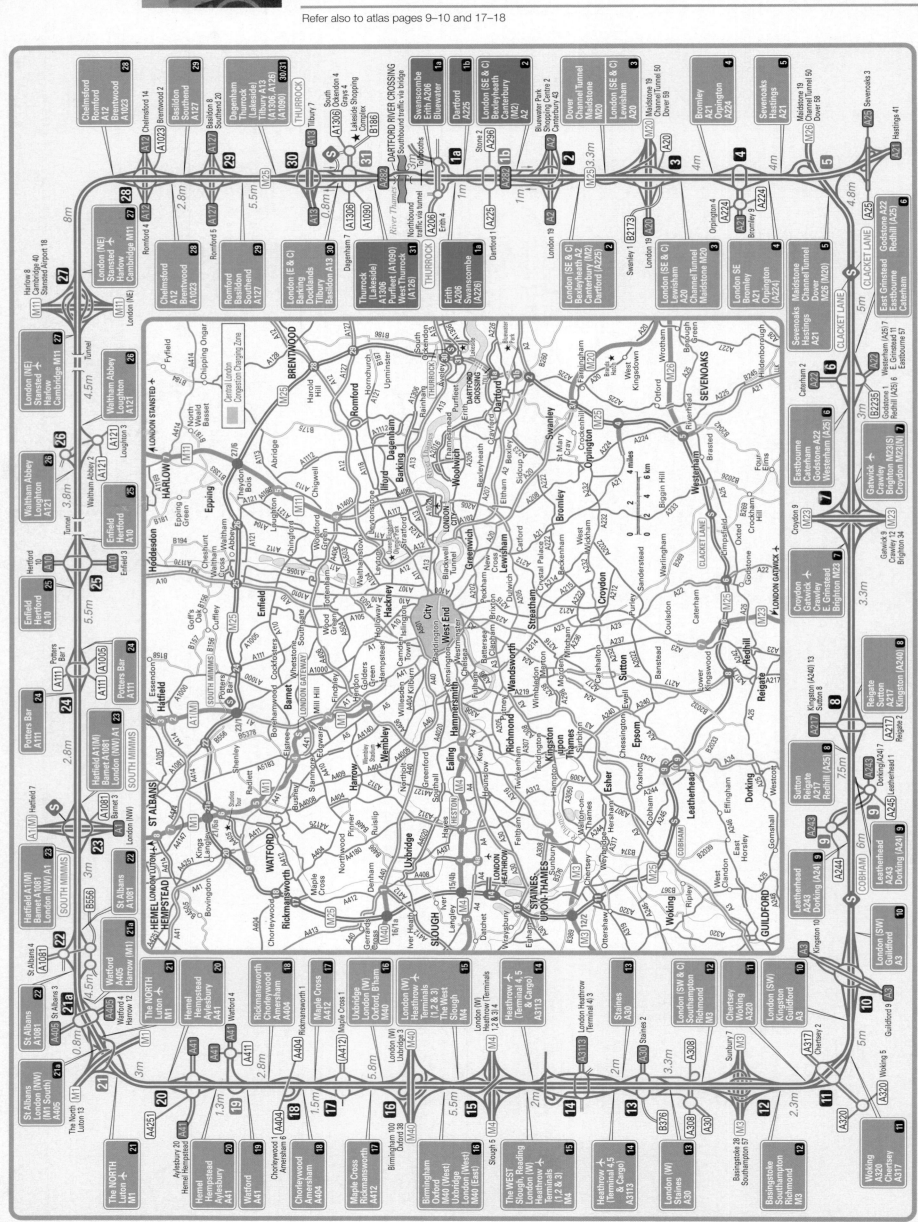

Isles of Scilly

Isles of Scilly Heritage Coast

White Island
ST. MARTIN'S
St Martin's Head
King Charles's Castle
BRYHER
Old Grimsby
New Grimsby
Lizard Point
Higher Town
Old Blockhouse
Great Ganilly
Cromwell's Castle
TRESCO
Innisidgen Tomb
Tresco Abbey
Great Arthur
Samson
Bant's Carn Burial
Harry's Walls
ST MARY'S
St Mary's Quay
Longstone
Deep Point
Hugh Town
Porth Hellick Downs Tombs
Garrison Walls
Isles of Scilly (St Mary's)
Old Town
Annet
Gugh
Peninnis Head
Middle Town
ST. AGNES
Horse Point
Western Rocks

North West Channel
Broad Sound
Crow Sound
St Mary's Sound
Smith Sound

| 0 | 1 | 2 | 3 | 4 miles |
| 0 | 1 | 2 | 3 | 4 | 5 kilometres |

a   b   c

Mainland Cornwall (east section)

Rumps Point
Port Quin
Kelland Head
Varley Head
Port Isaac
Pentire Point
Padstow Bay
Trevone
Polzeath
Rock
TREVOSE HEAD
Trevose Head Heritage Coast
Stepper Point
Gunver Head
Trebetherick
St Minver
Dinas Head
Mother Ivey's Bay
Harlyn
Hayle Bay
Chapel Amble
Constantine Bay
Windmill
Padstow
St Merryn
St Issey
Wadebridge
Porthcothan
Penrose
Little Petherick
Trenance
Park Head
St Ervan
Rumford
St Breock Downs Monolith
Bedruthan Steps
Trenance
St Eval
Nine Maidens
Great Western Adventure Park
Berryls Point
Mawgan Porth
St Mawgan
Talskiddy
Rosenannon
Griffins Point
Trevarrian
Watergate Bay
St Columb Major
St Wenn
Withiel
Newquay
St Columb Minor
A3059
Tregonetha
Towan Head
Colan
Victoria
Fistral Bay
Mountjoy
St Dennis
Kelsey Head
West Pentire
Quintrell Downs
St Columb Road
Roche
Pentire
Lane
Fraddon
Goss Moor
Holywell Bay
Crantock
Kestle Mill
Indian Queens
Penhale Point
Tresean
Treviel
Newlyn East
St Enoder
Summercourt
Whitemoor
Holywell
Cubert
Stenalees
Ligger Point
Nanpean
Carthew
Liggar or Perran Bay
Rose
Goonhavern
Fiddlers Green
Mitchell
Scarcewater
Foxhole
Perranporth
Bolingey
Mawla
Shortlanesend
Probus
Creed
St Stephen
High Street
St Austell
Cligga Point
Trevellas Downs
Penhallow
Callestick
Zelah
St Allen
Ladock
Grampound Road
Polgooth
St Agnes Heritage Coast
St Agnes
Perranzabuloe
St Erme
Trispen
Hewas Water
Sticker
ST AGNES HEAD
Goonvrea
Mithian
Barkla Shop
Grampound
St Ewe
Wheal Coates
Goonbell
Kenwyn
Creed
Porthtowan
Mount Hawke
Idless
Tresillian
Gardens
Blackwater
Chacewater
A390
Truro
St Clement
Tregony
Polmassick
South West Coast Path
Illogan
Scorrier
Threemilestone
Malpas
Ruan Lanihorne
Boswin
Godrevy-Portreath Heritage Coast
Portreath
South Tehidy
Mount Ambrose
St Day
Kea
St Michael Penkevil
Veryan
Portloe
Navax Point
Reskadinnick
Carharrack
Bissoe
Playing Place
Lamorran
Veryan Bay
Godrevy Island
Carn Brea
Twelveheads
Carnon Downs
Philleigh
Nare Head
DODMAN POINT
Godrevy Point
Redruth
Devoran
Trewithian
The Roseland Heritage Coast
Kehelland
Camborne
Lanner
Gwennap
Perranarworthal
Feock
St Just-in-Roseland
Gerrans Bay
Carn Naun Point
Penponds
Carnkie
Perranwell
Portscatho
The Island or St Ives Head
St Ives Bay
Gwithian
Connor Downs
Four Lanes
Penhalvean
Mylor Bridge
Gerrans
Zennor Head
St Ives
Carbis Bay
Phillack
Angarrack
Barripper
Carnhell Green
Stithians
Longdowns
Mabe Burnthouse
Mylor
Greeb Point
Gurnards Head
Lelant
Hayle
Troon
Penryn
Flushing
South West Coast Path
Zennor
Towednack
Realwar
Praze-an-Beeble
Carnkie
Rame
Penryn
St Mawes
Halsetown
High Gwinear Lanes
Crowan
Porkellis
Argal & College Water Park
Budock Water
Bohortha
Pendeen Watch
St Erth Praze
Leedstown
Wendron Mining District
Treverva
Pendennis Castle
ZONE POINT
Morvah
Chysauster Ancient Village
Canonstown
St Erth
Godolphin House
Godolphin Cross
Prospidnick
Trenear
Falmouth
Pendennis Point
Pendeen
New Mill
Crowlas
Townshend
Wendron
Sewogan
Falmouth Bay
Geevor Tin Mine
Ludgvan
Nancledra
Relubbus
Trescowe
Crowntown
Brill
Maenan Smith
Levant Mine and Beam Engine
Madron
Heamoor
St Hilary
Goldsithney
Carleen
Constantine
Porth Navas
ROSEMULLION HEAD
Botallack
St Just Mining District
Longrock
Marazion
Ashton
Sithney
Coverack Bridges
Gweek
Trebah
Mawnan
St Just
Newbridge
Chyandour
Perranuthnoe
St Michael's Mount
Breage
Helston
Helford Passage
Glendurgan
Mawnan Smith
Ballowall Barrow
Penzance
Cudden Point
Praa Sands
Porthleven
Seal Sanctuary
Helford
St Anthony
Kelynack
Sancreed
Drift
Newlyn
Rinsey Head
Trewavas Mining District
Mawgan
Manaccan
Carn Euny Ancient Village
Kerris
Paul
MOUNT'S BAY
Garras
St Martin
Porthallow
St Just
Crows-an-Wra
St Buryan
Mousehole
Gunwalloe
St Keverne
Porthoustock
Trethewey
Treen
Lamorna
White Cross
Cury
Manacle Point
Whitesand Bay
The Merry Maidens
Lamorna Cove
Goonhilly Downs
Sennen Cove
Sennen
Merthen Point
Lowland Point
Sennen
St Levan
Minack Open Air Theatre
Cribba Head
Poldhu Point
Coverack
LAND'S END
Porthcurno
Marconi Memorial
The Lizard Heritage Coast
Black Head
Trevescan
Telegraph
Mullion Cove
Mullion
St Keverne
Porthgwarra
Gwennap Head
Predannack Head
Ruan Major
Kuggar
Vellan Head
Ruan Minor
Cadgwith
Black Head
Devil's Frying Pan
South West Coast Path
The Lizard
Kynance Cove
Church Cove
Lizard
Bass Point
LIZARD POINT
Lizard Lighthouse & Heritage Centre

| 0 | 1 | 2 | 3 | 4 miles |
| 0 | 1 | 2 | 3 | 4 | 5 kilometres |

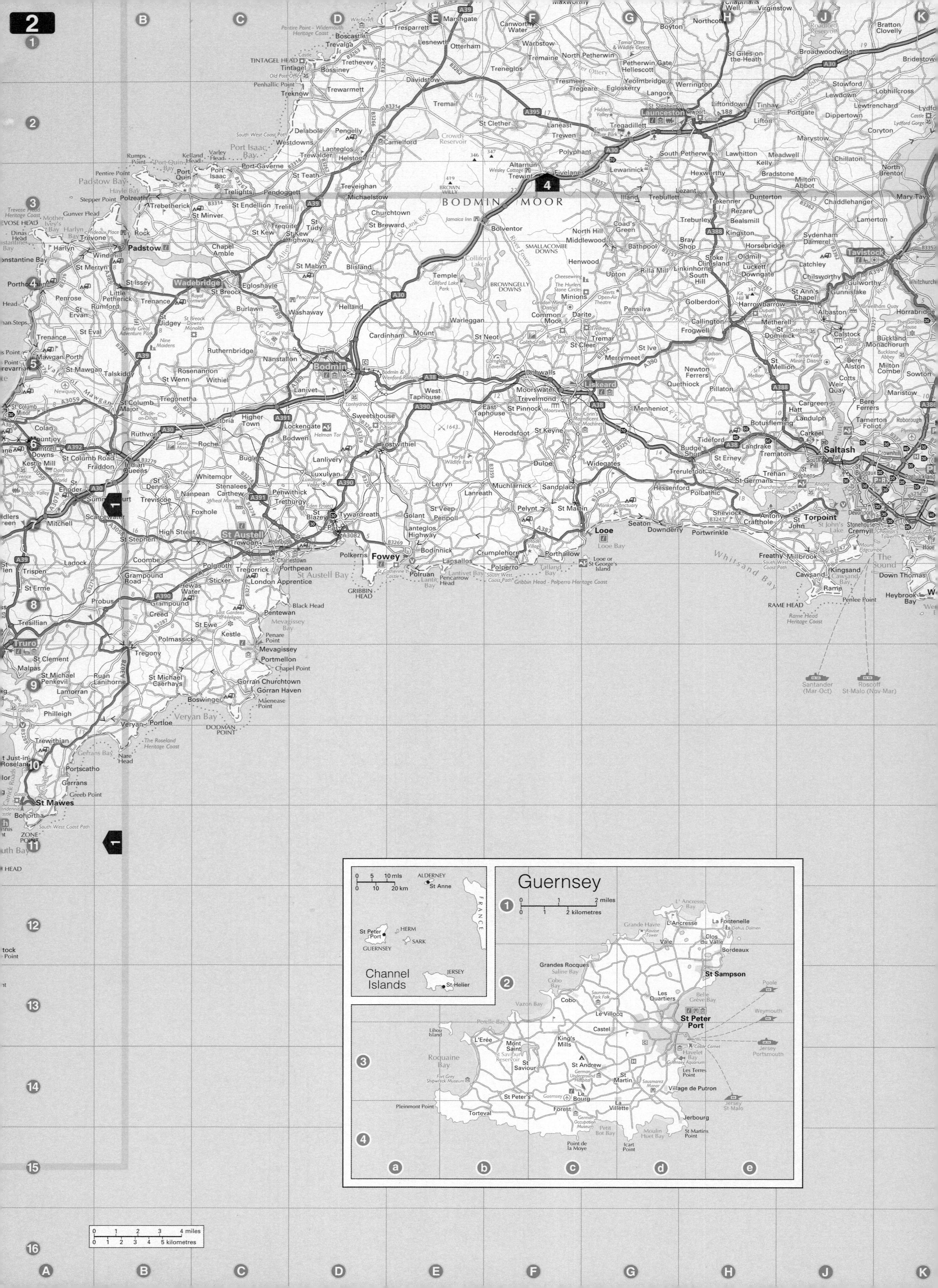
BODMIN MOOR
Bodmin
Launceston
Wadebridge
Padstow
Liskeard
Looe
Fowey
St Austell
Truro
Tavistock
Saltash
Torpoint
St Mawes
Lostwithiel
Camelford
Tintagel
Boscastle
Port Isaac
Camel Valley
Padstow Bay
Mevagissey
Polperro
Veryan Bay
Whitsand Bay
Mevagissey Bay
Gerrans Bay
Santander (Mar-Oct)
Roscoff St-Malo (Nov-Mar)
Guernsey
St Peter Port
St Sampson
Channel Islands
ALDERNEY
St Anne
HERM
SARK
GUERNSEY
JERSEY
St Helier
FRANCE
0 5 10 mls
0 10 20 km
0 1 2 miles
0 1 2 kilometres
0 1 2 3 4 miles
0 1 2 3 4 5 kilometres

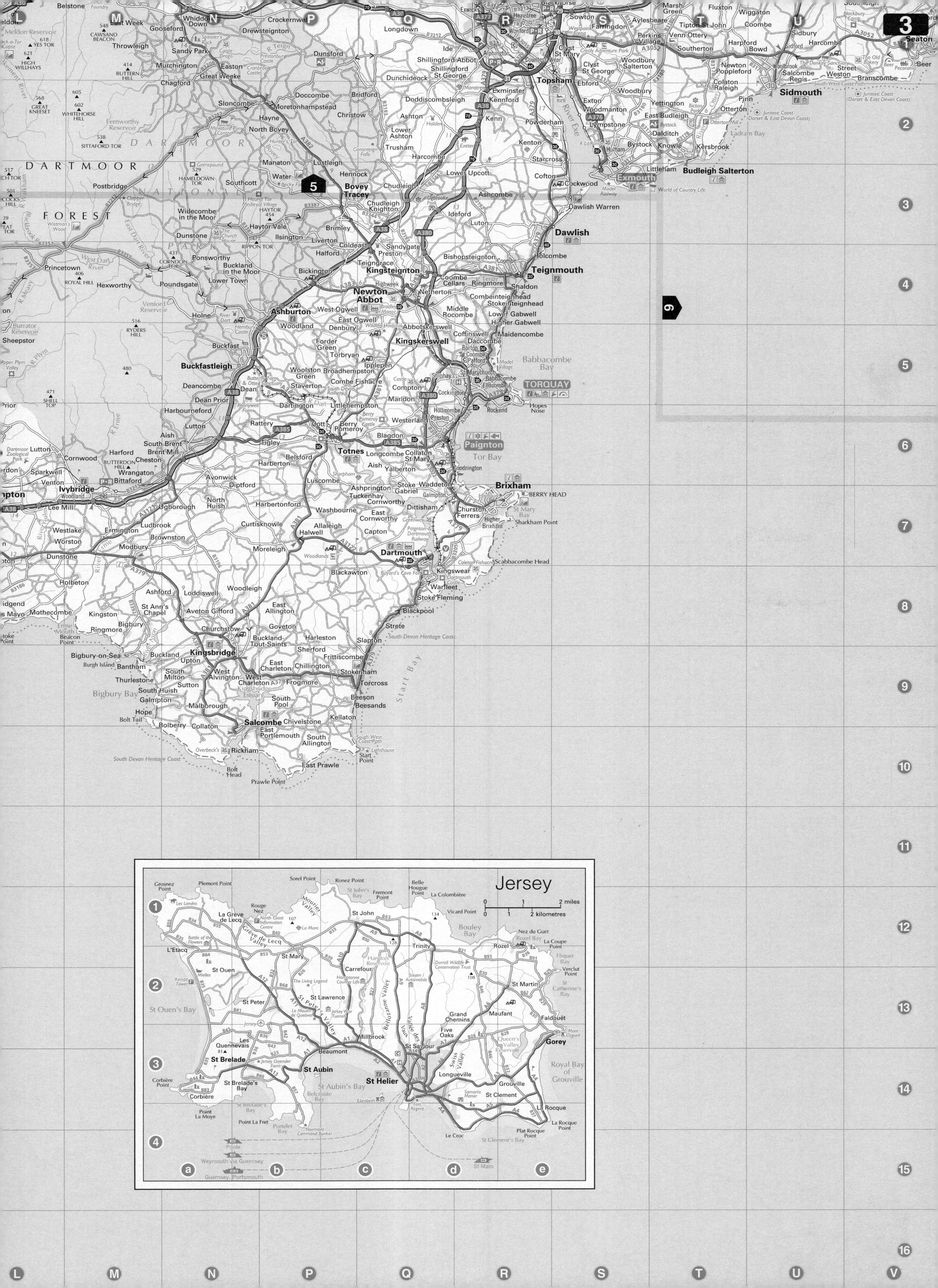
DARTMOOR
FOREST
Exeter
Topsham
Exmouth
Budleigh Salterton
Sidmouth
Seaton
Beer
Dawlish
Teignmouth
Bovey Tracey
Kingsteignton
Newton Abbot
Ashburton
Buckfastleigh
Kingskerswell
TORQUAY
Babbacombe Bay
Paignton
Tor Bay
Brixham
Totnes
Ivybridge
Dartmouth
Kingsbridge
Salcombe
Start Bay
Bigbury Bay
South Devon Heritage Coast
Prawle Point
Start Point
Bolt Head
Jersey
St Helier
St Aubin
St Brelade
Gorey
St Ouen's Bay
St Aubin's Bay
Royal Bay of Grouville
Bouley Bay
St Clement's Bay
La Rocque Point
Corbière Point
Grosnez Point
St John
St Mary
St Ouen
St Peter
St Lawrence
Trinity
St Martin
St Saviour
St Clement
Rozel
Poole
Weymouth via Guernsey
Guernsey, Portsmouth
St Malo
0 1 2 miles
0 1 2 kilometres

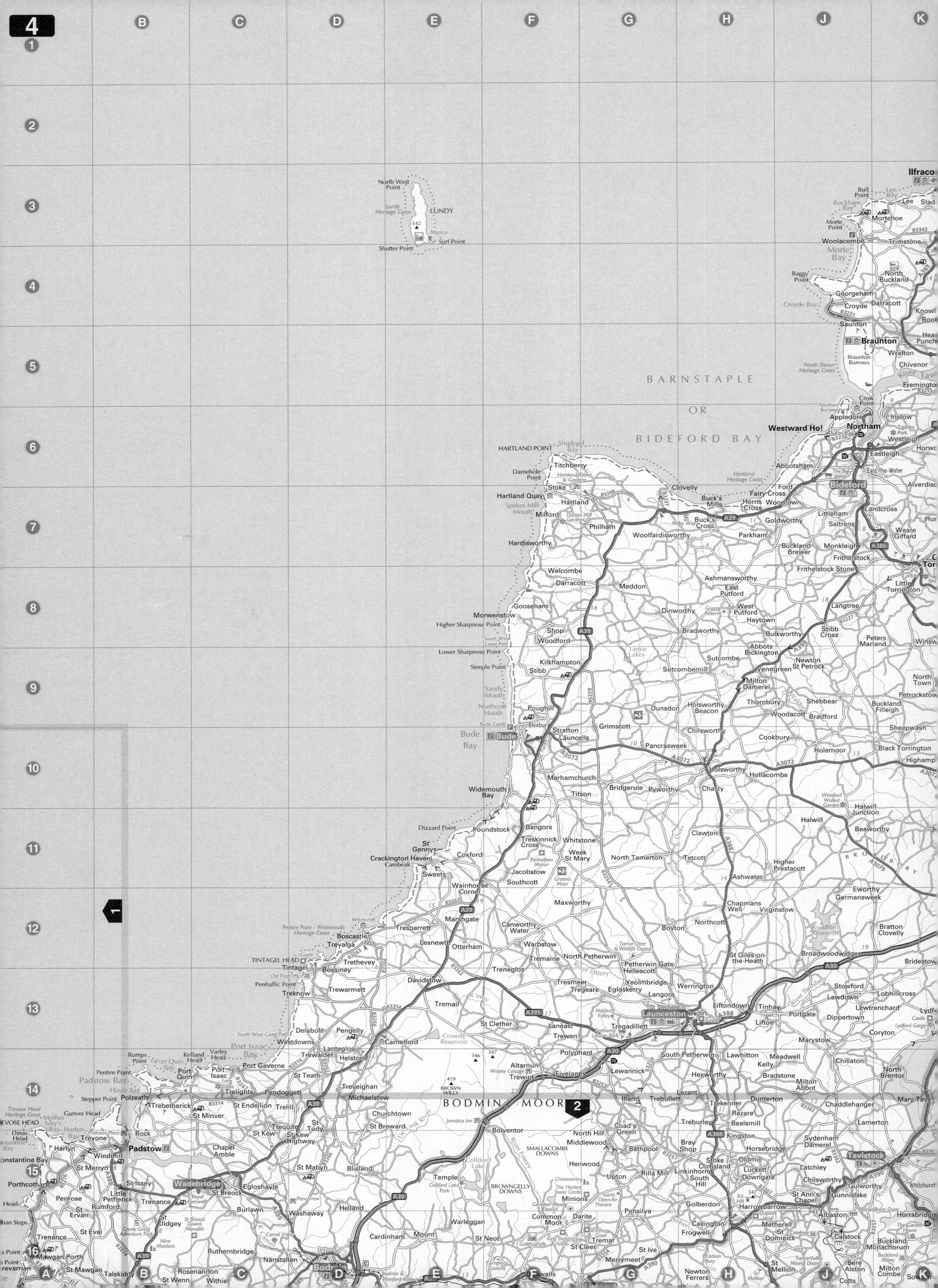

North West Point
Lundy Heritage Coast
LUNDY
Marisco
Surf Point
Shutter Point
Ilfraco
Bull Point
Lee Bay
Lee
Rockham Bay
Mortehoe
Morte Point
Woolacombe
Trimstone
Morte Bay
Baggy Point
North Buckland
Georgeham
Croyde
Croyde Bay
Darracott
Saunton
Braunton
Braunton Burrows
Wrafton
Chivenor
North Devon Heritage Coast
BARNSTAPLE
OR
BIDEFORD BAY
Fremington
Crow Point
Northam Burrows
Appledore
Instow
Northam
Westward Ho!
Westleigh
Eastleigh
HARTLAND POINT
Shipload Bay
Titchberry
Damehole Point
Hartland Abbey & Gardens
Stoke
Hartland
Hartland Quay
Spekes Mill Mouth
Milford
Docton Mill Gardens
Philham
Clovelly
Buck's Mills
Hartland Heritage Coast
Abbotsham
Ford
Fairy Cross
Horns Cross
Woodtown
Bideford
Buck's Cross
Goldworthy
Littleham
Landcross
Alverdisc
Woolfardisworthy
Parkham
Saltrens
Weare Giffard
Hardisworthy
Buckland Brewer
Monkleigh
Frithelstock
Frithelstock Stone
Welcombe
Darracott
Meddon
Ashmansworthy
East Putford
Little Torrington
Gooseham
Morwenstow
Higher Sharpnose Point
Dinworthy
West Putford
Haytown
Langtree
Shop
Woodford
Bradworthy
Bulkworthy
Stibb Cross
Peters Marland
Lower Sharpnose Point
Tamar Lakes
Abbots Bickington
Kilkhampton
Sutcombe
Newton St Petrock
Steeple Point
Stibb
Sutcombemill
Venngreen
Milton Damerel
North Town
Sandy Mouth
Northcott Mouth
Poughill
Dunsdon
Holsworthy Beacon
Thornbury
Shebbear
Buckland Filleigh
Petrockstow
Bude Castle
Flexbury
Stratton
Launcells
Grimscott
Chilsworthy
Woodacott
Bradford
Sheepwash
Bude
Bude Bay
Pancrasweek
Cookbury
Holemoor
Black Torrington
Highamp
Marhamchurch
Holsworthy
Hollacombe
Titson
Bridgerule
Pyworthy
Chasty
Widemouth Bay
Winsford Walled Garden
Halwill Junction
Halwill
Beaworthy
Dizzard Point
Poundstock
Bangors
Clawton
St Gennys
Treskinnick Cross
Whitstone
Crackington Haven
Cambeak
Coxford
Week St Mary
North Tamerton
Tetcott
Higher Prestacott
BROADBURY
Jacobstow
Sweets
Penhallam Manor
Greena Moor
Southcott
Ashwater
Wainhouse Corner
Maxworthy
Eworthy
Germansweek
Chapmans Well
Virginstow
Marshgate
Canworthy Water
Pentire Point - Widemouth Heritage Coast
Boscastle
Witchcroft
Tresparrett
Boyton
Northcott
Roadford Reservoir
Bratton Clovelly
Trevalga
Lesnewth
Otterham
Warbstow
Tamar Otter & Wildlife Centre
Castle
TINTAGEL HEAD
Tintagel
Old Post Office
Trethevey
Bossiney
Tremaine
North Petherwin
St Giles on the Heath
Broadwoodwidger
Bridestow
Penhallic Point
Treneglos
Petherwin Gate
Hellescott
River Ottery
Davidstow
Trewarmett
Treknow
Tresmeer
Tregeare
Yeolmbridge
Egloskerry
Werrington
Langore
Stowford
Lewdown
Lobhillcross
Tremail
Liftondown
Tinhay
Lewtrenchard
St Stephens
Launceston
Newport
Hidden Valley
Portgate
Dippertown
Lifton
Lydford Gorge
Coryton
St Clether
Laneast
Tregadillett
Trethorne Leisure Park
Delabole
Pengelly
South West Coast Path
Westdowns
Port Isaac Bay
Crowdy Reservoir
Camelford
Lanteglos
Trewen
Marystow
Varley Head
Kelland Head
Rumps Point
Port Quin Bay
Trewalder
Helstone
Polyphant
South Petherwin
Lawhitton
Meadwell
Chillaton
Port Gaverne
Pentire Point
Port Quin
Port Isaac
Altarnun
Wesley Cottage
Trewint
Fivelanes
Lewannick
Kelly
Bradstone
North Brentor
Padstow Bay
Hayle Bay
Rock Centre
Long Cross
Trelights
St Teath
Brown Willy
Hexworthy
Milton Abbot
Stepper Point
Pendoggett
Treveighan
Lezant
Polzeath
Trebetherick
St Endellion
Trelill
Michaelstow
BODMIN MOOR
Illand
Trebullett
Trekenner
Dunterton
Chaddlehanger
Mary Tavy
Trevose Head Heritage Coast
Gunver Head
Mother Ivey's Bay
St Minver
Churchtown
St Breward
Jamaica Inn
Bolventor
Coad's Green
Rezare
Bealsmill
Treburley
Lamerton
Harlyn Bay
Prideaux Place
Trevone
Rock
Trequite
St Tudy
St Kew
St Kew Highway
De Lank River
North Hill
Middlewood
Kingston
Bray Shop
Sydenham Damerel
Harlyn
Windmill
Padstow
Chapel Amble
SMALLACOMBE DOWNS
Bathpool
Horsebridge
Tavistock
Constantine Bay
St Merryn
St Mabyn
Blisland
Colliford Lake
River Fowey
Henwood
Stoke Climsland
Oldmill
Luckett
Latchley
Downgate
Chilsworthy
Porthcothan
Wadebridge
St Issey
Egloshayle
Temple
Colliford Lake Park
BROWNGELLY DOWNS
Cheesewring
The Hurlers Stone Circles
Upton
Rilla Mill
Linkinhorne
South Hill
Gulworthy
Whitchurch
Little Petherick
Penrose
Trenance
St Breock
Royal Cornwall
Minions
Sterts Open-Air Theatre
Kit Hill
Harrowbarrow
Gunnislake
St Ann's Chapel
St Ervan
Rumford
Burlawn
Washaway
Helland
Golberdon
Dupath Well
Horrabridge
St Jidgey
St Breock Downs Monolith
Pencarrow
Warleggan
Common Moor
Darite
Pensilva
Callington
Albaston
Crealy Great Adventure Park
Nine Maidens
Camel Valley
St Eval
Trethevy Quoit
Metherell
St Dominick
Frogwell
Calstock
Buckland Monachorum
Cardinham
Mount
St Neot
Golitha Falls
King Doniert's Stone
Tremar
St Cleer
St Ive
Rutherbridge
Mawgan Porth
Nanstallon
Bodmin
Carnglaze Caverns
Merrymeet
Cadson Bury
Tamar Valley Mining District
St Mellion
Bere Alston
Milton Combe
St Mawgan
Talskiddy
Rosenannon
St Wenn
Withiel
Bodmin & Wenford Railway
Newton Ferrers
Cotts
Trevose Head
Dinas Head
Trenance

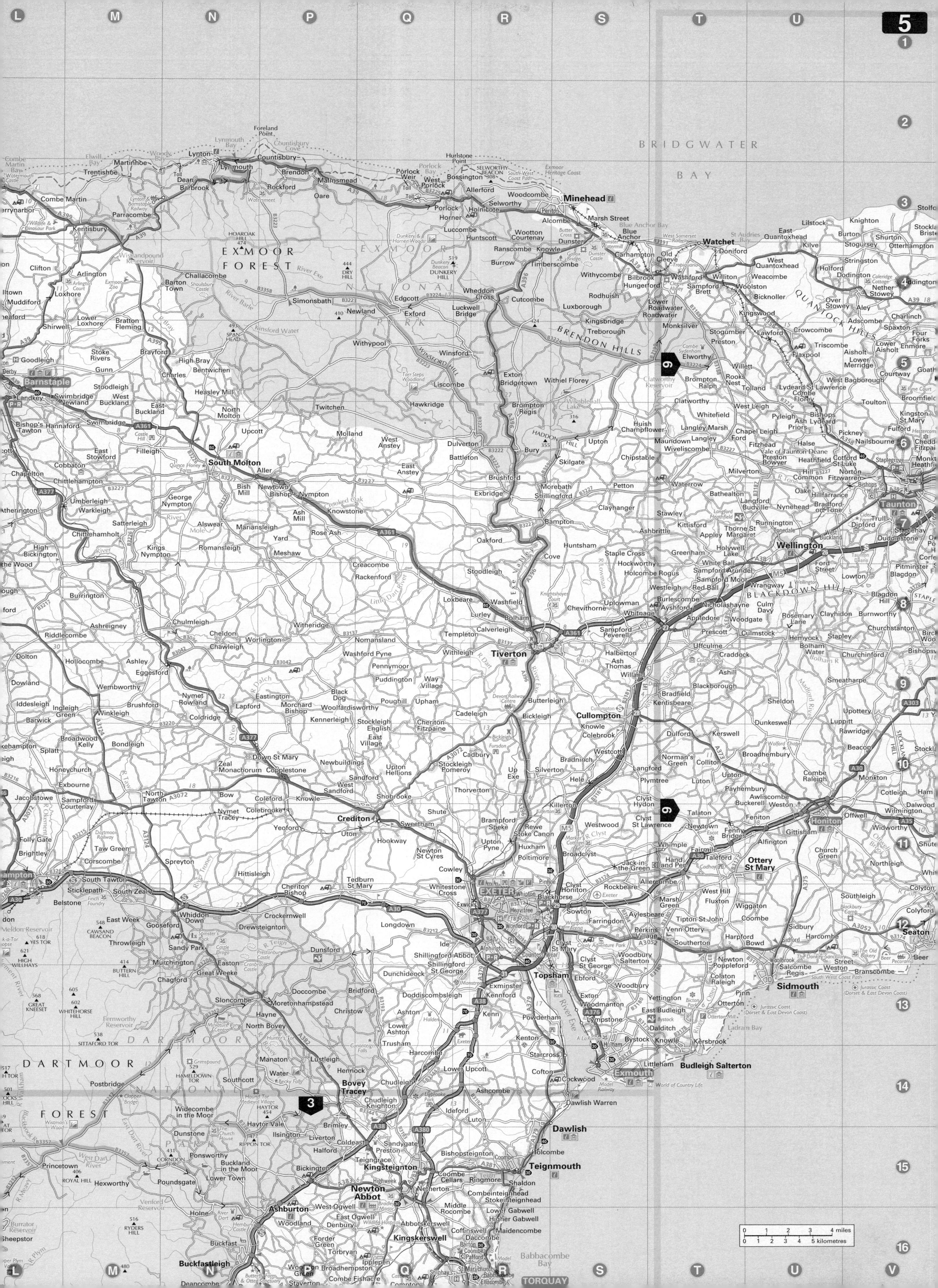
L
M
N
P
Q
R
S
T
U
V
1
2
3
4
5
6
7
8
9
10
11
12
13
14
15
16
BRIDGWATER
BAY
EXMOOR
FOREST
EXMOOR
NATIONAL
PARK
BRENDON HILLS
QUANTOCK HILLS
BLACKDOWN HILLS
DARTMOOR
FOREST
Foreland Point
Lynmouth Bay
Countisbury Cove
Hurlstone Point
Porlock Bay
Combe Martin Bay
Woody Bay
Lynton
Lynmouth
Countisbury
Brendon
Martinhoe
Trentishoe
Elwill Bay
Dean
Barbrook
Rockford
Malmsmead
Oare
Porlock
Porlock Weir
West Porlock
Bossington
Allerford
Selworthy
Holnicote
Horner
Luccombe
Woodcombe
Minehead
Alcombe
Marsh Street
Blue Anchor Bay
Blue Anchor
Dunster
Wootton Courtenay
Huntscott
Ranscombe
Knowle
Timberscombe
Burrow
Carhampton
Withycombe
Watchet
Doniford
Old Cleeve
Washford
Williton
Bilbrook
Hungerford
Sampford Brett
Woolston
Rodhuish
Luxborough
Lower Roadwater
Roadwater
Kingsbridge
Treborough
Monksilver
Stogumber
Elworthy
Combe Martin
Berrynarbor
Parracombe
Kentisbury
Arlington
Clifton
Challacombe
Barton Town
Loxhore
Muddiford
Lower Loxhore
Bratton Fleming
Shirwell
Simonsbath
Newland
Exford
Edgcott
Luckwell Bridge
Wheddon Cross
Cutcombe
Withypool
Winsford
Exton
Bridgetown
Withiel Florey
Brompton Regis
Liscombe
Hawkridge
Goodleigh
Stoke Rivers
Brayford
High Bray
Charles
Bentwichen
Gunn
Barnstaple
Landkey
Swimbridge
Newland
Stoodleigh
West Buckland
East Buckland
Heasley Mill
North Molton
Twitchen
Bishop's Tawton
Hannaford
Swimbridge
Filleigh
Upcott
South Molton
Molland
West Anstey
East Anstey
Dulverton
Battleton
Brushford
Exbridge
Bury
Skilgate
Upton
Huish Champflower
Chipstable
Morebath
Shillingford
Petton
Bampton
Clayhanger
Stawley
Kittisford
Ashbrittle
Huntsham
Oakford
Cove
Stoodleigh
Stoodleigh
Knowstone
Rose Ash
Ash Mill
Bish Mill
Aller
Newtown
Bishop's Nympton
George Nympton
Mariansleigh
Alswear
Yard
Meshaw
Romansleigh
Kings Nympton
Chapelton
Cobbaton
East Stowford
Chittlehampton
Umberleigh
Warkleigh
Satterleigh
Chittlehamholt
High Bickington
Atherington
Burrington
Chulmleigh
Ashreigney
Riddlecombe
Cheldon
Chawleigh
Worlington
Witheridge
Nomansland
Washford Pyne
Pennymoor
Puddington
Way Village
Templeton
Tiverton
Withleigh
Calverleigh
Loxbeare
Lurley
Washfield
Bolham
Creacombe
Rackenford
Dolton
Hollocombe
Ashley
Eggesford
Dowland
Wembworthy
Iddesleigh
Ingleigh Green
Winkleigh
Brushford
Nymet Rowland
Coldridge
Lapford
Eastington
Morchard Bishop
Black Dog
Woolfardisworthy
Poughill
Upham
Cadeleigh
Bickleigh
Butterleigh
Cullompton
Knowle
Colebrook
Westcott
Bradninch
Kennerleigh
Stockleigh English
Cheriton Fitzpaine
East Village
Barwick
Broadwood Kelly
Bondleigh
Splatt
Honeychurch
Exbourne
Zeal Monachorum
Down St Mary
Copplestone
Newbuildings
Sandford
Upton Hellions
Stockleigh Pomeroy
Cadbury
Up Exe
Silverton
Hele
Thorverton
Jacobstowe
Sampford Courtenay
North Tawton
Bow
Coleford
Colebrooke
Knowle
West Sandford
Shobrooke
Nymet Tracey
Yeoford
Crediton
Uton
Sweetham
Hookway
Shute
Brampford Speke
Rewe
Stoke Canon
Upton Pyne
Huxham
Poltimore
Newton St Cyres
Cowley
Folly Gate
Brightley
Taw Green
Corscombe
Spreyton
Hittisleigh
Cheriton Bishop
Tedburn St Mary
Whitestone Cross
Exwick
Exeter
Whipton
Heavitree
Wonford
Pinhoe
Blackhorse
Clyst Honiton
Sowton
Farringdon
Okehampton
Sticklepath
South Tawton
South Zeal
Belstone
Whiddon Down
Crockernwell
Drewsteignton
Gooseford
East Week
Throwleigh
Longdown
Ide
Dunsford
Shillingford Abbot
Shillingford St George
Alphington
Countess Wear
Topsham
Clyst St Mary
Clyst St George
Ebford
Woodbury Salterton
Woodbury
Sandy Park
Murchington
Chagford
Easton
Great Weeke
Dunchideock
Exminster
Kennford
Doddiscombsleigh
Bridford
Doccombe
Sloncombe
Moretonhampstead
Christow
Ashton
Lower Ashton
Trusham
Hayne
North Bovey
Kenn
Powderham
Kenton
Starcross
Cofton
Cockwood
Exton
Woodmanton
Lympstone
Exmouth
Littleham
Dawlish Warren
Dawlish
Holcombe
Teignmouth
Shaldon
Harcombe
Lower Upcott
Ashcombe
Ideford
Luton
Bishopsteignton
Chudleigh
Chudleigh Knighton
Lustleigh
Manaton
Water
Hennock
Bovey Tracey
Postbridge
Southcott
Widecombe in the Moor
Haytor Vale
Dunstone
Ponsworthy
Buckland in the Moor
Lower Town
Poundsgate
Princetown
Hexworthy
Ilsington
Liverton
Coldeast
Brimley
Halford
Sandygate
Preston
Teigngrace
Kingsteignton
Bickington
Newton Abbot
Coombe Cellars
Ringmore
Combeinteignhead
Stokeinteignhead
Netherton
Middle Rocombe
Lower Gabwell
Higher Gabwell
Maidencombe
Ashburton
West Ogwell
East Ogwell
Woodland
Denbury
Abbotskerswell
Kingskerswell
Coffinswell
Daccombe
Forder Green
Torbryan
Ipplepen
Broadhempston
Buckfast
Buckfastleigh
Holne
Staverton
Combe Fishacre
Compton
Deancombe
Babbacombe Bay
TORQUAY
Stolford
Knighton
Stockland Bristol
Lilstock
Burton
Shurton
Otterhampton
East Quantoxhead
Kilve
Stogursey
Stringston
West Quantoxhead
Holford
Dodington
Nether Stowey
Over Stowey
Adscombe
Alley
Charlinch
Spaxton
Four Forks
Enmore
Aisholt
Lower Aisholt
Courtway
Lower Merridge
Weacombe
Bicknoller
Kingswood
Crowcombe
Lawford
Triscombe
Flaxpool
Preston
Willett
Brompton Ralph
Rooks Nest
Tolland
Clatworthy
Whitefield
West Leigh
Lydeard St Lawrence
Combe Florey
West Bagborough
Toulton
Broomfield
Kingston St Mary
Pyleigh
Ash Priors
Bishops Lydeard
Fulford
Pickney
Nailsbourne
Langley Marsh
Langley
Maundown
Wiveliscombe
Chapel Leigh
Ford
Fitzhead
Halse
Preston Bowyer
Heathfield
Cotford St Luke
Vale of Taunton Deane
Milverton
Hill Common
Norton Fitzwarren
Staplegrove
Taunton
Waterrow
Bathealton
Oake
Hillfarrance
Langford Budville
Nynehead
Bradford-on-Tone
Trull
Dipford
Runnington
Thorne St Margaret
Appley
Greenham
Holywell Lake
White Ball
Sampford Arundel
Sampford Moor
Wellington
Staple Cross
Hockworthy
Holcombe Rogus
Westleigh
Red Ball
Wrangway
Burlescombe
Ayshford
Nicholashayne
Culm Davy
Pitminster
Blagdon
Lowton
Blagdon Hill
Uplowman
Chevithorne
Whitnage
Sampford Peverell
Appledore
Woodgate
Prescott
Culmstock
Rosemary Lane
Clayhidon
Burnworthy
Churchstanton
Hemyock
Stapley
Bolham Water
Churchinford
Uffculme
Craddock
Halberton
Ash Thomas
Willand
Ashill
Smeatharpe
Bradfield
Blackborough
Kentisbeare
Sheldon
Upottery
Dunkeswell
Luppitt
Rawridge
Dulford
Kerswell
Norman's Green
Colliton
Broadhembury
Beacon
Langford
Plymtree
Luton
Upton
Payhembury
Combe Raleigh
Monkton
Cotleigh
Clyst Hydon
Awliscombe
Buckerell
Weston
Killerton
Clyst St Lawrence
Talaton
Feniton
Honiton
Offwell
Wilmington
Widworthy
Westwood
Newtown
Fenny Bridges
Gittisham
Whimple
Fairmile
Alfington
Broadclyst
Hand and Pen
Jack-in-the-Green
Taleford
Ottery St Mary
Church Green
Northleigh
Rockbeare
Allercombe
West Hill
Marsh Green
Fluxton
Wiggaton
Aylesbeare
Tipton St John
Coombe
Southleigh
Colyton
Colyford
Perkins Village
Venn Ottery
Southerton
Harpford
Bowd
Sidbury
Harcombe
Seaton
Beer
Newton Poppleford
Colaton Raleigh
Salcombe Regis
Street
Weston
Branscombe
Sidford
Sidmouth
Pinn
Otterton
Yettington
East Budleigh
Dalditch
Bystock
Knowle
Kersbrook
Budleigh Salterton
Ladram Bay
Hulham
Exmoor Heritage Coast
Jurassic Coast (Dorset & East Devon Coast)
Meldon Reservoir
Burrator Reservoir
Venford Reservoir
Fernworthy Reservoir
Wimbleball Lake
Clatworthy Reservoir
Wistlandpound Reservoir
CAWSAND BEACON
YES TOR
HIGH WILLHAYS
BUTTERN HILL
GREAT KNEESET
WHITEHORSE HILL
SITTAFORD TOR
HAMELDOWN TOR
HAYTOR
RIPPON TOR
CORNDON TOR
ROYAL HILL
RYDERS HILL
HOAROAK HILL
DUNKERY HILL
SELWORTHY BEACON
SPAN HEAD
DRY HILL
0 1 2 3 4 miles
0 1 2 3 4 5 kilometres

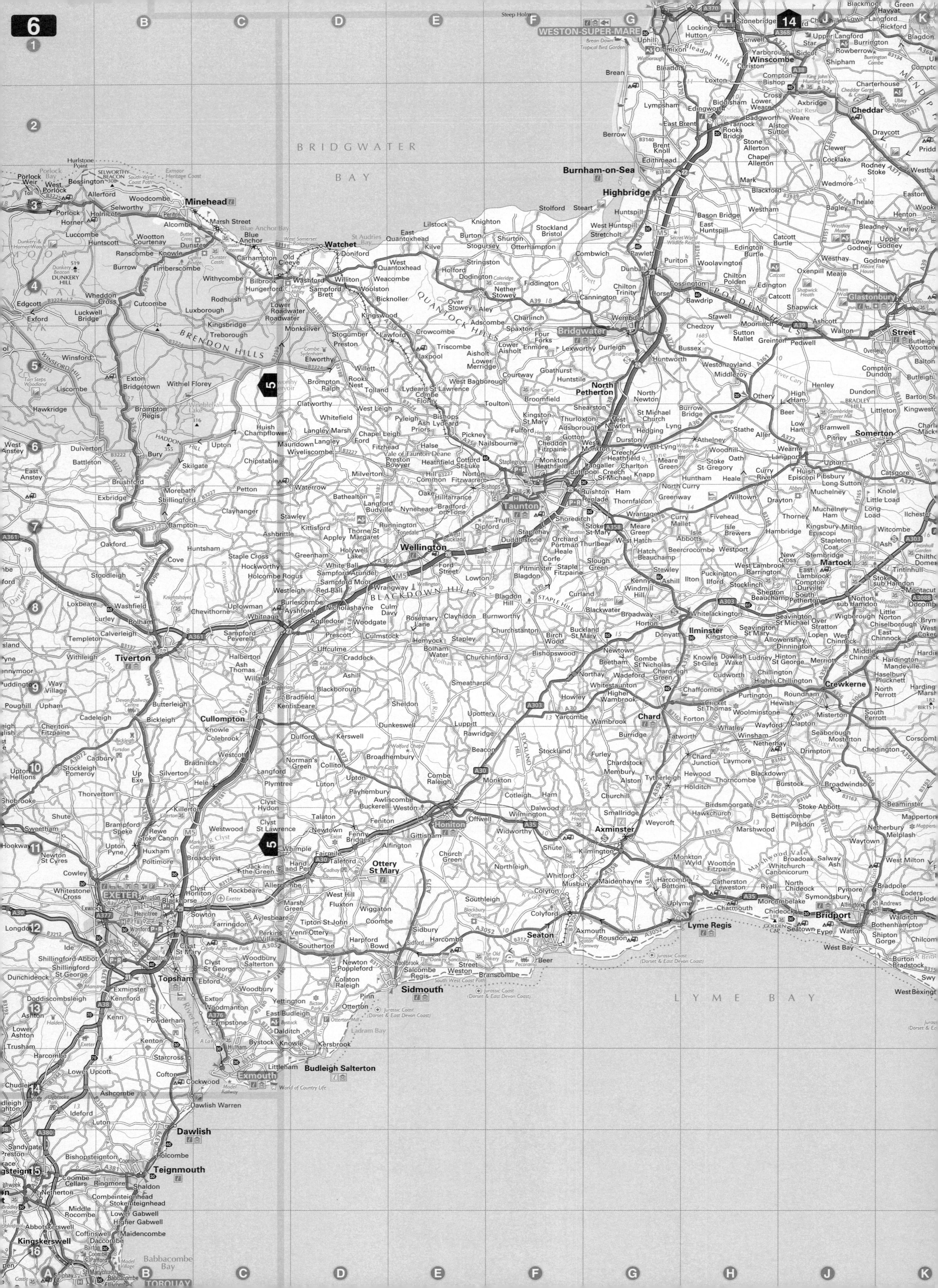

WESTON-SUPER-MARE
Steep Holm
BRIDGWATER BAY
Burnham-on-Sea
Highbridge
Minehead
Watchet
Porlock
Dunster
Williton
QUANTOCK HILLS
BRENDON HILLS
Bridgwater
North Petherton
Glastonbury
Street
Cheddar
Winscombe
Wedmore
Taunton
Wellington
BLACKDOWN HILLS
Wiveliscombe
Dulverton
Tiverton
Cullompton
Honiton
Ilminster
Chard
Crewkerne
Somerton
Martock
Axminster
Lyme Regis
Bridport
Seaton
Sidmouth
Ottery St Mary
Budleigh Salterton
Exmouth
EXETER
Topsham
Dawlish
Teignmouth
Kingskerswell
TORQUAY
Babbacombe Bay
LYME BAY
Ladram Bay
West Bay
Jurassic Coast (Dorset & East Devon Coast)
South West Coast Path
M5
A30
A35
A38
A39
A303
A358
A361
A373
A375
A376
A379
A380
A3052

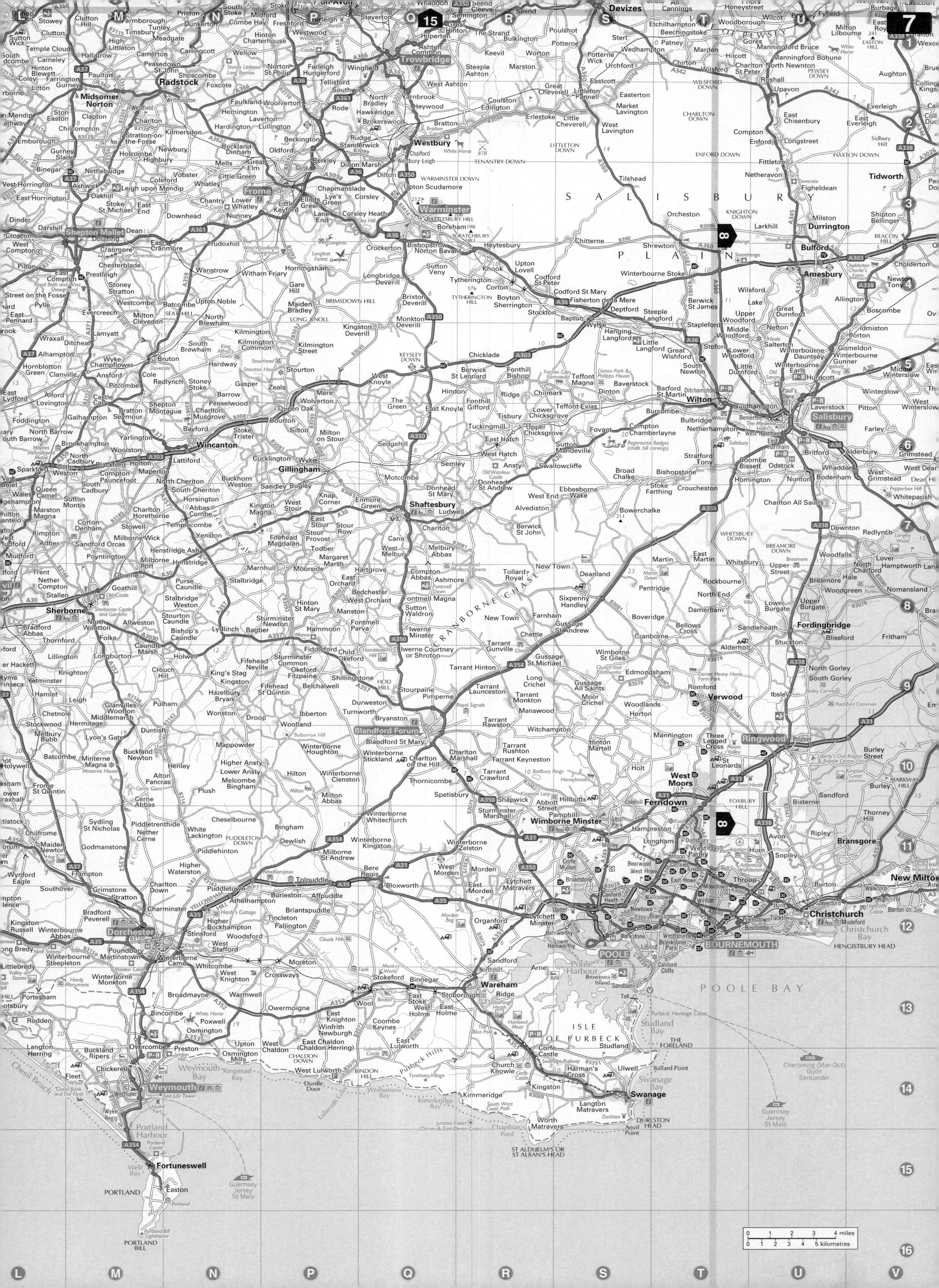
Devizes
Trowbridge
Westbury
Frome
Warminster
Shepton Mallet
Radstock
Midsomer Norton
SALISBURY PLAIN
Amesbury
Bulford
Durrington
Tidworth
Wilton
Salisbury
Wincanton
Gillingham
Shaftesbury
Sherborne
Fordingbridge
CRANBORNE CHASE
Blandford Forum
Verwood
Ringwood
West Moors
Ferndown
Wimborne Minster
POOLE
BOURNEMOUTH
Christchurch
Christchurch Bay
HENGISTBURY HEAD
POOLE BAY
Poole Harbour
Wareham
ISLE OF PURBECK
Swanage
Swanage Bay
Studland
DURLSTON HEAD
ST ALDHELM'S OR ST ALBAN'S HEAD
Dorchester
Weymouth
Weymouth Bay
Portland Harbour
Fortuneswell
PORTLAND
PORTLAND BILL
Chesil Beach
Cherbourg (Mar-Oct) Gijón Santander
Guernsey Jersey St-Malo
0 1 2 3 4 miles
0 1 2 3 4 5 kilometres
L M N P Q R S T U V
1 2 3 4 5 6 7 8 9 10 11 12 13 14 15 16

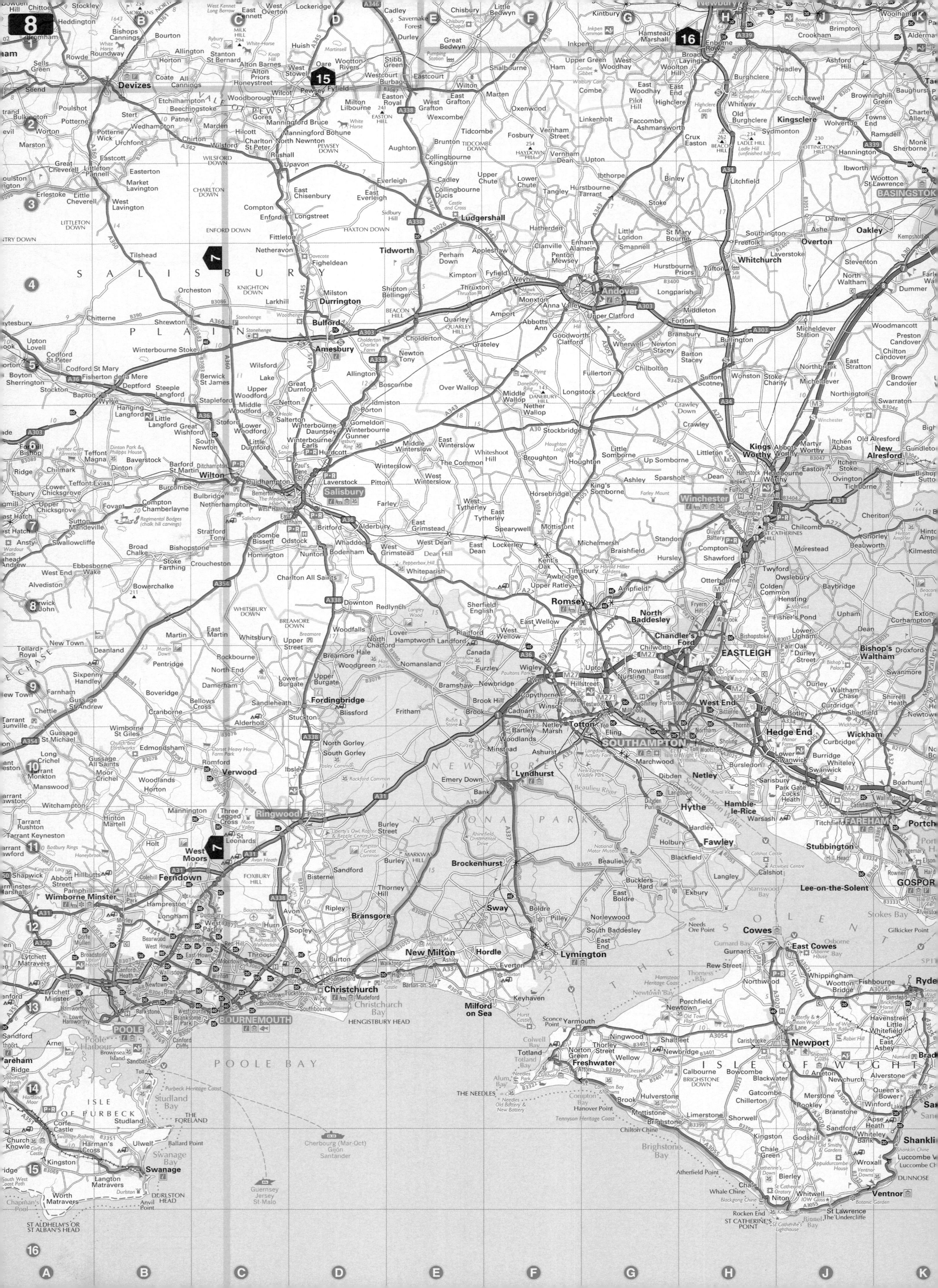

Devizes
Pewsey
Ludgershall
Tidworth
Andover
Whitchurch
Kingsclere
BASINGSTOKE
Overton
Oakley
Durrington
Bulford
Amesbury
SALISBURY PLAIN
Wilton
Salisbury
Stockbridge
Kings Worthy
Winchester
New Alresford
Romsey
North Baddesley
Chandler's Ford
EASTLEIGH
Bishop's Waltham
Totton
SOUTHAMPTON
West End
Hedge End
Netley
Hythe
Fawley
Lyndhurst
NEW FOREST NATIONAL PARK
Fordingbridge
Verwood
Ringwood
West Moors
Ferndown
Wimborne Minster
POOLE
BOURNEMOUTH
Christchurch
New Milton
Hordle
Milford on Sea
Brockenhurst
Lymington
Sway
FAREHAM
GOSPORT
Lee-on-the-Solent
Cowes
East Cowes
Newport
Ryde
Yarmouth
Freshwater
ISLE OF WIGHT
Shanklin
Ventnor
THE SOLENT
POOLE BAY
ISLE OF PURBECK
Swanage
Wareham

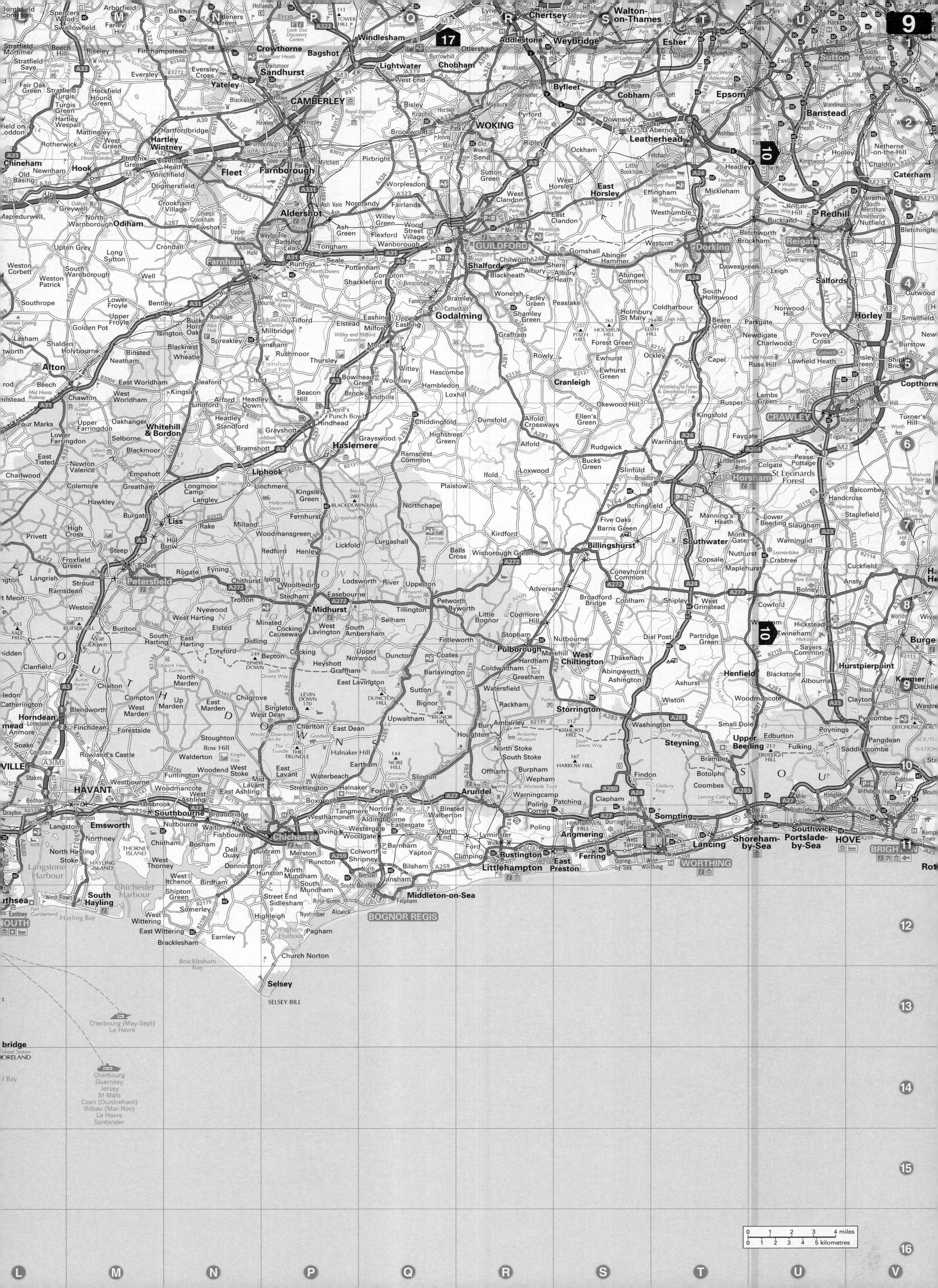
Windlesham
Bagshot
Crowthorne
Sandhurst
Yateley
CAMBERLEY
Lightwater
Chobham
Addlestone
Chertsey
Weybridge
Walton-on-Thames
Esher
Byfleet
Cobham
Epsom
Sutton
Banstead
WOKING
Leatherhead
Hartley Wintney
Fleet
Farnborough
Hook
Chineham
Odiham
Aldershot
Guildford
Shalford
Dorking
Reigate
Redhill
Caterham
East Horsley
Farnham
Godalming
Alton
Cranleigh
Horley
CRAWLEY
Whitehill & Bordon
Haslemere
Liphook
Liss
Petersfield
Midhurst
Horsham
Billingshurst
Southwater
Pulborough
West Chiltington
Storrington
Henfield
Hurstpierpoint
Steyning
Arundel
Chichester
HAVANT
Emsworth
Southbourne
South Hayling
Littlehampton
Rustington
Angmering
Ferring
WORTHING
Lancing
Sompting
Shoreham-by-Sea
Southwick
Portslade-by-Sea
HOVE
Middleton-on-Sea
BOGNOR REGIS
Selsey
SELSEY BILL
Chichester Harbour
Langstone Harbour
Hayling Bay
Bracklesham Bay
Cherbourg (May-Sept)
Le Havre
Cherbourg
Guernsey
Jersey
St Malo
Caen (Ouistreham)
Bilbao (Mar-Nov)
Le Havre
Santander
SOUTH DOWNS NATIONAL PARK
0 1 2 3 4 miles
0 1 2 3 4 5 kilometres
L M N P Q R S T U V
1 2 3 4 5 6 7 8 9 10 11 12 13 14 15 16

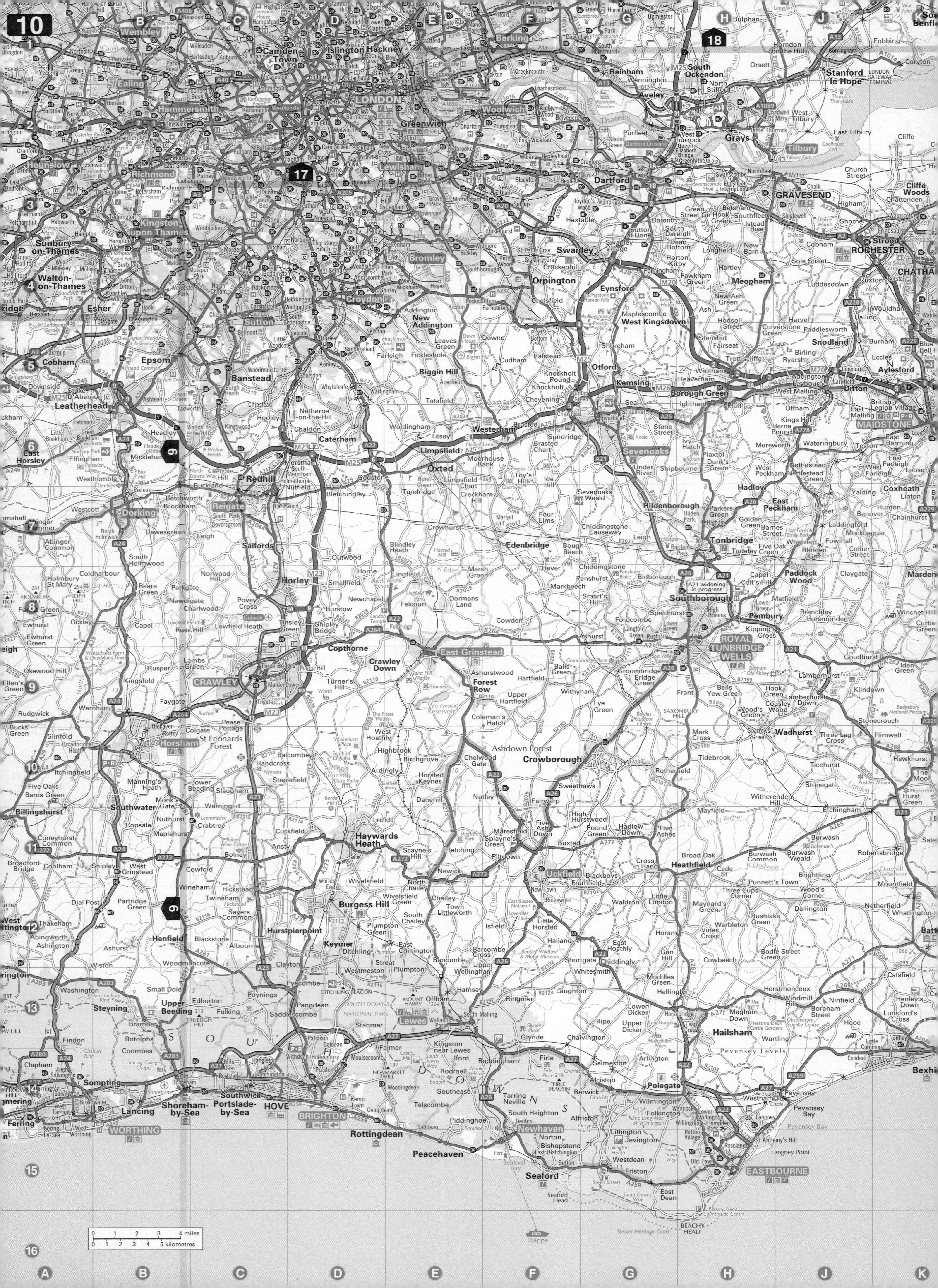

A
B
C
D
E
F
G
H
J
K
Wembley
Camden Town
Islington
Hackney
Barking
Ealing
Hammersmith
LONDON
Greenwich
Woolwich
Rainham
South Ockendon
Aveley
Stanford le Hope
Grays
Tilbury
Hounslow
Richmond
Lewisham
Dartford
GRAVESEND
Kingston upon Thames
Sunbury-on-Thames
Walton-on-Thames
Esher
Bromley
Swanley
Orpington
ROCHESTER
CHATHAM
Croydon
Sutton
Epsom
Cobham
Banstead
New Addington
Biggin Hill
West Kingsdown
Snodland
Otford
Kemsing
Borough Green
Aylesford
Ditton
Leatherhead
MAIDSTONE
Caterham
Westerham
Limpsfield
Oxted
Redhill
Reigate
Dorking
Sevenoaks
Hildenborough
Tonbridge
Hadlow
East Peckham
Edenbridge
Horley
Southborough
Pembury
Paddock Wood
ROYAL TUNBRIDGE WELLS
Crawley Down
East Grinstead
CRAWLEY
Forest Row
Horsham
St Leonards Forest
Ashdown Forest
Crowborough
Wadhurst
Billingshurst
Southwater
Haywards Heath
Uckfield
Heathfield
Burgess Hill
Hurstpierpoint
Henfield
Keymer
Steyning
Upper Beeding
Lewes
Hailsham
Polegate
Shoreham-by-Sea
Portslade-by-Sea
HOVE
BRIGHTON
Lancing
Sompting
WORTHING
Ferring
Rottingdean
Peacehaven
Newhaven
Seaford
EASTBOURNE
Pevensey
Pevensey Bay
BEACHY HEAD
Dieppe
Sussex Heritage Coast
SOUTH DOWNS NATIONAL PARK
17
18
9
A21 widening in progress
0 1 2 3 4 miles
0 1 2 3 4 5 kilometres
1
2
3
4
5
6
7
8
9
10
11
12
13
14
15
16

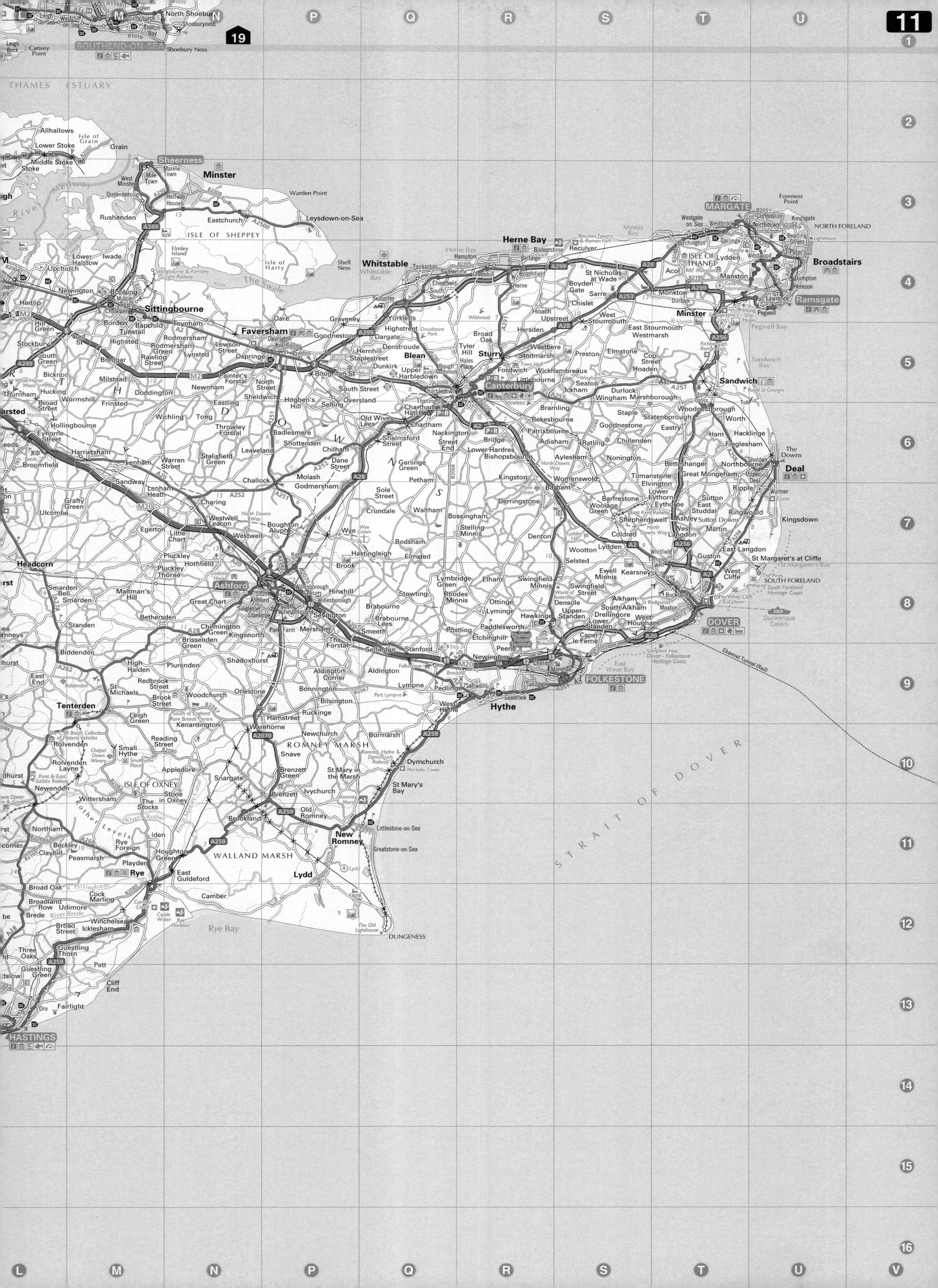
19
SOUTHEND-ON-SEA
Shoebury Ness
Canvey Point
Leigh Beck
THAMES ESTUARY
Allhallows
Isle of Grain
Grain
Lower Stoke
Middle Stoke
Sheerness
Minster
Warden Point
Queenborough
Halfway Houses
River Medway
Rushenden
Eastchurch
Leysdown-on-Sea
ISLE OF SHEPPEY
Elmley Island
Isle of Harty
Shell Ness
The Swale
Lower Halstow
Iwade
Upchurch
Newington
Bobbing
Milton Regis
Sittingbourne
Bapchild
Tunstall
Teynham
Oare
Faversham
Graveney
Goodnestone
Whitstable
Whitstable Bay
Tankerton
Seasalter
Yorkletts
Herne Bay
Reculver
Herne
Broomfield
St Nicholas at Wade
Minnis Bay
MARGATE
Westgate on Sea
Birchington
Garlinge
ISLE OF THANET
Acol
Manston
Broadstairs
NORTH FORELAND
Foreness Point
Ramsgate
Pegwell Bay
Minster
Monkton
Sarre
Chislet
Hoath
Upstreet
West Stourmouth
East Stourmouth
Westmarsh
Sturry
Fordwich
Blean
Canterbury
Harbledown
Boughton St
Dunkirk
Selling
Chartham
Bridge
Barham
Chilham
Wye
Ashford
Kennington
Charing
Lenham
Headcorn
Smarden
Biddenden
Tenterden
Woodchurch
Hamstreet
ROMNEY MARSH
Burmarsh
Dymchurch
St Mary's Bay
New Romney
Littlestone-on-Sea
Greatstone-on-Sea
Lydd
DUNGENESS
Rye Bay
Camber
Rye
WALLAND MARSH
ISLE OF OXNEY
Winchelsea
Icklesham
Pett
Cliff End
Fairlight
Ore
HASTINGS
Hythe
Sandgate
FOLKESTONE
Cheriton
Newington
Lympne
Saltwood
Elham
Lyminge
Hawkinge
Capel-le-Ferne
DOVER
St Margaret's at Cliffe
St Margaret's Bay
SOUTH FORELAND
Kingsdown
Walmer
Deal
The Downs
Sandwich
Sandwich Bay
Eastry
Ash
Wingham
Preston
Aylesham
Shepherdswell
Whitfield
River
STRAIT OF DOVER
Channel Tunnel (Rail)
Dunkerque
Calais
M2
M20
A2
A20
A28
A299
A256
A258
A259
A249
A251
A252
A262
A268
A2070
A2050
A257
A253
A2500

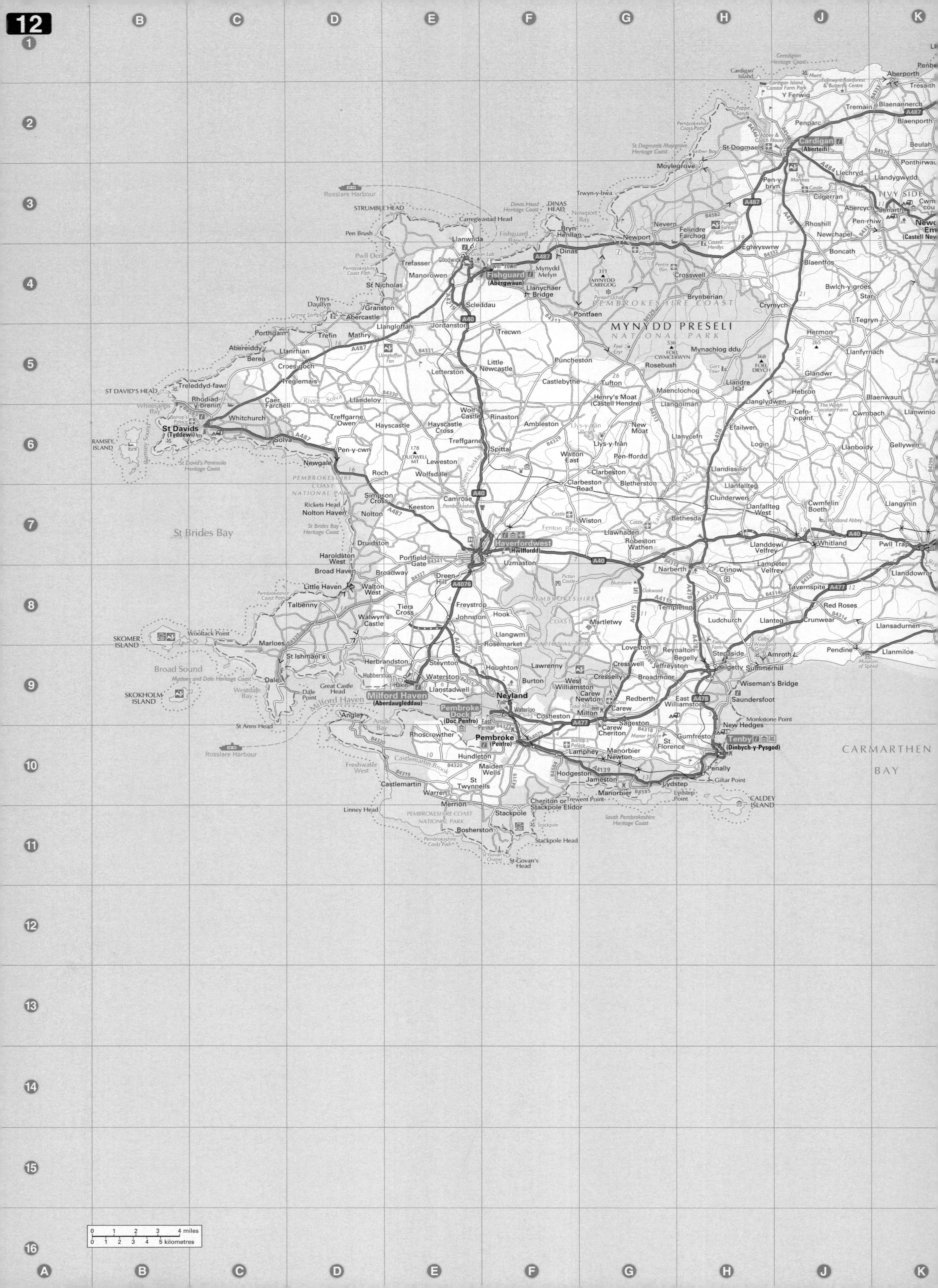

Cardigan Island
Aberporth
Y Ferwig
Tremain
Blaenannerch
Blaenporth
Penparc
Cardigan (Aberteifi)
St Dogmaels
Moylegrove
Beulah
Llechryd
Pontihirwaun
Llandygwydd
Cilgerran
Tivy Side
Abercych
Cenarth
Pen-rhiw
Newcastle Emlyn (Castell Newydd Emlyn)
Rhoshill
Newchapel
Boncath
Blaenffos
Pen-y-bryn
Trwyn-y-bwa
Nevern
Felindre Farchog
Eglwyswrw
Newport
Dinas
Bryn-Henllan
Dinas Head
Rosslare Harbour
Strumble Head
Carregwastad Head
Pen Brush
Llanwnda
Goodwick
Fishguard (Abergwaun)
Mynydd Melyn
Llanychaer Bridge
Trefasser
Manorowen
St Nicholas
Granston
Ynys Daullyn
Abercastle
Scleddau
Jordanston
Llangloffan
Trefin
Mathry
Porthgain
Abereiddy
Berea
Llanrhian
Croes-goch
Treglemais
Treleddyd-fawr
St David's Head
Rhodiad-y-brenin
St Davids (Tyddewi)
Whitchurch
Caer Farchell
Ramsey Island
Ramsey Sound
Solva
Pen-y-cwm
Newgale
Llandeloy
Treffgarne Owen
Hayscastle
Hayscastle Cross
Treffgarne
Wolf's Castle
Rinaston
Letterston
Little Newcastle
Trecwn
Pontfaen
Crosswell
Brynberian
Crymych
Mynydd Preseli
Pembrokeshire Coast National Park
Puncheston
Castlebythe
Tufton
Henry's Moat (Castell Hendre)
Maenclochog
Llangolman
Rosebush
Mynachlog ddu
Llandre Isaf
Glandwr
Hebron
Llanfyrnach
Hermon
Tegryn
Star
Bwlch-y-groes
Blaenwaun
Llanwinio
Cwmbach
Cefn-y-pant
Llanglydwen
Efailwen
Login
Llanboidy
Gellywen
Ambleston
Llys-y-frân
New Moat
Llanycefn
Spittal
Walton East
Pen-ffordd
Clarbeston
Clarbeston Road
Bletherston
Llandissilio
Llanfallteg
Clunderwen
Llanfallteg West
Cwmfelin Boeth
Llangynin
Roch
Simpson Cross
Keeston
Camrose
Wolfsdale
Leweston
Rickets Head
Nolton Haven
Nolton
St Brides Bay
Druidston
Haroldston West
Broad Haven
Little Haven
Walton West
Broadway
Portfield Gate
Haverfordwest (Hwlffordd)
Uzmaston
Wiston
Llawhaden
Robeston Wathen
Bethesda
Narberth
Crinow
Llanddewi Velfrey
Whitland
Pwll Trap
Lampeter Velfrey
Tavernspite
Llanddowror
Red Roses
Crunwear
Llansadurnen
Pendine
Llanmiloe
Dreen Hill
Freystrop
Johnston
Hook
Tiers Cross
Walwyn's Castle
Talbenny
Skomer Island
Wooltack Point
Marloes
St Ishmael's
Broad Sound
Dale
Skokholm Island
Dale Point
Great Castle Head
Herbrandston
Hubberston
Hakin
Milford Haven (Aberdaugleddau)
Steynton
Waterston
Llanstadwell
Neyland
Llangwm
Rosemarket
Houghton
Burton
Martletwy
Lawrenny
Templeton
Ludchurch
Llanteg
Loveston
Reynalton
Begelly
Jeffreyston
Cresswell
Stepaside
Amroth
Kilgetty
Summerhill
Wiseman's Bridge
Saundersfoot
Broadmoor
Cresselly
West Williamston
Carew Newton
Redberth
East Williamston
Milton
Carew
Cosheston
Sageston
Carew Cheriton
Pembroke Dock (Doc Penfro)
Pembroke (Penfro)
Angle
St Anns Head
Rhoscrowther
Hundleton
Maiden Wells
Lamphey
Manorbier Newton
St Florence
Gumfreston
Tenby (Dinbych-y-Pysgod)
Monkstone Point
New Hedges
Penally
Giltar Point
Caldey Island
Carmarthen Bay
Hodgeston
Jameston
Manorbier
Lydstep
Lydstep Point
Freshwater West
Castlemartin
Warren
St Twynnells
Merrion
Linney Head
Cheriton or Stackpole Elidor
Trewent Point
Stackpole
Bosherston
Stackpole Head
St Govan's Head
A40
A487
A477
A478
A4076
A4075
A4139
A484
0 1 2 3 4 miles
0 1 2 3 4 5 kilometres

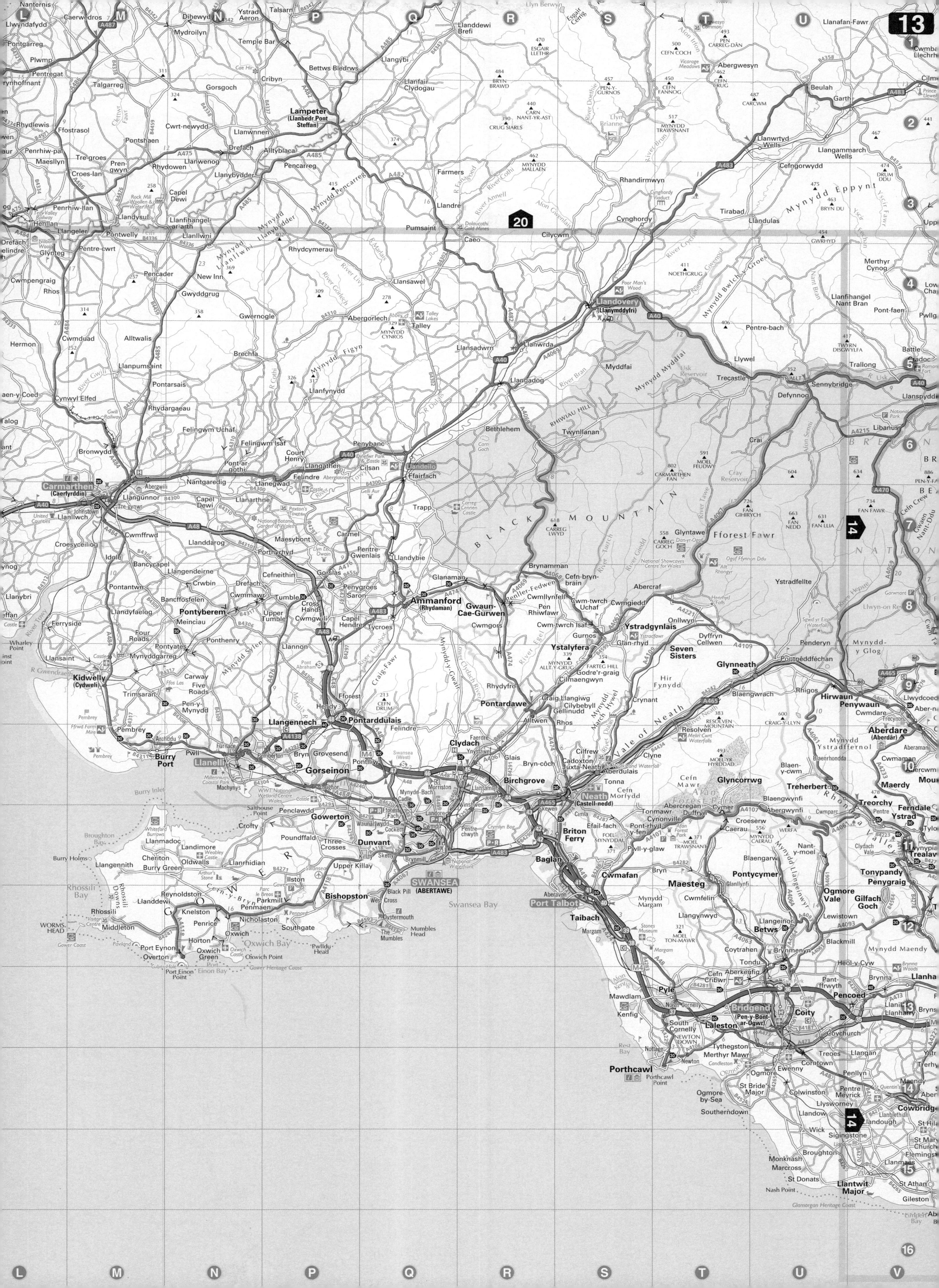

Lampeter (Llanbedr Pont Steffan)
Llanddewi Brefi
Llanwrtyd Wells
Llangammarch Wells
Beulah
Abergwesyn
Llandovery (Llanymddyfri)
Llandeilo
Ammanford (Rhydaman)
Carmarthen (Caerfyrddin)
Kidwelly (Cydweli)
Llanelli
Burry Port
Pontyberem
Llangennech
Pontarddulais
Gorseinon
Gowerton
Dunvant
Clydach
Pontardawe
Gwaun-Cae-Gurwen
Ystalyfera
Ystradgynlais
Seven Sisters
Glynneath
Neath (Castell-nedd)
Briton Ferry
Baglan
Port Talbot
Taibach
Cwmafan
Maesteg
Pyle
Porthcawl
Bridgend (Pen-y-Bont-ar-Ogwr)
Laleston
Coity
Pencoed
Cowbridge
Llantwit Major
Aberdare (Aberdâr)
Hirwaun
Penywaun
Treherbert
Treorchy
Ferndale
Maerdy
Tonypandy
Penygraig
Ogmore Vale
Gilfach Goch
Glyncorrwg
Pontycymer
Betws
SWANSEA (ABERTAWE)
Swansea Bay
Mumbles Head
Oystermouth
Bishopston
Port Eynon
Rhossili
Rhossili Bay
Llangennith
Burry Holms
Worms Head
Oxwich Bay
GOWER
Cefn-y-Bryn
Llanrhidian
Burry Inlet
Broughton Bay
BLACK MOUNTAIN
Fforest Fawr
Mynydd Eppynt
Llangadog
Llanwrda
Talley
Llansawel
Cynghordy
Myddfai
Trecastle
Sennybridge
Defynnog
Brynamman
Llandybie
Cross Hands
Tumble
Glanaman
Newcastle Emlyn
Llandysul
Henllan
Pencader
Alltwalis
Cynwyl Elfed
Bronwydd
Ferryside
Pembrey
Trimsaran
Four Roads
Vale of Neath
River Towy

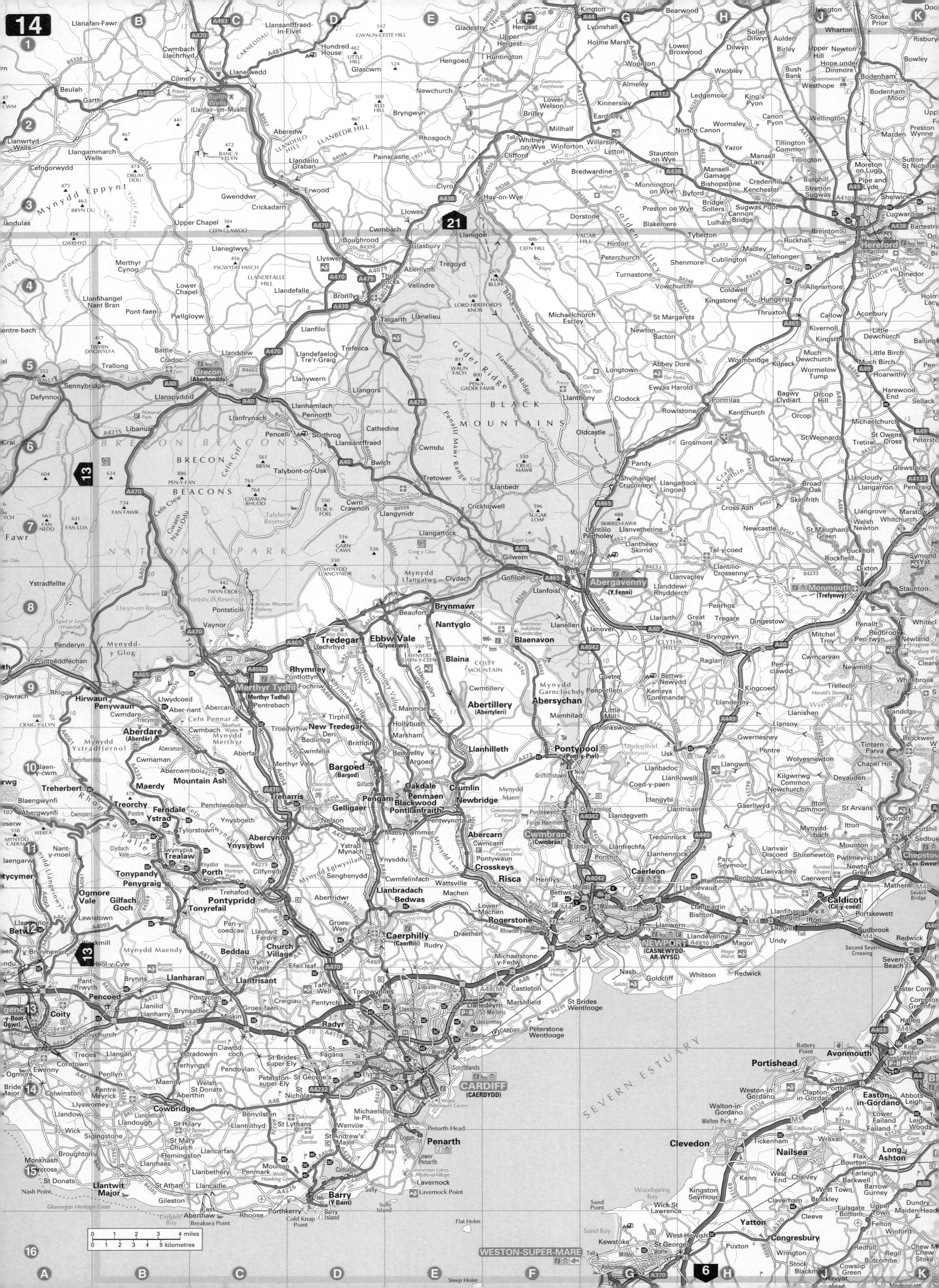

BRECON BEACONS
NATIONAL PARK
BLACK MOUNTAINS
SEVERN ESTUARY
Golden Valley
Brecon (Aberhonddu)
Builth Wells (Llanfair-ym-Muallt)
Hay-on-Wye
Hereford
Abergavenny (Y Fenni)
Monmouth (Trefynwy)
Merthyr Tydfil (Merthyr Tudful)
Aberdare (Aberdâr)
Ebbw Vale (Glynebwy)
Tredegar
Brynmawr
Nantyglo
Blaenavon
Abertillery (Abertyleri)
Pontypool (Pont-y-Pwl)
Cwmbran (Cwmbrân)
Caerleon
NEWPORT (CASNEWYDD-AR-WYSG)
Caldicot (Cil-y-coed)
Chepstow (Cas-Gwent)
Caerphilly (Caerffili)
Pontypridd
CARDIFF (CAERDYDD)
Penarth
Barry (Y Barri)
Cowbridge
Llantwit Major
Portishead
Clevedon
Nailsea
Yatton
Congresbury
WESTON-SUPER-MARE
Avonmouth
Severn Beach
Bridgend
Talgarth
Crickhowell
Raglan
Usk
Llandrindod
Llangynidr
Rhymney
Bargoed
Blackwood
Treharris
Treorchy
Porth
Tonypandy
Llantrisant
Risca
Crosskeys
Rogerstone
1 2 3 4 miles
0 1 2 3 4 5 kilometres

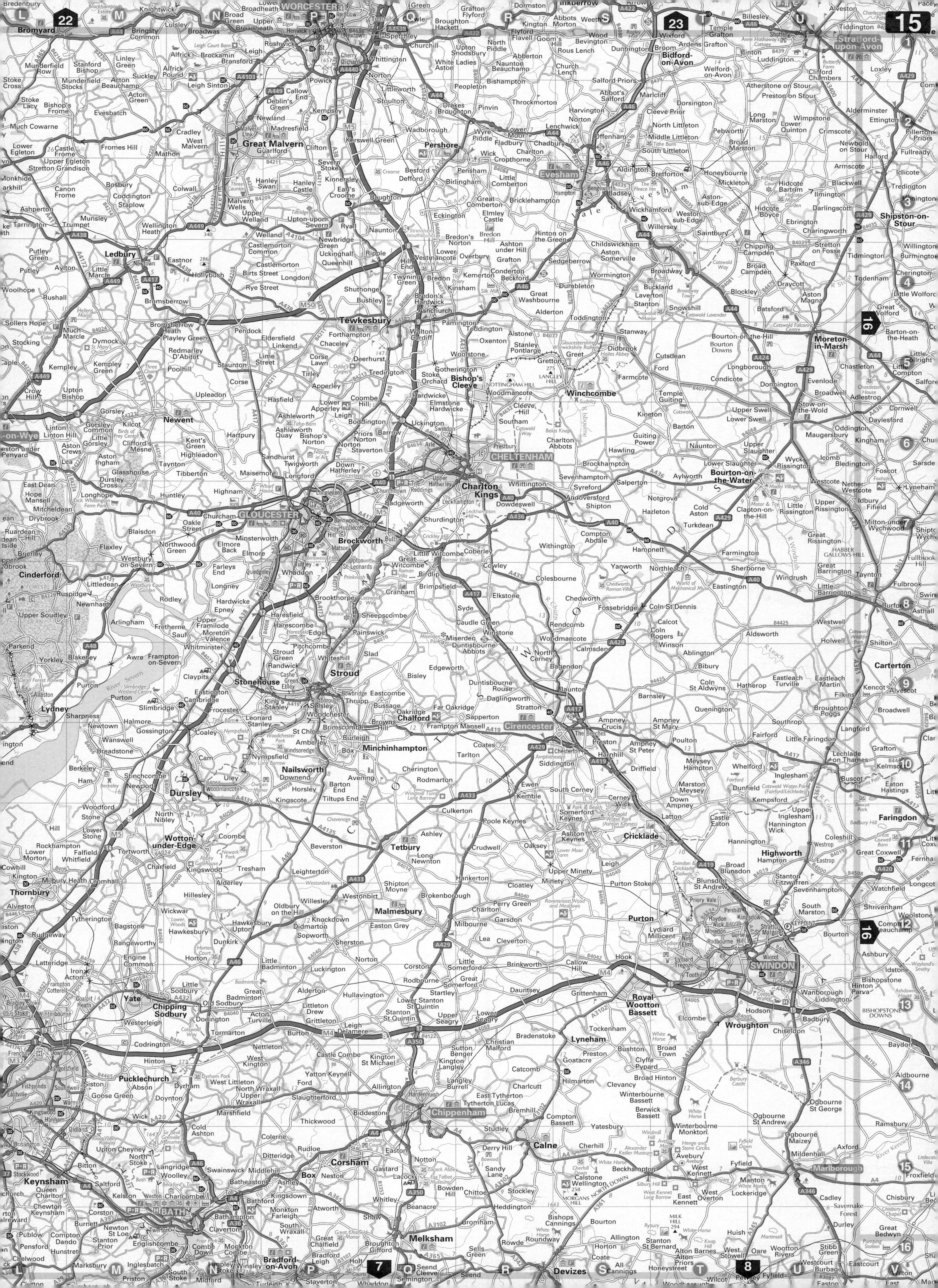
22
23
WORCESTER
Bromyard
Stratford-upon-Avon
Bidford-on-Avon
Great Malvern
Pershore
Evesham
Shipston-on-Stour
Ledbury
Tewkesbury
Moreton-in-Marsh
Bishop's Cleeve
Winchcombe
Newent
CHELTENHAM
Charlton Kings
Bourton-on-the-Water
GLOUCESTER
Brockworth
Cinderford
Lydney
Stonehouse
Stroud
Chalford
Cirencester
Minchinhampton
Nailsworth
Dursley
Carterton
Wotton-under-Edge
Tetbury
Cricklade
Faringdon
Highworth
Thornbury
Malmesbury
Purton
SWINDON
Yate
Chipping Sodbury
Royal Wootton Bassett
Wroughton
Lyneham
Pucklechurch
Chippenham
Calne
Keynsham
BATH
Corsham
Box
Marlborough
Melksham
Bradford-on-Avon
Devizes
16
7
8

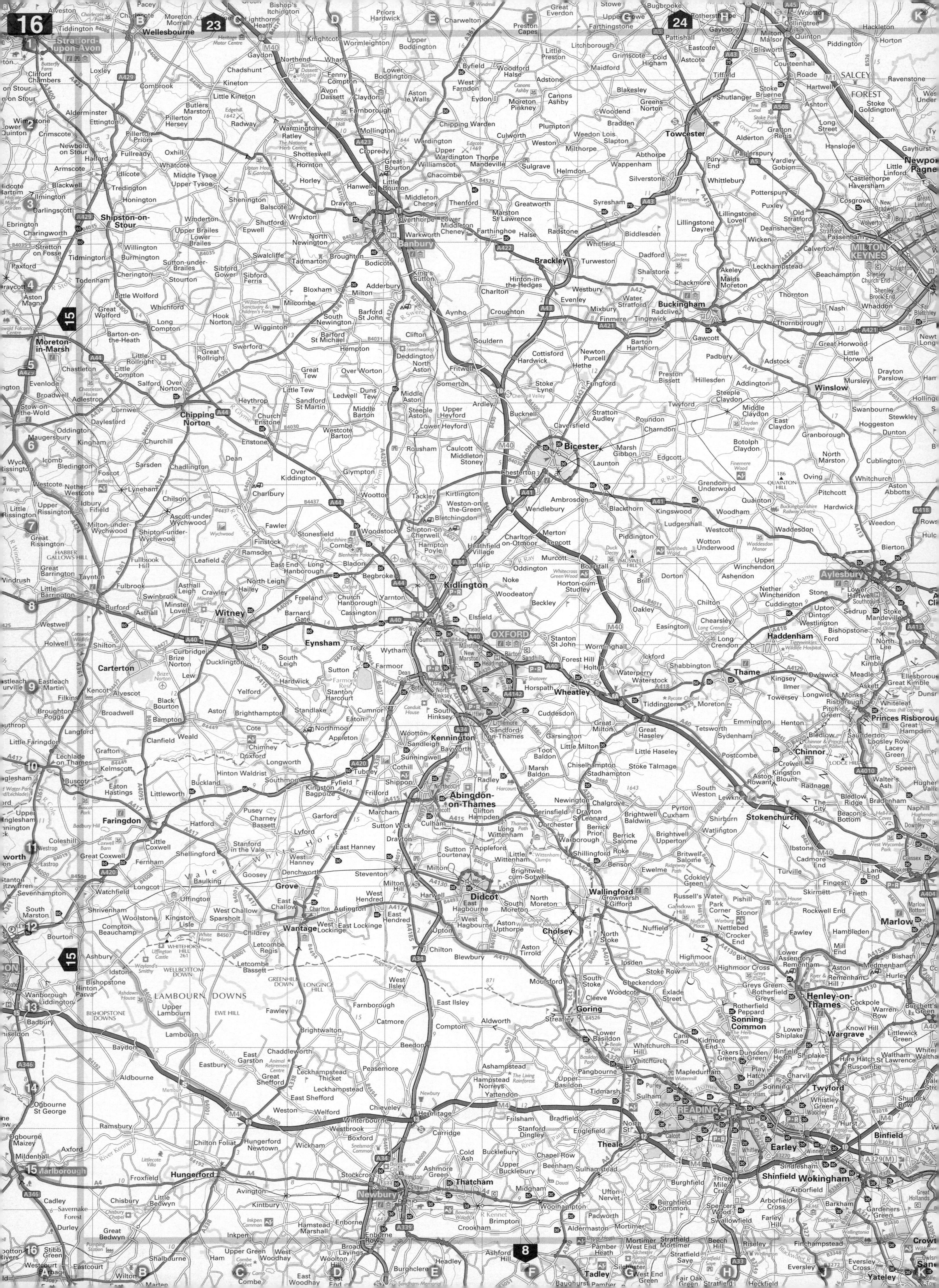
Stratford-upon-Avon
Wellesbourne
Banbury
Brackley
Towcester
Buckingham
Milton Keynes
Shipston-on-Stour
Moreton-in-Marsh
Chipping Norton
Bicester
Winslow
Aylesbury
Kidlington
Witney
Oxford
Carterton
Eynsham
Thame
Wheatley
Haddenham
Princes Risborough
Chinnor
Stokenchurch
Abingdon-on-Thames
Faringdon
Wantage
Didcot
Wallingford
Cholsey
Goring
Henley-on-Thames
Marlow
Reading
Wokingham
Newbury
Thatcham
Hungerford
Marlborough
Lambourn Downs
Vale of White Horse
Salcey Forest
23
24
15
8

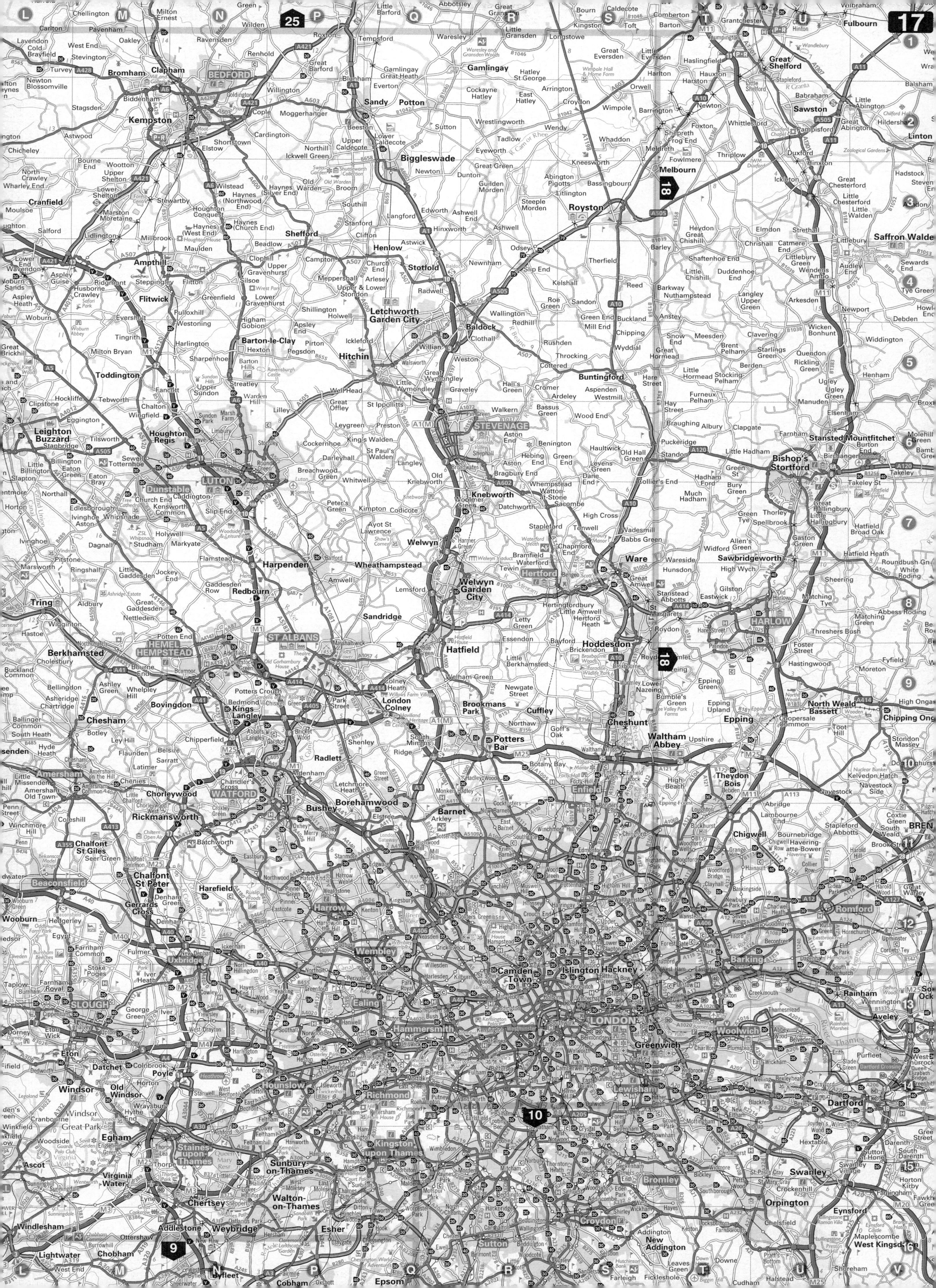
25
Bedford
Kempston
Sandy
Potton
Biggleswade
Gamlingay
Royston
Melbourn
18
Great Shelford
Sawston
Fulbourn
Linton
Saffron Walden
Shefford
Ampthill
Flitwick
Henlow
Stotfold
Letchworth Garden City
Baldock
Hitchin
Buntingford
Toddington
Leighton Buzzard
Houghton Regis
Dunstable
Luton
Stevenage
Knebworth
Welwyn
Harpenden
Welwyn Garden City
Hertford
Ware
Sawbridgeworth
Bishop's Stortford
Stansted Mountfitchet
Harlow
Tring
Berkhamsted
Hemel Hempstead
St Albans
Hatfield
Hoddesdon
Cheshunt
Waltham Abbey
Epping
Chesham
Amersham
Kings Langley
London Colney
Potters Bar
Radlett
Watford
Rickmansworth
Bushey
Borehamwood
Barnet
Enfield
Chigwell
Beaconsfield
Chalfont St Peter
Gerrards Cross
Harrow
Wembley
Uxbridge
Slough
Ealing
Hammersmith
Camden Town
Islington
Hackney
London
Greenwich
Woolwich
Barking
Romford
Rainham
Windsor
Eton
Hounslow
Richmond
Egham
Staines-upon-Thames
Kingston upon Thames
Sunbury-on-Thames
Walton-on-Thames
Chertsey
Weybridge
Esher
Epsom
Sutton
Croydon
Bromley
Lewisham
Dartford
Swanley
Orpington
New Addington
10
9

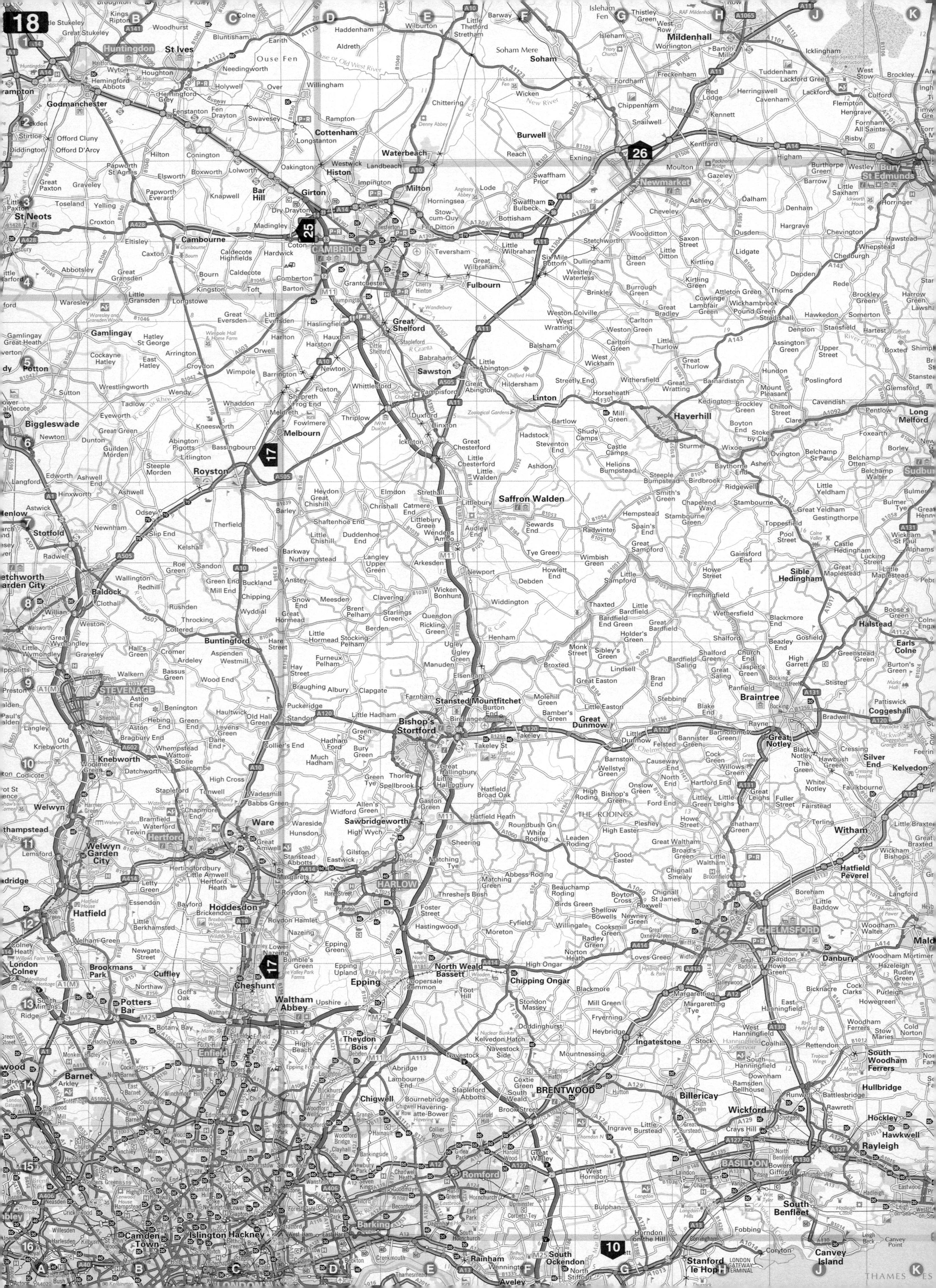
Huntingdon
St Ives
Godmanchester
St Neots
Cambourne
Bar Hill
Girton
Histon
Cottenham
Waterbeach
Milton
CAMBRIDGE
Burwell
Soham
Mildenhall
Newmarket
Bury St Edmunds
Fulbourn
Great Shelford
Sawston
Linton
Haverhill
Biggleswade
Potton
Gamlingay
Royston
Melbourn
Saffron Walden
Baldock
Letchworth Garden City
Stotfold
Buntingford
STEVENAGE
Knebworth
Welwyn
Welwyn Garden City
Hatfield
Hertford
Ware
Hoddesdon
Cheshunt
Waltham Abbey
Potters Bar
Enfield
Barnet
Bishop's Stortford
Stansted Mountfitchet
Sawbridgeworth
HARLOW
Epping
North Weald Bassett
Chipping Ongar
Great Dunmow
Braintree
Halstead
Sible Hedingham
Long Melford
Coggeshall
Witham
CHELMSFORD
Danbury
Ingatestone
BRENTWOOD
Billericay
Wickford
Rayleigh
BASILDON
South Benfleet
Canvey Island
Stanford le Hope
Romford
Barking
Chigwell
Theydon Bois
Islington
Hackney
Camden Town
Rainham
South Ockendon
THE RODINGS
M11
M25
A1(M)
A14
A10
A12
A120
A127
A13
25
26
17
10

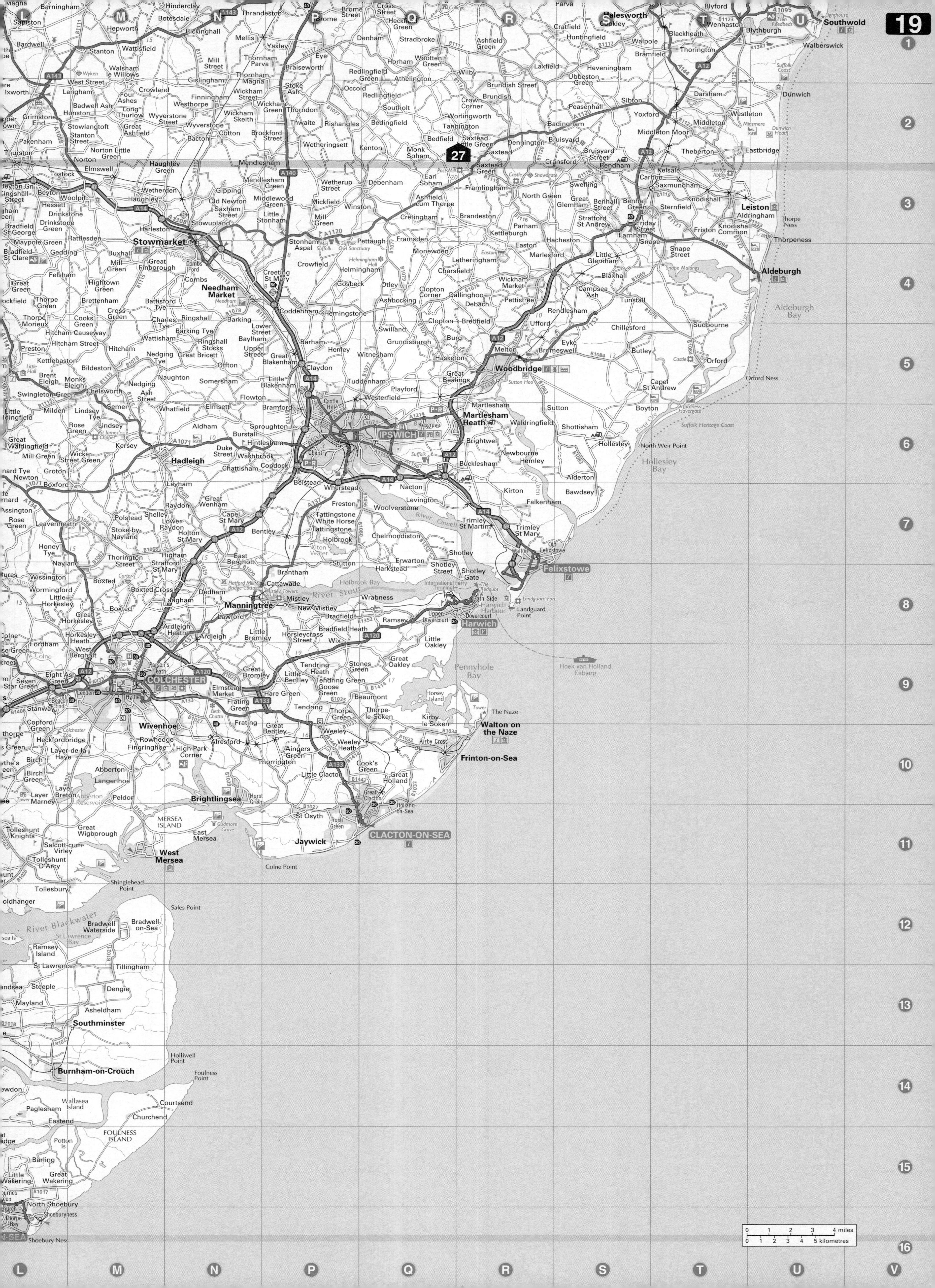
Southwold
Halesworth
Blythburgh
Walberswick
Dunwich
Stowmarket
Needham Market
Framlingham
Saxmundham
Leiston
Aldeburgh
Orford
Orford Ness
Aldeburgh Bay
Woodbridge
Martlesham Heath
IPSWICH
Hadleigh
Felixstowe
Hollesley Bay
Manningtree
Harwich
Hoek van Holland
Esbjerg
COLCHESTER
Wivenhoe
Brightlingsea
Walton on the Naze
Frinton-on-Sea
CLACTON-ON-SEA
Jaywick
West Mersea
MERSEA ISLAND
Pennyhole Bay
Holbrook Bay
River Stour
River Orwell
River Blackwater
Burnham-on-Crouch
Southminster
FOULNESS ISLAND
Wallasea Island
North Shoebury
Shoebury Ness
Colne Point
Sales Point
Holliwell Point
Foulness Point
27
0 1 2 3 4 miles
0 1 2 3 4 5 kilometres
L M N P Q R S T U V
1 2 3 4 5 6 7 8 9 10 11 12 13 14 15 16

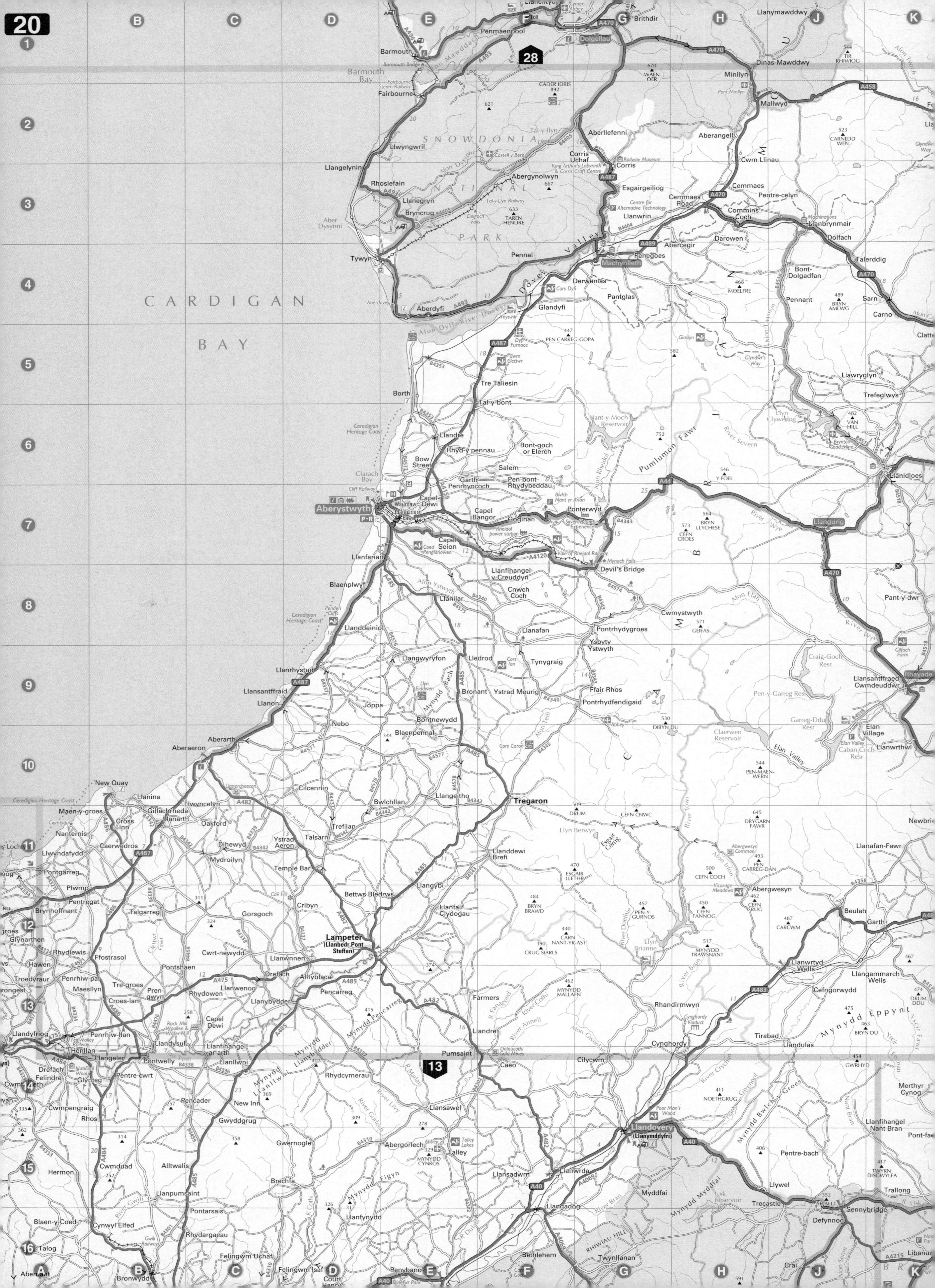

CARDIGAN
BAY
SNOWDONIA
NATIONAL
PARK
Barmouth
Penmaenpool
Dolgellau
Brithdir
Llanymawddwy
28
Barmouth Bay
Fairbourne
Fairbourne Steam Railway
CADER IDRIS 892
WAEN OER
Minllyn
Dinas-Mawddwy
Mallwyd
Pont Minllyn
Tal-y-llyn
Abergynolwyn
Castell y Bere
Llwyngwril
Llangelynin
Rhoslefain
Llanegryn
Bryncrug
Tal-y-Llyn Railway
TAREN HENDRE
Aber Dysynni
Tywyn
Pennal
Aberllefenni
Corris Uchaf
Corris
King Arthur's Labyrinth & Corris Craft Centre
Railway Museum
Esgairgeiliog
Centre for Alternative Technology
Llanwrin
Aberangell
Cwm Llinau
CARNEDD WEN
Cemmaes
Cemmaes Road
Commins Coch
Pentre-celyn
Llanbrynmair
Dolfach
Talerddig
Darowen
Abercegir
Penegoes
Machynlleth
Dovey Valley
Derwenlas
Cors Dyfi
Aberdovey
Aberdyfi
Ynys-hir
Afon Dyfi/River Dovey
Glandyfi
Pantglas
MOELFRE
Bont-Dolgadfan
Pennant
BRYN AMLWG
Sarn
Carno
Clatter
PEN CARREG-GOPA
Dyfi Furnace
Gwm Glettwr
Glaslyn
Glyndŵr's Way
Tre Taliesin
Borth
Tal-y-bont
Llawryglyn
Trefeglwys
Llyn Clywedog
VAN HILL
Bryntail Lead Mine
Nant-y-Moch Reservoir
Ceredigion Heritage Coast
Llandre
Rhyd-y pennau
Bont-goch or Elerch
Bow Street
Pumlumon Fawr
River Severn
Salem
Clarach Bay
Cliff Railway
Garth Penrhyncoch
Pen-bont Rhydybeddau
Bwlch Nant yr Arian
Y FOEL
Llanidloes
Aberystwyth
Waunfawr
Capel-Dewi
Llanbadarn Fawr
Capel Bangor
Goginan
Ponterwyd
Silver Mountain Experience
Rheidol power station
BRYN LLYCHESE
CEFN CROES
Llangurig
River Wye
Capel Seion
Coed Penglanowen
Vale of Rheidol Railway
Mynach Falls
Devil's Bridge
Llanfarian
Llanfihangel-y-Creuddyn
Blaenplwyf
Afon Ystwyth
Cnwch Coch
Llanilar
Afon Elan
Pant-y-dwr
Cwmystwyth
GEIFAS
Pontrhydygroes
Penderi Cliffs
Llanddeiniol
Llanafan
Ysbyty Ystwyth
Gilfach Farm
Craig-Goch Resr
Llangwyryfon
Lledrod
Cors Ian
Tynygraig
Llyn Eiddwen
Mynydd Bach
Llanrhystud
Bronant
Ystrad Meurig
Ffair Rhos
Pontrhydfendigaid
Rhayader
Llansantffraed-Cwmdeuddwr
Pen-y-Garreg Resr
Llansantffraid
Llanon
Joppa
Nebo
Bontnewydd
Blaenpennal
DIBYN DU
Abbey
Garreg-Ddu Resr
Claerwen Reservoir
Elan Village
Elan Valley
Caban Coch Resr
Llanwrthwl
Aberarth
Aberaeron
Cors Caron
Afon Teifi
PEN-MAEN-WERN
New Quay
Llanina
Ceredigion Heritage Coast
Maen-y-groes
Cwmtydu
Gilfachrheda
Llanarth
Llwyncelyn
Cilcennin
Llangeitho
Bwlchllan
Tregaron
DRUM
CEFN CNWC
DRYGARN FAWR
Newbridge
Cross Inn
Nanternis
Oakford
Afon Aeron
Trefilan
Llyn Berwyn
Esgair Cerrig
River Towy
Llwyndafydd
Caerwedros
Dihewyd
Ystrad Aeron
Talsarn
Llanddewi Brefi
Abergwesyn Common
Llanafan-Fawr
Pontgarreg
Mydroilyn
Temple Bar
ESGAIR LLETHR
CEFN COCH
PEN CARREG-DAN
Plwmp
Llangybi
Vicarage Meadows
Abergwesyn
Pentregat
Brynhoffnant
Cribyn
Bettws Bledrws
Llanfair Clydogau
BRYN BRAWD
PEN-Y-GURNOS
CEFN FANNOG
CEFN GRUG
Beulah
Talgarreg
Gorsgoch
CARCWM
Garth
Glynarthen
Lampeter (Llanbedr Pont Steffan)
CARN NANT-YR-AST
Llyn Brianne
MYNYDD TRAWSNANT
Rhydlewis
Ffostrasol
Cwrt-newydd
CRUG SIARLS
River Doethie
Hawen
Pontshaen
Llanwnnen
Llanwrtyd Wells
Troedyraur
Penrhiw-pal
Drefach
Alltyblaca
Tre-groes
Prengwyn
MYNYDD MALLAEN
Llangammarch Wells
Maesllyn
Rhydowen
Llanwenog
Llanybydder
Pencarreg
Farmers
Rhandirmwyn
Cefngorwydd
Croes-lan
Capel Dewi
Mynydd Pencarreg
River Cothi
Cynghordy Viaduct
DRUM DDU
Rock Mill Woollen & Water Mill
Mynydd Eppynt
Llandyfriog
Penrhiw-llan
Teifi Valley Railway
Henllan
Llandysul
Llanfihangel-ar-arth
Mynydd Llanybydder
Llandre
Pumsaint
Dolaucothi Gold Mines
Cynghordy
Tirabad
Llandulas
BRYN DU
Llangeler
Pontwelly
Llanllwni
Cilycwm
GWRHYD
Drefach Felindre
National Wool Museum
Glynteg
Pentre-cwrt
Rhydcymerau
13
Caeo
Mynydd Llanllwni
Cwmhiraeth
Cwmpengraig
Pencader
New Inn
River Crychan
NOETHGRUG
Merthyr Cynog
Rhos
Gwyddgrug
Llansawel
Poor Man's Wood
Mynydd Bwlch-y-Groes
Nant Bran
Llandovery (Llanymddyfri)
Llanfihangel Nant Bran
Pont-faen
Gwernogle
Abergorlech
Talley Lakes
Talley
MYNYDD CYNROS
Pentre-bach
Cwmduad
Alltwalis
Hermon
Llansadwrn
Llanwrda
TWYRN DISGWYLFA
Brechfa
Mynydd Figyn
Myddfai
Mynydd Myddfai
Usk Reservoir
Llywel
Trallong
Llanpumsaint
Llangadog
Trecastle
Sennybridge
Blaen-y-Coed
Cynwyl Elfed
Pontarsais
Llanfynydd
Defynnog
Gwili Railway
Rhydargaeau
RHIWIAU HILL
Talog
Felingwm Uchaf
Bethlehem
Twynllanan
Libanus
Abernant
Bronwydd
Felingwm Isaf
Court Henry
Penybanc
Crai
BRECON
A470
A493
A487
A489
A458
A44
A485
A4120
A482
A475
A486
A484
A40
A483
A4069
A4215
B4405
B4404
B4353
B4572
B4343
B4340
B4574
B4575
B4576
B4337
B4342
B4577
B4578
B4336
B4459
B4338
B4476
B4310
B4302
B4301
B4333
B4358
B4518

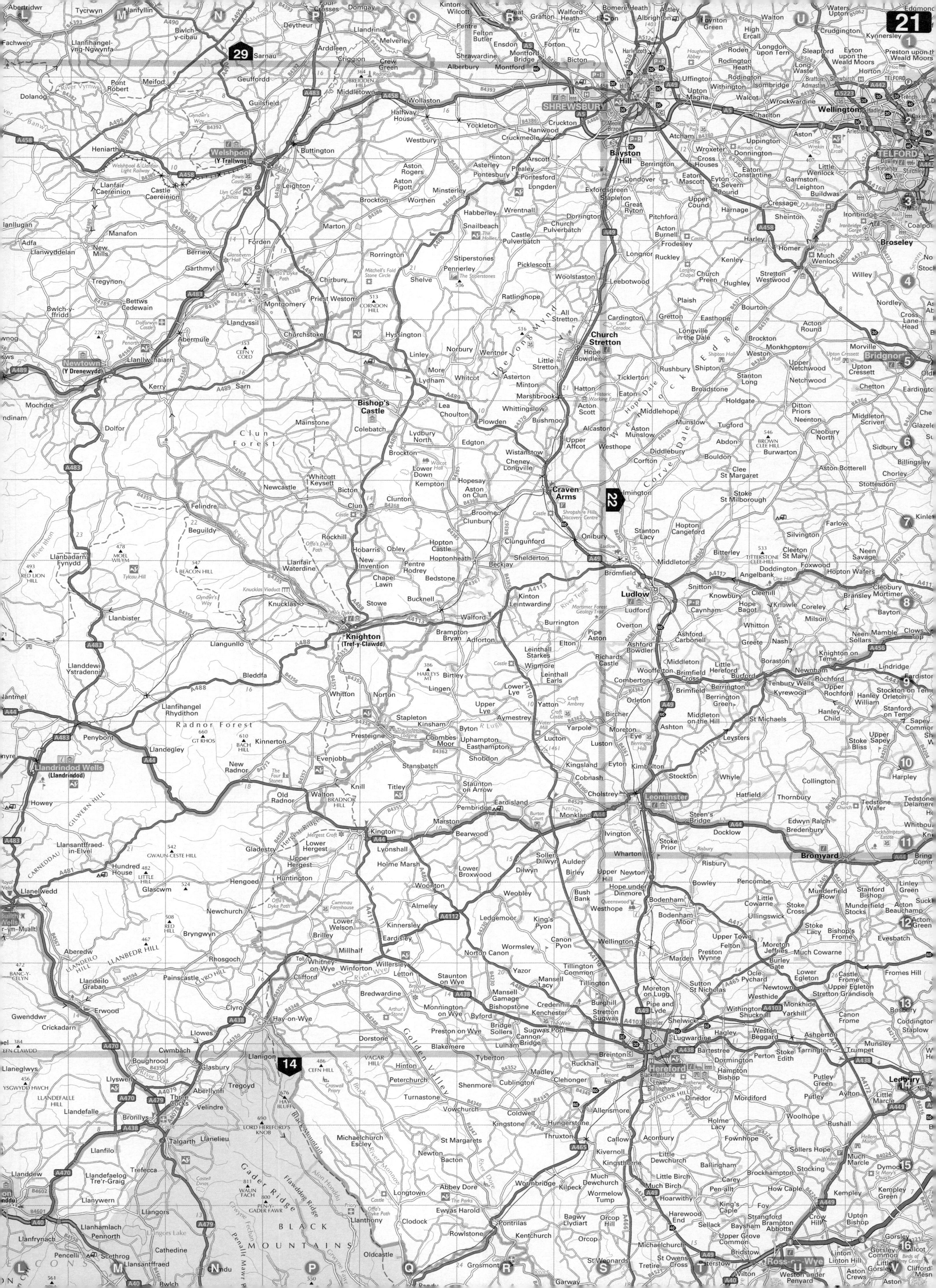
SHREWSBURY
Welshpool
(Y Trallwng)
Wellington
TELFORD
Bayston Hill
Church Stretton
Bishop's Castle
Craven Arms
Ludlow
Knighton
(Tref-y-Clawdd)
Leominster
Hereford
Ross-on-Wye
Ledbury
Bromyard
Bridgnorth
Broseley
Newtown
(Y Drenewydd)
Montgomery
Llandrindod Wells
(Llandrindod)
Kington
Presteigne
Hay-on-Wye
Talgarth
Clun Forest
Radnor Forest
The Long Mynd
Wenlock Edge
Corve Dale
Golden Valley
BLACK MOUNTAINS
Gader Ridge
29
22
14

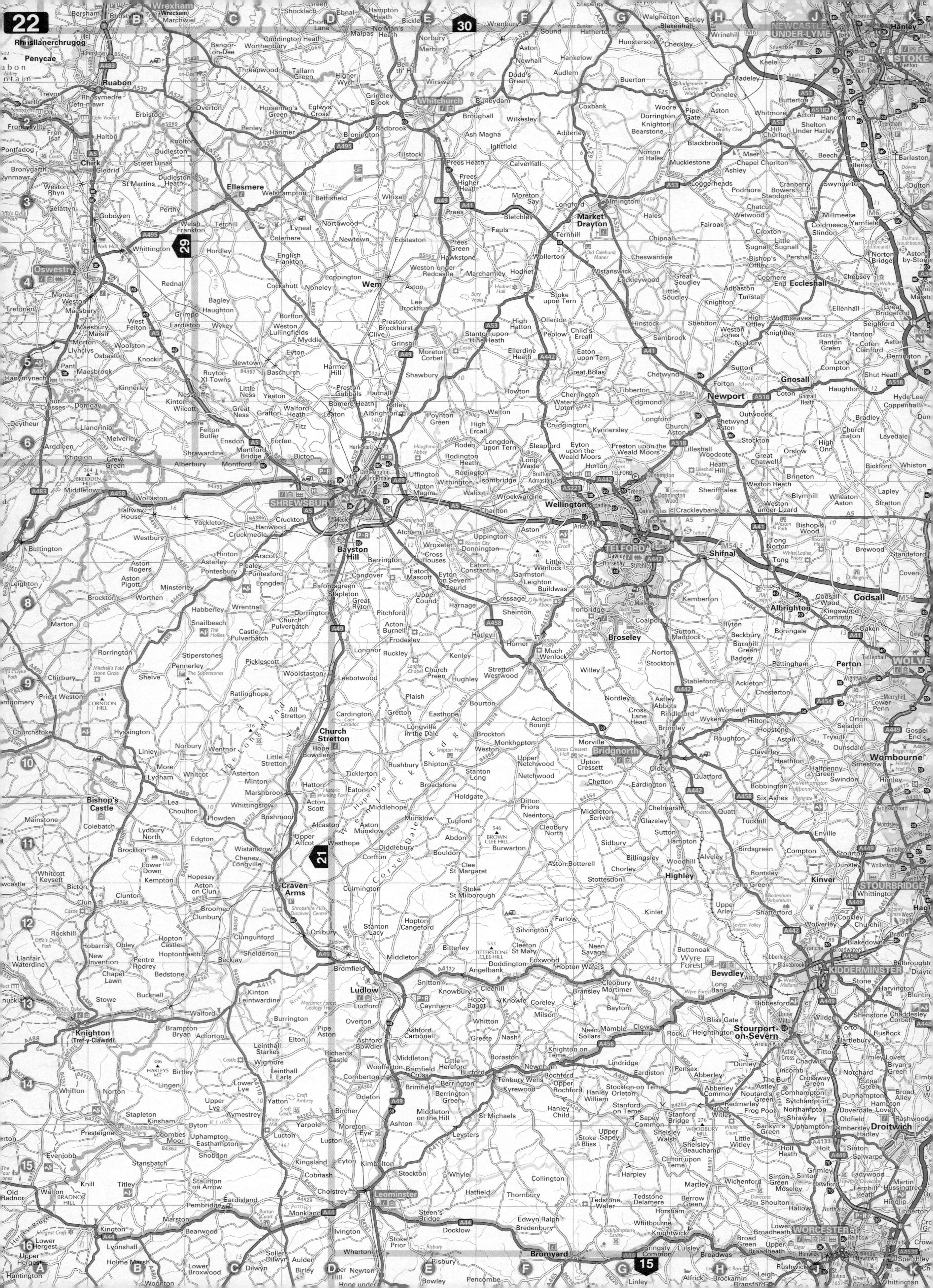
Wrexham
Whitchurch
Newcastle-under-Lyme
Stoke
Hanley
Ruabon
Chirk
Ellesmere
Oswestry
Wem
Market Drayton
Eccleshall
Newport
Gnosall
Shrewsbury
Wellington
Telford
Shifnal
Codsall
Albrighton
Bayston Hill
Broseley
Much Wenlock
Church Stretton
Bridgnorth
Wombourne
Bishop's Castle
Craven Arms
Highley
Kinver
Stourbridge
Ludlow
Cleobury Mortimer
Bewdley
Kidderminster
Knighton
Stourport-on-Severn
Tenbury Wells
Droitwich
Leominster
Bromyard
Worcester

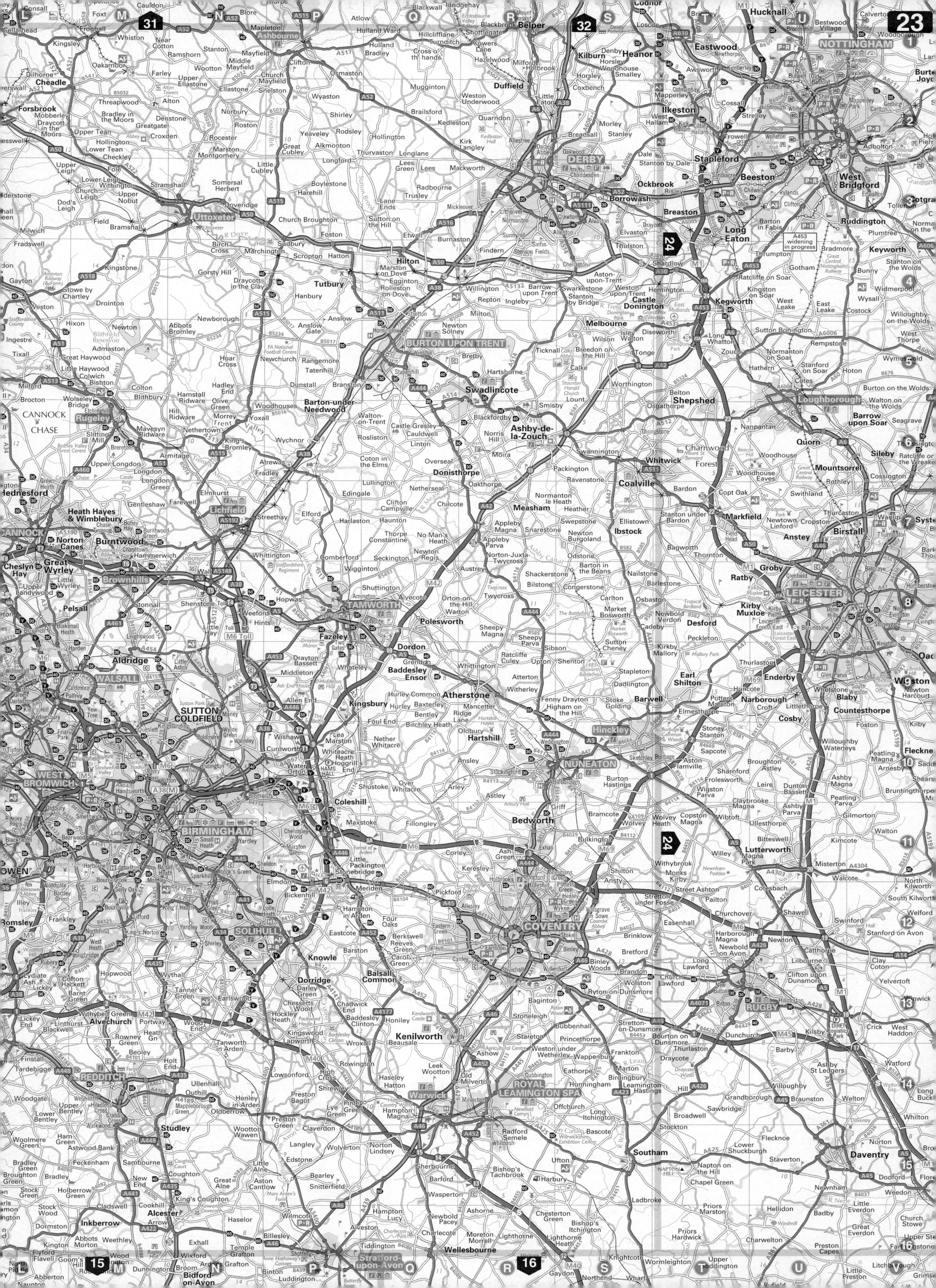
NOTTINGHAM
DERBY
BURTON UPON TRENT
Loughborough
LEICESTER
Hinckley
NUNEATON
COVENTRY
RUGBY
BIRMINGHAM
SOLIHULL
WALSALL
WEST BROMWICH
SUTTON COLDFIELD
TAMWORTH
Lichfield
Rugeley
CANNOCK CHASE
Uttoxeter
Ashbourne
Brownhills
REDDITCH
Warwick
ROYAL LEAMINGTON SPA
Stratford-upon-Avon
Daventry
Coalville
Ashby-de-la-Zouch
Swadlincote
Kenilworth
Long Eaton
West Bridgford
Ilkeston
Heanor
Belper
Cheadle
Hednesford
Alcester
Studley
Wellesbourne
Southam
Lutterworth
31
32
24
15
16

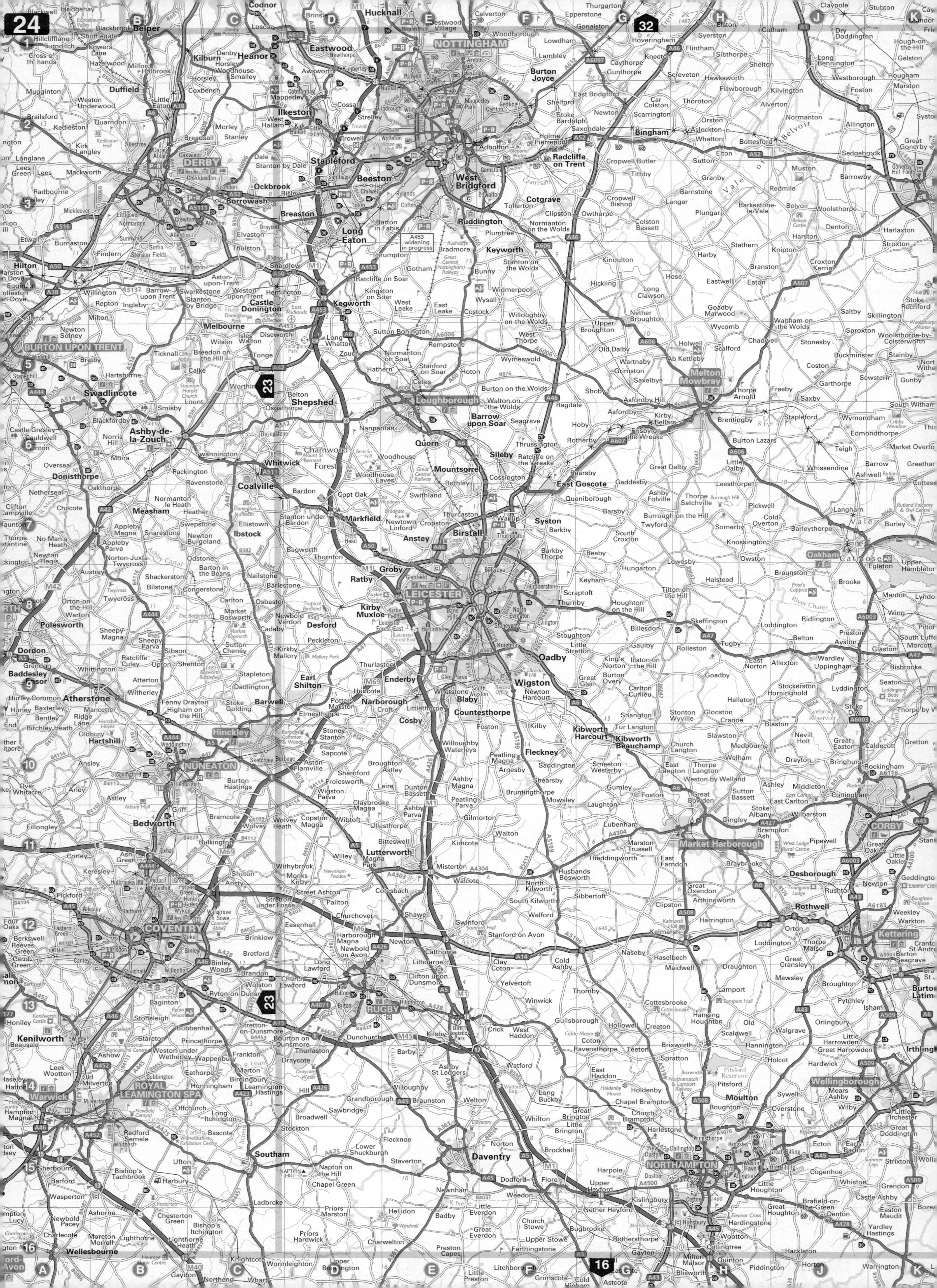
32
23
16
NOTTINGHAM
DERBY
LEICESTER
COVENTRY
NUNEATON
NORTHAMPTON
BURTON UPON TRENT
Loughborough
Melton Mowbray
Hinckley
RUGBY
Market Harborough
CORBY
Kettering
Wellingborough
ROYAL LEAMINGTON SPA
Warwick
Oakham
Hucknall
Belper
Heanor
Eastwood
Ilkeston
Stapleford
Beeston
West Bridgford
Long Eaton
Bingham
Radcliffe on Trent
Ruddington
Keyworth
Kegworth
Castle Donington
Melbourne
Swadlincote
Ashby-de-la-Zouch
Shepshed
Coalville
Whitwick
Quorn
Sileby
Mountsorrel
Syston
Birstall
Markfield
Anstey
Groby
Ratby
Kirby Muxloe
Desford
Oadby
Wigston
Blaby
Countesthorpe
Narborough
Enderby
Earl Shilton
Barwell
Atherstone
Polesworth
Bedworth
Lutterworth
Kibworth Harcourt
Kibworth Beauchamp
Fleckney
Desborough
Rothwell
Daventry
Southam
Kenilworth
Wellesbourne
Duffield
Borrowash
Cotgrave
Moulton
M1
M6
M69
M42
M45
A46
A6
A5
A14

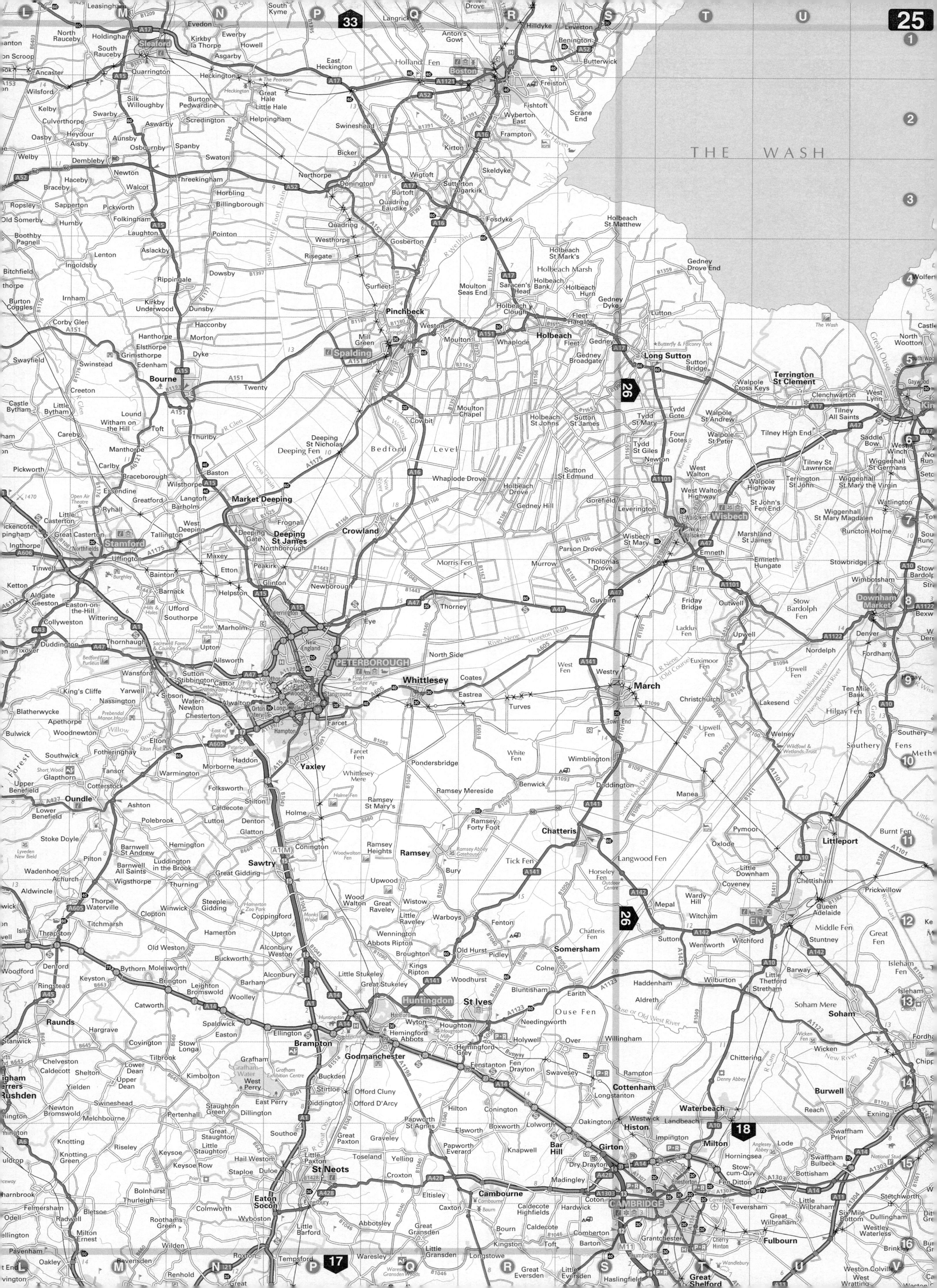
THE WASH
Sleaford
Boston
Spalding
Holbeach
Long Sutton
Bourne
Stamford
Market Deeping
Deeping St James
Crowland
Pinchbeck
PETERBOROUGH
Whittlesey
March
Wisbech
Downham Market
Oundle
Yaxley
Sawtry
Ramsey
Chatteris
Littleport
Ely
Huntingdon
St Ives
Somersham
Soham
Thrapston
Raunds
Rushden
Brampton
Godmanchester
St Neots
Eaton Socon
Cambourne
Cottenham
Histon
Girton
Milton
Waterbeach
Burwell
CAMBRIDGE
Fulbourn
Great Shelford
Bedford Level
Ouse Fen
Grafham Water

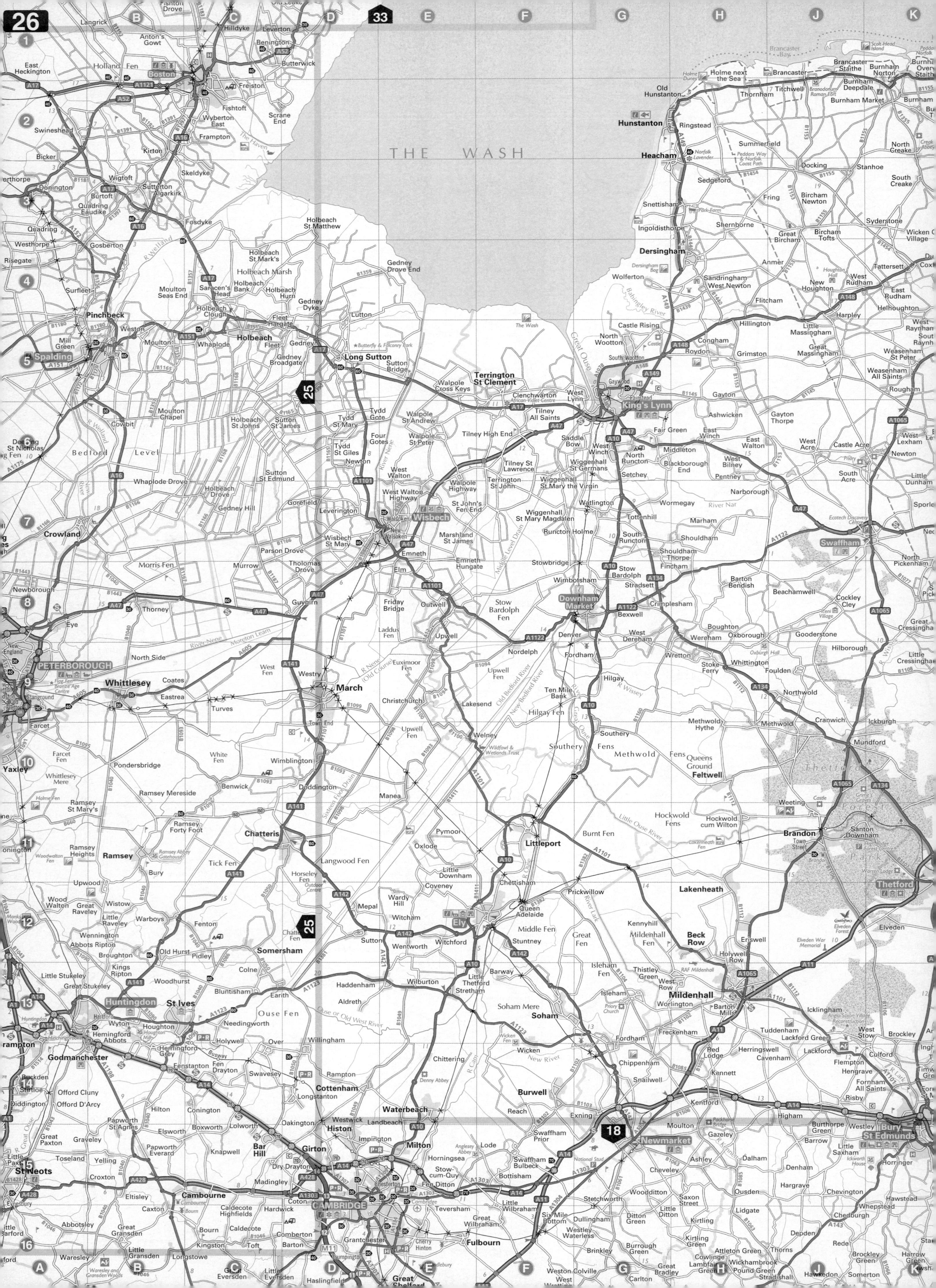
33
25
18
THE WASH
Boston
Spalding
PETERBOROUGH
Whittlesey
March
Wisbech
King's Lynn
Hunstanton
Heacham
Dersingham
Downham Market
Swaffham
Thetford
Brandon
Mundford
Feltwell
Methwold
Littleport
Ely
Soham
Mildenhall
Lakenheath
Newmarket
Bury St Edmunds
Cambridge
Huntingdon
St Ives
St Neots
Godmanchester
Chatteris
Ramsey
Yaxley
Crowland
Holbeach
Long Sutton
Pinchbeck
Terrington St Clement
Sutton Bridge
Gedney
Fleet
Whaplode
Moulton
Weston
Kirton
Frampton
Wyberton East
Fishtoft
Freiston
Butterwick
Benington
Leverton
Hilldyke
Anton's Gowt
Langrick
Holland Fen
East Heckington
Swineshead
Bicker
Donington
Quadring
Gosberton
Surfleet
Wigtoft
Sutterton
Algarkirk
Fosdyke
Scrane End
Skeldyke
Holbeach St Matthew
Holbeach St Mark's
Holbeach Marsh
Holbeach Bank
Holbeach Hurn
Holbeach Clough
Gedney Drove End
Gedney Dyke
Lutton
Moulton Seas End
Saracen's Head
Fleet Hargate
Gedney Broadgate
Moulton Chapel
Holbeach St Johns
Sutton St James
Sutton St Edmund
Whaplode Drove
Holbeach Drove
Gedney Hill
Cowbit
Deeping St Nicholas
Bedford Level
Tydd Gote
Tydd St Mary
Tydd St Giles
Four Gotes
Newton
Walpole Cross Keys
Walpole St Andrew
Walpole St Peter
Walpole Highway
West Walton
West Walton Highway
Clenchwarton
Tilney All Saints
Tilney High End
Tilney St Lawrence
Terrington St John
St John's Fen End
West Lynn
Saddle Bow
Wiggenhall St Germans
Wiggenhall St Mary the Virgin
Wiggenhall St Mary Magdalen
Watlington
Runcton Holme
Tottenhill
South Runcton
Stow Bardolph
Stowbridge
Wimbotsham
Marshland St James
Emneth Hungate
Emneth
Elm
Leverington
Gorefield
Wisbech St Mary
Parson Drove
Murrow
Tholomas Drove
Guyhirn
Morris Fen
Newborough
Thorney
Eye
North Side
Friday Bridge
Outwell
Upwell
Nordelph
Stow Bardolph Fen
Denver
Fordham
Hilgay
Ten Mile Bank
Hilgay Fen
Southery
Southery Fens
Methwold Fens
Methwold Hythe
Queens Ground
Welney
Lakesend
Christchurch
Upwell Fen
Euximoor Fen
Laddus Fen
West Fen
Westry
Coates
Eastrea
Turves
Farcet
Stanground
Pondersbridge
White Fen
Wimblington
Benwick
Doddington
Manea
Ramsey Mereside
Ramsey St Mary's
Ramsey Forty Foot
Ramsey Heights
Whittlesey Mere
Bury
Upwood
Tick Fen
Wood Walton
Great Raveley
Little Raveley
Wistow
Warboys
Fenton
Pidley
Somersham
Colne
Bluntisham
Earith
Woodhurst
Old Hurst
Wennington
Abbots Ripton
Broughton
Kings Ripton
Little Stukeley
Great Stukeley
Hartford
Wyton
Houghton
Hemingford Abbots
Hemingford Grey
Needingworth
Holywell
Over
Willingham
Fenstanton
Fen Drayton
Swavesey
Longstanton
Rampton
Cottenham
Oakington
Histon
Impington
Girton
Westwick
Landbeach
Waterbeach
Milton
Bar Hill
Dry Drayton
Madingley
Coton
Cambourne
Caldecote
Highfields
Hardwick
Comberton
Barton
Toft
Kingston
Bourn
Eltisley
Caxton
Great Gransden
Little Gransden
Abbotsley
Waresley
Longstowe
Croxton
Toseland
Yelling
Graveley
Papworth Everard
Papworth St Agnes
Hilton
Conington
Boxworth
Elsworth
Lolworth
Knapwell
Offord Cluny
Offord D'Arcy
Diddington
Buckden
Great Paxton
Little Paxton
Eynesbury
Sutton
Haddenham
Aldreth
Wilburton
Stretham
Little Thetford
Witchford
Wentworth
Witcham
Mepal
Wardy Hill
Coveney
Little Downham
Pymoor
Oxlode
Langwood Fen
Horseley Fen
Chettisham
Queen Adelaide
Prickwillow
Middle Fen
Stuntney
Barway
Soham Mere
Great Fen
Isleham Fen
Isleham
Thistley Green
West Row
Mildenhall Fen
Kennyhill
Beck Row
Burnt Fen
Hockwold Fens
Hockwold cum Wilton
Weeting
Santon Downham
Elveden
Eriswell
Holywell Row
Barton Mills
Worlington
Freckenham
Fordham
Chippenham
Snailwell
Wicken
Upware
Burwell
Reach
Exning
Swaffham Prior
Swaffham Bulbeck
Lode
Horningsea
Stow-cum-Quy
Fen Ditton
Bottisham
Teversham
Little Wilbraham
Great Wilbraham
Fulbourn
Cherry Hinton
Grantchester
Trumpington
Great Shelford
Haslingfield
Six Mile Bottom
Westley Waterless
Dullingham
Stetchworth
Woodditton
Cheveley
Ashley
Moulton
Gazeley
Dalham
Kentford
Kennett
Red Lodge
Herringswell
Cavenham
Tuddenham
Icklingham
Lackford
Flempton
Hengrave
Fornham All Saints
Risby
Higham
Barrow
Burthorpe Green
Little Saxham
Westley
Horringer
Denham
Hargrave
Chevington
Ousden
Lidgate
Saxon Street
Kirtling
Kirtling Green
Ditton Green
Little Ditton
Burrough Green
Brinkley
Weston Colville
Carlton
Great Bradley
Cowlinge
Lambfair Green
Wickhambrook
Attleton Green
Thorns
Depden
Rede
Chedburgh
Whepstead
Hawstead
Brockley
Hawkedon
Stradishall
Somerton
Harrow Green
Colford
Culford
West Stow
Ingham
Timworth
Fair Green
Middleton
Blackborough End
Setchey
North Runcton
West Winch
East Winch
Ashwicken
Gayton
Gayton Thorpe
West Bilney
Pentney
Narborough
Wormegay
Marham
Shouldham
Shouldham Thorpe
Fincham
Stradsett
Crimplesham
Bexwell
West Dereham
Wereham
Wretton
Stoke Ferry
Boughton
Oxborough
Barton Bendish
Beachamwell
Cockley Cley
Gooderstone
Hilborough
Whittington
Foulden
Northwold
Cranwich
Ickburgh
West Acre
Castle Acre
South Acre
Newton
Little Dunham
Sporle
North Pickenham
Great Cressingham
Little Cressingham
West Lexham
East Walton
Middleton
Congham
Roydon
Grimston
Hillington
Harpley
Great Massingham
Little Massingham
Flitcham
Anmer
West Newton
Sandringham
Wolferton
Castle Rising
North Wootton
South Wootton
Gaywood
Ingoldisthorpe
Snettisham
Sedgeford
Fring
Shernborne
Great Bircham
Bircham Newton
Bircham Tofts
Docking
Stanhoe
Ringstead
Old Hunstanton
Holme next the Sea
Thornham
Titchwell
Brancaster
Brancaster Staithe
Burnham Deepdale
Burnham Market
Burnham Norton
Burnham Overy Staithe
Summerfield
North Creake
South Creake
Syderstone
Tattersett
West Rudham
East Rudham
New Houghton
Helhoughton
Weasenham St Peter
Weasenham All Saints
Rougham
Wicken Village
Scolt Head Island
Brancaster Bay
Thetford Forest Park
Ouse Fen
New River
River Lark
River Nar
Great Ouse
Old Bedford River
New Bedford River
Sixteen Foot Drain
Middle Level Drain
Forty Foot
River Nene
River Welland
The Haven

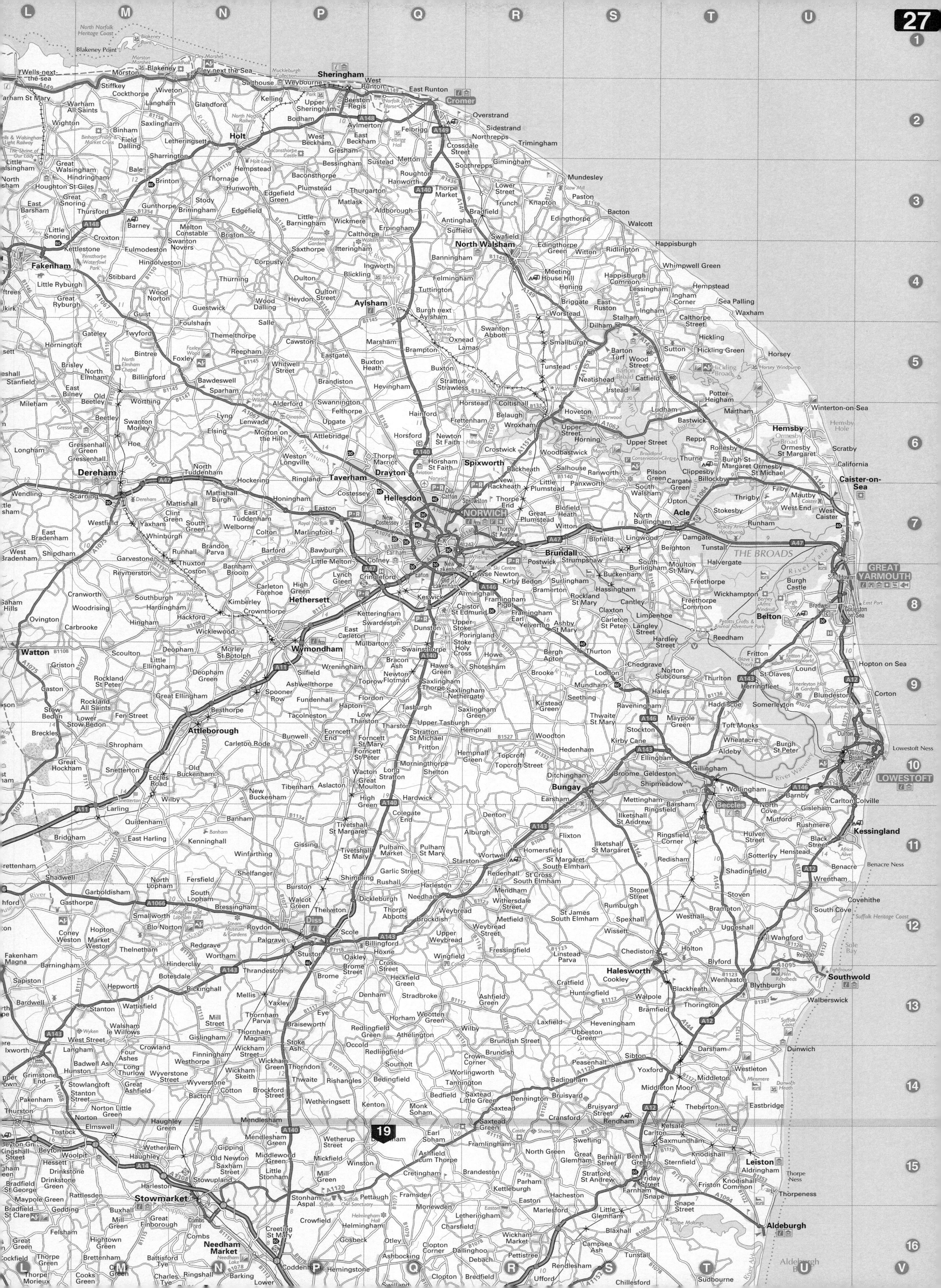
L
M
N
P
Q
R
S
T
U
V
North Norfolk Heritage Coast
Blakeney Point
Wells-next-the-sea
Sheringham
Cromer
Holt
Fakenham
Aylsham
North Walsham
Mundesley
Happisburgh
Sea Palling
Dereham
Taverham
Drayton
Hellesdon
NORWICH
Acle
Caister-on-Sea
GREAT YARMOUTH
THE BROADS
Brundall
Hethersett
Wymondham
Watton
Attleborough
Belton
Hopton on Sea
Corton
Lowestoft Ness
LOWESTOFT
Beccles
Bungay
Kessingland
Diss
Halesworth
Southwold
Walberswick
Dunwich
Stowmarket
Needham Market
Leiston
Saxmundham
Aldeburgh
19
1
2
3
4
5
6
7
8
9
10
11
12
13
14
15
16

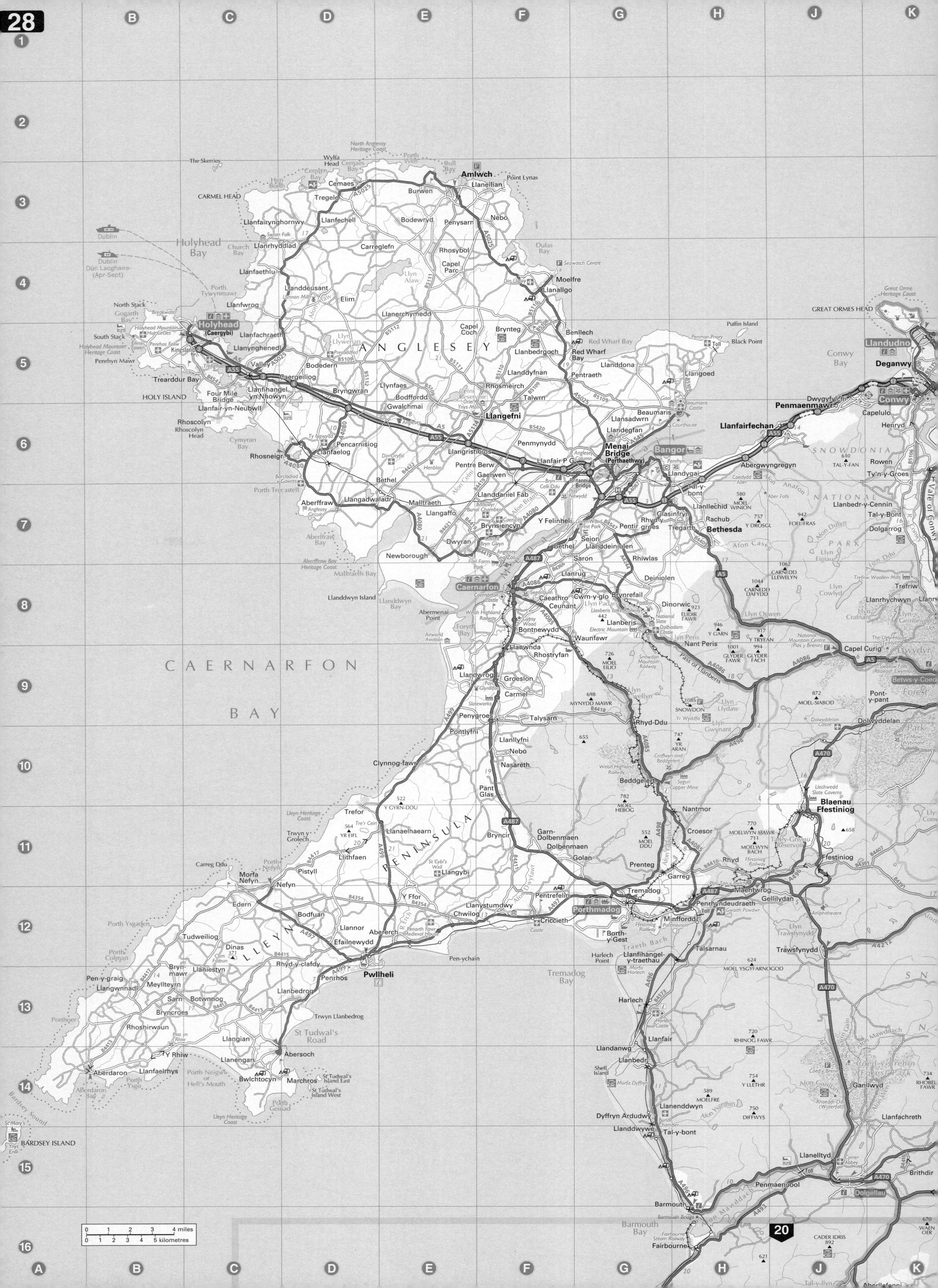
ANGLESEY
CAERNARFON BAY
LLEYN PENINSULA
SNOWDONIA NATIONAL PARK
Holyhead (Caergybi)
HOLY ISLAND
Holyhead Bay
Dublin
Dublin Dún Laoghaire (Apr-Sept)
The Skerries
CARMEL HEAD
Wylfa Head
Cemaes
Cemaes Bay
Amlwch
Llaneilian
Point Lynas
Bull Bay
Porth Wen
Burwen
Tregele
Llanfechell
Bodewryd
Penysarn
Nebo
Llanfairynghornwy
Llanrhyddlad
Carreglefn
Rhosybol
Capel Parc
Dulas Bay
Moelfre
Llanallgo
Llanfaethlu
Llanddeusant
Elim
Llanerchymedd
Capel Coch
Brynteg
Benllech
Red Wharf Bay
Puffin Island
Black Point
North Stack
Gogarth Bay
South Stack
Penrhyn Mawr
Llanfwrog
Llanfachraeth
Llanynghenedl
Kingsland
Valley
Trearddur Bay
Four Mile Bridge
Llanfihangel yn Nhowyn
Caergeiliog
Bodedern
Bryngwran
Llynfaes
Bodffordd
Gwalchmai
Llangefni
Rhosmeirch
Talwrn
Llanbedrgoch
Llanddyfnan
Pentraeth
Llanddona
Llangoed
Beaumaris
Llansadwrn
Llandegfan
Menai Bridge (Porthaethwy)
Bangor
Llanfair-yn-Neubwll
Rhoscolyn
Rhoscolyn Head
Cymyran Bay
Rhosneigr
Pencarnisiog
Llanfaelog
Llangristiolus
Pentre Berw
Gaerwen
Penmynydd
Llanfair P G
Bethel
Porth Trecastell
Aberffraw
Llangadwaladr
Malltraeth
Llanddaniel Fab
Llangaffo
Brynsiencyn
Dwyran
Newborough
Y Felinheli
Malltraeth Bay
Llanddwyn Island
Llanddwyn Bay
Abermenai Point
Foryd Bay
Caernarfon
Caeathro
Cwm-y-glo
Ceunant
Llanrug
Bethel
Saron
Llanddeiniolen
Pentir
Rhiwlas
Deiniolen
Brynrefail
Dinorwic
Llanberis
Bontnewydd
Waunfawr
Llanwnda
Rhostryfan
Llandwrog
Groeslon
Carmel
Penygroes
Talysarn
Pontllyfni
Llanllyfni
Nebo
Nasareth
Clynnog-fawr
Pant Glas
Trefor
Llanaelhaearn
Llithfaen
Trwyn y Gorlech
Carreg Ddu
Morfa Nefyn
Nefyn
Pistyll
Llangybi
Bryncir
Garn-Dolbenmaen
Dolbenmaen
Golan
Prenteg
Edern
Bodfuan
Y Ffor
Llanystumdwy
Chwilog
Pentrefelin
Criccieth
Porthmadog
Tremadog
Porth Ysgaden
Tudweiliog
Llannor
Abererch
Efailnewydd
Dinas
Rhyd-y-clafdy
Pwllheli
Penrhos
Porth Colmon
Bryn-mawr
Llaniestyn
Pen-y-graig
Llangwnnadl
Meyllteyrn
Sarn
Botwnnog
Llanbedrog
Bryncroes
Porthor
Rhoshirwaun
Trwyn Llanbedrog
St Tudwal's Road
Llangian
Y Rhiw
Llanengan
Abersoch
Aberdaron
Llanfaelrhys
Porth Neigwl or Hell's Mouth
Bwlchtocyn
Marchros
St Tudwal's Island East
St Tudwal's Island West
Aberdaron Bay
Porth Ysgo
Porth Ceiriad
Bardsey Sound
BARDSEY ISLAND
Pen-ychain
Tremadog Bay
Borth-y-Gest
Minffordd
Penrhyndeudraeth
Harlech Point
Llanfihangel-y-traethau
Talsarnau
Harlech
Llanfair
Llandanwg
Llanbedr
Shell Island
Dyffryn Ardudwy
Llanddwywe
Tal-y-bont
Llanenddwyn
Barmouth
Barmouth Bay
Fairbourne
Penmaenpool
Llanelltyd
Dolgellau
Brithdir
Llanfachreth
Ganllwyd
Trawsfynydd
Ffestiniog
Blaenau Ffestiniog
Maentwrog
Gellilydan
Rhyd
Croesor
Nantmor
Garreg
Beddgelert
Rhyd-Ddu
SNOWDON
Nant Peris
Capel Curig
Dolwyddelan
Pont-y-pant
Betws-y-Coed
Trefriw
Llanrhychwyn
Bethesda
Rachub
Tregarth
Glasinfryn
Llanllechid
Tal-y-bont
Llandygai
Abergwyngregyn
Llanfairfechan
Penmaenmawr
Dwygyfylchi
Conwy
Capelulo
Henryd
Rowen
Ty'n-y-Groes
Llanbedr-y-Cennin
Tal-y-Bont
Dolgarrog
Deganwy
Llandudno
GREAT ORMES HEAD
Conwy Bay
A5
A55
A487
A499
A497
A470
A496
A498
A4085
A4086
A4080
A5025
20

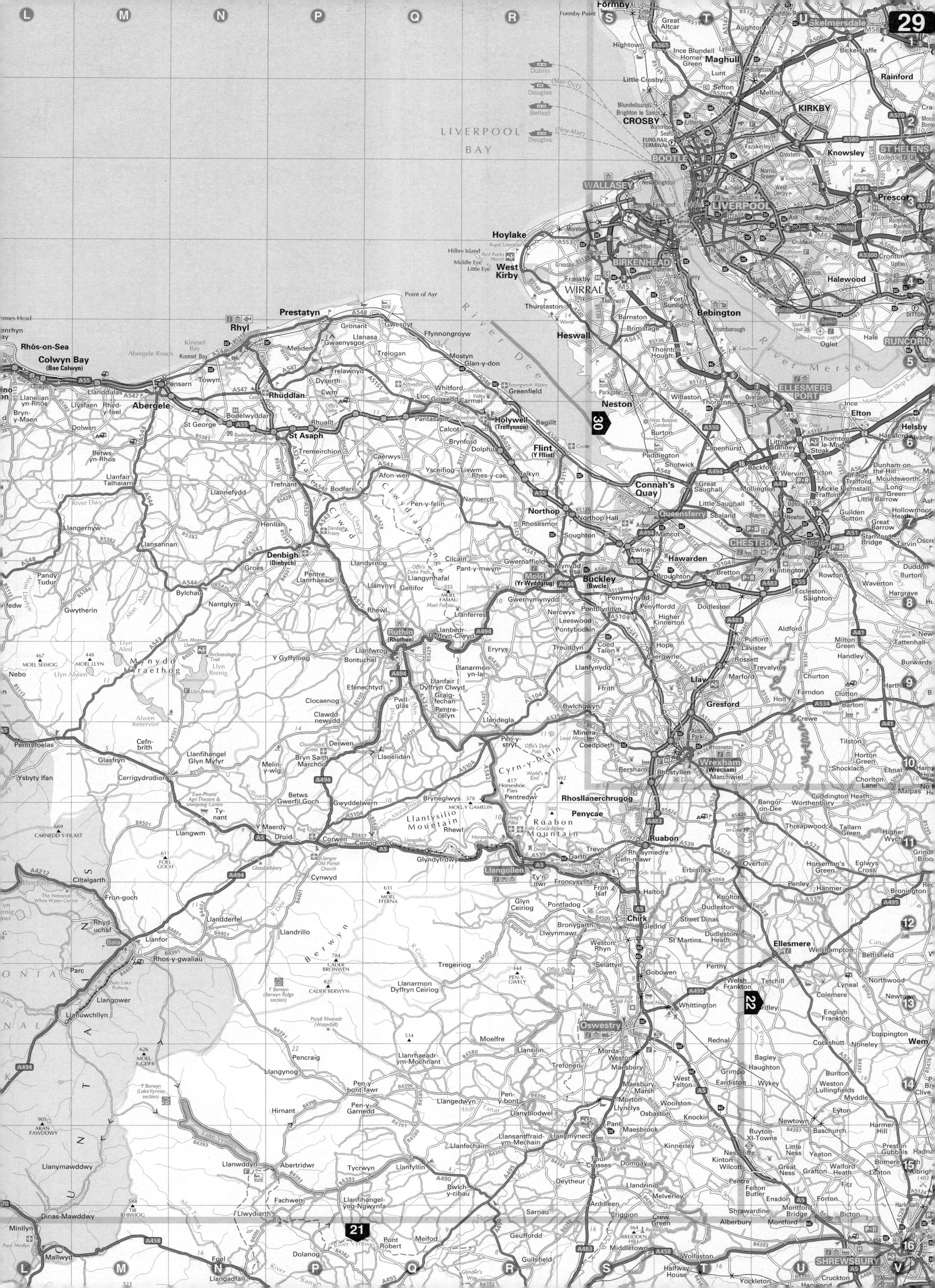
LIVERPOOL BAY
Formby
Formby Point
Great Altcar
Skelmersdale
Hightown
Ince Blundell
Homer Green
Maghull
Bickerstaffe
Rainford
Little Crosby
Lunt
Sefton
Melling
KIRKBY
Blundellsands
Brighton le Sands
CROSBY
Waterloo
Seaforth
Litherland
Orrell
Fazakerley
Croxteth
Knowsley
ST HELENS
Eccleston
BOOTLE
Norris Green
West Derby
Prescot
WALLASEY
New Brighton
Egremont
Everton
LIVERPOOL
Knotty Ash
Roby
Whiston
Rainhill
Rainhill Stoops
Moreton
Hoylake
Hilbre Island
Middle Eye
Little Eye
West Kirby
Upton
Claughton
BIRKENHEAD
Tranmere
Rock Ferry
Toxteth
Dingle
Allerton
Childwall
Halewood
Hunts Cross
Cronton
Hough Green
Greasby
Frankby
Irby
WIRRAL
Thingwall
Port Sunlight
Aigburth
Grassendale
Garston
Speke
Hale
Oglet
DITTON
Thurstaston
Heswall
Barnston
Brimstage
Bebington
Bromborough
Eastham
RUNCORN
Thornton Hough
Point of Ayr
Prestatyn
Gronant
Gwespyr
Ffynnongroyw
Rhyl
Llanasa
Meliden
Gwaenysgor
Trelogan
Mostyn
Glan-y-don
Rhôs-on-Sea
Colwyn Bay
(Bae Colwyn)
Kinmel Bay
Abergele Roads
Towyn
Pensarn
Dyserth
Trelawnyd
Cwm
Rhuddlan
Whitford
Greenfield
River Dee
River Mersey
Parkgate
Neston
Willaston
Childer Thornton
Overpool
ELLESMERE PORT
Ince
Elton
Helsby
Llanddulas
Llanelian-yn-Rhôs
Llysfaen
Rhyd-y-foel
Abergele
Bryn-y-Maen
Dolwen
St George
Bodelwyddan
St Asaph
Rhuallt
Tremeirchion
Gorsedd
Carmel
Lloc
Pantasaph
Calcot
Holywell
(Treffynnon)
Bagillt
Brynford
Dolphin
Flint
(Y Fflint)
Burton
Capenhurst
Puddington
Shotwick
Little Stanney
Stoak
Thornton-le-Moors
Hapsford
Alvanley
Betws-yn-Rhos
Llanfair Talhaiarn
Caerwys
Afon-wen
Ysceifiog
Lixwm
Rhes-y-cae
Halkyn
Backford
Wervin
Picton
Bridge Trafford
Dunham-on-the-Hill
Mouldsworth
Trefnant
Bodfari
Llannefydd
Vale of Clwyd
Clwydian Range
Pen-y-felin
Nannerch
Connah's Quay
Great Saughall
Mollington
Mickle Trafford
Plemstall
Long Green
Little Barrow
River Elwy
Llangernyw
Henllan
Northop
Northop Hall
Rhosesmor
Little Saughall
Queensferry
Sealand
Upton
Newton
Guilden Sutton
Hollowmoor Heath
Great Barrow
Soughton
Aston
Mancot
Llansannan
Denbigh
(Dinbych)
Cilcain
Pant-y-mwyn
Gwernaffield
Mynydd Isa
Ewloe
Hawarden
CHESTER
Littleton
Stamford Bridge
Tarvin
Pandy Tudur
Groes
Pentre Llanrhaeadr
Llandyrnog
Llangynhafal
Llanynys
Gellifor
Mold
(Yr Wyddgrug)
Buckley
(Bwcle)
Broughton
Bretton
Saltney
Handbridge
Huntington
Rowton
Duddon
Burton
Bylchau
Nantglyn
Moel Famau
Gwernymynydd
Penymynydd
Penyffordd
Dodleston
Eccleston
Saighton
Waverton
Hargrave
Gwytherin
Rhewl
Llanferres
Nercwys
Pontblyddyn
Leeswood
Pontybodkin
Higher Kinnerton
Aldford
Ruthin
(Rhuthun)
Llanbedr-Dyffryn-Clwyd
Eryrys
Treuddyn
Coed Talon
Hope
Pulford
Lavister
Milton Green
Tattenhall
Llyn Aled
Moel Seisiog
Moel Llyn
Mynydd Hiraethog
Llyn Brenig
Nebo
Llyn Alwen
Y Gyffylliog
Llanfwrog
Bontuchel
Llanarmon-yn-Ial
Llanfynydd
Caergwrle
Rossett
Trevalyn
Handley
Burwardsley
Efenechtyd
Llanfair Dyffryn Clwyd
Graig-fechan
Pentre-celyn
Ffrith
Llay
Marford
Churton
Farndon
Harthill
Clutton
Barton
Clocaenog
Clawdd-newydd
Pwll-glâs
Llandegla
Bwlchgwyn
Gresford
Holt
Crewe
Alwen Reservoir
Pentrefoelas
Cefn-brith
Derwen
Llanelidan
Pen-y-stryt
Minera
Coedpoeth
Acton Park
Rhosnesni
Wrexham
(Wrecsam)
Tilston
Horton Green
Shocklach
Chorlton Lane
Malpas
Glasfryn
Llanfihangel Glyn Myfyr
Bryn Saith Marchog
Melin-y-wig
Cyrn-y-brain
Bersham
Rhostyllen
Marchwiel
Ysbyty Ifan
Cerrigydrudion
Horseshoe Pass
Pentredwr
World's End
Rhosllanerchrugog
Penycae
Cuddington Heath
Bangor-on-Dee
Worthenbury
Betws Gwerfil Goch
Gwyddelwern
Bryneglwys
Moel y Gamelin
Llantysilio Mountain
Ruabon Mountain
Ty-nant
Threapwood
Tallarn Green
Higher Wych
Carnedd Y-Filast
Llangwm
Y Maerdy
Druid
Corwen
Carrog
Rhewl
Ruabon
Trevor
Rhosymedre
Garth
Cefn-mawr
Erbistock
Overton
Horseman's Green
Eglwys Cross
Grindley Brook
Moel Goch
Glyndyfrdwy
Llangollen
Ty'n-dwr
Froncysyllte
Fron Isaf
Cefn Viaduct
Penley
Hanmer
Bronington
Ciltalgarth
Llyn Celyn
The National White Water Centre
Cynwyd
Moel Fferna
Halton
Knolton
Fron-goch
Glyn Ceiriog
Pontfadog
Chirk
Dudleston
Street Dinas
Rhyd-uchaf
Llandderfel
Llandrillo
Bronygarth
Llwynmawr
Gledrid
St Martins
Dudleston Heath
Ellesmere
Welshampton
Bettisfield
Bala
Llanfor
Rhos-y-gwaliau
Berwyn
Cader Bronwen
Weston Rhyn
Selattyn
Gobowen
Perthy
Parc
Bala Lake Railway
Tregeiriog
Pen-y-Gwely
Offa's Dyke Path
Welsh Frankton
Tetchill
Lyneal
Northwood
Llangower
Cader Berwyn
Llanarmon Dyffryn Ceiriog
Colemere
Newtown
Llanuwchllyn
Y Berwyn (Berwyn Ridge section)
Pistyll Rhaeadr (Waterfall)
Whittington
Oswestry
English Frankton
Loppington
Moelfre
Rednal
Cockshutt
Noneley
Wem
Moel y Geifr
Pencraig
Llanrhaeadr-ym-Mochnant
Llansilin
Morda
Weston
Trefonen
Maesbury
Grimpo
Haughton
Bagley
Burlton
Llangynog
Maesbury Marsh
West Felton
Eardiston
Wykey
Weston Lullingfields
Myddle
Y Berwyn (Lake Vyrnwy section)
Pen-y-bont-fawr
Pen-y-bont
Llangedwyn
Llanyblodwel
Morton
Llynclys
Woolston
Osbaston
Knockin
Eyton
Aran Fawddwy
Hirnant
Pen-y-Garnedd
Pant
Maesbrook
Newtown
Baschurch
Harmer Hill
Lake Vyrnwy
Llanfechain
Llansantffraid-ym-Mechain
Llanymynech
Kinnerley
Ruyton-XI-Towns
Preston Gubbals
Little Ness
Yeaton
Bomere Heath
Llanymawddwy
Llanwddyn
Abertridwr
Tycrwyn
Llanfyllin
Four Crosses
Domgay
Nesscliffe
Kinton
Wilcott
Great Ness
Grafton
Walford Heath
Leaton
Albrighton
Fitz
Deytheur
Llandrinio
Felton Butler
Pentre
Melverley
Bwlch-y-cibau
Fachwen
Llanfihangel-yng-Ngwynfa
Ensdon
Forton
Montford Bridge
Arddleen
Shrawardine
Tir Rhiwiog
Dinas-Mawddwy
Llwydiarth
Sarnau
Criggion
Crew Green
Alberbury
Montford
Bicton
Harlescott
Minllyn
Mallwyd
Foel
Dolanog
River Vyrnwy
Pont Robert
Meifod
Geuffordd
Breidden Hill
Middletown
Wollaston
Halfway House
Guilsfield
SHREWSBURY
Llangadfan
Yockleton
Glyndŵr's Way
Dublin
Douglas
Belfast
(Mar-Oct)
(Nov-Mar)
30
21
22

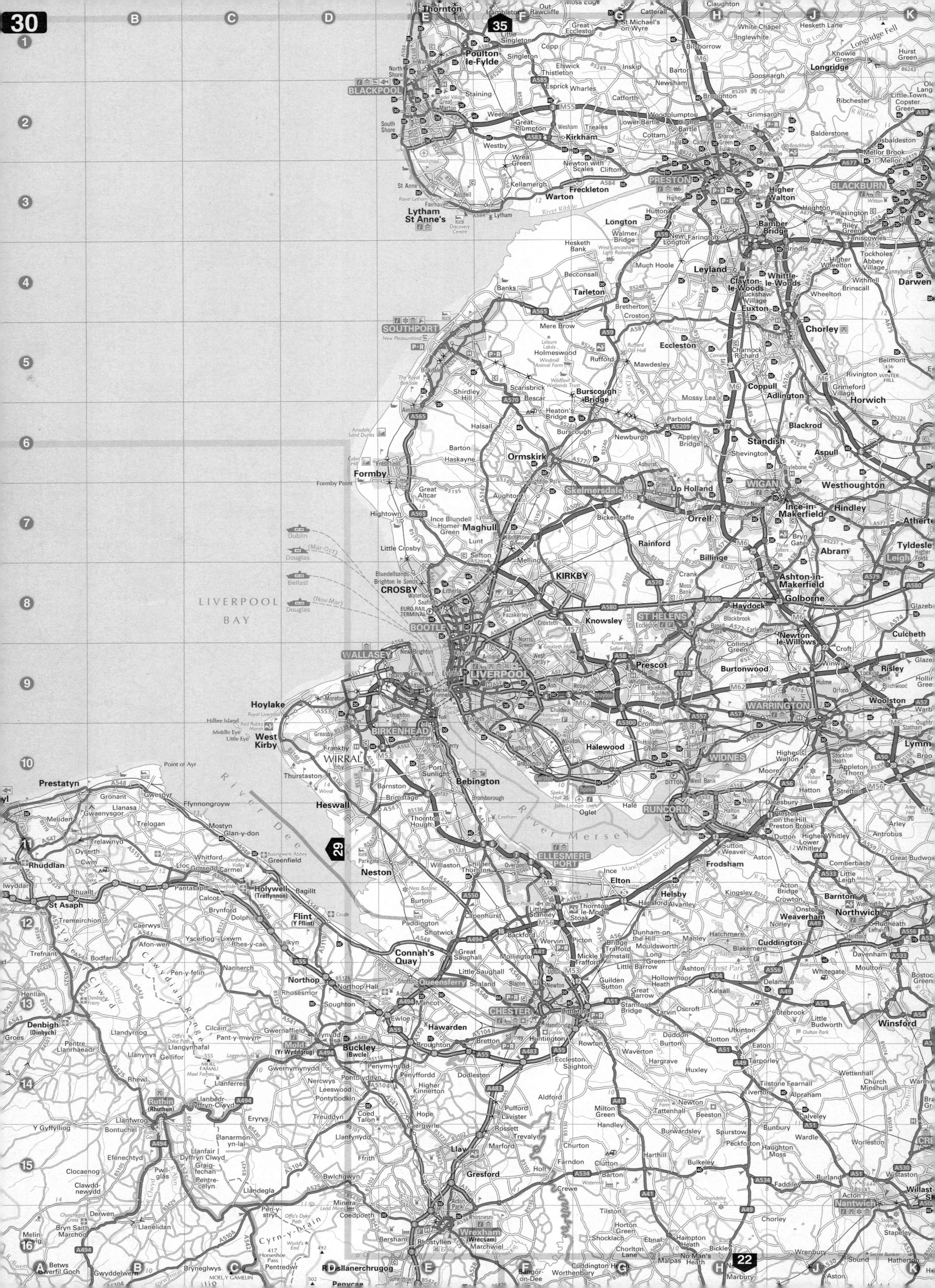
35
Thornton
Poulton-le-Fylde
BLACKPOOL
Kirkham
Lytham St Anne's
Warton
Freckleton
PRESTON
Longridge
BLACKBURN
Higher Walton
Bamber Bridge
Longton
Leyland
Darwen
Tarleton
SOUTHPORT
Chorley
Eccleston
Burscough Bridge
Horwich
Ormskirk
Formby
Standish
WIGAN
Skelmersdale
Up Holland
Westhoughton
Hindley
Orrell
Maghull
Rainford
Tyldesley
Leigh
KIRKBY
CROSBY
Ashton-in-Makerfield
Golborne
BOOTLE
ST HELENS
Knowsley
Newton-le-Willows
WALLASEY
LIVERPOOL
Prescot
Hoylake
West Kirby
BIRKENHEAD
WARRINGTON
WIRRAL
Halewood
WIDNES
Bebington
Prestatyn
Heswall
RUNCORN
River Mersey
River Dee
LIVERPOOL BAY
Rhuddlan
St Asaph
Holywell
ELLESMERE PORT
Neston
Frodsham
Flint
Helsby
Northwich
Connah's Quay
Queensferry
Cuddington
Northop
Denbigh (Dinbych)
Mold (Yr Wyddgrug)
Buckley (Bwcle)
Hawarden
CHESTER
Winsford
Ruthin (Rhuthun)
Llay
Gresford
Wrexham (Wrecsam)
Nantwich
29
22

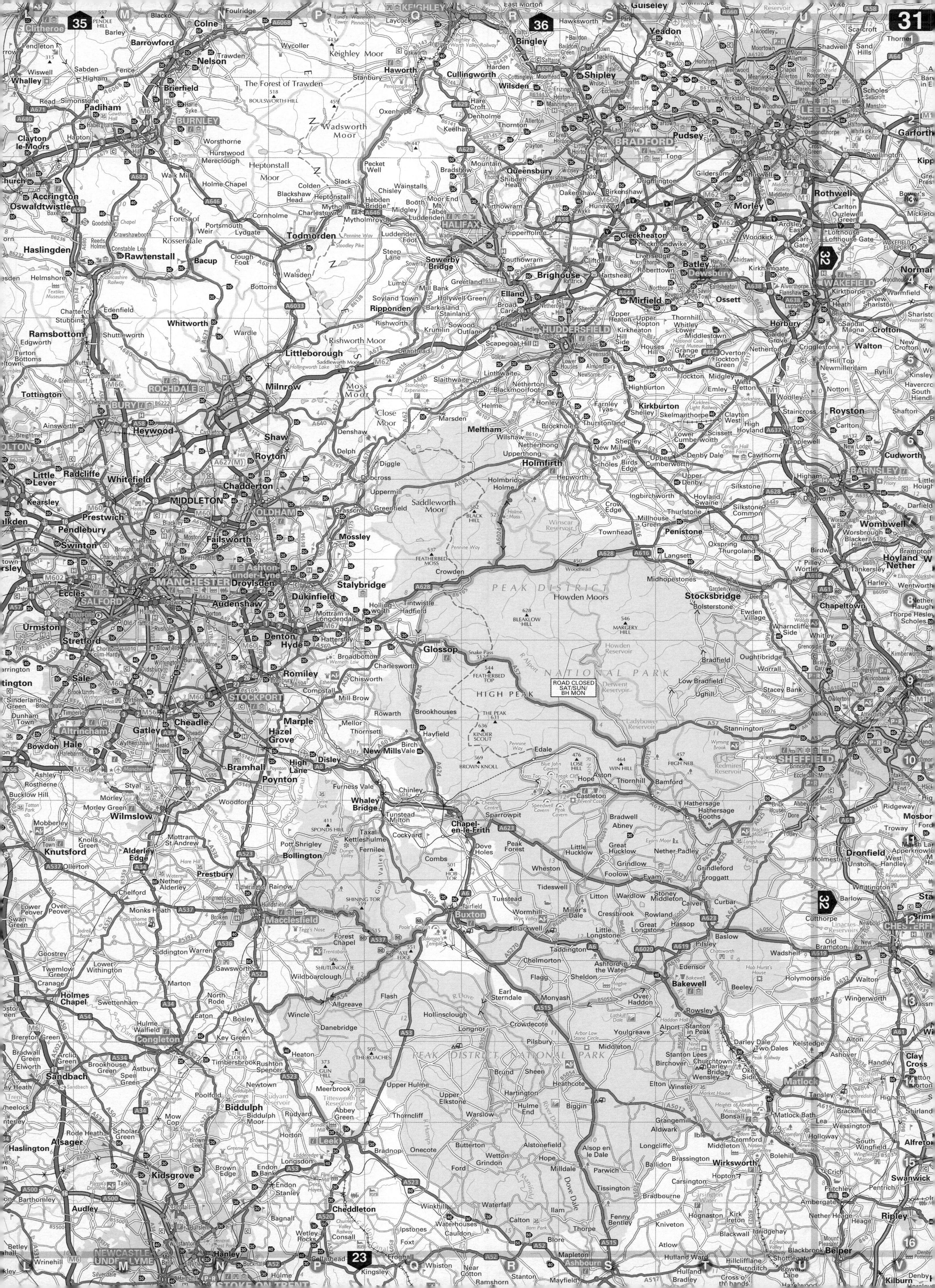
35
36
32
23
Clitheroe
Colne
Nelson
Burnley
Padiham
Accrington
Oswaldtwistle
Haslingden
Rawtenstall
Bacup
Todmorden
Haworth
Keighley
Bingley
Shipley
Yeadon
Guiseley
Leeds
Bradford
Pudsey
Halifax
Queensbury
Cleckheaton
Batley
Dewsbury
Morley
Rothwell
Wakefield
Brighouse
Elland
Huddersfield
Mirfield
Ossett
Horbury
Sowerby Bridge
Ripponden
Littleborough
Milnrow
Rochdale
Bury
Heywood
Ramsbottom
Whitworth
Shaw
Royton
Oldham
Chadderton
Middleton
Radcliffe
Whitefield
Prestwich
Failsworth
Manchester
Salford
Eccles
Swinton
Pendlebury
Urmston
Stretford
Sale
Altrincham
Hale
Gatley
Cheadle
Stockport
Ashton-under-Lyne
Droylsden
Audenshaw
Denton
Hyde
Dukinfield
Stalybridge
Mossley
Glossop
Romiley
Marple
Hazel Grove
Bramhall
Poynton
Disley
New Mills
Whaley Bridge
Chapel-en-le-Frith
Wilmslow
Knutsford
Alderley Edge
Macclesfield
Bollington
Buxton
Congleton
Sandbach
Alsager
Kidsgrove
Biddulph
Leek
Cheddleton
Newcastle-under-Lyme
Hanley
Stoke-on-Trent
Ashbourne
Belper
Ripley
Alfreton
Matlock
Bakewell
Chesterfield
Dronfield
Sheffield
Stocksbridge
Penistone
Barnsley
Royston
Wombwell
Holmfirth
Meltham
Marsden
Saddleworth Moor
Peak District National Park
High Peak
Kinder Scout
Howden Moors
Road closed Sat/Sun/BH Mon

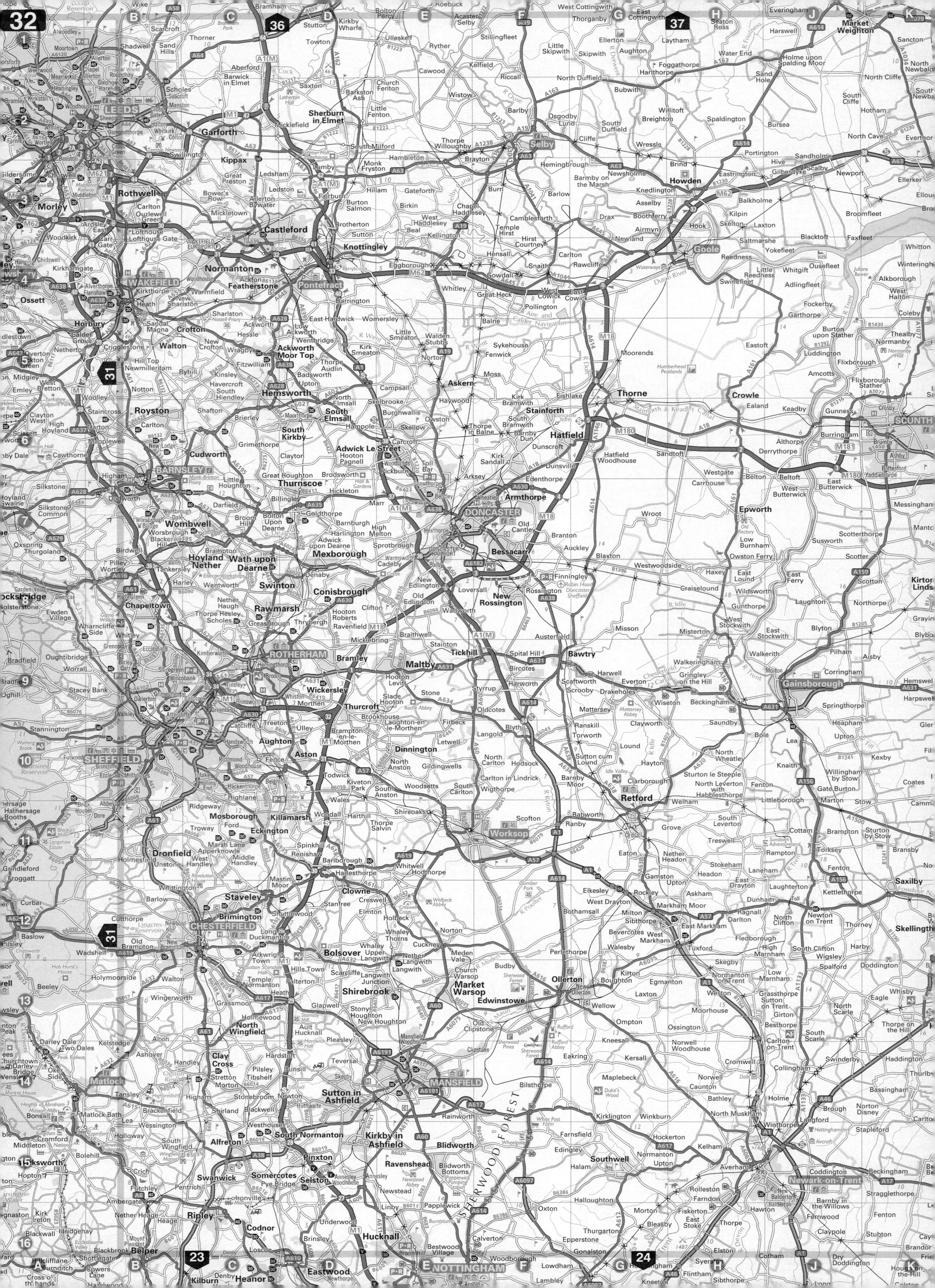
36
37
31
23
24
Leeds
Wakefield
Barnsley
Sheffield
Rotherham
Doncaster
Selby
Goole
Howden
Pontefract
Castleford
Normanton
Featherstone
Garforth
Rothwell
Morley
Ossett
Horbury
Royston
Hemsworth
South Elmsall
South Kirkby
Thurnscoe
Wombwell
Hoyland Nether
Wath upon Dearne
Mexborough
Conisbrough
Swinton
Rawmarsh
Maltby
Tickhill
Bawtry
Thorne
Hatfield
Armthorpe
Bessacarr
New Rossington
Epworth
Crowle
Scunthorpe
Gainsborough
Retford
Worksop
Dronfield
Staveley
Chesterfield
Bolsover
Shirebrook
Market Warsop
Edwinstowe
Ollerton
Mansfield
Sutton in Ashfield
Kirkby in Ashfield
Alfreton
Ripley
Belper
Heanor
Eastwood
Hucknall
Southwell
Newark-on-Trent
Nottingham
Matlock
Tuxford
Market Weighton
Sherwood Forest
Knottingley
Sherburn in Elmet
Eckington
Killamarsh
Chapeltown
Dinnington
Wickersley
Thurcroft
Bramley
Aston
Aughton
Cudworth
Askern
Stainforth

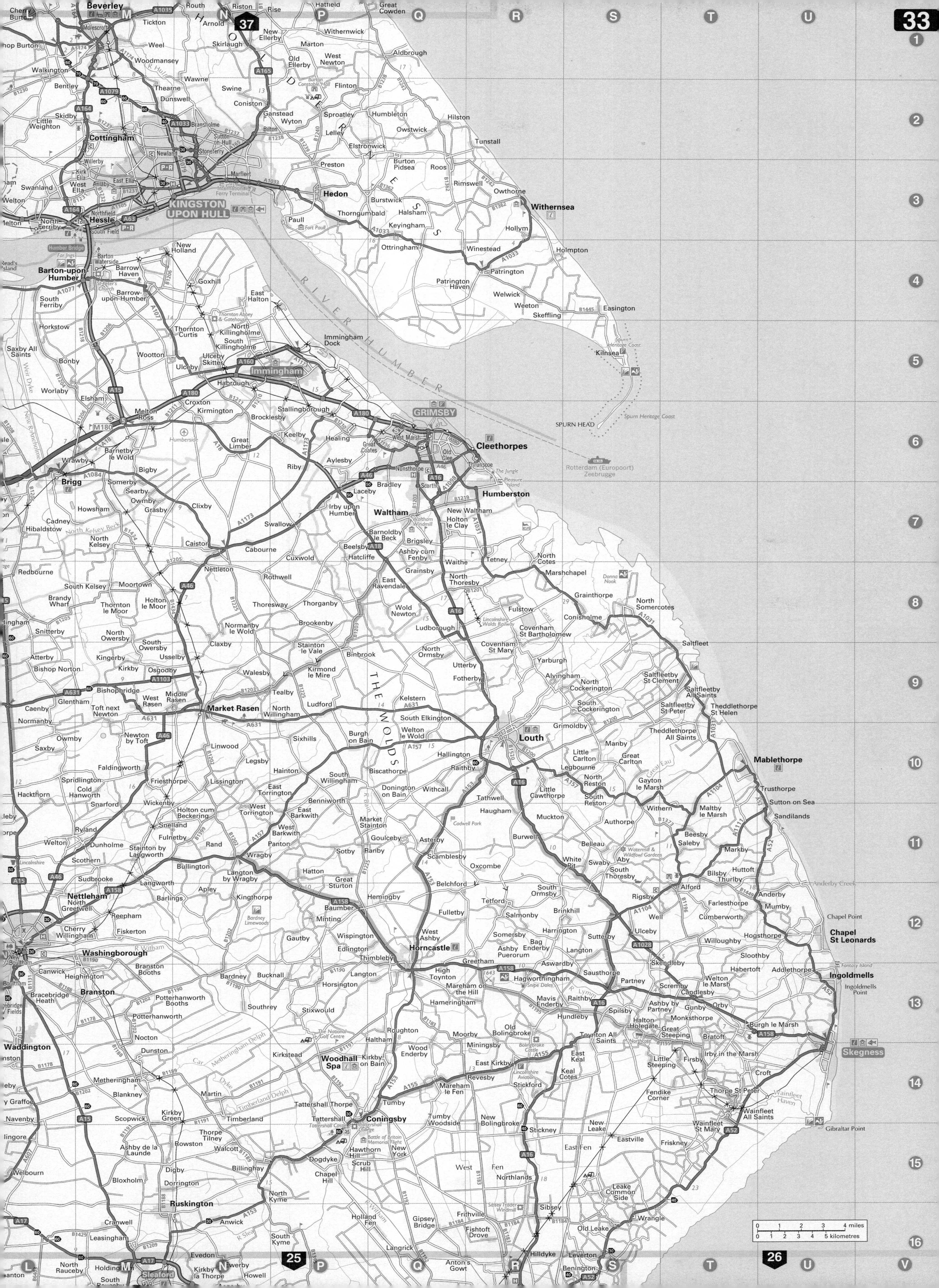

Beverley
37
Routh
Riston
Rise
Hatfield
Great Cowden
Tickton
Arnold
New Ellerby
Withernwick
Weel
Skirlaugh
Marton
Woodmansey
Aldbrough
Walkington
Old Ellerby
West Newton
Bentley
Wawne
Swine
Thearne
Flinton
Dunswell
Coniston
Skidby
Little Weighton
Ganstead
Wyton
Sproatley
Humbleton
Hilston
Bransholme
Lelley
Owstwick
Cottingham
Sutton-on-Hull
Stoneferry
Tunstall
Newland
Elstronwick
Willerby
Preston
Burton Pidsea
Roos
Kirk Ella
West Ella
Anlaby
East Ella
Marfleet
Swanland
Rimswell
Hedon
Owthorne
KINGSTON UPON HULL
Burstwick
Halsham
Withernsea
Hessle
North Ferriby
Thorngumbald
Paull
Keyingham
Hollym
Fort Paull
South Field
Ottringham
Winestead
Holmpton
Humber Bridge
New Holland
Barton Waterside
Barton-upon-Humber
Barrow Haven
Patrington
Patrington Haven
Goxhill
East Halton
Welwick
Barrow-upon-Humber
South Ferriby
Weeton
Skeffling
Easington
Thornton Abbey & Gatehouse
Horkstow
Thornton Curtis
North Killingholme
South Killingholme
Immingham Dock
Spurn Heritage Coast
Saxby All Saints
Kilnsea
Wootton
Ulceby Skitter
Bonby
Ulceby
Immingham
Habrough
RIVER HUMBER
Worlaby
Elsham
Croxton
Kirmington
Stallingborough
Melton Ross
Brocklesby
GRIMSBY
SPURN HEAD
Spurn Heritage Coast
Humberside
Keelby
Healing
West Marsh
Barnetby le Wold
Great Limber
Great Coates
Old Clee
Cleethorpes
Wrawby
Aylesby
Bigby
Riby
Nunsthorpe
Thrunscoe
The Jungle
Pleasure Island
Rotterdam (Europoort) Zeebrugge
Brigg
Somerby
Laceby
Bradley
Scartho
Humberston
Searby
Owmby
Howsham
Grasby
Clixby
Irby upon Humber
Waltham
New Waltham
Cadney
Hibaldstow
North Kelsey Beck
Swallow
Waltham Windmill
Holton le Clay
North Kelsey
Barnoldby le Beck
Brigsley
Caistor
Cabourne
Beelsby
Ashby cum Fenby
Cuxwold
Hatcliffe
Waithe
Tetney
North Cotes
Redbourne
Nettleton
Grainsby
Marshchapel
South Kelsey
Moortown
Rothwell
East Ravendale
North Thoresby
Donna Nook
Brandy Wharf
Thornton le Moor
Holton le Moor
Thoresway
Thorganby
Grainthorpe
North Somercotes
Wold Newton
Fulstow
Lincolnshire Wolds Railway
Conisholme
Snitterby
Normanby le Wold
Brookenby
Ludborough
Covenham St Bartholomew
North Owersby
South Owersby
Claxby
Stainton le Vale
North Ormsby
Covenham St Mary
Saltfleet
Atterby
Kingerby
Usselby
Binbrook
Utterby
Yarburgh
Bishop Norton
Kirkby
Osgodby
Walesby
Kirmond le Mire
Alvingham
North Cockerington
Saltfleetby St Clement
Fotherby
Bishopbridge
Tealby
Glentham
West Rasen
Middle Rasen
THE WOLDS
Kelstern
Saltfleetby All Saints
Caenby
Toft next Newton
Market Rasen
North Willingham
Ludford
South Cockerington
Saltfleetby St Peter
Theddlethorpe St Helen
Normanby
South Elkington
Louth
Grimoldby
Theddlethorpe All Saints
Owmby
Newton by Toft
Welton le Wold
Burgh on Bain
Sixhills
Manby
Saxby
Linwood
Hallington
Little Carlton
Great Carlton
Mablethorpe
Legsby
Raithby
Legbourne
Faldingworth
Hainton
Biscathorpe
North Reston
Great Eau
Gayton le Marsh
Spridlington
Friesthorpe
Lissington
South Willingham
Little Cawthorpe
Trusthorpe
Hackthorn
Cold Hanworth
East Torrington
Donington on Bain
Withcall
South Reston
Sutton on Sea
Snarford
Tathwell
Withern
Maltby le Marsh
Sandilands
Wickenby
Holton cum Beckering
West Torrington
Benniworth
Haugham
Ryland
Snelland
East Barkwith
Market Stainton
Cadwell Park
Muckton
Authorpe
Welton
Fulnetby
West Barkwith
Goulceby
Asterby
Burwell
Beesby
Saleby
Dunholme
Stainton by Langworth
Rand
Panton
Belleau
Markby
Scothern
Wragby
Sotby
Ranby
Scamblesby
Waterwill & Wildfowl Gardens
Aby
White Pit
Swaby
Huttoft
Bullington
Langton by Wragby
South Thoresby
Bilsby
Thurlby
Sudbrooke
Hatton
Oxcombe
Alford
Anderby Creek
Nettleham
Langworth
Great Sturton
Belchford
South Ormsby
Anderby
North Greetwell
Barlings
Apley
Kingthorpe
Hemingby
Tetford
Rigsby
Farlesthorpe
Reepham
Baumber
Brinkhill
Mumby
Bardney Limewoods
Fulletby
Salmonby
Well
Chapel Point
Cherry Willingham
Fiskerton
Minting
Harrington
Ulceby
Cumberworth
Chapel St Leonards
Gautby
West Ashby
Somersby
Sutterby
Hogsthorpe
Washingborough
Wispington
Edlington
Horncastle
Bag Enderby
Langton
Willoughby
Ashby Puerorum
Sloothby
Thimbleby
Greetham
Aswardby
Skendleby
New Boultham
Canwick
Heighington
Branston Booths
Bardney
Bucknall
High Toynton
Hagworthingham
Habertoft
Addlethorpe
Fantasy Island
Ingoldmells
Sausthorpe
Partney
Langton
Snipe Dales
Scremby
Welton le Marsh
Ingoldmells Point
Bracebridge Heath
Branston
Horsington
Mareham on the Hill
Candlesby
Potterhanworth Booths
Hameringham
Mavis Enderby
Raithby
Gunby
Orby
Southrey
Spilsby
Potterhanworth
Stixwould
Hundleby
Ashby by Partney
Monksthorpe
Roughton
Old Bolingbroke
Halton Holegate
Burgh le Marsh
Nocton
The National Golf Centre
Moorby
Toynton All Saints
Great Steeping
Bratoft
Waddington
Dunston
Haltham
Wood Enderby
Miningsby
Bolingbroke Castle
East Keal
Skegness
Kirkstead
Woodhall Spa
Kirkby on Bain
Little Steeping
Irby in the Marsh
Firsby
Metheringham Delph
East Kirkby
Lincolnshire Aviation
Keal Cotes
Metheringham
Revesby
Croft
Blankney
Martin
Mareham le Fen
Stickford
Fendike Corner
Thorpe St Peter
Wainfleet Haven
Timberland Delph
Kirkby Green
Tattershall Thorpe
Tumby
Wainfleet All Saints
Navenby
Scopwick
Timberland
Tattershall Castle
Coningsby
Tumby Woodside
New Bolingbroke
New Leake
Gibraltar Point
Thorpe Tilney
Tattershall College
Stickney
Eastville
Wainfleet St Mary
Ashby de la Launde
Rowston
Walcott
Battle of Britain Memorial Flight
Hawthorn Hill
New York
East Fen
Friskney
Welbourn
Dogdyke
Scrub Hill
Digby
Billinghay
West Fen
Bloxholm
Dorrington
Chapel Hill
Northlands
North Kyme
Leake Commonside
Ruskington
Sibsey Trader Windmill
Sibsey
Frithville
Wrangle
Cranwell
Anwick
Holland Fen
Gipsey Bridge
Leasingham
Fishtoft Drove
Old Leake
South Kyme
Langrick
Evedon
Hilldyke
Leverton
North Rauceby
Holdingham
Kirkby la Thorpe
Ewerby
Howell
Anton's Gowt
Benington
Sleaford
South Rauceby
25
26
0 1 2 3 4 miles
0 1 2 3 4 5 kilometres

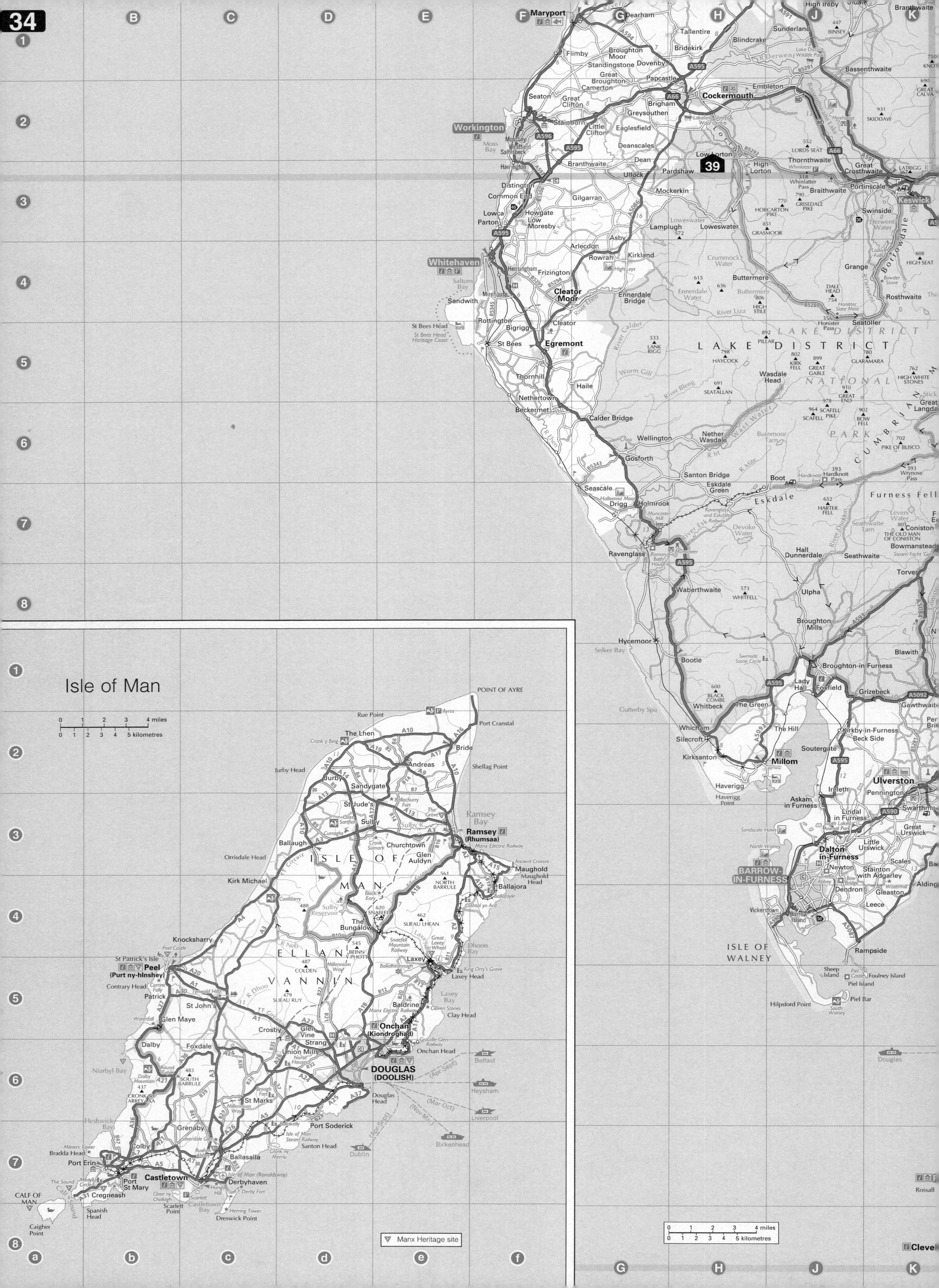
Maryport
Dearham
Tallentire
Bridekirk
Blindcrake
Sunderland
High Ireby
Branthwaite
Flimby
Broughton Moor
Standingstone
Dovenby
Papcastle
Great Broughton
Camerton
Seaton
Great Clifton
Cockermouth
Brigham
Greysouthen
Embleton
Bassenthwaite
SKIDDAW
Workington
Stainburn
Little Clifton
Eaglesfield
Deanscales
Dean
Low Lorton
High Lorton
39
Pardshaw
Ullock
Harrington
Branthwaite
Thornthwaite
Great Crosthwaite
Braithwaite
Portinscale
Keswick
Distington
Common End
Mockerkin
Gilgarran
Lowca
Parton
Howgate
Low Moresby
Lamplugh
Loweswater
Whinlatter Pass
HOBCARTON PIKE
GRISEDALE PIKE
GRASMOOR
Swinside
Derwent Water
Whitehaven
Arlecdon
Asby
Rowrah
Kirkland
Frizington
Cleator Moor
Crummock Water
Buttermere
Grange
Ennerdale Water
Ennerdale Bridge
Rosthwaite
Sandwith
Rottington
Bigrigg
Cleator
Egremont
St Bees Head
St Bees
Seatoller
Honister Pass
LAKE DISTRICT
PILLAR
HAYCOCK
KIRK FELL
GREAT GABLE
GLARAMARA
Thornhill
Haile
Wasdale Head
NATIONAL
HIGH WHITE STONES
SEATALLAN
GREAT END
Nethertown
Beckermet
SCAFELL PIKE
SCAFELL
BOW FELL
CUMBRIAN
Calder Bridge
Wellington
Nether Wasdale
Wast Water
PARK
PIKE OF BLISCO
Gosforth
Santon Bridge
Seascale
Eskdale Green
Boot
Hardknott Pass
Wrynose Pass
Drigg
Holmrook
Eskdale
Furness Fell
HARTER FELL
Devoke Water
Coniston
THE OLD MAN OF CONISTON
Bowmanstead
Ravenglass
Hall Dunnerdale
Seathwaite
Torver
Waberthwaite
WHITFELL
Ulpha
Broughton Mills
Hycemoor
Selker Bay
Bootle
Blawith
Broughton-in-Furness
Lady Hall
Foxfield
Grizebeck
Gawthwaite
BLACK COMBE
Whitbeck
The Green
Gutterby Spa
Whicham
The Hill
Kirkby-in-Furness
Beck Side
Silecroft
Kirksanton
Millom
Soutergate
Haverigg
Haverigg Point
Ulverston
Pennington
Ireleth
Askam in Furness
Lindal in Furness
Swarthmoor
Great Urswick
Little Urswick
Dalton-in-Furness
BARROW-IN-FURNESS
Newton
Stainton with Adgarley
Scales
Aldingham
Dendron
Gleaston
Leece
Vickerstown
Barrow Island
Rampside
ISLE OF WALNEY
Sheep Island
Piel Island
Foulney Island
Piel Bar
Hilpsford Point
Douglas
Rossall
Cleve
Isle of Man
0 1 2 3 4 miles
0 1 2 3 4 5 kilometres
POINT OF AYRE
Rue Point
Port Cranstal
The Lhen
Bride
Jurby Head
Jurby
Andreas
Shellag Point
Sandygate
St Jude's
Sulby
Ramsey Bay
Ramsey (Rhumsaa)
Ballaugh
Churchtown
Glen Auldyn
Orrisdale Head
ISLE OF MAN
Maughold
Maughold Head
Kirk Michael
NORTH BARRULE
Ballajora
SNAEFELL
The Bungalow
SLIEAU LHEAN
Knocksharry
ELLAN VANNIN
Dhoon Bay
BEINN Y PHOTT
COLDEN
St Patrick's Isle
Peel (Purt ny-h-Inshey)
Laxey
Laxey Head
Contrary Head
Patrick
SLIEAU RUY
Laxey Bay
St John's
Baldrine
Clay Head
Glen Maye
Crosby
Glen Vine
Onchan (Kiondroghad)
Dalby
Foxdale
Strang
Union Mills
Onchan Head
Belfast
Niarbyl Bay
SOUTH BARRULE
DOUGLAS (DOOLISH)
CRONK NY ARREY LAA
St Marks
Douglas Head
Heysham
Liverpool
Fleshwick Bay
Grenaby
Port Soderick
Birkenhead
Bradda Head
Colby
Santon Head
Dublin
Port Erin
Ballasalla
Castletown
Port St Mary
Derbyhaven
CALF OF MAN
Cregneash
Spanish Head
Scarlett Point
Castletown Bay
Dreswick Point
Caigher Point
Manx Heritage site

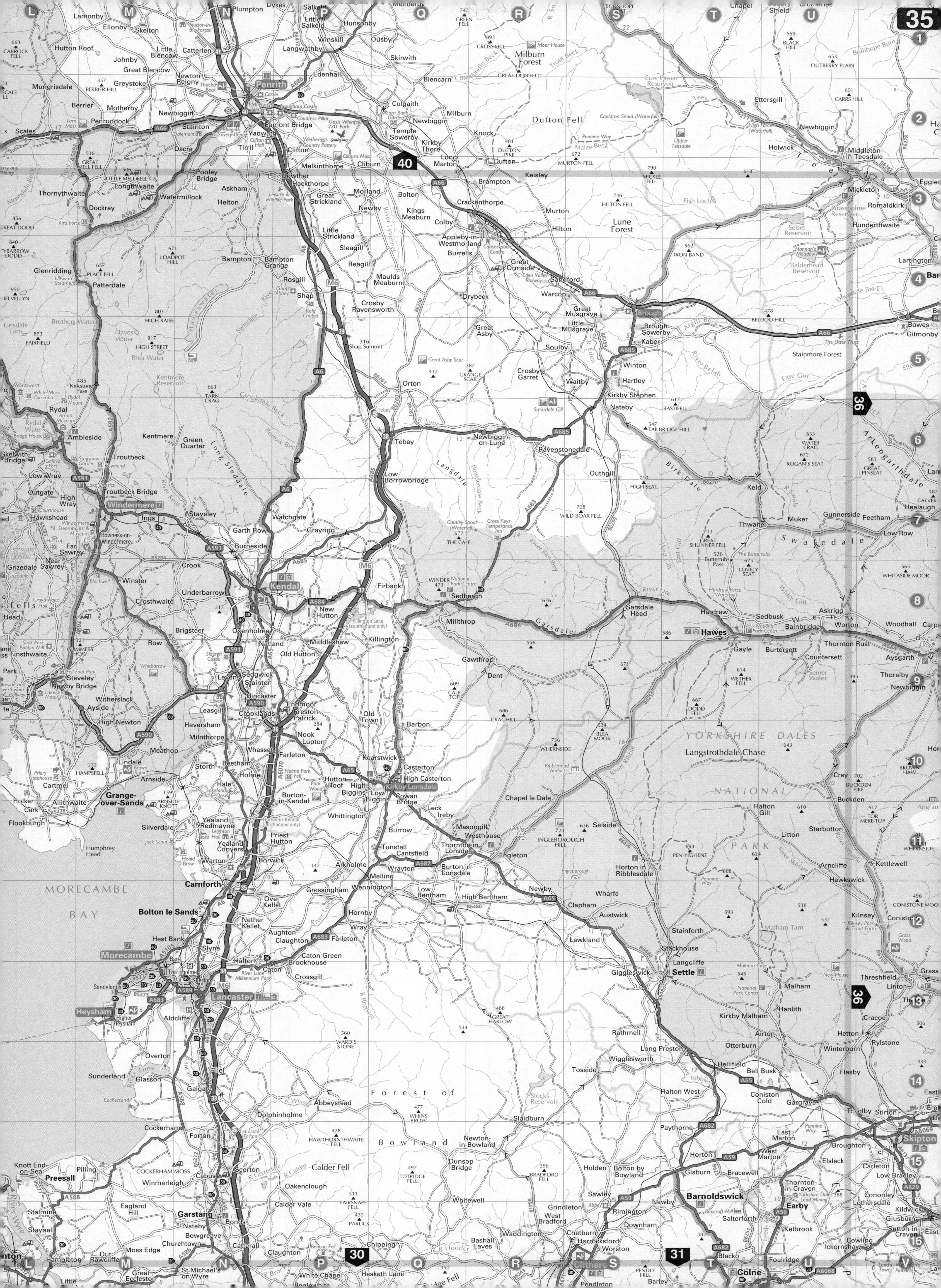
Penrith
Kendal
Windermere
Kirkby Lonsdale
Morecambe
Heysham
Lancaster
Skipton
Brough
Hawes
Settle
Barnoldswick
Colne
Clitheroe
Garstang
Carnforth
Bolton le Sands
Grange-over-Sands
MORECAMBE BAY
Forest of Bowland
YORKSHIRE DALES NATIONAL PARK
Langstrothdale Chase
Swaledale
Wensleydale
Garsdale
Dentdale
Lune Forest
Milburn Forest
Dufton Fell
Stainmore Forest
Appleby-in-Westmorland
Kirkby Stephen
Sedbergh
Tebay
Orton
Shap
Ambleside
Staveley
Troutbeck Bridge
Bowness-on-Windermere
Hawkshead
Glenridding
Patterdale
Pooley Bridge
Askham
Lowther
Eamont Bridge
Middleton-in-Teesdale
Ravenstonedale
Newbiggin-on-Lune
Dent
Ingleton
Horton in Ribblesdale
Giggleswick
Long Preston
Hellifield
Gargrave
Slaidburn
Dunsop Bridge
Chipping
Preesall
Knott End-on-Sea
Hest Bank
Arnside
Silverdale
Cartmel
Milnthorpe
Heversham
Levens
Oxenholme
Burneside
Grayrigg
Firbank
Killington
Casterton
Barbon
Burton-in-Kendal
Hornby
Wray
High Bentham
Clapham
Austwick
Malham
Kettlewell
Buckden
Askrigg
Bainbridge
Keld
Muker
Thwaite
Gunnerside
Low Row
Bowes
Warcop
Great Musgrave
Crosby Garrett
Kaber
Winton
Hartley
Nateby
Outhgill
A66
A6
A591
A590
A65
A684
A685
A683
A687
A682
A59
A56
A629
A589
A683
A588
A586
A6068
M6
30
31
36
40

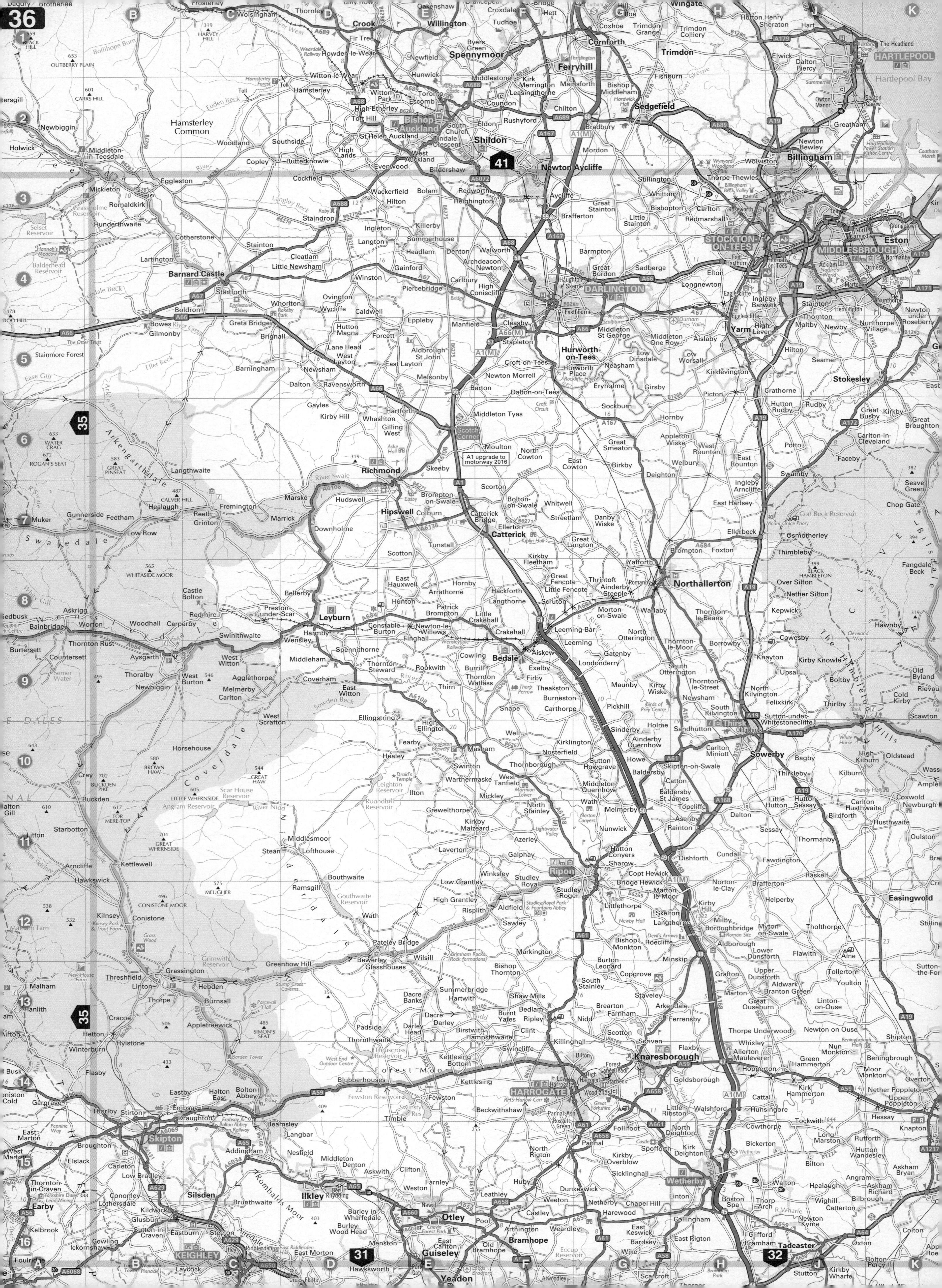
Crook
Willington
Spennymoor
Ferryhill
Cornforth
Trimdon
Wingate
HARTLEPOOL
Hartlepool Bay
Sedgefield
Bishop Auckland
Shildon
Newton Aycliffe
Billingham
STOCKTON-ON-TEES
MIDDLESBROUGH
Eston
DARLINGTON
Yarm
Stokesley
Barnard Castle
Hamsterley Common
Middleton-in-Teesdale
Richmond
Catterick
Scotch Corner
A1 upgrade to motorway 2016
Northallerton
Leyburn
Bedale
Thirsk
Sowerby
Ripon
Masham
Pateley Bridge
Knaresborough
HARROGATE
Wetherby
Skipton
Ilkley
Otley
KEIGHLEY
Guiseley
Tadcaster
Grassington
Swaledale
Wensleydale
Coverdale
Nidderdale
Arkengarthdale
Hambleton Hills
CLEVELAND
41
35
31
32

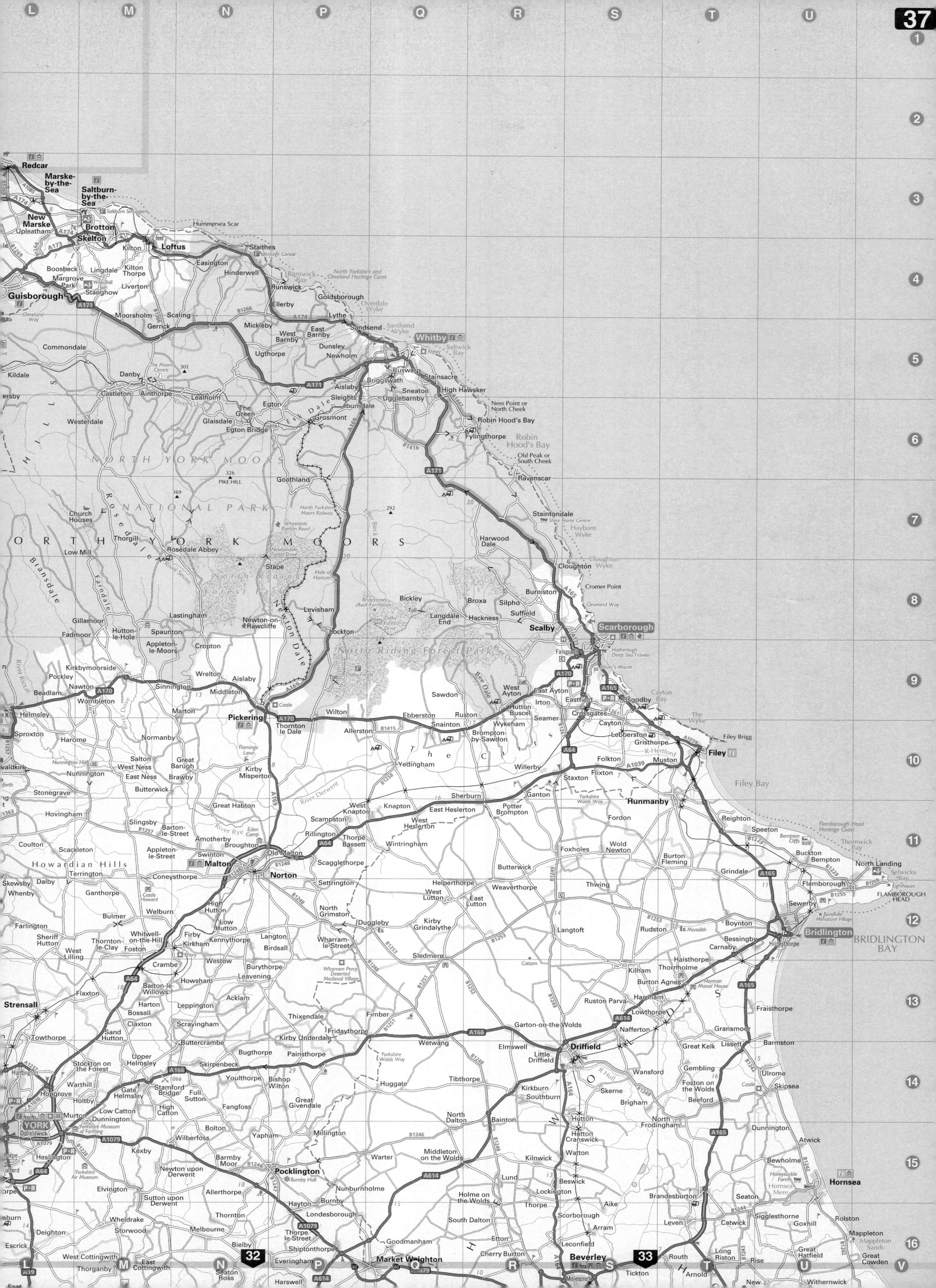

Redcar
Marske-by-the-Sea
Saltburn-by-the-Sea
New Marske
Upleatham
Brotton
Skelton
Loftus
Kilton
Hummersea Scar
Staithes
Easington
Hinderwell
Runswick
Runswick Bay
North Yorkshire and Cleveland Heritage Coast
Boosbeck
Lingdale
Kilton Thorpe
Margrove Park
Stanghow
Liverton
Guisborough
Goldsborough
Ellerby
Overdale Wyke
Lythe
Moorsholm
Scaling
Gerrick
Mickleby
Sandsend
Sandsend Wyke
West Barnby
East Barnby
Whitby
Saltwick Bay
Commondale
Dunsley
Ugthorpe
Newholm
Kildale
Danby
Ruswarp
Stainsacre
Castleton
Ainthorpe
Lealholm
Briggswath
Sneaton
High Hawsker
Aislaby
Sleights
Ugglebarnby
Ness Point or North Cheek
Westerdale
The Green
Egton
Iburndale
Glaisdale
Egton Bridge
Grosmont
Robin Hood's Bay
Fylingthorpe
Esk Dale
NORTH YORK MOORS
NATIONAL PARK
Old Peak or South Cheek
PIKE HILL
Goathland
Ravenscar
Church Houses
Rosedale
North Yorkshire Moors Railway
Wheeldale Roman Road
Staintondale
Shire Horse Centre
Hayburn Wyke
Thorgill
Harwood Dale
Low Mill
Rosedale Abbey
Newtondale Forest Drive
Cloughton
Cloughton Wyke
Stape
Bransdale
Farndale
Hole of Horcum
North Riding Forest Park
Cromer Point
Burniston
Cleveland Way
Bridestones (Rock Formation)
Bickley
Broxa
Silpho
Lastingham
Levisham
Langdale End
Hackness
Suffield
Gillamoor
Newton-on-Rawcliffe
Newton Dale
Scalby
Scarborough
Fadmoor
Hutton-le-Hole
Spaunton
Lockton
Appleton-le-Moors
Cropton
Dalby Forest Drive
Falsgrave
Hatherleigh Deep Sea Trawler
Oliver's Mount
Kirkbymoorside
Pockley
Wrelton
Aislaby
Beadlam
Nawton
Sinnington
Middleton
Sawdon
West Ayton
East Ayton
Osgodby
Cayton Bay
Wombleton
Helmsley
Marton
Pickering
Wilton
Ebberston
Ruston
Hutton Buscel
Irton
Eastfield
Crossgates
Sproxton
Thornton le Dale
Allerston
Snainton
Wykeham
Seamer
Cayton
The Wyke
Harome
Normanby
Brompton-by-Sawdon
Lebberston
Gristhorpe
Filey Brigg
Filey
Nunnington Hall
Salton
Great Barugh
Flamingo Land
Kirby Misperton
Yedingham
The Carrs
Willerby
Folkton
Muston
West Ness
East Ness
Nunnington
Brawby
Flixton
Staxton
Filey Bay
Stonegrave
Butterwick
River Derwent
Sherburn
Ganton
Great Habton
Knapton
West Knapton
East Heslerton
Potter Brompton
Yorkshire Wolds Way
Hunmanby
Hovingham
Slingsby
Barton-le-Street
Scampston
West Heslerton
Fordon
Reighton
Eden Camp
Rillington
Flamborough Head Heritage Coast
Amotherby
Broughton
Thorpe Bassett
Wintringham
Wold Newton
Speeton
Coulton
Scackleton
Appleton-le-Street
Swinton
Old Malton
Bempton Cliffs
Thornwick Bay
Howardian Hills
Malton
Norton
Scagglethorpe
Foxholes
Burton Fleming
Buckton
Bempton
North Landing
Terrington
Butterwick
Grindale
Selwicks Bay
Skewsby
Dalby
Coneysthorpe
Settrington
Helperthorpe
Weaverthorpe
Thwing
Flamborough
Lighthouse
Whenby
Ganthorpe
Castle Howard
West Lutton
East Lutton
FLAMBOROUGH HEAD
High Hutton
North Grimston
Sewerby
Welburn
Bondville Miniature Village
Bulmer
Low Hutton
Duggleby
Kirby Grindalythe
Langtoft
Rudston
Monolith
Boynton
Farlington
Whitwell-on-the-Hill
Firby
Langton
Wharram-le-Street
Bridlington
BRIDLINGTON BAY
Sheriff Hutton
Thornton-le-Clay
Kirkham
Kennythorpe
Birdsall
Bessingby
Carnaby
Hilderthorpe
West Lilling
Foston
Priory
Sledmere
Cottam
Haisthorpe
Crambe
Westow
Burythorpe
Wharram Percy Deserted Medieval Village
Thornholme
Kilham
Leavening
Burton Agnes
Norman Manor House
Howsham
Barton-le-Willows
Harpham
Flaxton
Acklam
Ruston Parva
Lowthorpe
Fraisthorpe
Strensall
Harton
Leppington
Thixendale
Fimber
Bossall
Garton-on-the-Wolds
Nafferton
Claxton
Scrayingham
Fridaythorpe
Gransmoor
Sand Hutton
Towthorpe
Buttercrambe
Kirby Underdale
Wetwang
Elmswell
Driffield
Lissett
Barmston
Great Kelk
Bugthorpe
Painsthorpe
Little Driffield
Upper Helmsley
Stockton on the Forest
Huntington
Skirpenbeck
Gembling
Youlthorpe
Bishop Wilton
Tibthorpe
Wansford
Ulrome
Warthill
Foston on the Wolds
Stamford Bridge
Huggate
R Hull
Skipsea
Heworth
Gate Helmsley
Full Sutton
Kirkburn
Skerne
Southburn
Brigham
Beeford
Holtby
Great Givendale
Murton
Low Catton
Fangfoss
High Catton
North Dalton
Bainton
Hutton
North Frodingham
YORK
Osbaldwick
Dunnington
Yorkshire Museum of Farming
Bolton
Cranswick
Dunnington
Atwick
Wilberfoss
Yapham
Millington
Middleton on the Wolds
Heslington
Kexby
Barmby Moor
Warter
Kilnwick
Watton
Bewholme
Newton upon Derwent
Pocklington
Burnby Hall
Yorkshire Air Museum
Lund
Beswick
Honeysuckle Farm
Hornsea Mere
Hornsea
Elvington
Allerthorpe
Nunburnholme
Holme on the Wolds
Lockington
Aike
Brandesburton
Seaton
Sutton upon Derwent
Hayton
Burnby
Thorpe
Scorborough
Wheldrake
Thornton
Londesborough
South Dalton
Leven
Catwick
Sigglesthorne
Goxhill
Rolston
Storwood
Deighton
Melbourne
Thorpe le Street
Arram
Goodmanham
Etton
Leconfield
Mappleton
Mappleton Sands
Bielby
Shiptonthorpe
Escrick
Cherry Burton
Beverley
Routh
Long Riston
Great Hatfield
Great Cowden
West Cottingwith
East Cottingwith
Thorganby
Seaton Ross
Everingham
Market Weighton
Molescroft
Tickton
Arnold
Rise
Harswell
New
Withernwick

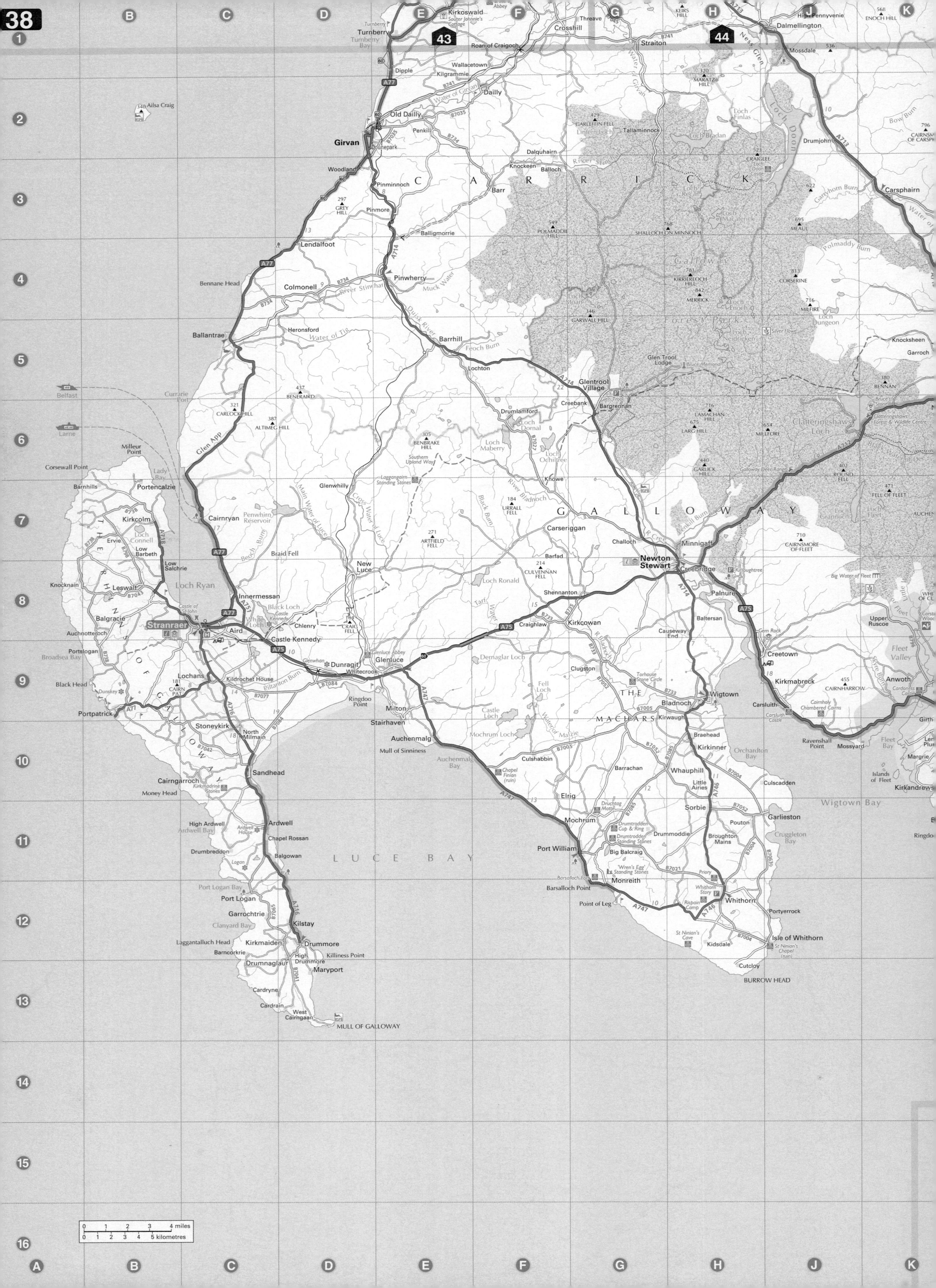
43
44
Turnberry
Turnberry Bay
Kirkoswald
Souter Johnnie's Cottage
Crosshill
Threave
Keirs Hill
High Pennyvenie
Dalmellington
568 Enoch Hill
Roan of Craigoch
Straiton
Ness Glen
Mossdale
536
Wallacetown
Dipple
Kilgrammie
Water of Girvan
Dailly
320 Maratz Hill
Loch Doon
Loch Finlas
Bow Burn
796 Cairnsmore of Carsphairn
340 Ailsa Craig
Old Dailly
Penkill
429 Garleffin Fell
Tallaminnock
Loch Bradan
Drumjohn
Girvan
Dounepark
Dalquhairn
Woodland
Knockeen
Balloch
River Stinchar
523 Craiglee
Loch Doon Castle
Pinminnoch
C A R R I C K
Barr
Loch Recar
622
Garryhorn Burn
Carsphairn
297 Grey Hill
Pinmore
Loch Macaterick
695 Meaul
Water of Ken
Balligmorrie
549 Polmaddie Hill
768 Shalloch on Minnoch
Lendalfoot
Polmaddy Burn
Galloway
781 Kirriereoch Hill
813 Corserine
Pinwherry
Muck Water
842 Merrick
Bennane Head
Colmonell
River Stinchar
Loch Moan
Loch Enoch
716 Milfire
346 Garwall Hill
Loch Dungeon
Forest Park
Duisk River
Heronsford
Water of Tig
Silver Flowe
Loch Neldricken
Knockshen
Ballantrae
Barrhill
Feoch Burn
Garroch
Glen Trool Lodge
Bruce Memorial
Lochton
Loch Trool
Belfast
Currarie Port
437 Beneraird
Glentrool Village
Bargrennan
380 Bennan
Creebank
Drumlamford
Loch Dornal
716 Lamachan Hill
Clatteringshaws Forest & Wildlife Centre
321 Carlock Hill
387 Altimeg Hill
675 Larg Hill
654 Millfore
Clatteringshaws Loch
Larne
Glen App
305 Benbrake Hill
Loch Maberry
Loch Ochiltree
Millreur Point
Southern Upland Way
Corsewall Point
Lady Bay
Laggangairn Standing Stones
Knowe
440 Garlick Hill
Galloway Deer Range
402 Round Fell
Barnhills
Portencalzie
Glenwhilly
Black Water of Dee
471 Fell of Fleet
Kirkcolm
184 Urrall Fell
River Bladnoch
Cairnryan
Penwhirn Reservoir
G A L L O W A Y
Loch Connell
Main Water of Luce
Cross Water of Luce
Black Burn
Carseriggan
Penkiln Burn
Auchen
Ervie
Low Barbeth
271 Artfield Fell
Challoch
Minnigaff
710 Cairnsmore of Fleet
Beoch Burn
Braid Fell
Barfad
Newton Stewart
Low Salchrie
New Luce
214 Culvennan Fell
Creebridge
Kirroughtree
Big Water of Fleet
Knocknain
Leswalt
Loch Ryan
Loch Ronald
Shennanton
Palnure
Innermessan
Black Loch
Balgracie
Castle of St John
White Loch
Castle Kennedy
Chlenry
184 Craig Fell
Craighlaw
Kirkcowan
Baltersan
Upper Ruscoe
Auchnotteroch
Stranraer
Aird
Castle Kennedy
Causeway End
Gem Rock
Portslogan
Broadsea Bay
Dernaglar Loch
Creetown
Fleet Valley
Glenluce Abbey
Glenwhan
Dunragit
Glenluce
Whitecrook
Clugston
Torhouse Stone Circle
Kirkmabreck
455 Cairnharrow
Anwoth
Black Head
Lochans
Kildrochet House
Piltanton Burn
181 Cairn Pat
Dunskey
Fell Loch
T H E
Wigtown
Carsluith
Cairnholy Chambered Cairns
Ringdoo Point
Portpatrick
Carsluith Castle
Milton
Castle Loch
Bladnoch
Stoneykirk
Stairhaven
M A C H A R S
Kirwaugh
Braehead
North Milmain
Mochrum Loch
Water of Malzie
Auchenmalg
Ravenshall Point
Mossyard
Fleet Bay
Kirkinner
Orchardton Bay
Mull of Sinniness
Auchenmalg Bay
Culshabbin
Margrie
Barrachan
Whauphill
Islands of Fleet
Sandhead
Chapel Finian (ruin)
Cairngarroch
Kirkmadrine Stones
Little Airies
Culscadden
Kirkandrews
Money Head
Elrig
Druchtag Motte
Sorbie
Wigtown Bay
Drumtrodden Cup & Ring
High Ardwell
Ardwell Bay
Ardwell
Ardwell House
Mochrum
Pouton
Garlieston
Drumtrodden Standing Stones
Drummoddie
Chapel Rossan
Broughton Mains
Cruggleton Bay
Ringdo
Port William
Big Balcraig
Drumbreddon
Balgowan
L U C E B A Y
Logan
'Wren's Egg' Standing Stones
Priory
Barsalloch Fort
Monreith
Port Logan Bay
Barsalloch Point
Whithorn Story
Whithorn
Port Logan
Point of Leg
Rispain Camp
Garrochtrie
Portyerrock
Clanyard Bay
Kilstay
St Ninian's Cave
Isle of Whithorn
Laggantalluch Head
Kirkmaiden
Drummore
Kidsdale
St Ninian's Chapel (ruin)
Barncorkrie
Killiness Point
High Drummore
Drumnaglaur
Maryport
Cutcloy
Burrow Head
Cardryne
Cardrain
West Cairngaan
Mull of Galloway
A77
A714
A75
A747
A746
A716
A713
A712
A718
A751
B7035
B734
B741
B7045
B7027
B7043
B738
B798
B7077
B7084
B7042
B7065
B7041
B733
B735
B7052
B7005
B7085
B7004
B7021
B7063
0 1 2 3 4 miles
0 1 2 3 4 5 kilometres
A B C D E F G H J K

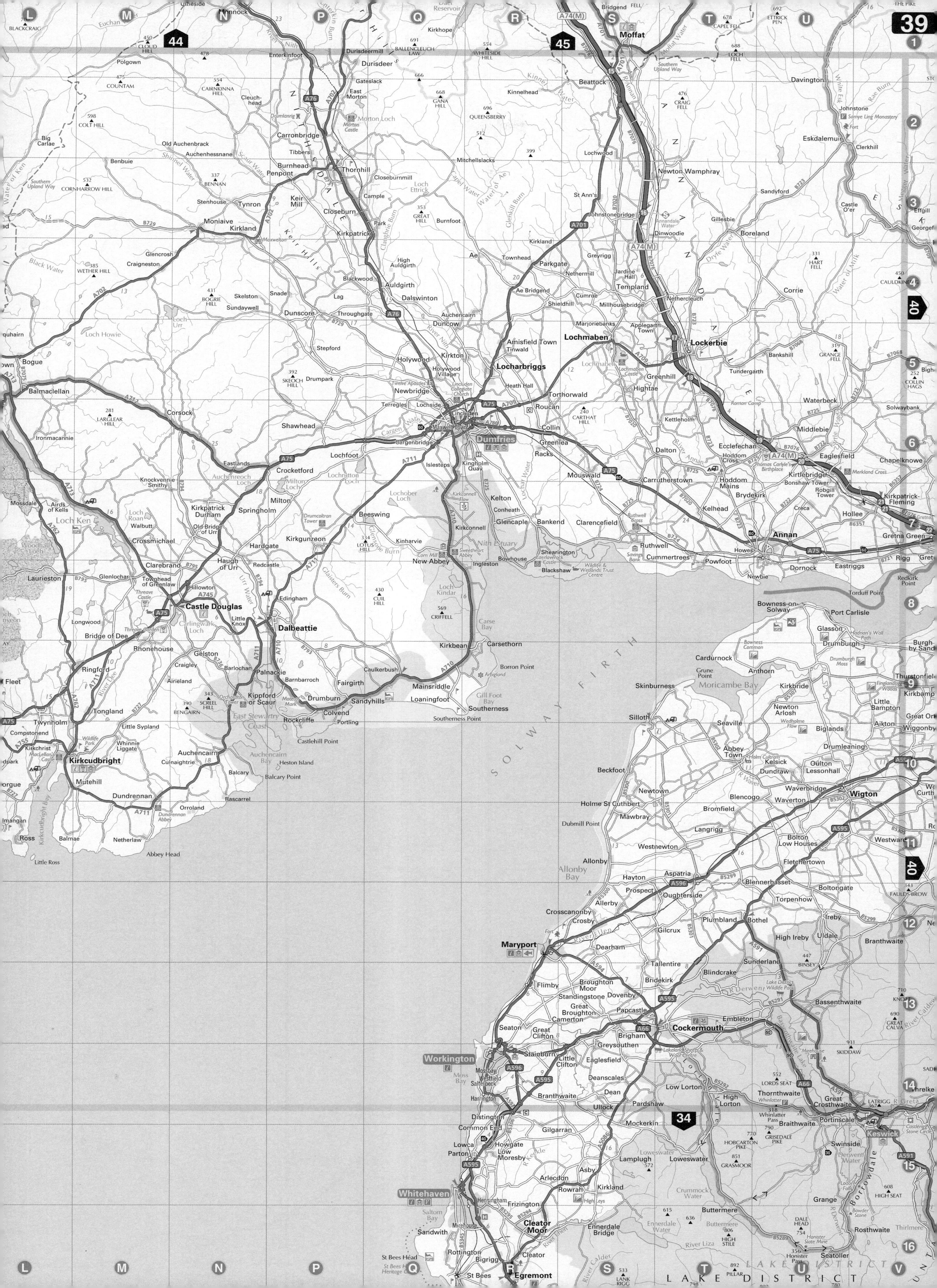
39
44
45
40
34
L
M
N
P
Q
R
S
T
U
V
1
2
3
4
5
6
7
8
9
10
11
12
13
14
15
16
BLACKCRAIG
CLOUD HILL
Polgown
COUNTAM
CAIRNKINNA HILL
COLT HILL
Big Carlae
Benbuie
CORNHARROW HILL
BENNAN
Old Auchenbrack
Auchenhessnane
Southern Upland Way
Stenhouse
Tynron
Moniaive
Kirkland
Maxwelton
Glencrosh
Craigneston
WETHER HILL
Black Water
Skelston
Sundaywell
BOGRIE HILL
Loch Urr
Loch Howie
Bogue
Balmaclellan
LARGLEAR HILL
Ironmacannie
Corsock
Mossdale
Airds of Kells
Loch Ken
Woodhall Loch
Laurieston
Glenlochar
Threave Castle
Townhead of Greenlaw
Clarebrand
Castle Douglas
Carlingwark Loch
Longwood
Bridge of Dee
Threave Garden
Rhonehouse
Ringford
River Dee
Tongland
Twynholm
Compstonend
Kirkchrist
Wildlife Park
Kirkcudbright
MacLellan's Castle
Mutehill
Dundrennan
Dundrennan Abbey
Kirkcudbright Bay
Ross
Balmae
Netherlaw
Abbey Head
Little Ross
Little Sypland
Whinnie Liggate
BENGAIRN
SCREEL HILL
Orchardton Tower
Auchencairn
Culnaightrie
Balcary
Balcary Point
Heston Island
Auchencairn Bay
Rascarrel
Orroland
East Stewartry Coast
Castlehill Point
Craigley
Airieland
Gelston
Barlochan
Palnackie
Kippford or Scaur
Motte of Mark
Rockcliffe
Colvend
Portling
Dalbeattie
Little Knox
Haugh of Urr
Hillowton
Old Bridge of Urr
Crossmichael
Walbutt
Loch Roan
Kirkpatrick Durham
Knockvennie Smithy
Auchenreoch Loch
Springholm
Milton
Milton Loch
Crocketford
Eastlands
Lochfoot
Lochrutton Loch
Drumcoltran Tower
Hardgate
Redcastle
Kirkgunzeon
Edingham
Glaisters Burn
Barnbarroch
Fairgirth
Drumburn
Sandyhills
Caulkerbush
Mainsriddle
Loaningfoot
Southerness
Southerness Point
Gill Foot Bay
Arbigland
Borron Point
Carsethorn
Kirkbean
CRIFFELL
CUIL HILL
Loch Kindar
Carse Bay
New Abbey
Corn Mill
Sweetheart Abbey
Kinharvie
LOTUS HILL
Beeswing
Lochober Loch
Kirkconnell
Kirkconnell Flow
Nith Estuary
Ingleston
Islesteps
Kingholm Quay
Dumfries
Maxwelltown
Lincluden
Lincluden Collegiate Church
Cargenbridge
Cargen Water
Terregles
Lochside
Newbridge
Twelve Apostles
Holywood
Holywood Village
Kirkton
Shawhead
Drumpark
SKEOCH HILL
Stepford
Duncow
Auchencairn
Dunscore
Throughgate
Lag
Dalswinton
Auldgirth
Blackwood
High Auldgirth
Snade
Ae
Kirkpatrick
Closeburn
Cample
Park
Closeburnmill
Loch Ettrick
GREAT HILL
Burnfoot
Thornhill
Burnhead
Penpont
Keir Mill
Tibbers
Carronbridge
Drumlanrig
Morton Loch
Morton Castle
East Morton
Gateslack
Durisdeer
Durisdeermill
Enterkinfoot
Cleuchhead
GANA HILL
QUEENSBERRY
BALLENCLEUCH LAW
WHITESIDE HILL
Kirkhope
Daer Reservoir
Mitchellslacks
Kinnelhead
Capel Water
Water of Ae
Glenkiln Burn
St Ann's
Johnstonebridge
Kirkland
Townhead
Parkgate
Ae Bridgend
Greyrigg
Nethermill
Shieldhill
Cumrue
Millhousebridge
Templand
Jardine Hall
Marjoriebanks
Amisfield Town
Tinwald
Lochmaben
Lochmaben Castle
Locharbriggs
Heath Hall
Torthorwald
Roucan
Collin
CARTHAT HILL
Greenlea
Racks
Mouswald
Kelton
Conheath
Glencaple
Bankend
Lochar Water
Clarencefield
Caerlaverock Castle
Shearington
Blackshaw
Bowhouse
Wildlife & Wetlands Trust Centre
Ruthwell
Ruthwell Cross
Savings Bank
Cummertrees
Powfoot
Annan
Howes
Newbie
Dornock
Eastriggs
Rigg
Gretna Green
Kirkpatrick-Fleming
Hollee
Creca
Kelhead
Brydekirk
Carrutherstown
Hoddom Mains
Hoddom Cross
Thomas Carlyle's Birthplace
Ecclefechan
Dalton
River Annan
Kettleholm
Greenhill
Hightae
Applegarth Town
Lockerbie
Nethercleuch
Dinwoodie
Annandale Water
Lochwood
Newton Wamphray
Beattock
Moffat
Bridgend
Southern Upland Way
Moffat Water
CAPEL FELL
ETTRICK PEN
LOCH FELL
CRAIG FELL
Davington
Johnstone
Samye Ling Monastery
Eskdalemuir
Clerkhill
Sandyford
Castle O'er
Gillesbie
Boreland
Dryfe Water
HART FELL
Corrie
CAULDKINE
Bankshill
GRANGE FELL
Tundergarth
Roman Camp
Waterbeck
COLLIN HAGS
Solwaybank
Middlebie
Eaglesfield
Merkland Cross
Chapelknowe
Kirtlebridge
Bonshaw Tower
Robgill Tower
Effgill
Georgefield
Redkirk Point
Torduff Point
Bowness-on-Solway
Port Carlisle
Glasson
Hadrian's Wall Path
Drumburgh
Bowness Common
Drumburgh Moss
Burgh by Sands
Cardurnock
Anthorn
Grune Point
Moricambe Bay
Skinburness
Kirkbride
Finglandrigg Woods
Thurstonfield
Kirkbampton
Newton Arlosh
Little Bampton
Great Orton
Aikton
Wiggonby
Silloth
Seaville
Wedholme Flow
Biglands
Abbey Town
Holm Cultram Abbey
Kelsick
Oulton
Lessonhall
Dundraw
Drumleaning
Wigton
Waverbridge
Waverton
Beckfoot
Newtown
Blencogo
Holme St Cuthbert
Mawbray
Bromfield
Dubmill Point
Langrigg
Westnewton
Bolton Low Houses
Westward
Allonby
Allonby Bay
Fletchertown
Hayton
Aspatria
Blennerhasset
Prospect
Oughterside
Boltongate
Allerby
Torpenhow
Crosscanonby
Crosby
Plumbland
Bothel
Ireby
Uldale
High Ireby
Branthwaite
Maryport
Fort
River Ellen
Dearham
Gilcrux
Tallentire
Sunderland
BINSEY
Flimby
Broughton Moor
Bridekirk
Blindcrake
Lake District Wildlife Park
Standingstone
Dovenby
Great Broughton
Camerton
Papcastle
Bassenthwaite
Seaton
Great Clifton
Brigham
Cockermouth
Embleton
GREAT CALVA
KNOTT
Workington
Stainburn
Little Clifton
Greysouthen
Lakeland Sheep & Wool Centre
Eaglesfield
Mossbay
Moss Bay
Salterbeck
Deanscales
Dean
SKIDDAW
LORDS SEAT
Mirehouse
Bassenthwaite Lake
Harrington
Branthwaite
Low Lorton
High Lorton
Thornthwaite
Whinlatter
Whinlatter Pass
Great Crosthwaite
LATRIGG
Keswick
Castlerigg Stone Circle
Portinscale
Braithwaite
Distington
Ullock
Pardshaw
Common End
Gilgarran
Mockerkin
HOBCARTON PIKE
GRISEDALE PIKE
Swinside
Derwent Water
Lowca
Parton
Howgate
Low Moresby
Lamplugh
Loweswater
GRASMOOR
Whitehaven
Arlecdon
Asby
Rowrah
Kirkland
High Leys
Crummock Water
Lodore Falls
Grange
Borrowdale
HIGH SEAT
Bowder Stone
Hensingham
Frizington
Saltom Bay
Cleator Moor
Ennerdale Bridge
Ennerdale Water
Buttermere
DALE HEAD
Honister Slate Mine
Honister Pass
HIGH STILE
River Liza
Rosthwaite
Thirlmere
Sandwith
Mirehouse
Rottington
Cleator
St Bees Head
St Bees Heritage Centre
Bigrigg
Egremont
St Bees
LANK RIGG
PILLAR
Seatoller
LAKE DISTRICT
Solway Firth
Nithsdale
Annandale
Kerr Hills
Mennock
Dalveen Pass

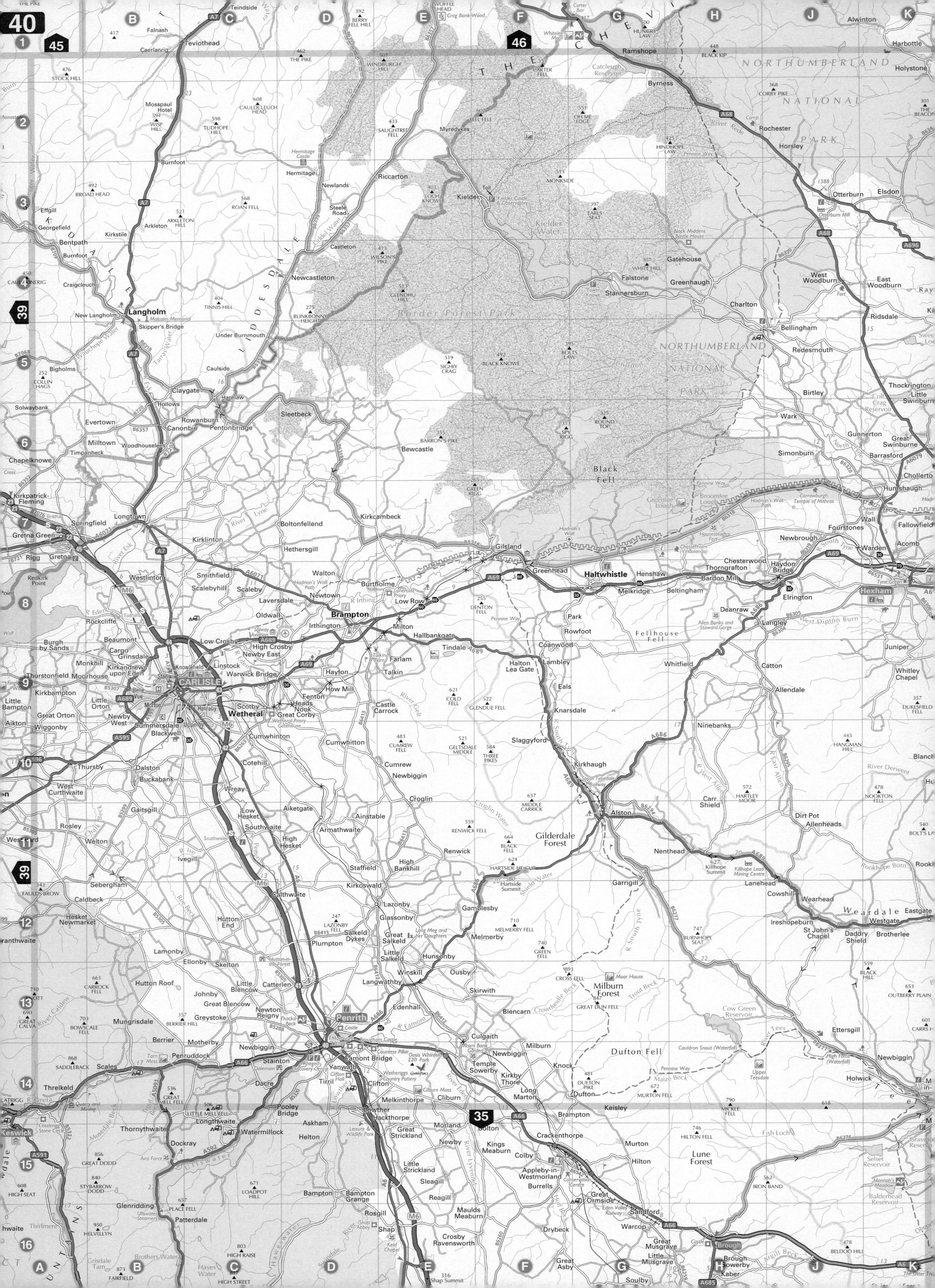
45
46
39
35
NORTHUMBERLAND NATIONAL PARK
Border Forest Park
Kielder Water
LIDDESDALE
ESKDALE
THE CHEVIOTS
Black Fell
Gilderdale Forest
Dufton Fell
Milburn Forest
Lune Forest
Weardale
Teviothead
Langholm
Newcastleton
Kielder
Riccarton
Hermitage
Byrness
Rochester
Otterburn
Elsdon
Bellingham
Falstone
Stannersburn
Gatehouse
Greenhaugh
Charlton
Redesmouth
Wark
Simonburn
Humshaugh
Chollerton
Fourstones
Newbrough
Hexham
Haydon Bridge
Bardon Mill
Haltwhistle
Greenhead
Gilsland
Bewcastle
Kirkcambeck
Longtown
Gretna
Gretna Green
Springfield
Canonbie
Rowanburn
Penton Bridge
Brampton
CARLISLE
Wetheral
Dalston
Thursby
Low Hesket
High Hesket
Kirkoswald
Alston
Nenthead
Allendale
Allenheads
Garrigill
Melmerby
Langwathby
Penrith
Eamont Bridge
Temple Sowerby
Kirkby Thore
Appleby-in-Westmorland
Dufton
Brough
Kirkby Stephen
Keswick
Pooley Bridge
Patterdale
Glenridding
Shap
Shap Summit
Ullswater
Haweswater
Thirlmere
Cow Green Reservoir
Selset Reservoir
Balderhead Reservoir
Catcleugh Reservoir
Middleton-in-Teesdale
Westgate
Eastgate
St John's Chapel
Wearhead
Cowshill
Ireshopeburn
Daddry Shield
Holwick
Newbiggin
M6
A7
A68
A69
A66
A686
A689
A6
A595
A591
A592
A6071
A74

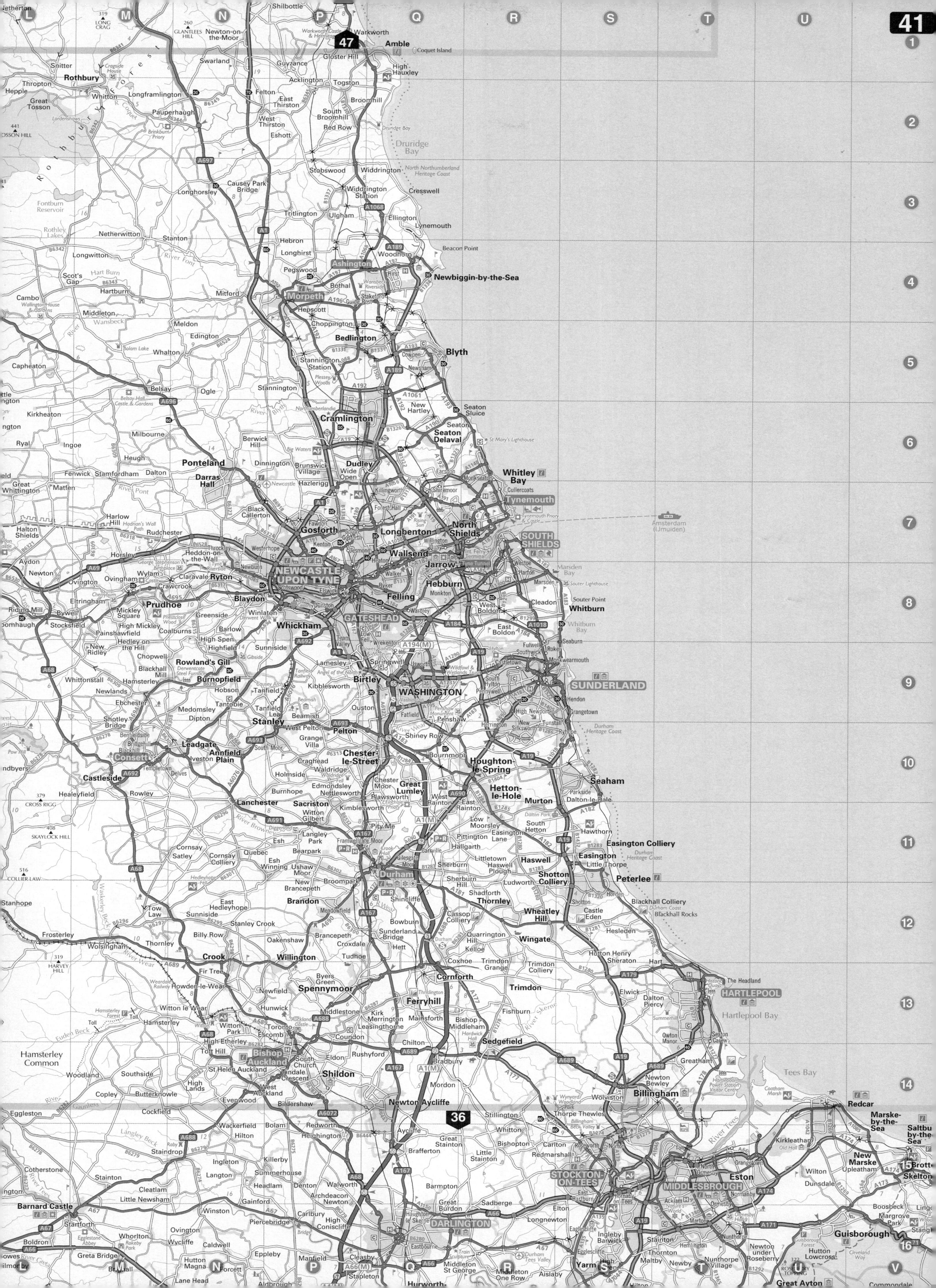
L
M
N
O
P
Q
R
S
T
U
1
2
3
4
5
6
7
8
9
10
11
12
13
14
15
16
V
47
36
Amble
Coquet Island
Warkworth
Shilbottle
High Hauxley
Rothbury
Thropton
Hepple
Snitter
Whitton
Great Tosson
Longframlington
Pauperhaugh
Swarland
Newton-on-the-Moor
Guyzance
Acklington
Togston
Broomhill
Felton
East Thirston
West Thirston
South Broomhill
Red Row
Eshott
Druridge Bay
Widdrington
Stobswood
Widdrington Station
Cresswell
Ulgham
Ellington
Lynemouth
Tritlington
Hebron
Longhirst
Causey Park Bridge
Longhorsley
Fontburn Reservoir
Rothley Lakes
Netherwitton
Stanton
Longwitton
Scot's Gap
Hartburn
Cambo
Middleton
Mitford
Pegswood
Ashington
Woodhorn
Newbiggin-by-the-Sea
Beacon Point
Morpeth
Bothal
Hepscott
Choppington
Bedlington
Blyth
Meldon
Edington
Whalton
Capheaton
Stannington Station
Stannington
Belsay
Ogle
Kirkheaton
Milbourne
Cramlington
New Hartley
Seaton Sluice
Seaton Delaval
Ryal
Ingoe
Berwick Hill
Heugh
Ponteland
Darras Hall
Dinnington
Brunswick Village
Hazlerigg
Dudley
Wide Open
Whitley Bay
Cullercoats
Tynemouth
Fenwick
Stamfordham
Dalton
Great Whittington
Matfen
Harlow Hill
Black Callerton
Halton Shields
Rudchester
Gosforth
Longbenton
North Shields
Amsterdam (IJmuiden)
South Shields
Heddon-on-the-Wall
Horsley
Wallsend
Jarrow
Marsden
Aydon
Newton
Ovington
Ovingham
Wylam
Clara Vale
Ryton
Crawcrook
NEWCASTLE UPON TYNE
Hebburn
Felling
Cleadon
Whitburn
Blaydon
Riding Mill
Bywell
Eltringham
Prudhoe
Mickley Square
Greenside
Winlaton
GATESHEAD
West Boldon
East Boldon
Stocksfield
Painshawfield
High Mickley
Coalburns
Whickham
Barlow
Hedley on the Hill
New Ridley
High Spen
Highfield
Sunniside
Chopwell
Rowland's Gill
Blackhall Mill
Burnopfield
Lamesley
Birtley
WASHINGTON
Sunderland
Whittonstall
Hamsterley
Newlands
Hobson
Tanfield
Kibblesworth
Ebchester
Medomsley
Dipton
Tantobie
Stanley
Tanfield Lea
Beamish
Ouston
Fatfield
Penshaw
Shotley Bridge
Leadgate
Pelton
Grange Villa
Shiney Row
Consett
Annfield Plain
Iveston
South Moor
Chester-le-Street
Houghton-le-Spring
Seaham
Castleside
Delves
Craghead
Waldridge
Holmside
Bournmoor
Healeyfield
Rowley
Burnhope
Edmondsley
Chester Moor
Great Lumley
Hetton-le-Hole
Murton
Dalton-le-Dale
Lanchester
Sacriston
Witton Gilbert
Nettlesworth
Kimblesworth
West Rainton
East Rainton
Cross Rigg
Skylock Hill
Pity Me
Low Moorsley
South Hetton
Hawthorn
Easington Colliery
Easington
Little Thorpe
Peterlee
Esh
Langley Park
Bearpark
Framwellgate Moor
Pittington
Hallgarth
Cornsay
Satley
Cornsay Colliery
Quebec
Esh Winning
Ushaw Moor
Durham
Sherburn
Littletown
Haswell
Haswell Plough
Shotton Colliery
Collier Law
New Brancepeth
Broompark
Sherburn Hill
Ludworth
Shadforth
Thornley
Stanhope
Brandon
Shincliffe
Wheatley Hill
Castle Eden
Blackhall Colliery
Blackhall Rocks
Tow Law
East Hedleyhope
Sunniside
Stanley Crook
Bowburn
Cassop Colliery
Wingate
Hesleden
Billy Row
Brancepeth
Croxdale
Sunderland Bridge
Hett
Quarrington Hill
Kelloe
Frosterley
Wolsingham
Thornley
Oakenshaw
Tudhoe
Harvey Hill
Crook
Fir Tree
Willington
Coxhoe
Trimdon Grange
Trimdon Colliery
Hutton Henry
Sheraton
Hart
The Headland
Howden-le-Wear
Byers Green
Spennymoor
Cornforth
Trimdon
Newfield
Ferryhill
HARTLEPOOL
Hartlepool Bay
Elwick
Dalton Piercy
Hunwick
Middlestone
Kirk Merrington
Witton le Wear
Hamsterley
Witton Park
Toronto
Leasingthorne
Mainsforth
Fishburn
Bishop Middleham
Hamsterley Common
High Etherley
Escomb
Coundon
Sedgefield
Owton Manor
Seaton Carew
Toft Hill
Bishop Auckland
Chilton
Eldon
Rushyford
Greatham
Woodland
Southside
St Helen Auckland
South Church
Tindale Crescent
Shildon
Bradbury
Tees Bay
Copley
Butterknowle
High Lands
West Auckland
Evenwood
Mordon
Newton Bewley
Billingham
Wolviston
Redcar
Marske-by-the-Sea
Eggleston
Cockfield
Bildershaw
Newton Aycliffe
Stillington
Thorpe Thewles
Wackerfield
Bolam
Redworth
Heighington
Hilton
Aycliffe
Great Stainton
Whitton
Bishopton
Carlton
Kirkleatham
Saltburn-by-the-Sea
Staindrop
Ingleton
Killerby
Summerhouse
Brafferton
Little Stainton
Redmarshall
Norton
New Marske
Upleatham
Brotton
Skelton
Cotherstone
Stainton
Langton
Headlam
Denton
Walworth
Barmpton
STOCKTON-ON-TEES
MIDDLESBROUGH
Eston
Wilton
Dunsdale
Cleatlam
Little Newsham
Gainford
Archdeacon Newton
Great Burdon
Sadberge
Barnard Castle
Startforth
Winston
Carlbury
Piercebridge
High Coniscliffe
Haughton le Skerne
DARLINGTON
Longnewton
Elton
Ingleby Barwick
Eaglescliffe
Acklam
Ormesby
Nunthorpe
Boosbeck
Margrove Park
Guisborough
Boldron
Whorlton
Ovington
Wycliffe
Caldwell
Eppleby
Manfield
Cleasby
Stapleton
Middleton St George
Eastbourne
Stainton
Thornton
Maltby
Newby
Nunthorpe Village
Newton under Roseberry
Hutton Lowcross
Greta Bridge
Rokeby Park
Hutton Magna
Forcett
Aldbrough
Lane Head
Hurworth
Middleton One Row
Aislaby
Yarm
Hilton
Great Ayton
Commondale

48

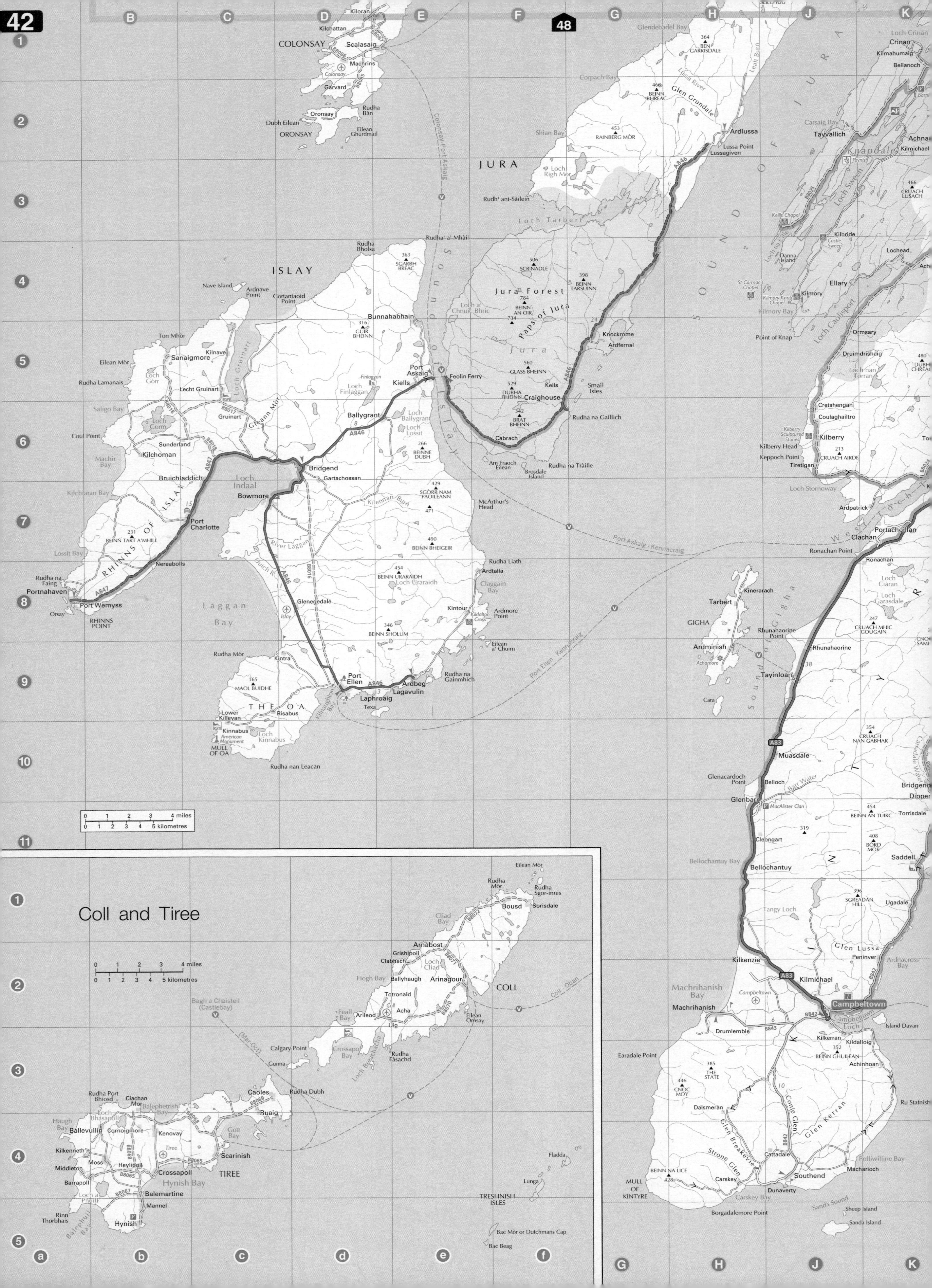

COLONSAY
Kiloran
Kilchattan
Scalasaig
Machrins
Garvard
Oronsay
Rudha Bàn
Dubh Eilean
ORONSAY
Eilean Ghurdmail
Colonsay-Port Askaig
JURA
Glendebadel Bay
364 BEN GARRISDALE
Lussa River
466 BEINN BHREAC
Glen Grundale
Corpach Bay
Leaf Burn
Shian Bay
453 RAINBERG MÒR
Ardlussa
Lussa Point
Lussagiven
Loch Righ Mor
Rudh' ant-Sàilein
Loch Tarbert
Rudha' a' Mhàil
506 SCRINADLE
398 BEINN TARSUINN
Jura Forest
784 BEINN AN OIR
734
Paps of Jura
Loch a' Chnuic Bhric
Knockrome
Ardfernal
560 GLASS BHEINN
529 DUBHA BHEINN
Craighouse
Keils
Small Isles
Rudha na Gaillich
442 BRAT BHEINN
Cabrach
Am Fraoch Eilean
Brosdale Island
Rudha na Tràille
Feolin Ferry
Sound of Islay
SOUND OF JURA
ISLAY
Rudha Bholsa
363 SGARBH BREAC
Nave Island
Ardnave Point
Gortantaoid Point
Bunnahabhain
316 GUIR-BHEINN
Ton Mhòr
Kilnave
Loch Gruinart
Eilean Mòr
Sanaigmore
Rudha Lamanais
Loch Gorr
Lecht Gruinart
Port Askaig
Finlaggan
Loch Finlaggan
Kiells
Saligo Bay
Gruinart
Loch Gorm
Glenn Mòr
Ballygrant
Loch Ballygrant
Loch Lossit
Coul Point
Sunderland
Kilchoman
266 BEINNE DUBH
Machir Bay
Bridgend
Gartachossan
Loch Indaal
Bruichladdich
429 SGÒRR NAM FAOILEANN
Kilchiaran Bay
Bowmore
Kilennan Burn
471
McArthur's Head
RHINNS OF ISLAY
Port Charlotte
231 BEINN TART A'MHILL
490 BEINN BHEIGEIR
River Laggan
Lossit Bay
Port Askaig - Kennacraig
Nereabolls
Rudha Liath
Ardtalla
454 BEINN URARAIDH
Loch Uaraidh
Rudha na Faing
Portnahaven
Port Wemyss
Orsay
RHINNS POINT
Duich
Claggain Bay
Laggan Bay
Glenegedale
Kintour
Ardmore Point
Kildalton Cross
346 BEINN SHOLUM
Eilean a' Chuirn
Rudha Mòr
Kintra
Port Ellen - Kennacraig
165 MAOL BUIDHE
Port Ellen
Ardbeg
Lagavulin
Laphroaig
Rudha na Gainmhich
Texa
THE OA
Risabus
Lower Killeyan
Kinnabus
American Monument
Loch Kinnabus
MULL OF OA
Rudha nan Leacan
Kilnaughton Bay
A846
A847
B8016
B8017
B8018
A83
B842
B843
B8025
B8024
Loch Crinan
Crinan
Kilmahumaig
Bellanoch
Carsaig Bay
Tayvallich
Achnamara
Kilmichael
Knapdale
Loch Sween
466 CRUACH LUSACH
Keills Chapel
Kilbride
Castle Sween
Loch na Cille
Danna Island
Lochead
St Cormac's Chapel
Kilmory Knap Chapel
Kilmory
Kilmory Bay
Ellary
Point of Knap
Loch Caolisport
Ormsary
Druimdrishaig
480 DUBH CHREAG
Loch nan Torran
Cretshengan
Coulaghailtro
Kilberry Sculptured Stones
Kilberry
Kilberry Head
Keppoch Point
213 CRUACH AIRDE
Tiretigan
Loch Stornoway
Ardpatrick
West Loch Tarbert
Portachoillan
Clachan
Ronachan Point
Ronachan
Loch Ciaran
Loch Garasdale
Kinerarach
Tarbert
GIGHA
247 CRUACH MHIC GOUGAIN
Rhunahaorine Point
Ardminish
Achamore
Rhunahaorine
Sound of Gigha
Tayinloan
Cara
354 CRUACH NAN GABHAR
Muasdale
Glenacardoch Point
Belloch
Barr Water
Glenbarr
MacAlister Clan
Bridgend
454 BEINN AN TUIRC
Torrisdale
319
408 BORD MOR
Cleongart
Saddell
Bellochantuy Bay
Bellochantuy
396 SGREADAN HILL
Ugadale
Tangy Loch
KINTYRE
Glen Lussa
Peninver
Ardnacross Bay
Kilkenzie
Kilmichael
Machrihanish Bay
Campbeltown
Machrihanish
Drumlemble
Campbeltown Loch
Island Davarr
Kilkerran
Kildalloig
352 BEINN GHUILEAN
Achinhoan
Earadale Point
385 THE STATE
446 CNOC MOY
Ru Stafnish
Dalsmeran
Glen Breakerie
Conie Glen
Glen Kerran
Strone Glen
Cattadale
Polliwilline Bay
Southend
Macharioch
BEINN NA LICE 428
MULL OF KINTYRE
Carskey
Dunaverty
Carskey Bay
Sanda Sound
Sheep Island
Sanda Island
Borgadalemore Point
0 1 2 3 4 miles
0 1 2 3 4 5 kilometres
Coll and Tiree
Eilean Mòr
Rudha Mòr
Rudha Sgor-innis
Bousd
Sorisdale
Cliad Bay
Arnabost
Grishipoll
Clabhach
Loch Cliad
Hogh Bay
Ballyhaugh
Arinagour
COLL
Coll - Oban
Bagh a Chaisteil (Castlebay)
Totronald
Feall Bay
Arileod
Acha
Uig
Eilean Ornsay
Calgary Point
Crossapol Bay
Rudha Fasachd
Gunna
Loch Breachacha
Rudha Port Bhiosd
Clachan Mor
Balephetrish Bay
Caoles
Rudha Dubh
Loch Bhasapoll
Haugh Bay
Ballevullin
Cornaigmore
Ruaig
Kenovay
Gott Bay
Kilkenneth
Tiree
Scarinish
Middleton
Moss
Heylipoll
Crossapoll
TIREE
Barrapoll
Hynish Bay
Balemartine
Loch a' Phuill
Mannel
Rinn Thorbhais
Hynish
Fladda
Lunga
TRESHNISH ISLES
Bac Mòr or Dutchmans Cap
Bac Beag

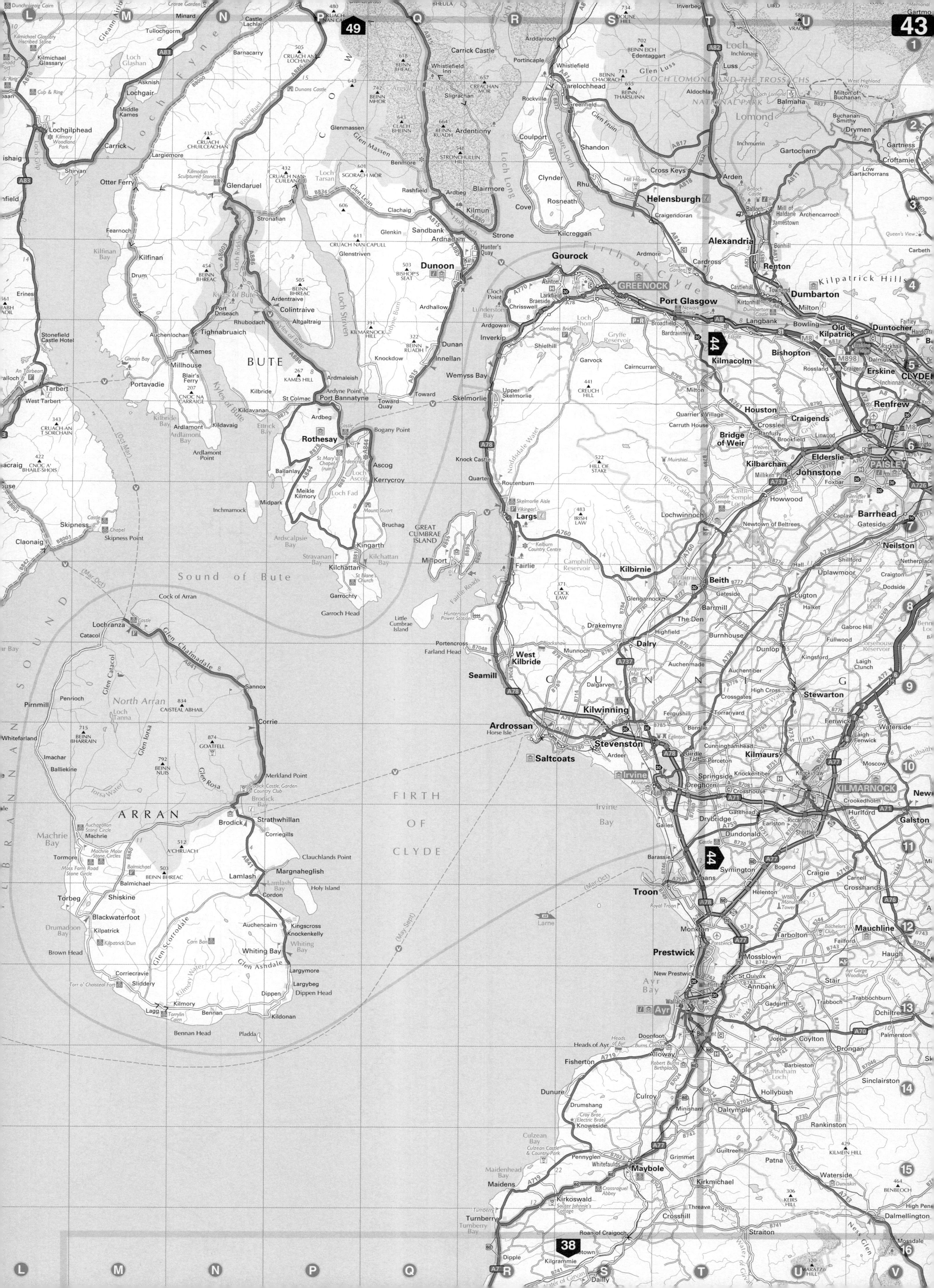

49
44
38
LOCH LOMOND AND THE TROSSACHS NATIONAL PARK
Lochgilphead
Ardrishaig
Tarbert
West Tarbert
Skipness
Claonaig
Otter Ferry
Glendaruel
Kilfinan
Tighnabruaich
Kames
Portavadie
Millhouse
Colintraive
Rothesay
Port Bannatyne
Ardbeg
Ascog
Kerrycroy
Kingarth
Kilchattan
Garroch Head
BUTE
Dunoon
Sandbank
Strone
Kilmun
Blairmore
Ardentinny
Carrick Castle
Strachur
Toward
Innellan
Gourock
GREENOCK
Port Glasgow
Helensburgh
Dumbarton
Alexandria
Balloch
Renton
Cardross
Kilcreggan
Cove
Rosneath
Garelochhead
Arrochar
Luss
Inverbeg
Balmaha
Drymen
Gartocharn
Kilmacolm
Bishopton
Erskine
Renfrew
Houston
Bridge of Weir
Kilbarchan
Johnstone
PAISLEY
Elderslie
Howwood
Lochwinnoch
Barrhead
Neilston
Kilbirnie
Beith
Dalry
Largs
Fairlie
Skelmorlie
Wemyss Bay
Inverkip
Millport
GREAT CUMBRAE ISLAND
West Kilbride
Seamill
Ardrossan
Saltcoats
Stevenston
Kilwinning
Irvine
Dreghorn
KILMARNOCK
Kilmaurs
Stewarton
Dunlop
Galston
Hurlford
Troon
Prestwick
Ayr
Symington
Tarbolton
Mauchline
Annbank
Alloway
Dalrymple
Maybole
Kirkoswald
Turnberry
Maidens
Crosshill
Kirkmichael
Straiton
Dunure
Patna
Dalmellington
Drongan
Ochiltree
Coylton
ARRAN
North Arran
Lochranza
Catacol
Pirnmill
Machrie
Blackwaterfoot
Lagg
Kilmory
Whiting Bay
Lamlash
Brodick
Corrie
Sannox
Holy Island
Pladda
Sound of Bute
KILBRANNAN SOUND
FIRTH OF CLYDE
Firth of Clyde
Irvine Bay
Ayr Bay
Larne
(Mar-Oct)
(May-Sept)

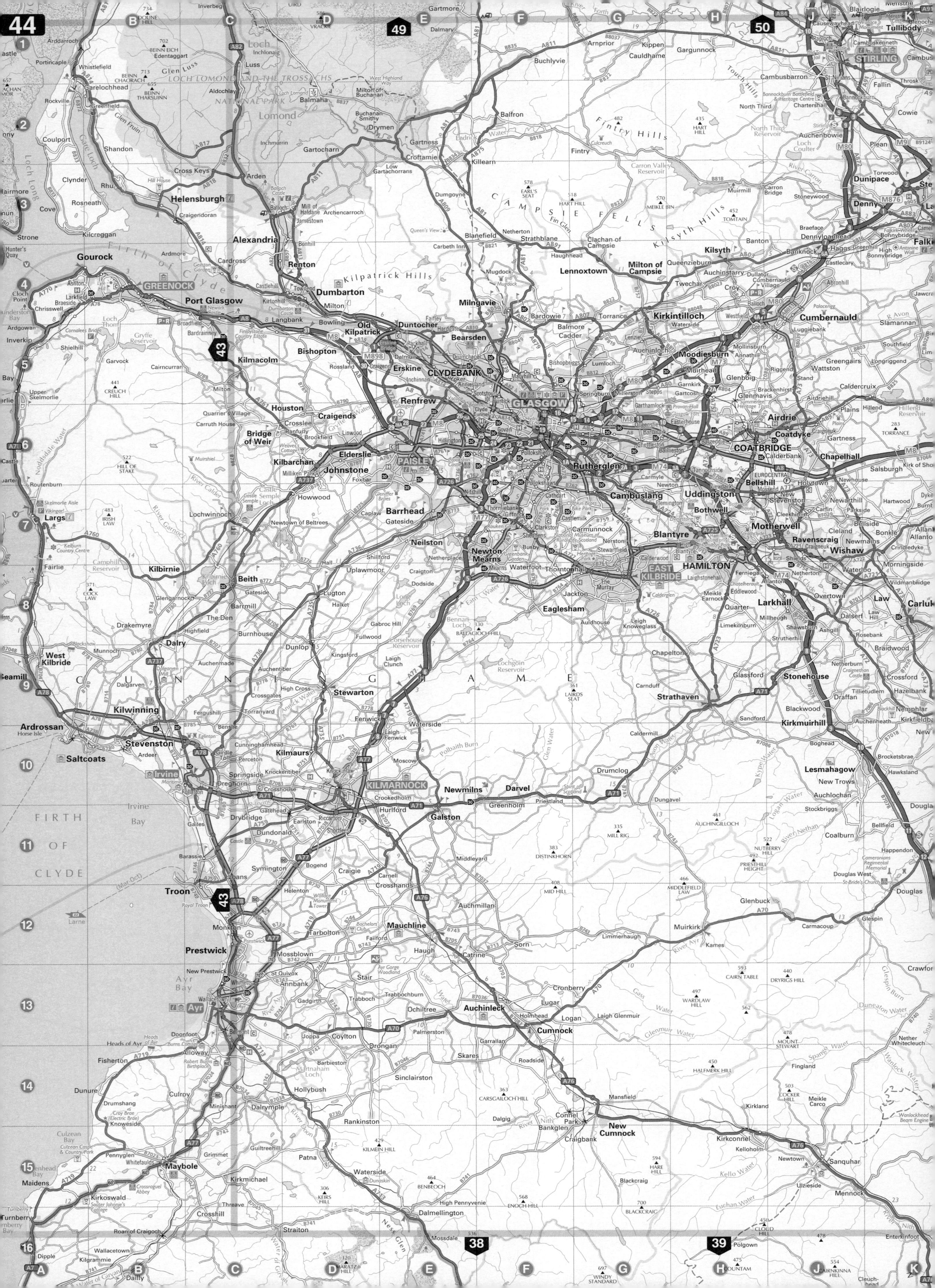
49
50
43
38
39
STIRLING
Tullibody
Cambuskenneth
Bannockburn
Gartmore
Arnprior
Kippen
Gargunnock
Buchlyvie
Touch Hills
Fintry Hills
Fintry
Balfron
Drymen
Killearn
Gartness
Croftamie
Balmaha
Milton of Buchanan
LOCH LOMOND AND THE TROSSACHS NATIONAL PARK
Loch Lomond
Luss
Glen Luss
Arrochar
Inverbeg
Aldochlay
Garelochhead
Whistlefield
Portincaple
Rosneath
Kilcreggan
Cove
Clynder
Rhu
Shandon
Glen Fruin
Loch Long
Gare Loch
Helensburgh
Cardross
Arden
Balloch
Alexandria
Renton
Dumbarton
Kilpatrick Hills
Gourock
GREENOCK
Port Glasgow
Firth of Clyde
Inverkip
Wemyss Bay
Skelmorlie
Largs
Kilmacolm
Bishopton
Erskine
Old Kilpatrick
Duntocher
Bearsden
Milngavie
CLYDEBANK
Renfrew
GLASGOW
Paisley
PAISLEY
Johnstone
Elderslie
Kilbarchan
Bridge of Weir
Houston
Craigends
Barrhead
Neilston
Newton Mearns
Rutherglen
Cambuslang
Blantyre
EAST KILBRIDE
HAMILTON
Motherwell
Wishaw
Bellshill
Uddingston
Bothwell
COATBRIDGE
Airdrie
Coatdyke
Chapelhall
Cumbernauld
Kilsyth
Kirkintilloch
Lennoxtown
Milton of Campsie
CAMPSIE FELLS
Kilsyth Hills
Denny
Dunipace
Larbert
Falkirk
Carron Valley Reservoir
Moodiesburn
Stepps
Lochwinnoch
Kilbirnie
Beith
Dalry
Howwood
Fairlie
West Kilbride
Ardrossan
Saltcoats
Stevenston
Kilwinning
Irvine
Dreghorn
Kilmaurs
Stewarton
Dunlop
KILMARNOCK
Hurlford
Galston
Newmilns
Darvel
Strathaven
Eaglesham
Larkhall
Stonehouse
Lesmahagow
Kirkmuirhill
Coalburn
Douglas
Glenbuck
Muirkirk
Sorn
Catrine
Mauchline
Tarbolton
Symington
Troon
Prestwick
Monkton
Ayr
Ayr Bay
Auchinleck
Cumnock
New Cumnock
Ochiltree
Drongan
Coylton
Dalrymple
Maybole
Kirkmichael
Crosshill
Straiton
Patna
Dalmellington
Kirkoswald
Turnberry
Maidens
Dunure
Culzean Bay
Kirkconnel
Sanquhar
Kelloholm
FIRTH OF CLYDE
Irvine Bay
CUNNINGHAME

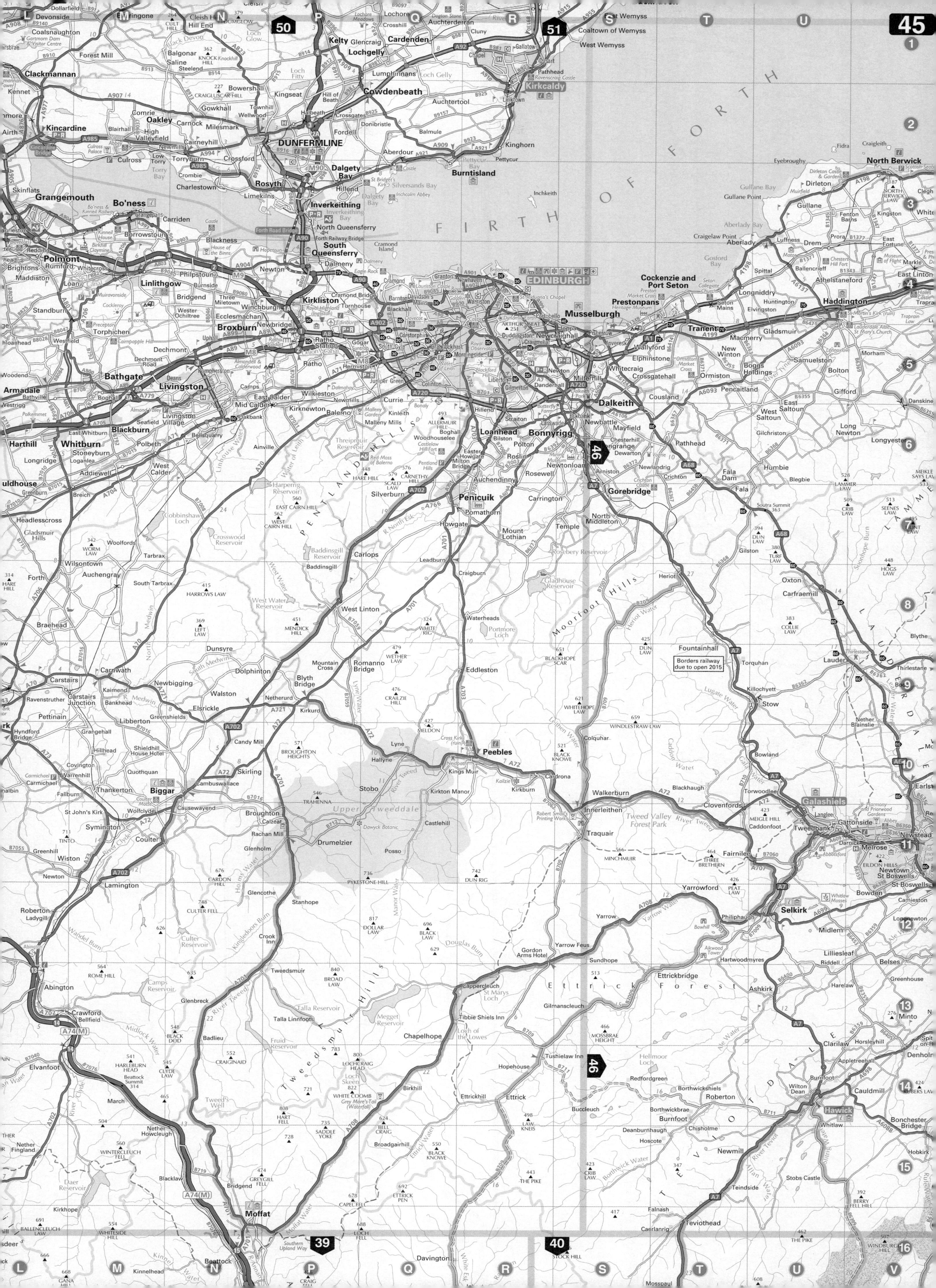
FIRTH OF FORTH
EDINBURGH
DUNFERMLINE
Kirkcaldy
Galashiels
Hawick
Kincardine
Clackmannan
Polmont
Grangemouth
Bo'ness
Linlithgow
Broxburn
Bathgate
Livingston
Armadale
Whitburn
Blackburn
Harthill
Kirkliston
South Queensferry
Dalmeny
Inverkeithing
Rosyth
Dalgety Bay
Aberdour
Burntisland
Kinghorn
Cowdenbeath
Lochgelly
Kelty
Cardenden
Auchterderran
Oakley
High Valleyfield
Culross
Charlestown
Limekilns
Musselburgh
Prestonpans
Cockenzie and Port Seton
Tranent
Haddington
North Berwick
Dirleton
Gullane
Aberlady
Longniddry
Dalkeith
Bonnyrigg
Loanhead
Penicuik
Gorebridge
Newtongrange
Mayfield
Pathhead
Peebles
Innerleithen
Walkerburn
Traquair
Selkirk
Melrose
Newtown St Boswells
St Boswells
Lauder
Stow
Biggar
Moffat
Abington
Crawford
Carnwath
Carstairs
West Linton
Carlops
Eddleston
Broughton
Stobo
Lamington
Symington
Coulter
Tweedsmuir
Ettrick
Ettrickbridge
Yarrow
Ashkirk
Denholm
Minto
PENTLAND HILLS
Moorfoot Hills
Tweedsmuir Hills
Ettrick Forest
LAUDERDALE
TEVIOTDALE
Upper Tweeddale
Tweed Valley Forest Park
Borders railway due to open 2015
50
51
46
39
40

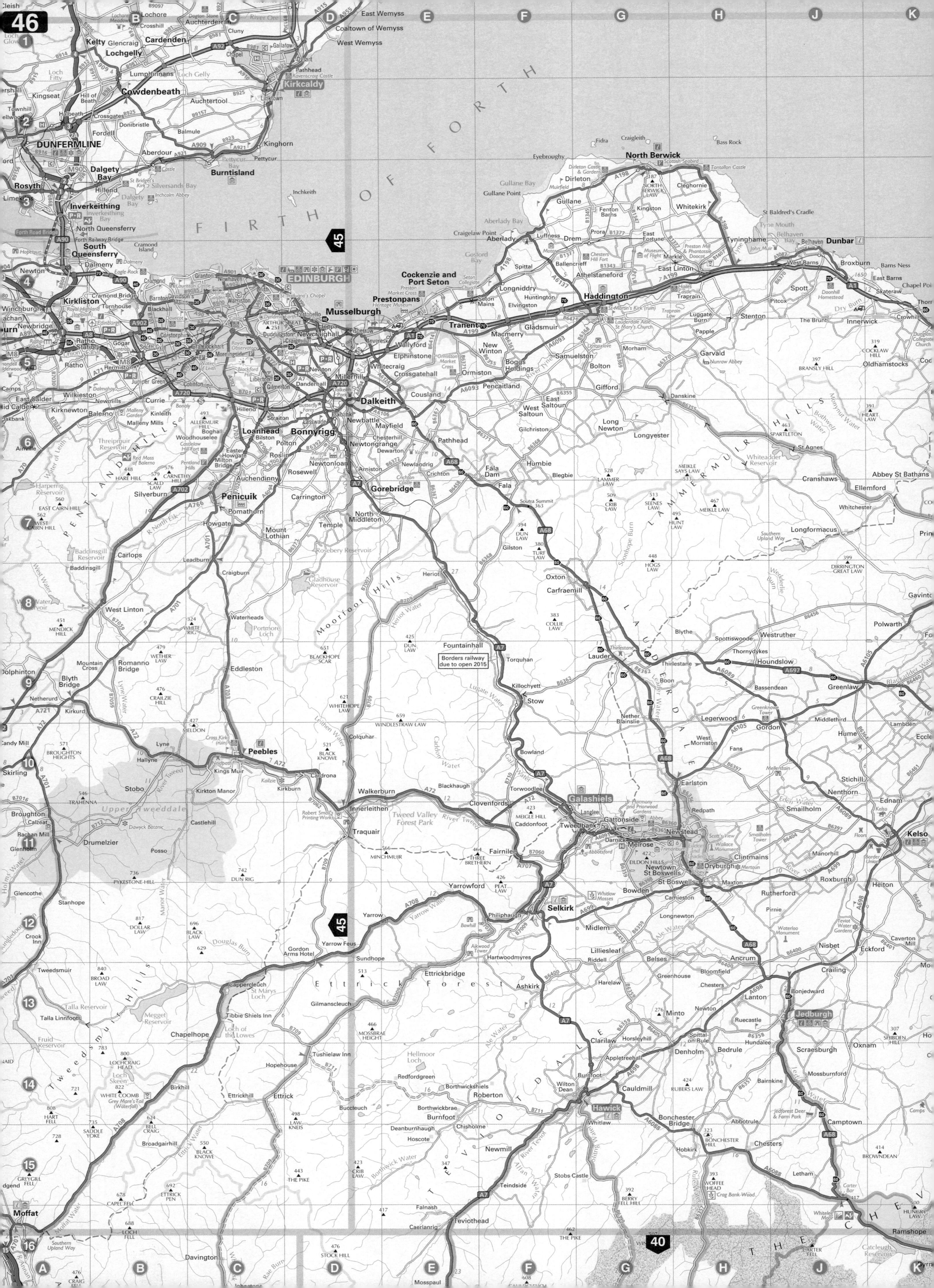
FIRTH OF FORTH
Kirkcaldy
East Wemyss
Coaltown of Wemyss
West Wemyss
Lochore
Auchterderran
Cardenden
Kelty
Lochgelly
Lumphinnans
Cowdenbeath
Auchtertool
Kinghorn
DUNFERMLINE
Aberdour
Dalgety Bay
Burntisland
Rosyth
Inverkeithing
North Queensferry
South Queensferry
Dalmeny
Kirkliston
Ratho
EDINBURGH
Musselburgh
Prestonpans
Cockenzie and Port Seton
Tranent
Dalkeith
Bonnyrigg
Loanhead
Penicuik
Gorebridge
North Berwick
Dirleton
Gullane
Aberlady
Haddington
East Linton
Dunbar
Innerwick
Gifford
Pathhead
Fala
Lauder
Stow
Peebles
Innerleithen
Walkerburn
Traquair
Galashiels
Melrose
Newstead
St Boswells
Earlston
Kelso
Selkirk
Jedburgh
Hawick
Denholm
Ancrum
West Linton
Moffat
Tweedsmuir
Yarrow
Ettrick
Pentland Hills
Moorfoot Hills
Lammermuir Hills
Lauderdale
Teviotdale
Ettrick Forest
Tweedsmuir Hills
Borders railway due to open 2015

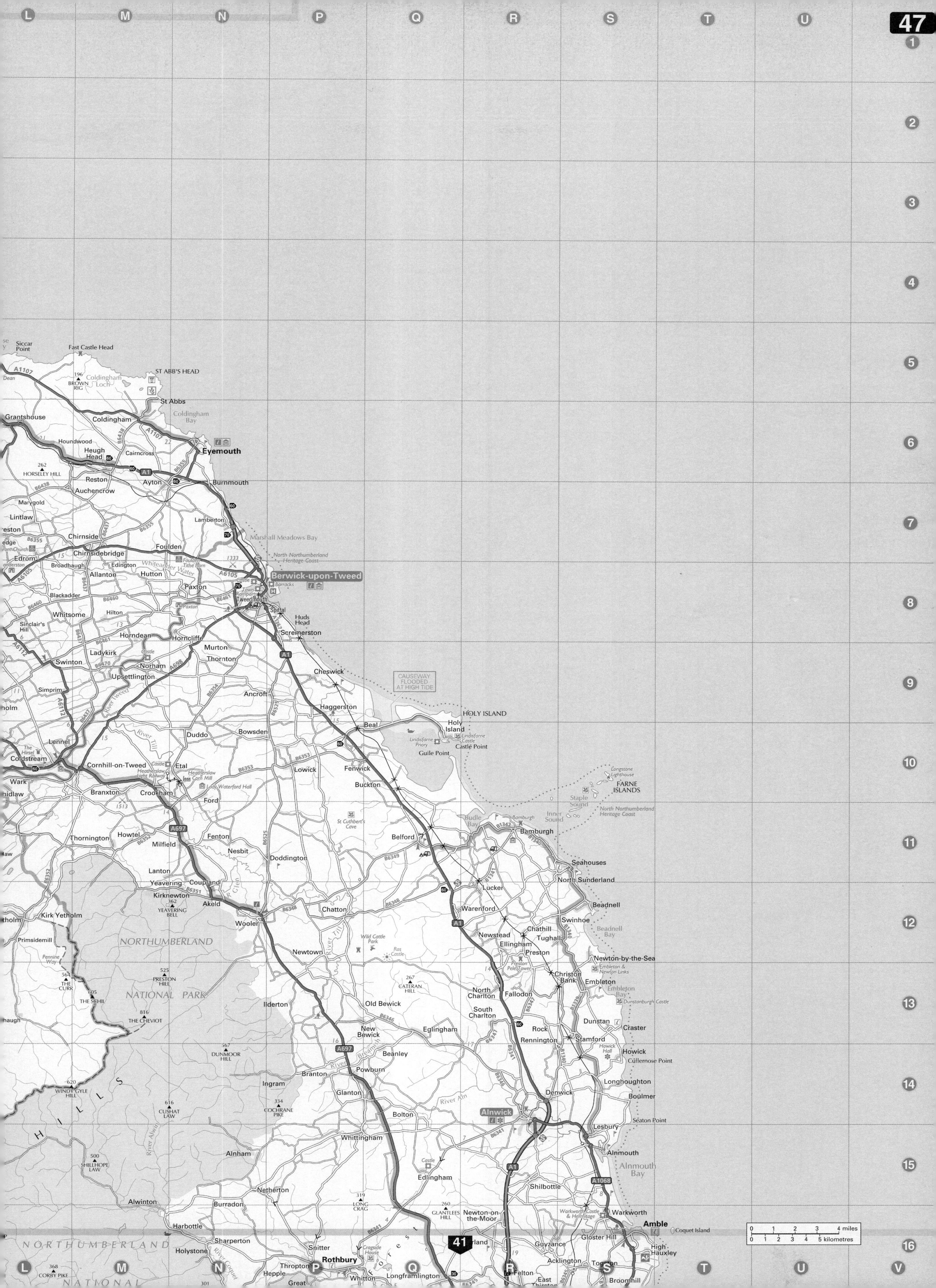
L M N P Q R S T U
Siccar Point
Fast Castle Head
ST ABB'S HEAD
Coldingham Loch
196 BROWN RIG
St Abbs
Coldingham Bay
Grantshouse
Coldingham
Houndwood
Heugh Head
Cairncross
Eyemouth
262 HORSELEY HILL
Reston
Ayton
Burnmouth
Auchencrow
Marygold
Lintlaw
Lamberton
Chirnside
Marshall Meadows Bay
Foulden
Chirnsidebridge
Edrom
North Northumberland Heritage Coast
Broadhaugh
Edington
Whiteadder Water
Allanton
Hutton
Berwick-upon-Tweed
Paxton
Blackadder
Tweedmouth
Whitsome
Hilton
Spittal
Sinclair's Hill
Huds Head
Horndean
Scremerston
Horncliffe
Murton
Ladykirk
Thornton
Norham
Swinton
Upsettlington
Cheswick
CAUSEWAY FLOODED AT HIGH TIDE
Simprim
Ancroft
River Tweed
Haggerston
HOLY ISLAND
Holy Island
Beal
Lennel
Duddo
Bowsden
Lindisfarne Priory
Lindisfarne Castle
Castle Point
Guile Point
The Hirsel
Coldstream
Cornhill-on-Tweed
Etal
Heatherslaw Light Railway
Heatherslaw Corn Mill
Lady Waterford Hall
Lowick
Fenwick
Longstone Lighthouse
FARNE ISLANDS
Wark
Branxton
Crookham
Buckton
Ford
Staple Sound
Inner Sound
North Northumberland Heritage Coast
Bamburgh
Budle Bay
St Cuthbert's Cave
Thornington
Howtel
Fenton
Belford
Milfield
Nesbit
Doddington
Seahouses
Lanton
North Sunderland
Yeavering
Coupland
Lucker
Kirknewton
Akeld
362 YEAVERING BELL
Beadnell
Kirk Yetholm
Wooler
Chatton
Warenford
Swinhoe
Beadnell Bay
Chathill
Newstead
Tughall
Primsidemill
NORTHUMBERLAND
Ellingham
Wild Cattle Park
Ros Castle
Preston
Newtown
Newton-by-the-Sea
Preston Pele Tower
Pennine Way
Embleton & Newton Links
525 PRESTON HILL
Christon Bank
Embleton
267 CATERAN HILL
564 THE CURR
North Charlton
Fallodon
Embleton Bay
605 THE SCHIL
NATIONAL PARK
Dunstanburgh Castle
South Charlton
Ilderton
Old Bewick
816 THE CHEVIOT
Dunstan
Craster
New Bewick
Rock
Eglingham
Rennington
Stamford
Howick Hall
Howick
567 DUNMOOR HILL
Beanley
Cullernose Point
Powburn
River Breamish
Branton
620 WINDY GYLE HILL
Longhoughton
Ingram
Glanton
Denwick
Boulmer
616 CUSHAT LAW
334 COCHRANE PIKE
River Aln
Alnwick
HILLS
Bolton
Seaton Point
Lesbury
River Alwin
Whittingham
Alnmouth
500 SHILLHOPE LAW
Alnham
Alnmouth Bay
Edlingham
Shilbottle
Netherton
319 LONG CRAG
Alwinton
Burradon
260 GLANTLEES HILL
Newton-on-the-Moor
Warkworth Castle & Hermitage
Warkworth
Amble
Coquet Island
Harbottle
Gloster Hill
Sharperton
NORTHUMBERLAND
Snitter
Cragside House
Guyzance
Holystone
High Hauxley
Rothbury
Acklington
Togston
Thropton
368 CORBY PIKE
Hepple
Whitton
Longframlington
Felton
Broomhill
NATIONAL
Great
East Thirston
A1 A1107 A697 A698 A6105 A6112 A1068 B6438 B6355 B6437 B6460 B6461 B6470 B6354 B6525 B6353 B6349 B6348 B6351 B6352 B6346 B6347 B6341 B6345 B1342 B1340 B1339 A1167
41
0 1 2 3 4 miles
0 1 2 3 4 5 kilometres
1 2 3 4 5 6 7 8 9 10 11 12 13 14 15 16
V

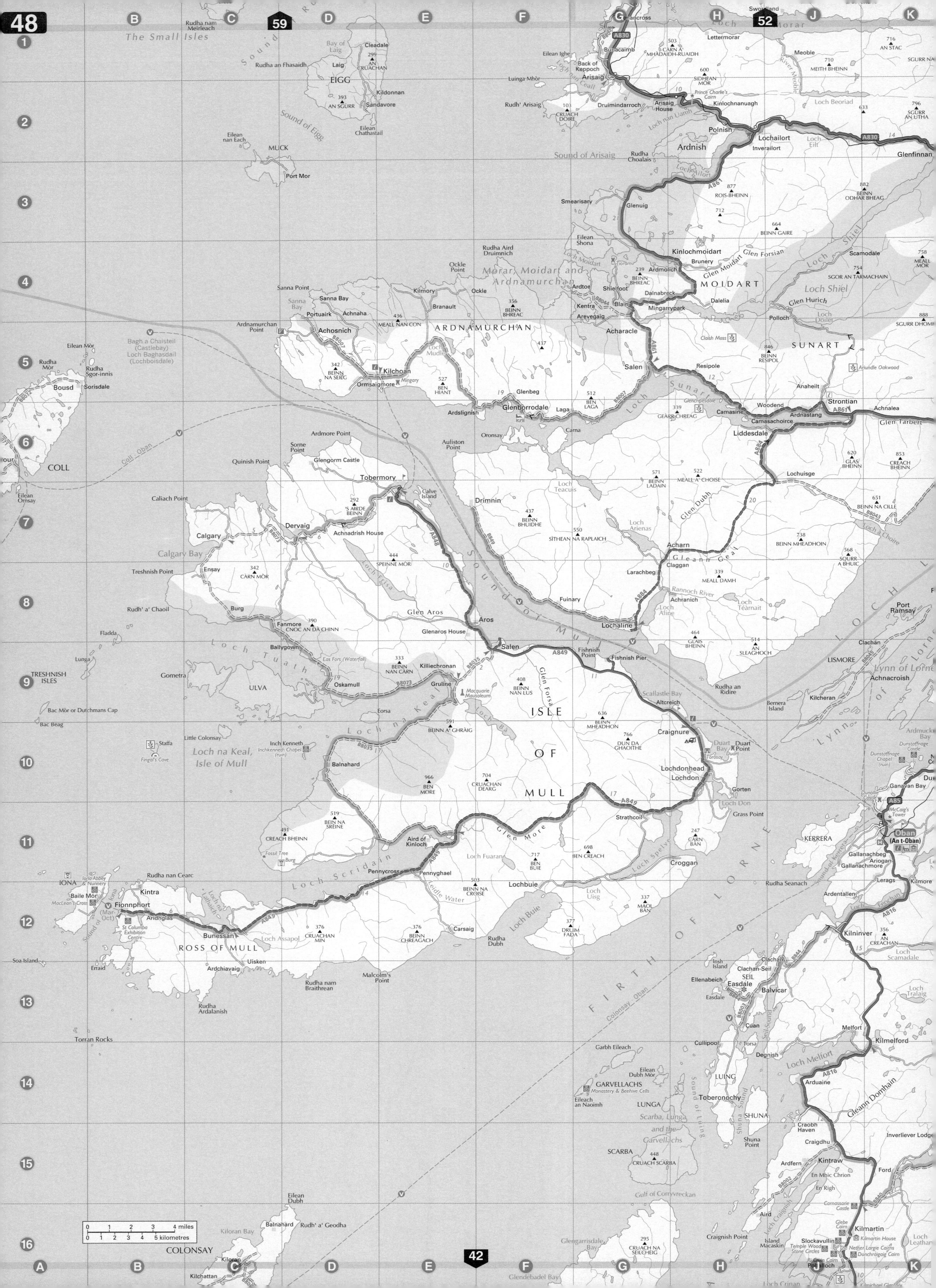
The Small Isles
Rudha nam Meirleach
Sound of Rum
Rudha an Fhasaidh
Bay of Laig
Cleadale
299 AN CRUACHAN
Laig
EIGG
Kildonnan
393 AN SGURR
Sandavore
Sound of Eigg
Eilean Chathastail
Eilean nan Each
MUCK
Port Mor
Mallaig
A830
Bunacaimb
503 CARN A' MHADAIDH-RUAIDH
Lettermorar
Loch Morar
Swordland
Meoble
716 AN STAC
SGURR NA
710 MEITH BHEINN
River Meoble
Eilean Ighe
Back of Keppoch
Arisaig
Loch nan Ceall
Luinga Mhòr
600 SIDHEAN MÒR
Prince Charlie's Cairn
Kinlochnanuagh
Loch Beoriad
633
796 SGURR AN UTHA
Rudh' Arisaig
103 CRUACH DOIRE
Druimindarroch
Arisaig House
Loch nan Uamh
Polnish
Lochailort
Inverailort
Loch Eilt
Glenfinnan
Ardnish
Sound of Arisaig
Rudha Choalais
Loch Ailort
A861
877 ROIS-BHEINN
882 BEINN ODHAR BHEAG
Smearisary
Glenuig
712
664 BEINN GAIRE
Eilean Shona
Rudha Aird Druimnich
Loch Moidart
Kinlochmoidart
Glen Forsian
Glen Moidart
Brunery
Ardmolich
Scamodale
758 MEALL MÒR
Loch Shiel
754 SGOR AN TARMACHAIN
Ockle Point
Morar, Moidart and Ardnamurchan
239 BEINN BHREAC
Tioram
Ardtoe
Shielfoot
Dalnabreck
MOIDART
Loch Shiel
Glen Hurich
Sanna Point
Sanna Bay
Kilmory
Ockle
356 BEINN BHREAC
Kentra
Blain
Arevegaig
Mingarrypark
Dalelia
Polloch
Loch Doilet
888 SGURR DHOMHNUILL
Portuairk
Achnaha
Branault
436 MEALL NAN CON
ARDNAMURCHAN
Acharacle
Ardnamurchan Point
Achosnich
B8007
437
Claish Moss
SUNART
Bagh a Chaisteil (Castlebay)
Loch Baghasdail (Lochboisdale)
Eilean Mòr
Rudha Mòr
Rudha Sgor-innis
Loch Mudle
342 BEINN NA SEILG
Kilchoan
Mingary
527 BEN HIANT
Salen
846 BEINN RESIPOL
Resipole
Ariundle Oakwood
Bousd
Sorisdale
B8072
Ormsaigmore
Glenbeg
512 BEN LAGA
Loch Sunart
Anaheilt
Strontian
Ardslignish
Glenborrodale
Laga
339 GEARR CHREAG
Glenchpesdole
Camasine
Woodend
Camasachoirce
Ardnastang
A861
Achnalea
Glen Tarbert
Ardmore Point
Oronsay
Carna
Liddesdale
Auliston Point
COLL
Coll-Oban
Sorne Point
Glengorm Castle
Quinish Point
Tobermory
Calve Island
571 BEINN LADAIN
522 MEALL A' CHOISE
Loch Teacuis
A884
620 GLAS BHEINN
853 CREACH BHEINN
Lochuisge
Eilean Ornsay
Caliach Point
292 'S AIRDE BEINN
Drimnin
Glen Dubh
651 BEINN NA CILLE
B8043
Dervaig
Achnadrish House
437 BEINN BHUIDHE
Loch Arienas
Calgary
B8073
550 SITHEAN NA RAPLAICH
Acharn
738 BEINN MHEADHOIN
Loch a' Choire
Calgary Bay
A848
B849
Gleann Geal
568 SGURR A' BHUIC
Treshnish Point
Ensay
342 CARN MÒR
444 SPEINNE MÒR
Loch Frisa
Claggan
Larachbeg
339 MEALL DAMH
Sound of Mull
Rannoch River
Achranich
Loch Tearnait
Loch Aline
Funiary
Rudh' a' Chaoil
Burg
Glen Aros
Aros
Lochaline
Port Ramsay
Fanmore
390 CNOC AN DÀ CHINN
Glenaros House
LOCH LINNHE
Fladda
Loch Tuath
Ballygown
Salen
Fishnish Point
Fishnish Pier
464 GLAIS BHEINN
514 AN SLEAGHOCH
Clachan
TRESHNISH ISLES
Lunga
Gometra
Eas Fors (Waterfall)
333 BEINN NAN CARN
Killiechronan
B8035
A849
Glen Forsa
LISMORE
Lynn of Lorne
Achnacroish
ULVA
Oskamull
B8073
Gruline
Macquarie Mausoleum
408 BEINN NAN LUS
Scallastle Bay
Rudha an Ridire
Kilcheran
Bernera Island
Bac Mòr or Dutchmans Cap
Bac Beag
Eorsa
Loch na Keal
Loch Ba
ISLE
636 BEINN MHEADHON
Altcreich
591 BEINN A' GHRAIG
Craignure
Ardmucknish Bay
Little Colonsay
Staffa
Fingal's Cave
Inch Kenneth
Inchkenneth Chapel (ruin)
Loch na Keal, Isle of Mull
B8035
766 DUN DA GHAOITHE
OF
Duart Bay
Duart Point
Torosay
Dunstaffnage Castle
Dunstaffnage Chapel (ruin)
Balnahard
966 BEN MORE
704 CRUACHAN DEARG
MULL
Lochdonhead
Lochdon
Gorten
Ganavan Bay
A85
Dunollie Castle
McCaig's Tower
Oban (An t-Oban)
519 BEINN NA SREINE
A849
Strathcoil
Loch Don
Grass Point
491 CREACH BHEINN
Fossil Tree
Burg
Aird of Kinloch
Glen More
247 CARN BAN
698 BEN CREACH
KERRERA
Gallanachbeg
Ariogan
Gallanachmore
Loch Fuaran
717 BEN BUIE
Loch Spelve
Croggan
IONA
Iona Abbey & Nunnery
Rudha nan Cearc
Loch Scridain
Pennycross
Pennyghael
503 BEINN NA CROISE
Lochbuie
Rudha Seanach
Lerags
Kilmore
Baile Mòr
MacLean's Cross
Kintra
Fionnphort
Sound of Iona
Aridhglas
Leidle Water
Loch Uisg
337 MAOL BAN
Ardentallen
Loch Feochan
St Columba Exhibition Centre
Bunessan
Loch Assapol
376 CRUACHAN MIN
376 BEINN CHREAGACH
Carsaig
Loch Buie
Rudha Dubh
377 DRUIM FADA
FIRTH OF LORNE
Kilninver
A816
356 AN CREACHAN
ROSS OF MULL
Loch Scamadale
Soa Island
Erraid
Ardchiavaig
Uisken
Insh Island
Clachan
Clachan-Seil
SEIL
Easdale
Balvicar
Ellenabeich
Rudha nam Braithrean
Malcolm's Point
Colonsay-Oban
Loch Tralaig
Rudha Ardalanish
B8003
B844
Cuan
Torran Rocks
Garbh Eileach
Cullipool
Torsa
Melfort
Kilmelford
Degnish
Loch Melfort
Eilean Dubh Mòr
GARVELLACHS
Monastery & Beehive Cells
LUING
A816
Arduaine
Eileach an Naoimh
LUNGA
Scarba, Lunga and the Garvellachs
Toberonochy
Sound of Luing
SHUNA
Gleann Domhain
Craobh Haven
Inverliever Lodge
SCARBA
448 CRUACH SCARBA
Shuna Point
Craigdhu
Ardfern
Kintraw
En Mhic Chrion
Ford
B8002
Gulf of Corryvreckan
Eilean Dubh
En Righ
Carnassarie Castle
Balnahard
Rudh' a' Geodha
Aird
Kilmartin
Glebe Cairn
Kilmartin House
Kiloran Bay
295 CRUACH NA SEILCHEIG
Craignish Point
Island Macaskin
Slockavullin
Temple Wood Stone Circles
Nether Largie Cairns
Dunchraigaig Cairn
Loch Leathan
COLONSAY
Glengarrisdale Bay
Kiloran
Kilchattan
Glendebadel Bay
Poltalloch
0 1 2 3 4 miles
0 1 2 3 4 5 kilometres

59
52
42

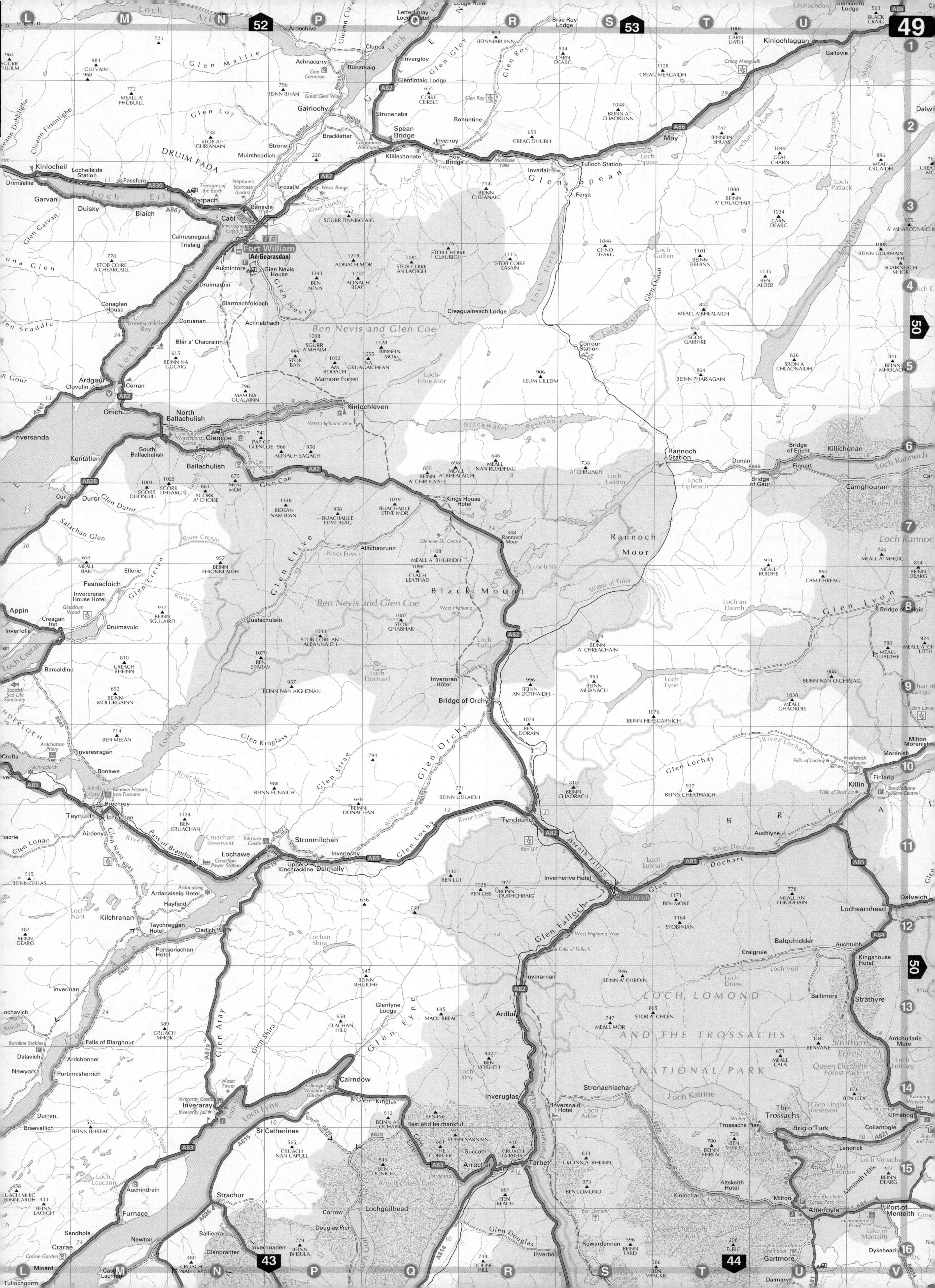
52
53
43
44
50
Fort William
(An Gearasdan)
Kinlochleven
Glencoe
Ballachulish
North Ballachulish
Onich
Corran
Ardgour
Clovulin
Inversanda
Kentallen
Duror
Cuil
Appin
Creagan Inn
Inverfolla
Barcaldine
Bonawe
Taynuilt
Brochroy
Airds Bay
Lochawe
Dalmally
Stronmilchan
Upper Kinchrackine
Inverlochy
Tyndrum
Bridge of Orchy
Inveroran Hotel
Kings House Hotel
Crianlarich
Inverherive Hotel
Inverarnan
Ardlui
Inveruglas
Tarbet
Arrochar
Succoth
Cairndow
Inveraray
St Catherines
Strachur
Furnace
Lochgoilhead
Crarae
Newton
Glenbranter
Kilchrenan
Taychreggan Hotel
Portsonachan Hotel
Cladich
Inverinan
Dalavich
Kinlochleven
Corpach
Banavie
Caol
Kinlocheil
Fassfern
Duisky
Blaich
Garvan
Drimsallie
Gairlochy
Spean Bridge
Roy Bridge
Inverroy
Tulloch Station
Fersit
Moy
Kinlochlaggan
Gallovie
Corrour Station
Rannoch Station
Dunan
Finnart
Bridge of Gaur
Camghouran
Killichonan
Killin
Finlarig
Auchlyne
Lochearnhead
Balquhidder
Strathyre
Kingshouse Hotel
Brig o'Turk
The Trossachs
Trossachs Pier
Stronachlachar
Inversnaid Hotel
Kinlochard
Aberfoyle
Port of Menteith
Gartmore
Rowardennan
Milton
Kilmahog
Callander
Glen Nevis
Ben Nevis and Glen Coe
Mamore Forest
Blackwater Reservoir
Rannoch Moor
Black Mount
Glen Coe
Glen Etive
Glen Orchy
Glen Lochay
Glen Lyon
Glen Falloch
Glen Spean
Glen Roy
Loch Linnhe
Loch Eil
Loch Leven
Loch Etive
Loch Awe
Loch Fyne
Loch Lomond
Loch Katrine
Loch Rannoch
Loch Treig
Loch Ossian
Loch Ericht
Loch Tulla
LOCH LOMOND AND THE TROSSACHS NATIONAL PARK
BREADALBANE
West Highland Way
1343 BEN NEVIS
1148 BIDEAN NAM BIAN
1130 BEN LUI
1174 BEN MORE
973 BEN LOMOND
884 BEN VORLICH
A82
A85
A86
A830
A819
A83
A815
A84
A821
A828
A861
B8004
B8005
B846
B845
B840
B828
B839

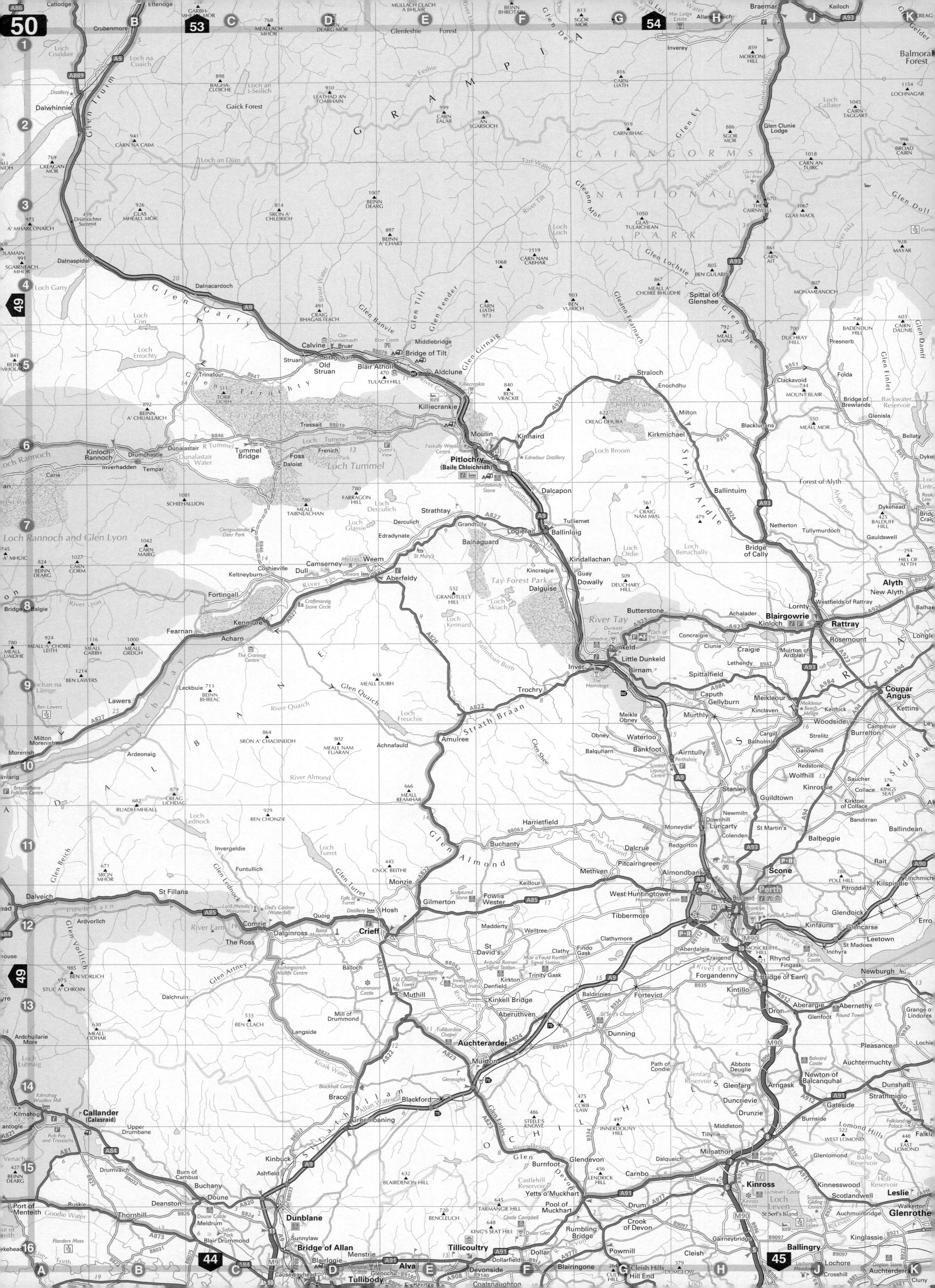
53
54
49
44
45
Dalwhinnie
Gaick Forest
G R A M P I A N
CAIRNGORMS NATIONAL PARK
Braemar
Inverey
Glen Clunie Lodge
Spittal of Glenshee
Glen Shee
Dalnaspidal
Drumochter Summit
Dalnacardoch
Glen Garry
Calvine
Bruar
Blair Atholl
Bridge of Tilt
Old Struan
Struan
Trinafour
Glen Errochty
Tay Forest Park
Killiecrankie
Moulin
Kinnaird
Pitlochry
(Baile Chloichridh)
Loch Tummel
Tummel Bridge
Kinloch Rannoch
Loch Rannoch
Drumchastle
Dunalastair
Tempar
Inverhadden
Foss
Dalcapon
Straloch
Enochdhu
Kirkmichael
Strath Ardle
Ballintuim
Bridge of Cally
Blairgowrie
Rattray
Alyth
New Alyth
Coupar Angus
Strathtay
Ballinluig
Logierait
Grandtully
Balnaguard
Weem
Aberfeldy
Dull
Coshieville
Keltneyburn
Fortingall
Kenmore
Loch Tay
Fearnan
Acharn
Lawers
Ardeonaig
Killin
River Tay
Dunkeld
Little Dunkeld
Birnam
Inver
Trochry
Amulree
Strath Braan
Glen Quaich
Glen Almond
Butterstone
Caputh
Murthly
Stanley
Luncarty
Bankfoot
Methven
Almondbank
Scone
Perth
Bridgend
Harrietfield
Buchanty
Monzie
Gilmerton
Fowlis Wester
Crieff
St Fillans
Comrie
Dalginross
Loch Earn
Lochearnhead
Dalveich
Ardvorlich
The Ross
Muthill
St David's
Kinkell Bridge
Aberuthven
Auchterarder
Gleneagles
Blackford
Braco
Greenloaning
Dunning
Forteviot
Bridge of Earn
Abernethy
Newburgh
Glenfarg
Milnathort
Kinross
Loch Leven
Callander
(Calasraid)
Kilmahog
Doune
Dunblane
Bridge of Allan
Deanston
Thornhill
Port of Menteith
Tillicoultry
Alva
Dollar
Menstrie
Tullibody
Rumbling Bridge
Yetts o'Muckhart
Glendevon
Ochil Hills
Ballingry
Glenrothes
Auchtermuchty
Strathmiglo
Lomond Hills
Leslie
Kinnesswood
Scotlandwell
Falkland
Ben Lawers
Schiehallion
Ben Vorlich
Ben Chonzie
Sidlaw Hills
Forest of Alyth
Glenisla
A9
A93
A924
A827
A822
A823
A85
A91
A912
M90
A84
A873
A977
A923
A984

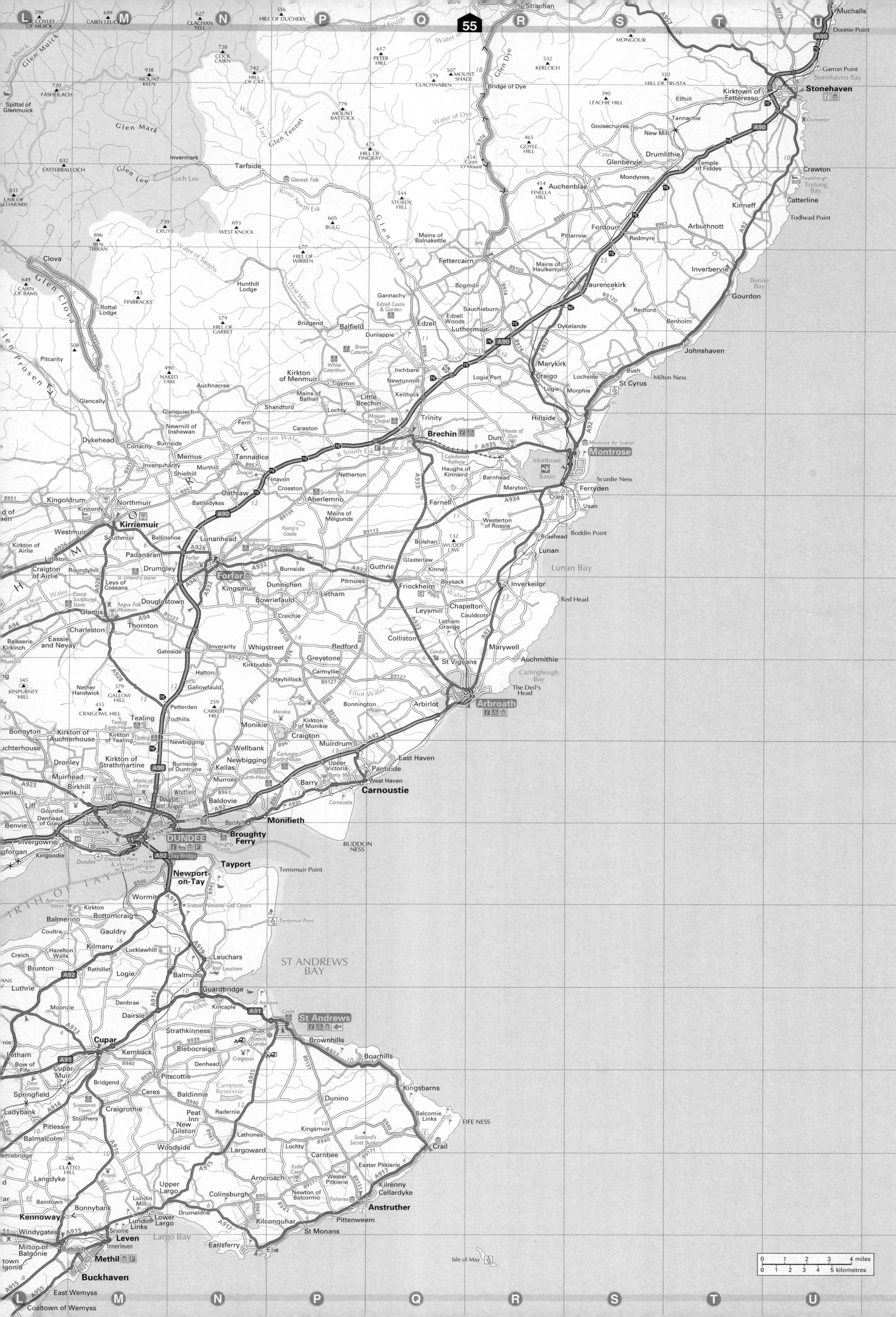
55
Stonehaven
Muchalls
Doonie Point
Garron Point
Stonehaven Bay
Kirktown of Fetteresso
Dunnottar
Crawton
Catterline
Todhead Point
Kinneff
Arbuthnott
Inverbervie
Bervie Bay
Gourdon
Johnshaven
Benholm
Milton Ness
St Cyrus
Lochside
Bush
Marykirk
Craigo
Logie
Morphie
Hillside
Montrose
Montrose Basin
Ferryden
Scurdie Ness
Usan
Boddin Point
Lunan
Lunan Bay
Inverkeilor
Red Head
Auchmithie
Carlingheugh Bay
The Deil's Head
Arbroath
St Vigeans
Marywell
Colliston
Friockheim
Letham
Forfar
Kirriemuir
Brechin
Edzell
Fettercairn
Laurencekirk
Auchenblae
Fordoun
Drumlithie
Glenbervie
Luthermuir
Tarfside
Invermark
Loch Lee
Clova
Glen Clova
Glen Prosen
Dykehead
Memus
Tannadice
Finavon
Aberlemno
Guthrie
Carmyllie
Carnoustie
East Haven
Panbride
Monifieth
Broughty Ferry
DUNDEE
Tay Bridge
Invergowrie
Newport-on-Tay
Tayport
Tentsmuir Point
Buddon Ness
Wormit
Balmerino
Leuchars
ST ANDREWS BAY
Guardbridge
St Andrews
Strathkinness
Cupar
Boarhills
Kingsbarns
Fife Ness
Crail
Anstruther
Pittenweem
St Monans
Elie
Earlsferry
Largo Bay
Lower Largo
Upper Largo
Leven
Methil
Buckhaven
Kennoway
Windygates
East Wemyss
Coaltown of Wemyss
Isle of May
A90
A92
A94
A933
A932
A934
A935
A926
A91
A914
A915
A916
A917
A919
A913
A930
B9120
B974
0 1 2 3 4 miles
0 1 2 3 4 5 kilometres
L M N P Q R S T U V

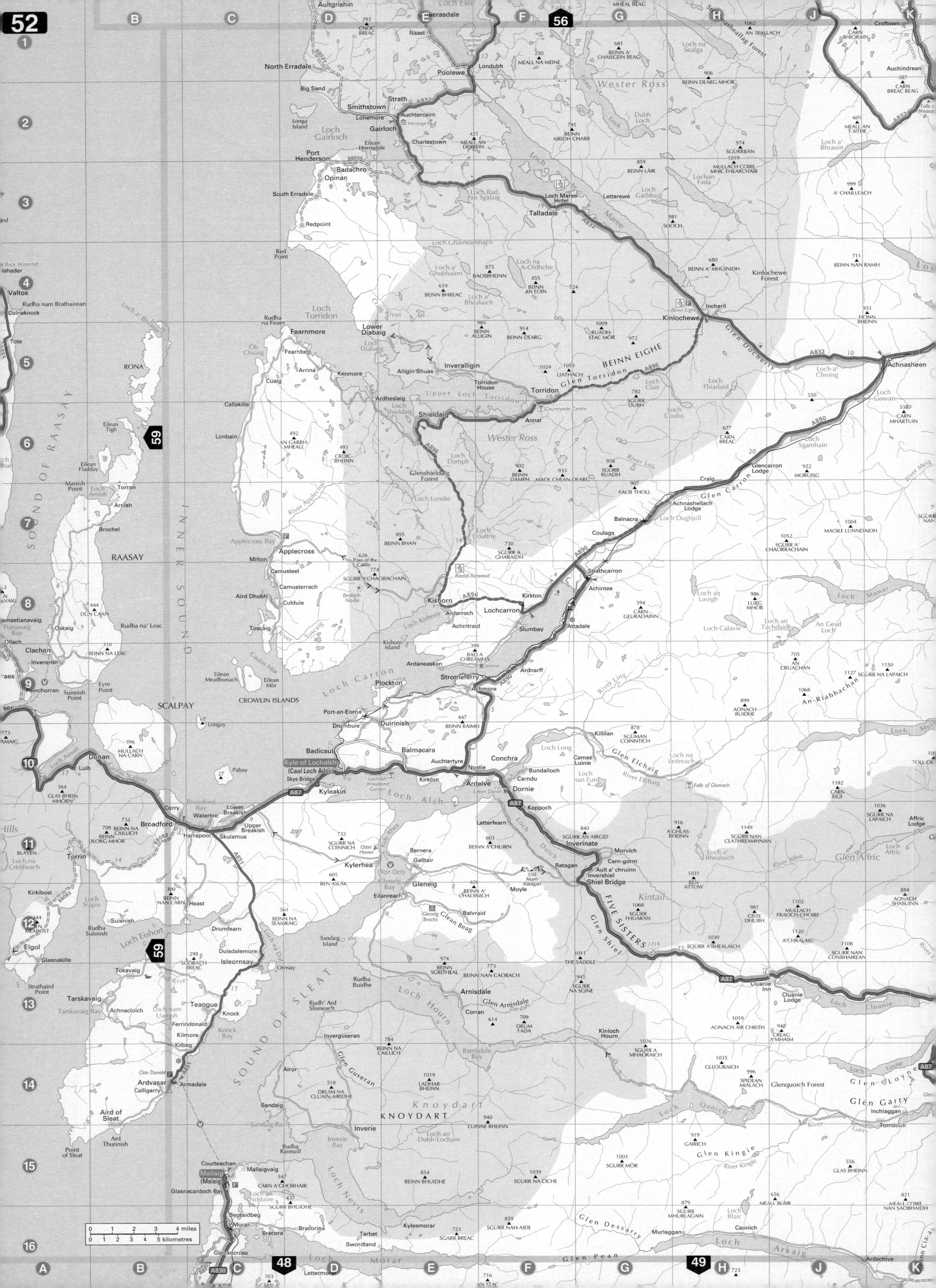
Aultgrishin
Everasdale
Naast
Inverewe Garden
North Erradale
Poolewe
Londubh
Big Sand
Strath
Smithstown
Lonemore
Auchtercairn
Longa Island
Loch Gairloch
Gairloch
Charlestown
Eilean Horrisdale
Port Henderson
Badachro
Opinan
South Erradale
Redpoint
Red Point
Loch Bad an Sgalaig
Loch Maree Hotel
Talladale
Letterewe
Loch Garbhaig
Loch Maree
Wester Ross
Dubh Loch
Fionn Loch
Loch na Sealga
Loch Fada
Lochan Fada
Sithasheallag Forest
AN TEALLACH
CARN BHIORAIN
Croftown
Auchindrean
CARN BREAC BEAG
MEALL AN T-SITHE
Loch a' Bhraoin
BEINN A' CHAISGEIN BEAG
MEALL NA MEINE
BEINN DEARG MHOR
BEINN AIRIDH CHARR
MEALL AN DOIREIN
SGURRBAN
MULLACH COIRE MHIC FHEARCHAIR
BEINN LAIR
SLIOCH
A' CHAILLEACH
Loch Ghaineamhach
Loch a' Ghobhainn
BAOSBHEINN
Loch na h-Oidhche
BEINN AN EOIN
BEINN BHREAC
Loch a' Bhealaich
BEINN A' MHUINIDH
Kinlochewe Forest
BEINN NAN RAMH
Kinlochewe
Incheril
Beinn Eighe
FIONN BHEINN
Glen Docherty
Achnasheen
Loch a' Chroisg
Loch Gowan
CARN MHARTUIN
Loch Torridon
Rudha na Feam
Fearnmore
Lower Diabaig
Loch Diabaig
Craig River
BEINN ALLIGIN
BEINN DEARG
RUADH-STAC MOR
BEINN EIGHE
Inveralligin
Alligin Shuas
Torridon House
Upper Loch Torridon
Torridon
Glen Torridon
LIATHACH
Loch Clair
Loch Fhiarlaid
Loch Coulin
SGURR DUBH
Countryside Centre
Annat
Shieldaig
Loch Shieldaig
Ardheslaig
Kenmore
Arrina
Fearnbeg
Cuaig
Òb Chuaig
Callakille
Lonbain
RONA
Eilean Tigh
SOUND OF RAASAY
AN GARBH-MHEALL
CROIC-BHEINN
Loch Damph
Glenshieldaig Forest
BEINN DAMPH
MAOL CHEAN-DEARG
SGORR RUADH
FAUR THOLL
River Lair
Loch Sgamhain
CARN BREAC
Glencarron Lodge
Craig
Glen Carron
MORUISG
River Meig
Achnashellach Lodge
Loch Dughaill
Balnacra
Coulags
MAOILE LUNNDAIDH
SGURR A' CHAORACHAIN
River Applecross
Loch Lundie
Loch Coultrie
BEINN BHAN
SGURR A' GHARAIDH
Applecross Bay
Applecross
Pass of the Cattle
SGURR A' CHAORACHAIN
Milton
Camusteel
Camusterrach
Culduie
Bealach-Na-Ba
Rassal Ashwood
Strathcarron
Achintee
Loch an Laoigh
LURG MHOR
Loch Monar
Kishorn
Kirkton
Lochcarron
Ardarroch
Achintraid
Slumbay
Attadale
CARN GEURADAINN
Loch Calavie
Loch an Tachdaidh
An Gead Loch
Aird Dhubh
Toscaig
River Toscaig
Loch Kishorn
Kishorn Island
BAD A' CHREAMHA
Strome
Ardaneaskan
Ardnarff
AN CRUACHAN
SGURR NA LAPAICH
An Riabhachan
RAASAY
Manish Point
Loch Arnish
Torran
Arnish
Eilean Fladday
Brochel
DUN CAAN
Rudha na' Leac
Oskaig
BEINN NA LEAC
Clachan
Inverarish
Eyre Point
Peinchorran
Suisnish Point
Eilean Meadhonach
Caolas Mòr
Eilean Mòr
CROWLIN ISLANDS
Loch Carron
Plockton
Stromeferry
Achmore
River Ling
AONACH BUIDHE
SCALPAY
Longay
INNER SOUND
Port-an-Eorna
Drumbuie
Duirinish
BEINN RAIMH
MULLACH NA CARN
Pabay
Badicaul
Kyle of Lochalsh
(Caol Loch Ailse)
Skye Bridge
Balmacara
Auchtertyre
Conchra
Killilan
SGUMAN COINNTICH
Loch Long
Glen Elchaig
Loch na Leitreach
Camas Luinie
Loch nan Eun
River Elchaig
Falls of Glomach
Dunan
Luib
Loch Ainort
Caolas Scalpay
GLAS BHEIN MHÒRN
Kyleakin
Lochalsh Woodland Garden
Kirkton
Nostie
Ardelve
Bundalloch
Carndu
Dornie
Eilean Donan
Loch Alsh
CARN EIGE
Corry
Broadford Bay
Lower Breakish
Waterloo
Upper Breakish
Broadford
Harrapool
Skulamus
BEINN NA CAILLICH
BEINN DEARG MHOR
BLAVEN
Torrin
Loch na Creitheach
SGURR NA COINNICH
Otter Haven
Kyle Rhea
Keppoch
Letterfearn
Loch Duich
BEINN A' CHUIRN
SGURR AN AIRGID
Inverinate
A' GHLAS-BHEINN
SGURR NAN CEATHREANNHAN
SGURR NA LAPAICH
Affric Lodge
Loch Affric
Glen Affric
River Affric
Loch a' Bhealaich
Kylerhea
Bernera
Galltair
Glenelg Bay
Glenelg
Ratagan
Mam Ratagan
Moyle
Morvich
Carn-gorm
Ault a' chruinn
Invershiel
Shiel Bridge
Kintail
BEN ATTOW
BEN ASLAK
BEINN A' CHAOINICH
Eilanreach
Balvraid
Glenelg Brochs
Glean Beag
Kirkibost
Loch Slapin
BEINN NAN CARN
Heast
Suisnish
BEINN NA SEAMRAIG
Sandaig Island
Rudha Suisnish
Loch Eishort
Drumfearn
Duisdalemore
Isleornsay
Ornsay
Elgol
Glasnakille
SGORACH BREAC
Tokavaig
Ord River
Strathaird Point
Tarskavaig
Tarskavaig Bay
Achnacloich
Loch nam Uamph
Teangue
Knock
Knock Bay
Ferrindonald
Kilmore
Kilbeg
Clan Donald
Ardvasar
Calligarry
Armadale
Aird of Sleat
Ard Thurinish
Point of Sleat
SOUND OF SLEAT
Loch na Dal
BEINN SGRITHEAL
BEINN NAN CAORACH
SGURR NA SGINE
THE SADDLE
Glen Shiel
FIVE SISTERS
SGURR FHUARAN
CISTE DHUBH
MULLACH FRAOCH-CHOIRE
A' CHRALAIG
SGURR A' BHEALAICH
SGURR NAN CONBHAIREAN
AONACH SHASUINN
Cluanie Inn
Cluanie Lodge
Loch Cluanie
Rudha Buidhe
Rudh' Ard Slisneach
Loch Hourn
Arnisdale
Glen Arnisdale
Corran
DRUIM FADA
Kinloch Hourn
SGURR A' MHAORAICH
AONACH AIR CHRITH
CREAG A' MHAIM
GLEOURAICH
SPIDEAN MIALACH
Glenquoich Forest
Loch Quoich
Glen Loyne
Loch Loyne
Glen Garry
Inchlaggan
Tomdoun
River Garry
Inverguseran
BEINN NA CAILLICH
Barrisdale Bay
Airor
Glen Guseran
DRUIM NA CLUAIN-AIRIDHE
LADHAR BHEINN
Sandaig
Sandaig Bay
Knoydart
KNOYDART
LUINNE BHEINN
Inverie
Inverie Bay
Loch an Dubh-Lochain
Rudha Raonuill
GAIRICH
Glen Kingie
River Kingie
SGURR MÒR
GLAS BHEINN
Courteachan
Mallaig
Mallaigvaig
CARN A' GHOBHAIR
Glasnacardoch Bay
Loch an Nostaire
SGURR BHUIDHE
Loch Nevis
BEINN BHUIDHE
SGURR NA CICHE
MEALL BLAIR
MEALL COIRE NAN SAOBHAIDH
SGURR MHURLAGAIN
Loch Blair
Caonich
Beoraidbeg
Morar
Bracora
Bracorina
Tarbet
Swordland
Kylesmorar
SGARR BREAC
SGURR NAH-AIDE
Glen Dessarry
Murlaggan
Loch Arkaig
Ardechive
Glenancross
Loch Morar
Lettermorar
Glen Pean
AN STAC
Bunacaimb
0 1 2 3 4 miles
0 1 2 3 4 5 kilometres

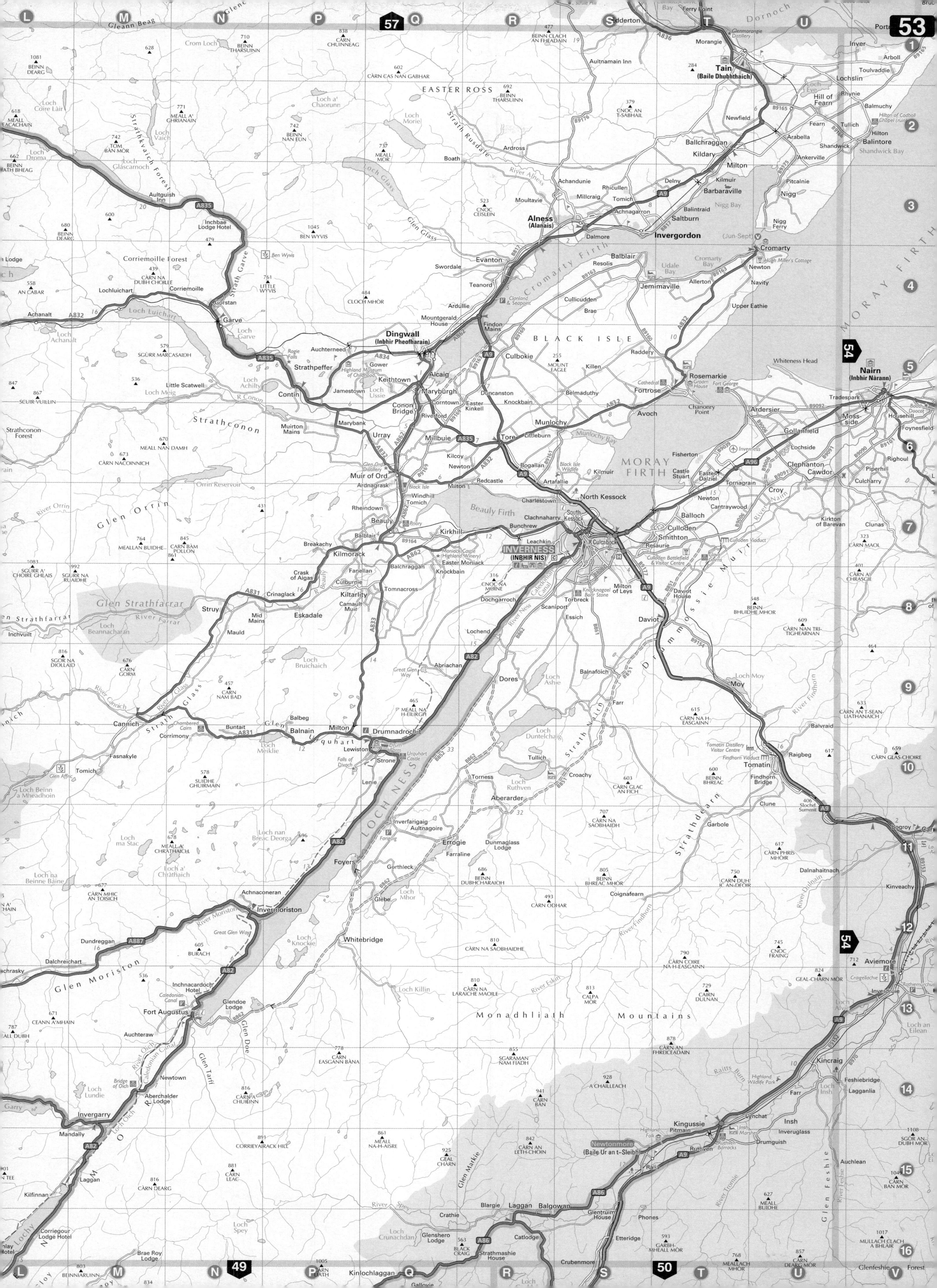
57
49
50
54
Gleann Beag
Crom Loch
BEINN THARSUINN
CARN CHUINNEAG
BEINN CLACH AN FHEADAIN
Edderton
Ferry Point
Dornoch
Glenmorangie Distillery
Morangie
Portmahomack
Inver
Arboll
Toulvaddie
Tain
(Baile Dhubhthaich)
Aultnamain Inn
Lochslin
Rhynie
Hill of Fearn
Balmuchy
Fearn
Tullich
Hilton of Cadboll
Chapel (ruin)
Hilton
Balintore
Shandwick
Shandwick Bay
Arabella
Newfield
Ballchraggan
Kildary
Ankerville
Milton
Kilmuir
Pitcalnie
Delny
Barbaraville
Nigg
Nigg Bay
Nigg Ferry
Balintraid
Saltburn
Invergordon
Cromarty
Hugh Miller's Cottage
Newton
Navity
CARN CAS NAN GABHAR
EASTER ROSS
BEINN THARSUINN
CNOC AN T-SABHAIL
Loch a' Chaorunn
Loch Morie
Strath Rusdale
Ardross
Boath
River Alness
Achandunie
Rhicullen
Millcraig
Tomich
Achnagarron
Moultavie
CNOC CEISLEIN
Alness
(Alanais)
Dalmore
BEINN DEARG
MEALL A' GHRIANAIN
MEALL TEACHAIN
Loch Coire Lair
Loch Droma
TOM BAN MOR
BEINN NAN EUN
MEALL MOR
Loch Glass
Glen Glass
Loch Vaich
Loch Glascarnoch
Strathvaich Forest
Aultguish Inn
A835
Inchbae Lodge Hotel
BEN WYVIS
Ben Wyvis
Corriemoille Forest
CARN NA DUBH CHOILLE
LITTLE WYVIS
Corriemoille
Lochluichart
AN CABAR
Achanalt
A832
Loch Luichart
Gorstan
Garve
Strath Garve
Loch Garve
Loch Achanalt
Evanton
Swordale
Teanord
Ardullie
Cromarty Firth
Balblair
Resolis
Udale Bay
Cromarty Bay
Jemimaville
Allerton
Upper Eathie
Clanland & Seaport
Cullicudden
Brae
CLOCH MHOR
Mountgerald House
Findon Mains
Dingwall
(Inbhir Pheofharain)
BLACK ISLE
Raddery
SGURR MARCASAIDH
Rogie Falls
Auchterneed
Strathpeffer
Gower
Highland Museum of Childhood
Keithtown
Alcaig
Culbokie
MOUNT EAGLE
Killen
Rosemarkie
Groam House
Fortrose
Cathedral
Fort George
Chanonry Point
Whiteness Head
MORAY FIRTH
Nairn
(Inbhir Narann)
Tradespark
Little Scatwell
Loch Achilty
Loch Meig
Contin
Jamestown
Loch Ussie
Maryburgh
Conon Bridge
Duncanston
Belmaduthy
Knockbain
Cornton
Easter Kinkell
Riverford
SCUIR VUILLIN
Strathconon
Strathconon Forest
Muirton Mains
Marybank
Urray
Millbuie
Tore
Munlochy
Munlochy Bay
Avoch
Ardersier
Moss-side
Househill
Foynesfield
Gollanfield
MEALL NAN DAMH
CARN NACOINNICH
Kilcoy
Newton
Muir of Ord
Glen Ord Distillery
Ardnagrask
Black Isle
Milton
Redcastle
Bogallan
Black Isle Wildlife
Kilmuir
MORAY FIRTH
Fisherton
Inverness
Castle Stuart
Easter Dalziel
Lochside
Clephanton
Cawdor
Righoul
Piperhill
Culcharry
Tornagrain
Croy
Orrin Reservoir
River Orrin
Glen Orrin
Windhill
Tomich
Rheindown
Charlestown
North Kessock
Beauly Firth
Beauly
Priory
Clachnaharry
South Kessock
Balloch
Cantraywood
Kirkton of Barevan
Clunas
Balblair
Kirkhill
Bunchrew
Culloden
Smithton
Culloden Viaduct
Culloden Battlefield & Visitor Centre
Clava Cairns
Resaurie
Leachkin
INVERNESS
(INBHIR NIS)
Culcabock
CARN MAOL
MEALLAN BUIDHE
CARN BAN POLLON
Breakachy
Kilmorack
Moniack Castle (Highland Winery)
Easter Moniack
Balchraggan
Knockbain
SGURR A' CHOIRE GHLAIS
SGURR NA RUAIDHE
Crask of Aigas
Fanellan
Culburnie
Kiltarlity
Tomnacross
CNOC NA MOINE
Dochgarroch
Knocknagael Boar Stone
Milton of Leys
CARN A' CHRASGIE
Glen Strathfarrar
River Farrar
Strathfarrar
Loch Beannacharan
Inchvuilt
Struy
A831
Cringlack
Mid Mains
Eskadale
Camault Muir
A833
Mauld
Caledonian Canal
Torbreck
Scaniport
Essich
Daviot House
Daviot
BEINN BHUIDHE MHOR
CARN NAN TRI-TIGHEARNAN
Lochend
River Ness
Drummossie Muir
SGOR NA DIOLLAID
CARN GORM
Loch Bruichaich
Abriachan
Great Glen Way
A82
Dores
Loch Ashie
Balnafoich
Loch Moy
Moy
River Glass
River Cannich
CARN NAM BAD
MEALL NA H-EILRIGH
Strath Nairn
Farr
Cannich
Strath Glass
Chambered Cairn
Buntait
Corrimony
Balbeg
Balnain
Glen Urquhart
Milton
Drumnadrochit
Loch Meiklie
Lewiston
Drum Farm
Urquhart Castle
Strone
Loch Duntelchaig
CARN NA H-EASGAINN
Balvraid
Tomatin Distillery Visitor Centre
Findhorn Viaduct
Tomatin
Raigbeg
River Findhorn
CARN AN T-SEAN-LIATHANAICH
CARN GLAS-CHOIRE
Fasnakyle
Glen Affric
Tomich
SUIDHE GHUIRMAIN
Falls of Divach
Lenie
LOCH NESS
Tullich
Croachy
Torness
Loch Ruthven
CARN GLAC AN FICH
BEINN BHREAC
Findhorn Bridge
Clune
Slochd Summit
Loch Beinn a' Mheadhoin
Aberarder
Inverfarigaig
Aultnagoire
Farigaig
Loch nan Breac Dearga
Loch ma Stac
MEALL A' CHRATHAICH
Errogie
Farraline
Dunmaglass Lodge
CARN NA SAOBHAIDHE
Strathdearn
Garbole
Bogroy
Carrbridge
CARN PHRIS MHOIR
Loch a' Chrathaich
Loch na Beinne Baine
Foyers
Gorthleck
BEINN DUBHCHARAIDH
BEINN BHREAC MHOR
CARN DUBH 'IC AN DEOIR
Dalnahaitnach
River Dulnain
Kinveachy
CARN MHIC AN TOISICH
Achnaconeran
Invermoriston
River Moriston
Glebe
Loch Mhor
Coignafearn
CARN ODHAR
Great Glen Way
Loch Knockie
Whitebridge
Dundreggan
A887
BURACH
Dalchreichart
Glen Moriston
CARN NA SAOBHAIDHE
River Findhorn
CARN COIRE NA H-EASGAINN
CNOC FRAING
Aviemore
GEAL-CHARN MOR
Craigellachie
Rothiemurchus
Inverdruie
Inchnacardoch Hotel
Caledonian Canal
Fort Augustus
Glendoe Lodge
Loch Killin
CARN NA LARAICHE MAOILE
River Eskin
CALPA MOR
CAIRN DULNAIN
Monadhliath Mountains
CEANN A' MHAIM
Auchteraw
Glen Doe
Glen Tarff
CARN EASGANN BANA
SGARAMAN NAM FIADH
CARN AN FHREICEADAIN
Kincraig
Raitts Burn
Highland Wildlife Park
Feshiebridge
Loch Insh
Lagganlia
Farr
Newtown
Bridge of Oich
Loch Lundie
Aberchalder Lodge
CARN A' CHUILINN
A' CHAILLEACH
CARN BAN
Lynchat
Insh
Kingussie
Pitmain
Insh Marshes
Inveruglass
Drumguish
Highland Folk
Ruthven Barracks
Ruthven
SGOR AN DUBH MOR
Invergarry
Mandally
Loch Oich
CORRIEYAIRACK HILL
MEALL NA H-AISRE
CARN AN LETH-CHOIN
GEAL CHARN
Newtonmore
(Baile Ur an t-Sleibh)
Ralia
Glen Markie
Auchlean
CARN BAN MOR
Glen Feshie
Laggan
CARN LEAC
CARN DEARG
Kilfinnan
A86
River Tromie
MEALL BUIDHE
River Spey
Blargie
Laggan
Balgowan
Gleantruim House
Phones
Crathie
Corriegour Lodge Hotel
Loch Spey
Loch Crunachdan
Glenshero Lodge
Catlodge
Etteridge
BLACK CRAIG
Strathmashie House
GARBH-MHEALL MOR
MULLACH CLACH A BHLAIR
Brae Roy Lodge
BEINN IARUINN
CARN DEARG
CARN DEARG MOR
MEALL CHUAICH
Crubenmore
Glenfeshie
Forest
Kinlochlaggan
Gallovie
Loch Lochy
A9
A82
A86
A96
A862
A834
A832
A835
B9163
B9160
B9161
B9169
B9164
B9006
B9091
B9090
B9101
B9092
B851
B852
B862
B861
B9154
B9152
B970
B9165
B9166
B9175
B9176
B817

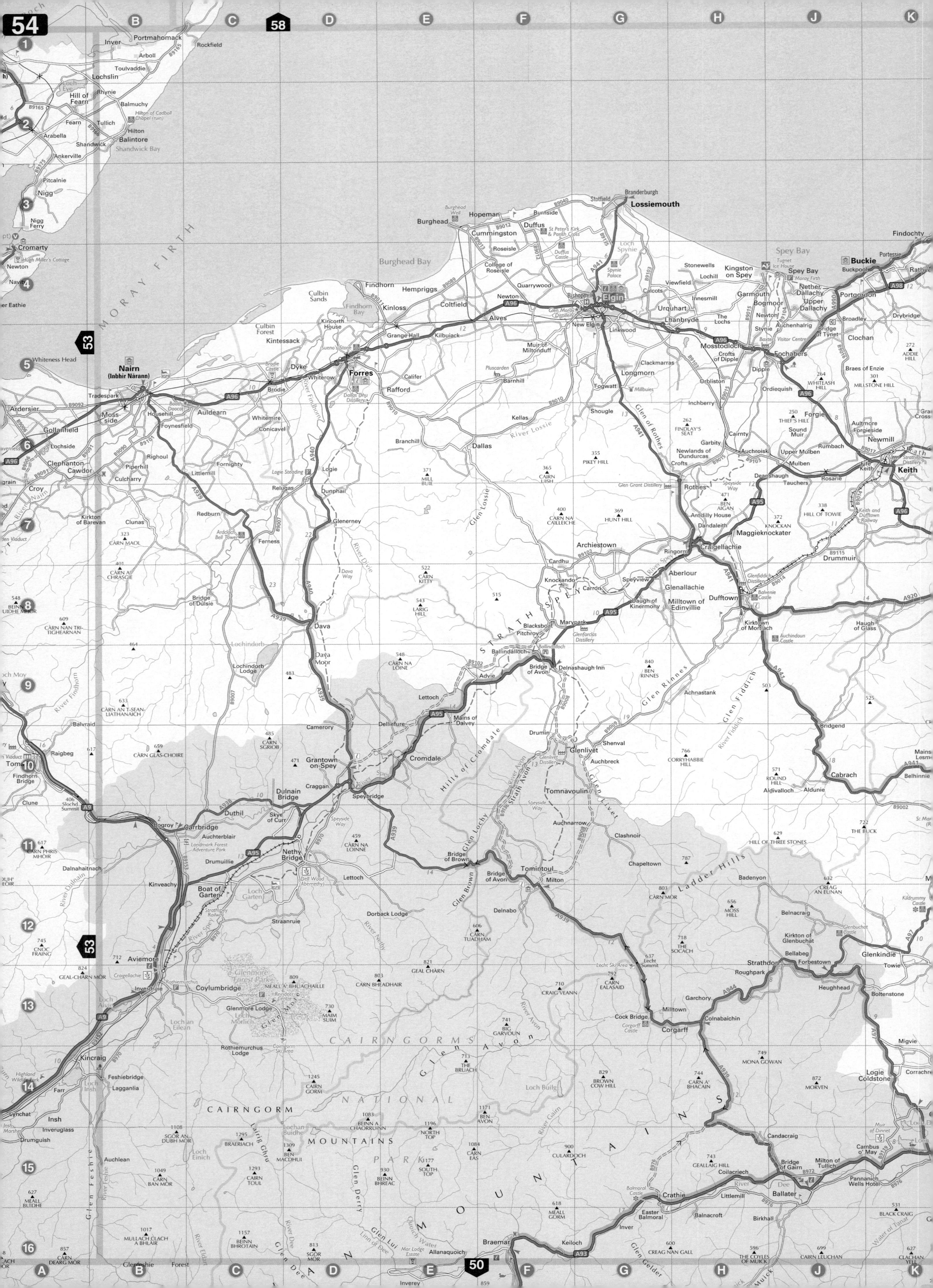

58
53
50
MORAY FIRTH
Burghead Bay
Spey Bay
Portmahomack
Rockfield
Inver
Arboll
Toulvaddie
Lochslin
Rhynie
Hill of Fearn
Balmuchy
Fearn
Tullich
Arabella
Hilton
Balintore
Shandwick
Shandwick Bay
Ankerville
Pitcalnie
Nigg
Nigg Ferry
Cromarty
Hugh Miller's Cottage
Newton
Navity
Whiteness Head
Nairn
(Inbhir Nàrann)
Tradespark
Ardersier
Gollanfield
Mosstodloch
Househill
Foynesfield
Auldearn
Lochside
Clephanton
Cawdor
Croy
Kirkton of Barevan
Culbin Sands
Culbin Forest
Kintessack
Findhorn
Findhorn Bay
Kinloss
Hempriggs
Coltfield
Burghead
Hopeman
Cummingston
Duffus
Roseisle
College of Roseisle
Quarrywood
Newton
Alves
Kincorth House
Grange Hall
Kilbuiack
Sueno's Stone
Forres
Dyke
Whiterow
Brodie
Califer
Rafford
Dallas Dhu Distillery
Whitemire
Conicavel
Branchill
Dallas
Kellas
Barnhill
Pluscarden
Muir of Miltonduff
Stotfield
Branderburgh
Lossiemouth
Burnside
Spynie Palace
Loch Spynie
Elgin
Bishopmill
New Elgin
Linkwood
Glen Moray Distillery
Calcots
Urquhart
Lhanbryde
Stonewells
Lochill
Kingston on Spey
Viewfield
Innesmill
Garmouth
Bogmoor
The Lochs
Mosstodloch
Fochabers
Newton
Stynie
Nether Dallachy
Upper Dallachy
Auchenhalrig
Bridge of Tynet
Buckie
Buckpool
Portgordon
Portessie
Findochty
Rathven
Drybridge
Broadley
Clochan
Braes of Enzie
ADDIE HILL
WHITEASH HILL
MILLSTONE HILL
Longmorn
Clackmarras
Fogwatt
Millbuies
Shougle
Orbliston
Crofts of Dipple
Dipple
Ordiequish
Inchberry
FINDLAY'S SEAT
THIEF'S HILL
Forgie
Sound Muir
Aultmore
Forgieside
Newmill
Garbity
Cairnty
Auchroisk
Upper Mulben
Mulben
Rumbach
Keith
Fife Keith
Newlands of Dundurcas
Crofts
Rothes
Glen Grant Distillery
Glen of Rothes
PIKEY HILL
CARN LUISH
MILL BUIE
Logie
Dunphail
Relugas
Logie Steading
Righoul
Piperhill
Culcharry
Littlemill
Fornighty
Redburn
Clunas
CARN MAOL
CARN A' CHRASGIE
Ardclach Bell Tower
Ferness
Glenerney
Dava Way
River Divie
CARN KITTY
LARIG HILL
Glen Lossie
CARN NA CAILLEICH
HUNT HILL
Archiestown
Cardhu
Knockando
Carron
Speyview
Aberlour
Glenallachie
Ringorm
Craigellachie
Dandaleith
Arndilly House
Maggieknockater
BEN AIGAN
KNOCKAN
HILL OF TOWIE
Deanshaugh
Tauchers
Rosarie
Drummuir
Dufftown
Balvenie Castle
Glenfiddich Distillery
Kirktown of Mortlach
Haugh of Glass
Auchindoun Castle
Daugh of Kinermony
Milltown of Edinvillie
Marypark
Blacksboat
Pitchroy
Glenfarclas Distillery
Ballindalloch
Bridge of Avon
Delnashaugh Inn
Advie
STRATH SPEY
BEN RINNES
Glen Rinnes
Achnastank
Glen Fiddich
River Fiddich
Bridgend
Cabrach
Aldivalloch
Aldunie
ROUND HILL
CORRYHABBIE HILL
Shenval
Glenlivet
Auchbreck
Drumin
Glen Livet
Tomnavoulin
Auchnarrow
Clashnoir
Bridge of Dulsie
BEINN UIDHE MHOR
CARN NAN TRI-TIGHEARNAN
Dava
Dava Moor
Lochindorb
Lochindorb Lodge
CARN NA LOINNE
Lettoch
Mains of Dalvey
Dellefure
Camerory
CARN SGRIOB
CARN AN T-SEAN-LIATHANAICH
CARN GLAS-CHOIRE
Balvraid
Raigbeg
Tomatin
Findhorn Bridge
River Findhorn
Clune
Slochd Summit
Grantown-on-Spey
Cromdale
Hills of Cromdale
Craggan
Speybridge
Dulnain Bridge
Skye of Curr
Duthil
Bogroy
Carrbridge
Auchterblair
Landmark Forest Adventure Park
Drumuillie
Nethy Bridge
Lettoch
Dell Wood Abernethy
CARN NA LOINNE
Bridge of Brown
Glen Brown
Bridge of Avon
Tomintoul
Milton
Glen Lochy
Strath Avon
River Avon
Chapeltown
Ladder Hills
Badenyon
CARN MOR
Lecht Ski Area
Lecht Summit
THE SOCACH
MOSS HILL
Belnacraig
Kirkton of Glenbuchat
Glenbuchat Castle
Bellabeg
Forbestown
Strathdon
Roughpark
Glenkindie
Towie
Heughhead
Boltenstone
CREAG AN EUNAN
Kildrummy Castle
HILL OF THREE STONES
THE BUCK
CARN PHRIS MHOIR
Dalnahaitnach
Kinveachy
Boat of Garten
Loch Garten
Strathspey Railway
Straanruie
Dorback Lodge
River Nethy
Delnabo
CARN TUADHAM
CNOC FRAING
Aviemore
GEAL-CHARN MOR
Craigellachie
Rothiemurchus
Inverdruie
Coylumbridge
Glenmore Forest Park
MEALL A' BHUACHAILLE
Glenmore Lodge
Glenmore
Reindeer Centre
Loch Morlich
Glen More
Loch an Eilein
MAIM SUIM
CARN BHEADHAIR
GEAL CHARN
CRAIG VEANN
CARN EALASAID
Garchory
Cock Bridge
Corgarff Castle
Milltown
Corgarff
Colnabaichin
Rothiemurchus Lodge
Cairngorm Ski Area
CAIRNGORMS
NATIONAL PARK
BIG GARVOUN
Glen Avon
THE BRUACH
Kincraig
Highland Wildlife Park
Feshiebridge
Lagganlia
Loch Insh
Farr
Lynchat
Insh
Insh Marshes
Inveruglass
Drumguish
CAIRN GORM
CAIRNGORM MOUNTAINS
BEINN A' CHAORRUINN
NORTH TOP
BEN AVON
Loch Builg
BROWN COW HILL
CARN A' BHACAIN
MONA GOWAN
MORVEN
Migvie
Logie Coldstone
Corrachree
SGOR AN DUBH MOR
BRAERIACH
Lairig Ghru
Lochan Buidhe
BEN MACDHUI
Loch Etchachan
CARN ETCHACHAN
CARN EAS
CULARDOCH
GEALLAIG HILL
Candacraig
Bridge of Gairn
Milton of Tullich
Cambus o' May
Muir of Dinnet
Pannanich Wells Hotel
Auchlean
CARN BAN MOR
CAIRN TOUL
BEINN BHREAC
SOUTH TOP
Glen Derry
Glen Feshie
MEALL BUIDHE
MEALL GORM
Crathie
Balmoral Castle
Easter Balmoral
Coilacriech
Littlemill
Ballater
Balnacroft
Birkhall
Inver
BLACK CRAIG
Water of Tanar
MULLACH CLACH A' BHLAIR
BEINN BHROTAIN
SGOR MOR
Glen Lui
Linn of Dee
Mar Lodge Estate
Quoich Water
Allanaquoich
Braemar
Keiloch
CREAG NAN GALL
Glen Gelder
THE COYLES OF MUICK
CAIRN LEUCHAN
CLACHAN YELL
CARN DEARG MOR
Glenfeshie
Forest
River Eidart
River Dee
Inverey
Glen Muick

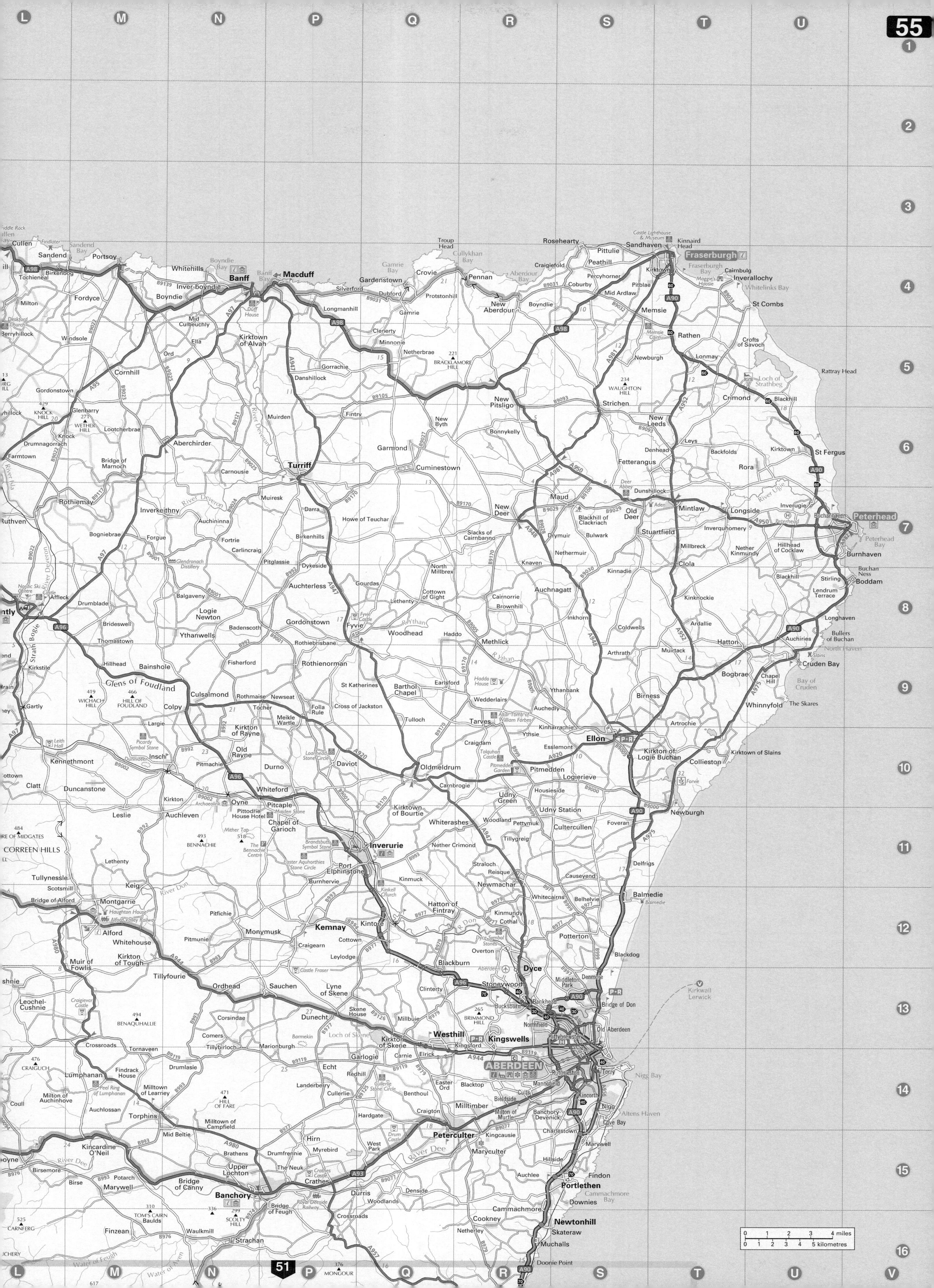
Cullen
Sandend
Portsoy
Whitehills
Banff
Macduff
Gardenstown
Crovie
Pennan
Rosehearty
Sandhaven
Kinnaird Head
Fraserburgh
Inverallochy
St Combs
Rathen
Memsie
New Aberdour
Troup Head
Cullykhan Bay
Gamrie Bay
Boyndie Bay
Inverboyndie
Boyndie
Fordyce
Tochieneal
Milton
Deskford Church
Windsole
Cornhill
Gordonstown
Knock
Glenbarry
Lootcherbrae
Drumnagorrach
Bridge of Marnoch
Aberchirder
Kirktown of Alvah
Ord
Mid Culbeuchly
Ella
Longmanhill
Gamrie
Clenerty
Minnonie
Netherbrae
Protstonhill
Dubford
Silverford
Gorrachie
Danshillock
Muirden
Fintry
New Byth
Garmond
Turriff
Cuminestown
New Pitsligo
Strichen
New Leeds
Bonnykelly
Fetterangus
Mintlaw
Longside
Inverugie
St Fergus
Peterhead
Burnhaven
Boddam
Stuartfield
Old Deer
Maud
New Deer
Cairnbulg
Crimond
Rattray Head
Loch of Strathbeg
Blackhill
Crofts of Savoch
Lonmay
Kirktown
Rora
Leys
Backfolds
Denhead
Dunshillock
Inverquhomery
Nether Kinmundy
Hillhead of Cocklaw
Stirling
Lendrum Terrace
Longhaven
Bullers of Buchan
Cruden Bay
Hatton
Auchiries
Bay of Cruden
The Skares
Whinnyfold
Chapel Hill
Bogbrae
Birness
Ellon
Collieston
Newburgh
Forvie
Kirkton of Logie Buchan
Kirktown of Slains
Artrochie
Ythanbank
Auchnagatt
Arthrath
Coldwells
Ardallie
Kinknockie
Clola
Millbreck
Kinnadie
Nethermuir
Drymuir
Bulwark
Blackhill of Clackriach
Knaven
Slacks of Cairnbanno
Methlick
Haddo
Woodhead
Fyvie
Gordonstown
Auchterless
Rothienorman
Rothiebrisbane
Fisherford
Badenscoth
Ythanwells
Logie Newton
Balgaveny
Forgue
Inverkeithny
Auchininna
Rothiemay
Huntly
Drumblade
Brideswell
Thomastown
Hillhead
Bainshole
Kirkstile
Gartly
Glens of Foudland
Culsalmond
Colpy
Largie
Insch
Kennethmont
Clatt
Duncanstone
Leslie
Kirkton
Oyne
Auchleven
Pitcaple
Chapel of Garioch
Inverurie
Port Elphinstone
Kintore
Kemnay
Monymusk
Alford
Montgarrie
Bridge of Alford
Keig
Tullynessle
Lethenty
Bennachie
Correen Hills
Whitehouse
Kirkton of Tough
Muir of Fowlis
Tillyfourie
Ordhead
Sauchen
Lyne of Skene
Dunecht
Echt
Garlogie
Kirkton of Skene
Westhill
Kingswells
Aberdeen
Dyce
Bucksburn
Bankhead
Bridge of Don
Old Aberdeen
Torry
Nigg Bay
Cove Bay
Kincorth
Cults
Bieldside
Milltimber
Peterculter
Maryculter
Banchory
Crathes
Durris
Portlethen
Newtonhill
Muchalls
Skateraw
Findon
Balmedie
Blackdog
Potterton
Udny Station
Udny Green
Pitmedden
Tarves
Oldmeldrum
Daviot
Old Rayne
Kirkton of Rayne
Durno
Whiteford
Kinmuck
Hatton of Fintray
Newmachar
Blackburn
Stoneywood
Clinterty
Skene House
Echt
Torphins
Lumphanan
Crossroads
Kincardine O'Neil
Birsemore
Marywell
Bridge of Canny
Strachan
Finzean
Bridge of Feugh
Crossroads
Cookney
Netherley
Downies
Doonie Point
Kirkwall Lerwick
River Dee
River Don
River Ythan
River Deveron
River Ugie
0 1 2 3 4 miles
0 1 2 3 4 5 kilometres
L M N P Q R S T U V
1 2 3 4 5 6 7 8 9 10 11 12 13 14 15 16
51

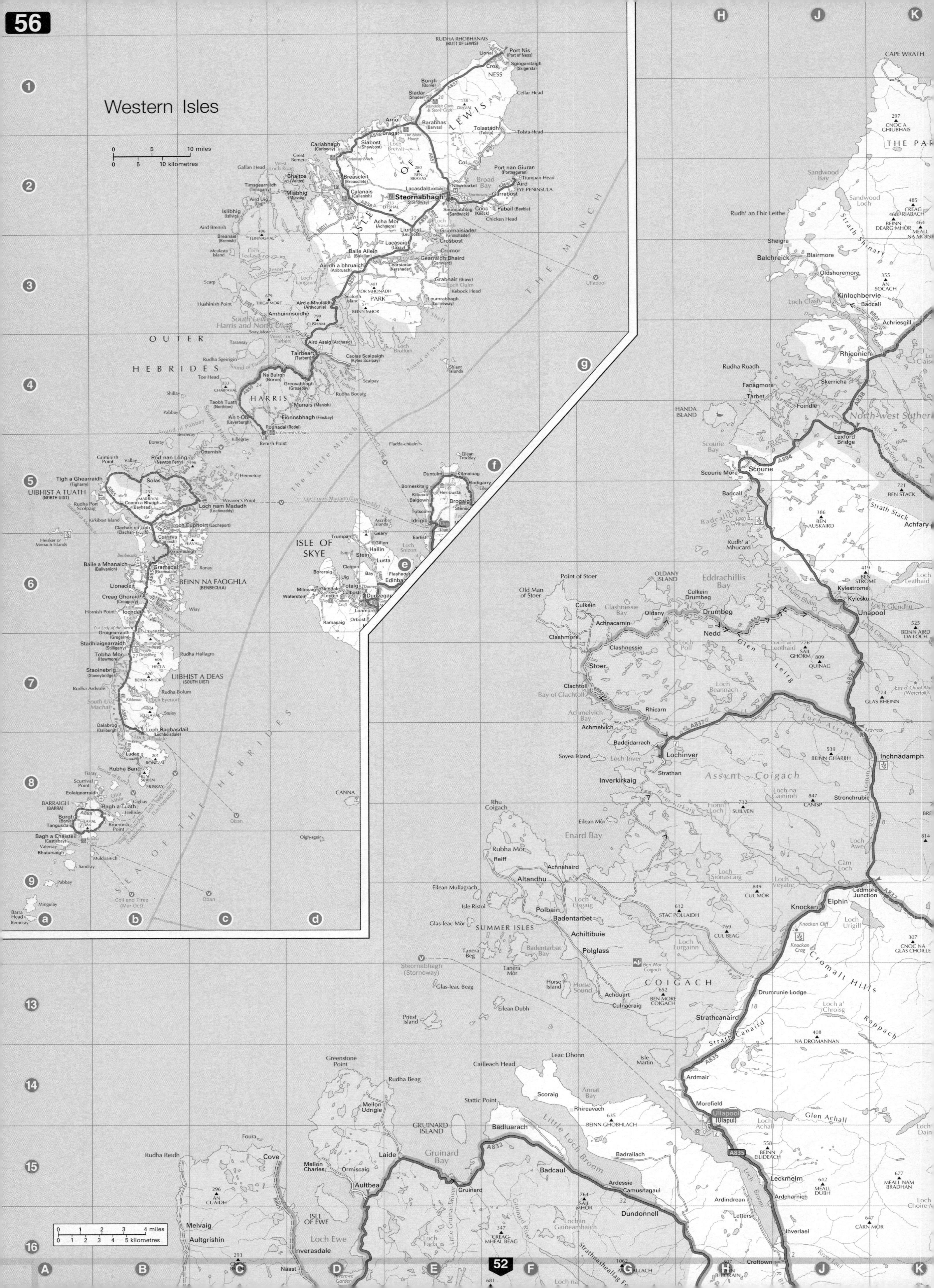
Western Isles
0 5 10 miles
0 5 10 kilometres
RUDHA RHOBHANAIS (BUTT OF LEWIS)
Port Nis (Port of Ness)
Lional
Cros
NESS
Sgiogarstaigh (Skigersta)
Borgh (Borve)
Siadar (Shader)
Cellar Head
Barabhas (Barvas)
Arnol
Bragar
Siabost (Shawbost)
Carlabhagh (Carloway)
Tolastadh (Tolsta)
Tolsta Head
ISLE OF LEWIS
Col
Port nan Giuran (Portnaguran)
Tiumpan Head
Aird
EYE PENINSULA
Broad Bay
Newmarket
Great Bernera
Gallan Head
West Loch Roag
Bhaltos (Valtos)
Breascleit (Breasclete)
Calanais (Callanish)
Miabhig (Miavaig)
Timsgearraidh (Timsgarry)
Aird Uig (Uig)
Islibhig (Islivig)
Lacasdal (Laxdale)
Steornabhagh (Stornoway)
Garrabost
Pabail (Bayble)
Cnoc (Knock)
Chicken Head
Sandwick
Acha Mor (Achmore)
Liurbost (Leurbost)
Griomsiadair (Grimshader)
Crosbost
Cromor
Lacasaigh (Laxay)
Baile Ailein (Balallan)
Gearraidh Bhaird (Garyvard)
Cearsiadar (Kershader)
Airidh a bhruaich (Arnbruaich)
Aird Brenish
Breanais (Brenish)
Mealasta Island
Loch Resort
Grabhair (Gravir)
Kebock Head
Leumrabhagh (Lemreway)
PARK
Ullapool
Scarp
Hushinish Point
Amhuinnsuidhe
CLISHAM
Aird a Mhulaidh (Ardvourlie)
Seaforth Island
BEINN MHOR
MOR MHONADH
THE MINCH
OUTER HEBRIDES
Taransay
Aird Asaig (Ardhasaig)
Tairbeart (Tarbert)
Caolas Scalpaigh (Kyles Scalpay)
Scalpay
Shiant Islands
Sound of Shiant
Rudha Sgeirigin
Toe Head
HARRIS
Na Buirgh (Borve)
Greosabhagh (Grosebay)
Manais (Manish)
Fionnsbhagh (Finsbay)
Rudha Bocaig
CHAIPAVAL
Taobh Tuath (Northton)
An t-Ob (Leverburgh)
Roghadal (Rodel)
Renish Point
Shillay
Pabbay
Sound of Pabbay
Sound of Harris
Berneray
Boreray
Killegray
Otternish
Griminish Point
Vallay
Port nan Long (Newton Ferry)
Fladda-chuain
Eilean Trodday
Tigh a Ghearraidh (Tigharry)
UIBHIST A TUATH (NORTH UIST)
Solas
MARRIVAL
Ceann a Bhaigh (Bayhead)
Rudha Port Scolpaig
Kirkibost Island
Loch nam Madadh (Lochmaddy)
Weaver's Point
Hermetray
The Little Minch
Loch Euphoirt (Locheport)
Clachan na Luib (Clachan-a-Luib)
Heisker or Monach Islands
Cairinis (Carinish)
Griomsaigh
Benbecula
Baile a Mhanaich (Balivanich)
Gramsdal (Gramsdale)
Ronay
BEINN NA FAOGHLA (BENBECULA)
Lionacleit
Creag Ghoraidh (Creagorry)
Iochdar
Hornish Point
Wiay
Groigearraidh (Gerogarry)
Stadhlaigearraidh (Stilligarry)
Tobha Mor (Howmore)
Rudha Hallagro
HECLA
Staoinebrig (Stoneybridge)
BEINN MHOR
UIBHIST A DEAS (SOUTH UIST)
Rudha Ardvule
Rudha Bolum
Loch Eynort
South Uist Machair
STULAVAL
Stuley
Dalabrog (Daliburgh)
Loch Baghasdail (Lochboisdale)
Ludag
RONEVAL
Rubha Ban
ERISKAY
Fuaray
Scurrival Point
Eolaigearraidh
BARRAIGH (BARRA)
Bagh a Tuath
Hellisay
Gighay
Borgh (Borve)
HEAVAL
Tangusdale
Bruernish Point
Bagh a Chaisteil (Castlebay)
Vatersay
Bhatarsaigh
Muldoanich
Sandray
Pabbay
Mingulay
Barra Head
Berneray
SEA OF THE HEBRIDES
Coll and Tiree (Mar Oct)
Oban
CANNA
Oigh-sgeir
Duntulm
Kilmaluag
Flodigarry
Borneskitaig
Kilvaxter
Balgown
Hunish
Brogaig
Totscore
Idrigil
Uig
Earlish
ISLE OF SKYE
Trumpan
Ascrib Islands
Geary
Gillen
Hallin
Stein
Isay
Lusta
Loch Snizort
Boreraig
Claigan
Uig
Bay
Flashader
Edinbane
Milovaig
Glendale
Waterstein
Totaig
Colbost
Lephin
Dunvegan
Lonmore
Ramasaig
Orbost
CAPE WRATH
CNOC A GHIUBHAIS
THE PARPH
Sandwood Bay
Sandwood Loch
CREAG RIABACH
BEINN DEARG MHOR
MEALL NA MOINE
Rudh' an Fhir Leithe
Sheigra
Balchreick
Blairmore
Strath Shinary
Oldshoremore
AN SOCACH
Loch Clash
Kinlochbervie
Badcall
Achriesgill
Rhiconich
Rudha Ruadh
Fanagmore
Tarbet
HANDA ISLAND
Skerricha
Foindle
Laxford Bridge
North-west Sutherland
Scourie Bay
Scourie More
Scourie
Badcall
BEN STACK
Strath Stack
Achfary
Badcall Bay
BEN AUSKAIRD
Rudh' a' Mhucard
BEN STROME
OLDANY ISLAND
Eddrachillis Bay
Point of Stoer
Kylestrome
Kylesku
Old Man of Stoer
Culkein
Culkein Drumbeg
Oldany
Drumbeg
Unapool
Clashnessie Bay
Achnacarnin
Nedd
Clashmore
Clashnessie
Glen Leirg
SAIL GHORM
QUINAG
BEINN AIRD DA LOCH
Stoer
Loch Beannach
Clachtoll
Bay of Clachtoll
GLAS BHEINN
Achmelvich Bay
Achmelvich
Rhicarn
Loch Assynt
Ardvreck
Baddidarrach
Soyea Island
Loch Inver
Lochinver
BEN GHARBH
Inchnadamph
Strathan
Assynt - Coigach
Inverkirkaig
Fionn Loch
SUILVEN
Loch na Gainimh
CANISP
Stronchrubie
Rhu Coigach
Eilean Mòr
Enard Bay
Rubha Mòr
Reiff
Loch Awe
Cam Loch
Achnahaird
Altandhu
Eilean Mullagrach
Loch Sionascaig
CUL MOR
Loch Veyatie
Ledmore Junction
Elphin
Knockan
Knockan Cliff
Loch Urigill
Isle Ristol
Polbain
Badentarbet
STAC POLLAIDH
Glas-leac Mòr
SUMMER ISLES
Achiltibuie
CUL BEAG
Loch Lurgainn
CNOC NA GLAS CHOILLE
Cromalt Hills
Tanera Beg
Badentarbat Bay
Polglass
Ben Mòr Coigach
Steornabhagh (Stornoway)
Tanera Mòr
Horse Island
Horse Sound
COIGACH
Glas-leac Beag
Achduart
BEN MORE COIGACH
Culnacraig
Drumrunie Lodge
Loch a' Chroisg
Rappach
Eilean Dubh
Strathcanaird
Priest Island
Strath Canaird
NA DROMANNAN
Greenstone Point
Cailleach Head
Leac Dhonn
Isle Martin
Ardmair
Rudha Beag
Scoraig
Annat Bay
Morefield
Static Point
Mellon Udrigle
Rhireavach
BEINN GHOBHLACH
Ullapool (Ulapul)
Glen Achall
GRUINARD ISLAND
Badluarach
Little Loch Broom
Loch Achall
Foura
Gruinard Bay
BEINN EILIDEACH
Rudha Reidh
Cove
Laide
Badrallach
Mellon Charles
Ormiscaig
Badcaul
Leckmelm
MEALL NAM BRADHAN
AN CUAIDH
Aultbea
Gruinard
Ardessie
Camusnagaul
MEALL DUBH
SAIL MHOR
Ardindrean
Ardcharnich
ISLE OF EWE
Dundonnell
Letters
Loch Broom
Melvaig
Loch Ewe
Loch Fada
CREAG-MHEAL BEAG
Lochan Gaineamhaich
Inverlael
CARN MOR
Aultgrishin
Inverasdale
Little Gruinard River
Gruinard River
Strathnashealag Forest
River Lael
Naast
Inverewe Garden
Croftown
Choire Mhor
0 1 2 3 4 miles
0 1 2 3 4 5 kilometres
52
A B C D E F G H J K
1 2 3 4 5 6 7 8 9 13 14 15 16
a b c d e f g

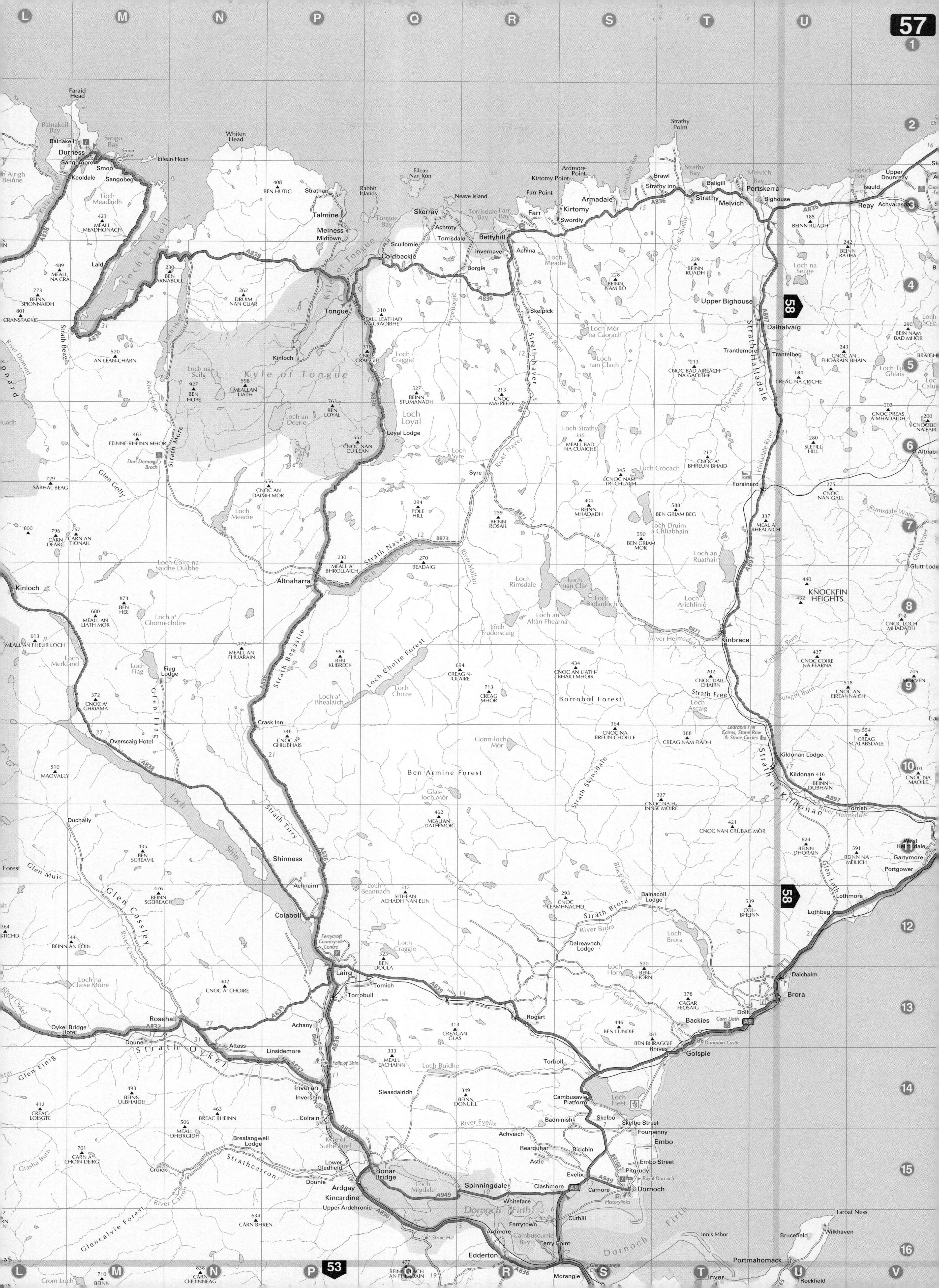

Faraid Head
Balnakeil Bay
Durness
Sangomore
Smoo
Sango Bay
Eilean Hoan
Whiten Head
Loch Eriboll
Laid
Tongue
Kyle of Tongue
Strath More
Loch Loyal
Loyal Lodge
Skerray
Bettyhill
Farr
Armadale
Strathy Point
Strathy
Melvich
Portskerra
Reay
Strath Naver
Syre
Altnaharra
Strath Halladale
Forsinard
Kinbrace
KNOCKFIN HEIGHTS
Borrobol Forest
Ben Armine Forest
Strath of Kildonan
Kildonan Lodge
Helmsdale
Strath Skinsdale
Loch Shin
Lairg
Rosehall
Strath Oykel
Inveran
Rogart
Strath Brora
Brora
Golspie
Dornoch
Embo
Skelbo
Bonar Bridge
Ardgay
Spinningdale
Dornoch Firth
Tain
Portmahomack
Edderton
A836
A838
A897
A9
A949
A839
B871
B873
58
53

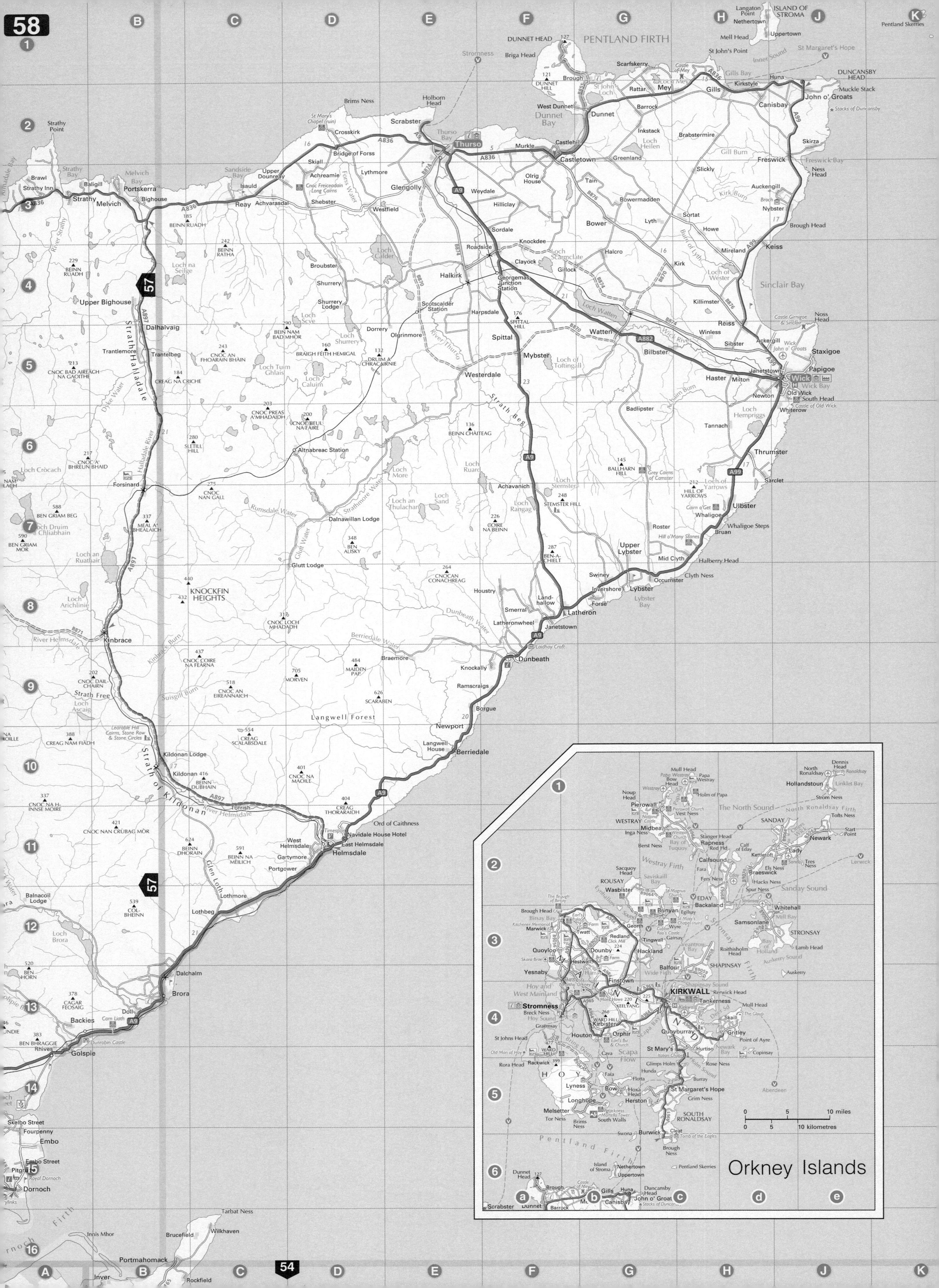
PENTLAND FIRTH
DUNNET HEAD
Dunnet Bay
Thurso
Scrabster
Wick
John o' Groats
DUNCANSBY HEAD
ISLAND OF STROMA
Pentland Skerries
Sinclair Bay
Castletown
Halkirk
Watten
Bilbster
Keiss
Reiss
Staxigoe
Papigoe
Thrumster
Ulbster
Upper Lybster
Lybster
Latheron
Dunbeath
Berriedale
Helmsdale
Brora
Golspie
Dornoch
Embo
Portmahomack
Tarbat Ness
Melvich
Portskerra
Strathy
Reay
Forsinard
Kinbrace
Kildonan Lodge
Altnabreac Station
KNOCKFIN HEIGHTS
Langwell Forest
MORVEN
Strath Halladale
Strath of Kildonan
Loch Watten
Loch Calder
Loch More
Loch Hempriggs
Orkney Islands
KIRKWALL
Stromness
HOY
SOUTH RONALDSAY
SANDAY
WESTRAY
ROUSAY
EDAY
STRONSAY
SHAPINSAY
St Margaret's Hope
Scapa Flow
10 miles
10 kilometres
54
57

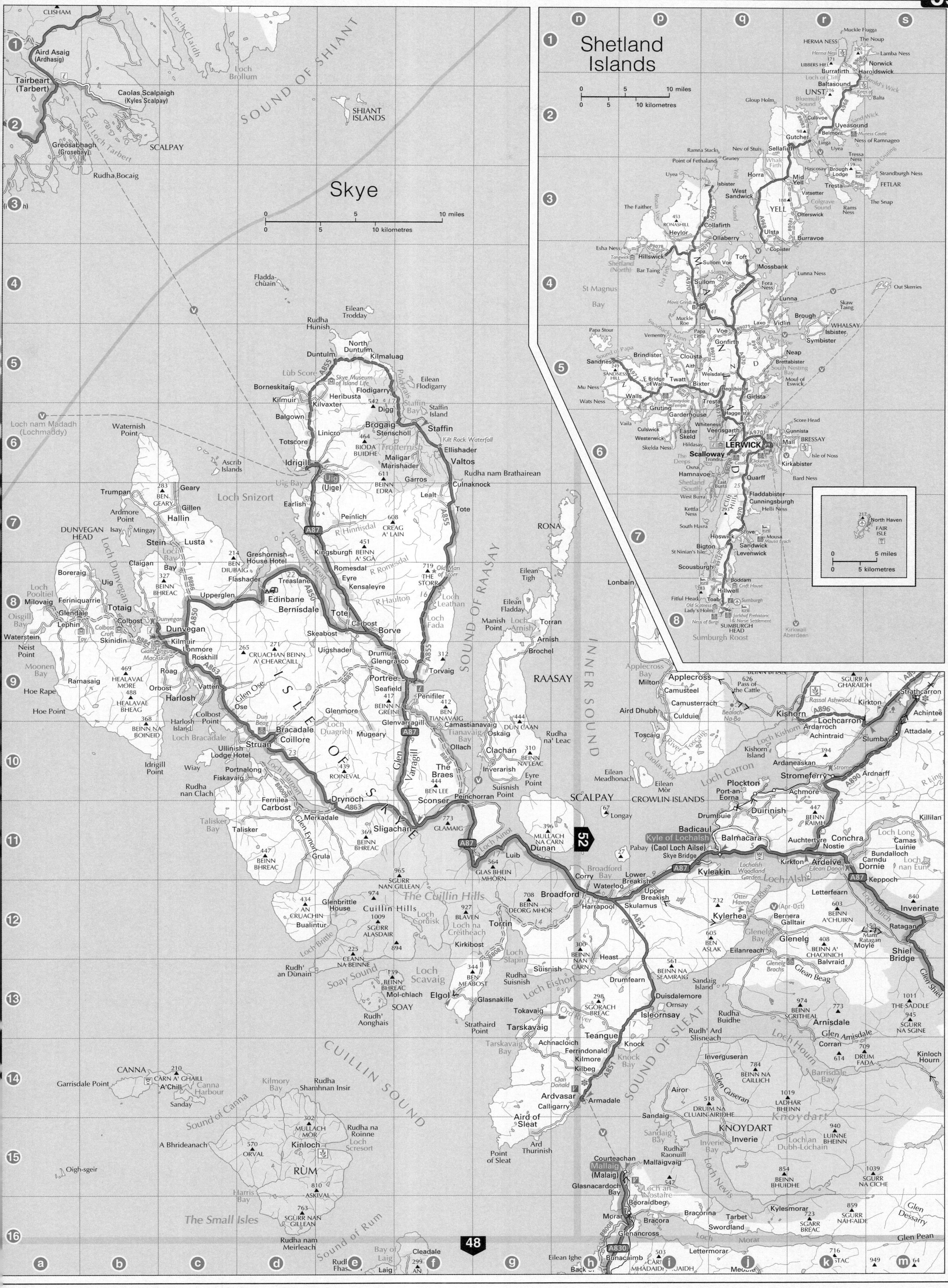

Skye

Shetland Islands

Scale: 0 — 5 — 10 miles / 0 — 5 — 10 kilometres

Harris / Tarbert area
CLISHAM
Aird Asaig (Ardhasig)
Tairbeart (Tarbert)
Caolas Scalpaigh (Kyles Scalpay)
Greosabhagh (Grosebay)
SCALPAY
Rudha Bocaig
East Loch Tarbert
Loch Claidh
Loch Brollum
SOUND OF SHIANT
SHIANT ISLANDS

Shetland Islands
HERMA NESS
The Noup
Muckle Flugga
LIBBERS HILL
Burrafirth
Lamba Ness
Loch of Cliff
Norwick
Haroldswick
UNST
Baltasound
Sand Wick
Muness Castle
Ness of Ramnageo
Uyeasound
Belmont
Gutcher
Cullivoe
Ness of Queyon
Uyea
Tressa Ness
Hascosay
Brough Lodge
Strandburgh Ness
FETLAR
Point of Fethaland
Ramna Stacks
Nev of Stuis
Gruney
Whale Firth
Mid Yell
Vatsetter
The Snap
Rams Ness
Colgrave Sound
Isbister
Horra
YELL
Otterswick
Gloup Holm
Sellafirth
RONASHILL
Collafirth
Heylor
Ollaberry
Ulsta
Burravoe
Copister
The Faither
West Sandwick
Esha Ness
Hillswick
Sullom Voe
Toft
Mossbank
Fora Ness
Lunna Ness
St Magnus Bay
Bar Taing
Sullom
Brae
Lunna
Skaw Taing
Out Skerries
Papa Stour
Muckle Roe
Papa Little
Laxo
Vidlin
Brough
WHALSAY
Sandness
Brindister
Clousta
Voe
Gonfirth
Isbister
Symbister
Neap
Brettabister
Sandsting
Aith
Twatt
Weisdale
South Nesting Bay
Mool of Eswick
Walls
Vementry
Bixter
Garderhouse
Tresta
Haggersta
Girlsta
Gunnista
Mu Ness
Vaila
Culswick
Whiteness
Veensgarth
Easter Skeld
Gardie
Wats Ness
Hildasay
LERWICK
Mail
BRESSAY
Isle of Noss
SCALLOWAY
Trondra
Hamnavoe
Oxna
East Burra
Quarff
Bard Ness
Skelda Ness
West Burra
Fladdabister
Cunningsburgh
Helli Ness
Kettla Ness
The Deeps
South Havra
St Ninian's Isle
Hoswick
Sandwick
Mousa
Bigton
Levenwick
Lonbain
Fitful Head
Old Scatness
Scousburgh
Boddam
Hillwell
Lady's Holm
Sumburgh Roost
Jarlshof Prehistoric
Norse Settlement
Ness of Burgi
SUMBURGH HEAD

Fair Isle inset
North Haven
FAIR ISLE

Skye
Rudha Hunish
Eilean Trodday
North Duntulm
Duntulm
Kilmaluag
Lub Score
Skye Museum of Island Life
Flodigarry
Eilean Flodigarry
Borneskitaig
Heribusta
Staffin Bay
Kilmuir
Kilvaxter
Digg
Staffin Island
Balgown
Linicro
Stenscholl
Staffin
Totscore
Brogaig
Ellishader
Valtos
Idrigill
BIODA BUIDHE
Maligar
Marishader
Rudha nam Brathairean
Kilt Rock Waterfall
Trotternish
Garros
Culnaknock
Uig Bay
BEINN EDRA
Uig (Uige)
Earlish
Peinlich
Lealt
Tote
Loch Snizort
R Hinnisdal
CREAG A' LAIN
Kingsburgh
BEINN A' SGA
Romesdal
Old Man of Storr
Eyre
R Romesdal
Kensaleyre
THE STORR
Waternish Point
Trumpan
Geary
Gillen
Hallin
Loch Snizort
Ascrib Islands
Ardmore Point
DUNVEGAN HEAD
Stein
Lusta
Greshornish House Hotel
Treaslane
Flashader
Isay
Mingay
Claigan
Loch Bay
BEN DIUBAIG
Loch Dunvegan
Borreraig
Uig
BEINN BHREAC
Upperglen
Edinbane
Bernisdale
Tote
Carbost
Skeabost
Borve
Feriniquarrie
Colbost
Dunvegan
Kilmuir
Lonmore
Roskhill
Uigshader
Drumuie
Glengrasco
Galtrigill
Skinidin
CRUACHAN BEINN A' CHEARCAILL
Milovaig
Glendale
Lephin
Waterstein
Ose
Bracadale
Coillore
Portree
Seafield
Penifiler
BEINN NA GREINE
BEN TIANAVAIG
Healaval More
Orbost
Roag
Vatten
Glen Ose
Glenmore
Glenvarragill
Camastianavaig
DUN CAAN
RAASAY
Harlosh
Ullinish Lodge Hotel
Struan
ISLE OF SKYE
Loch Duagrich
Mugeary
Tianavaig Bay
Oskaig
Clachan
BEINN NA'LEAC
Idrigill Point
Wiay
Portnalong
Fiskavaig
ROINEVAL
Inverarish
Glen Drynoch
The Braes
Eyre Point
Suisnish Point
Rudha nan Clach
Ferniilea
Carbost
Sconser
Peinchorran
SCALPAY
CROWLIN ISLANDS
Talisker Bay
Talisker
Merkadale
BEINN BHREAC
Sligachan
GLAMAIG
Longay
INNER SOUND
Grula
SGURR NAN GILLEAN
Luib
Broadford Bay
Glenbrittle House
Cuillin Hills
BLAVEN
GLAS BHEIN MHOR
Dunan
Pabay
Skye Bridge
Kyle of Lochalsh (Caol Loch Aluis)
Corry
Lower Breakish
Upper Breakish
AN CRUACHAN
Bualintur
Loch Coruisk
BEINN DEARG MHOR
Broadford
Harrapool
Skulamus
Kyleakin
Kirkton
Eilean Donan
SGURR ALASDAIR
CEANN NA BEINNE
Kirkibost
Tortin
Waterloo
Kylerhea
Bernera Galltair
BEN ASLAK
Eilanreach
Glenelg
The Cuillin Hills
BEINN BHREAC
Loch Slapin
Suisnish
Heast
BEINN NAN CARN
Drumfearn
Glenelg Bay
Loch Brittle
BEN MEABOST
Mol-chlach
Elgol
Glasnakille
Tokavaig
BEINN NA SEAMRAIG
Sandaig Island
Rudha Buidhe
Rudh' an Dunain
Loch Scavaig
SOAY
Rudh' Aonghais
Strathaird Point
Tarskavaig
Teangue
Knock
Corran
Arnisdale
Ord
SGORACH BREAC
Isleornsay
Duisdalemore
Ornsay
Soay Sound
Sound of Rum
Tarskavaig Bay
Achnacloich
Ferrindonald
Kilmore
Kilbeg
Clan Donald
Airor
Inverguseran
DRUM NA CLUAIN-AIRIDHE
Ardvasar
Calligarry
Armadale
Aird of Sleat
Sandaig
Rudha Raonuill
KNOYDART
Inverie
Ard Thurinish
Point of Sleat
Courteachan
Mallaig (Mallaig)
Mallaigvaig
Inverie Bay
Loch Nevis
BEINN BHUIDHE
Glasnacardoch Bay
Bracorina
Tarbet
Swordland
SGURR BREAC
Beoraidbeg
Morar
Bracora
Kylesmorar
Glen Dessary
Glenancross
Lettermorar
Glen Pean

Raasay / Applecross area
Applecross
Camusteel
Camusterrach
Culduie
Milton
Toscaig
Aird Dhubh
BEINN BHAN
SGURR A GHARAIDH
Pass of the Cattle
Bealach-Na-Ba
Rassal Ashwood
Kishorn
Kirkton
Strathcarron
Achintee
A896
Ardarroch
Lochcarron
Achintraid
Slumbay
Attadale
Kishorn Island
A890
Ardaneaskan
Stromeferry
Ardnarff
R Ling
Plockton
Port-an-Eorna
Achmore
Duirinish
BEINN RAIMH
Killilan
Drumbuie
Loch Carron
Loch Long
Badicaul
Balmacara
Auchtertyre
Conchra
Nostie
Camas Luinie
Bundalloch
Carndu
Dornie
Loch nan Eun
Kirkton
Ardelve
Keppoch
Letterfearn
Loch Duich
Inverinate
Kyleakin
Otter Haven
BEINN A'CHUIRN
Mam Ratagan
Moyle
Ratagan
Shiel Bridge
Glenelg Brochs
Glean Beag
Balvraid
Glen Shiel
Arnisdale
Corran
Glen Amisdale
THE SADDLE
SGURR NA SGINE
DRUM FADA
Kinloch Hourn
Sound of Sleat
Loch Hourn
BEINN NA CAILLICH
LADHAR BHEINN
KNOYDART
Inverie
LUINNE BHEINN
SGURR NA CICHE
LOCH QUOICH

Small Isles
CANNA
Garrisdale Point
CARN A' GHAILL
A'Chill
Canna Harbour
Sanday
Kilmory Bay
Rudha Shamhnan Insir
Rudha na Roinne
Sound of Canna
MULLACH MOR
Kinloch
ORVAL
A Bhrideanach
Loch Scresort
RUM
Harris Bay
ASKIVAL
SGURR NAN GILLEAN
The Small Isles
Sound of Rum
Rudha nam Meirleach
Bay of Laig
Cleadale
EIGG
Laig
CANNA
SGURR OF EIGG

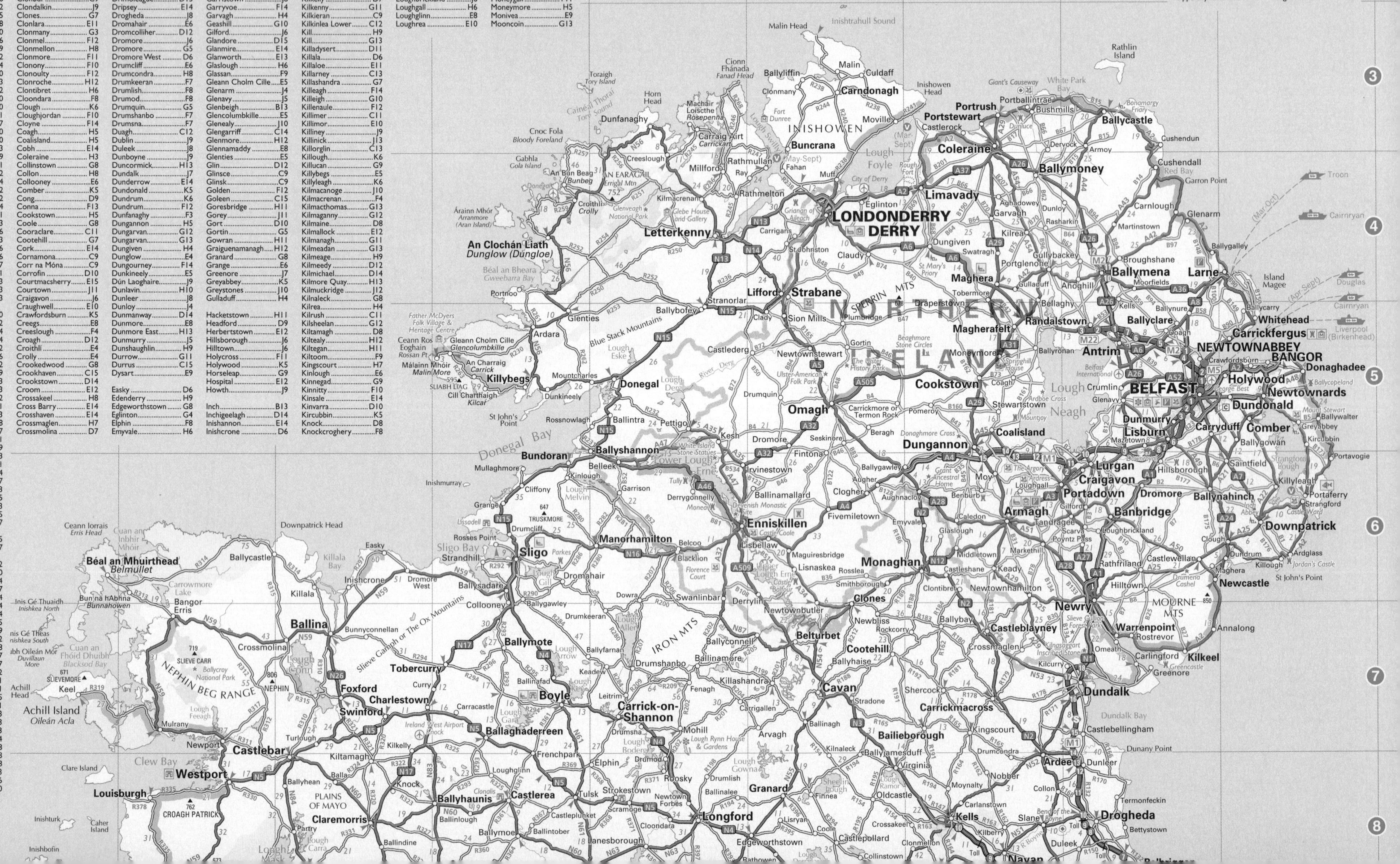
Malin Head
Inishtrahull Sound
Rathlin Island
Toraigh
Tory Island
Horn Head
INISHOWEN
Giant's Causeway
White Park Bay
Portrush
Portstewart
Bushmills
Ballycastle
Coleraine
Ballymoney
Limavady
LONDONDERRY
DERRY
Letterkenny
Buncrana
Carndonagh
Moville
Lough Foyle
Lough Swilly
Dunfanaghy
An Clochán Liath
Dunglow (Dungloe)
Strabane
Lifford
Ballybofey
Stranorlar
Glenties
Ardara
Killybegs
Donegal
Blue Stack Mountains
SPERRIN MTS
NORTHERN IRELAND
Omagh
Cookstown
Dungannon
Magherafelt
Randalstown
Antrim
Ballymena
Larne
Whitehead
Carrickfergus
NEWTOWNABBEY
BANGOR
Donaghadee
Holywood
BELFAST
Newtownards
Dundonald
Lisburn
Comber
Lough Neagh
Lurgan
Craigavon
Portadown
Banbridge
Armagh
Newry
Downpatrick
Newcastle
MOURNE MTS
Kilkeel
Warrenpoint
Dundalk
Drogheda
Donegal Bay
Bundoran
Ballyshannon
Sligo
Sligo Bay
Enniskillen
Monaghan
Clones
Cavan
Manorhamilton
Carrick-on-Shannon
Boyle
Ballymote
IRON MTS
Ballina
Castlebar
Westport
Achill Island
Clew Bay
NEPHIN BEG RANGE
Béal an Mhuirthead
Belmullet
Longford
Kells
Navan
Troon
Cairnryan
Douglas
Liverpool (Birkenhead)

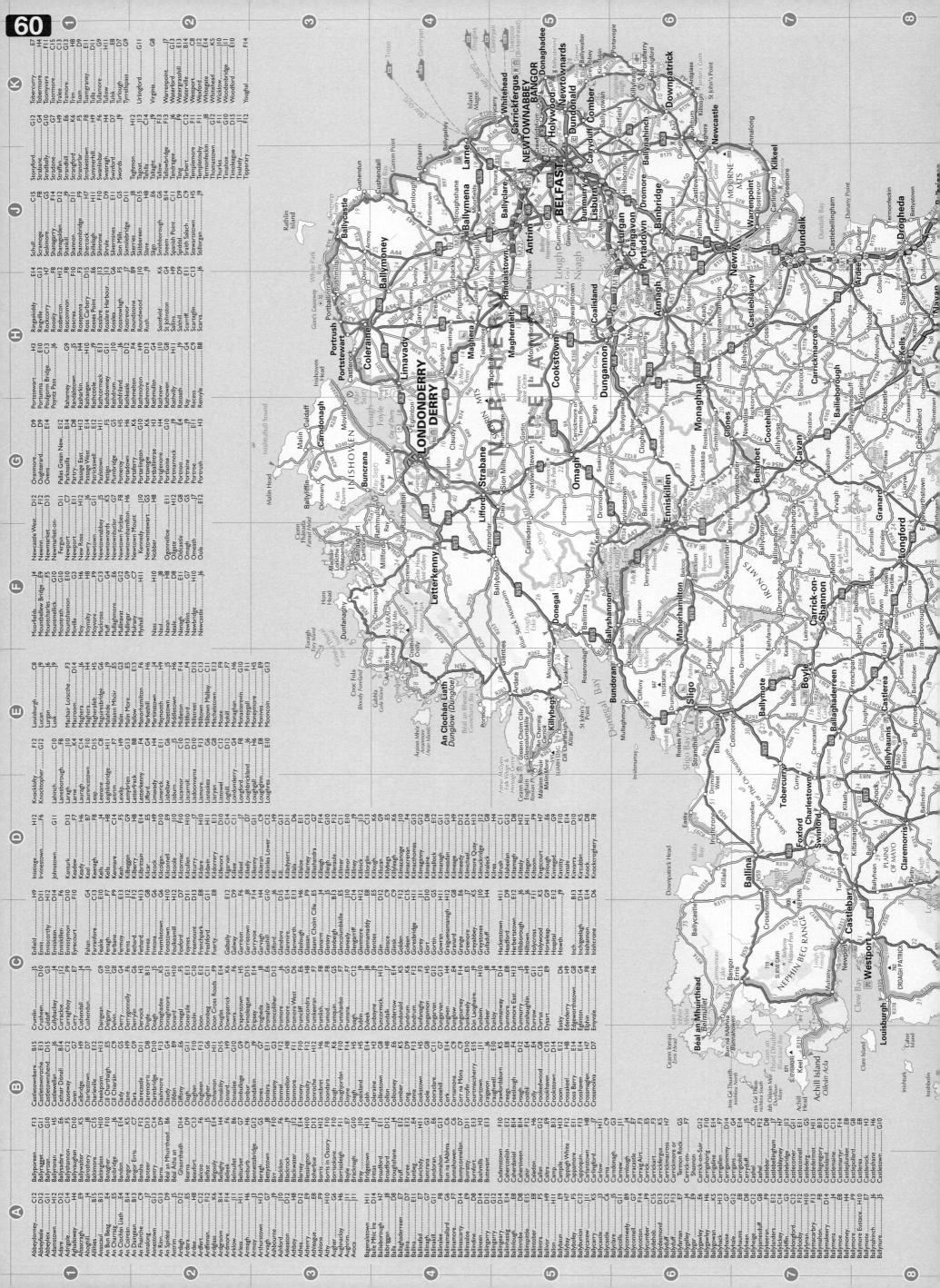

Ireland

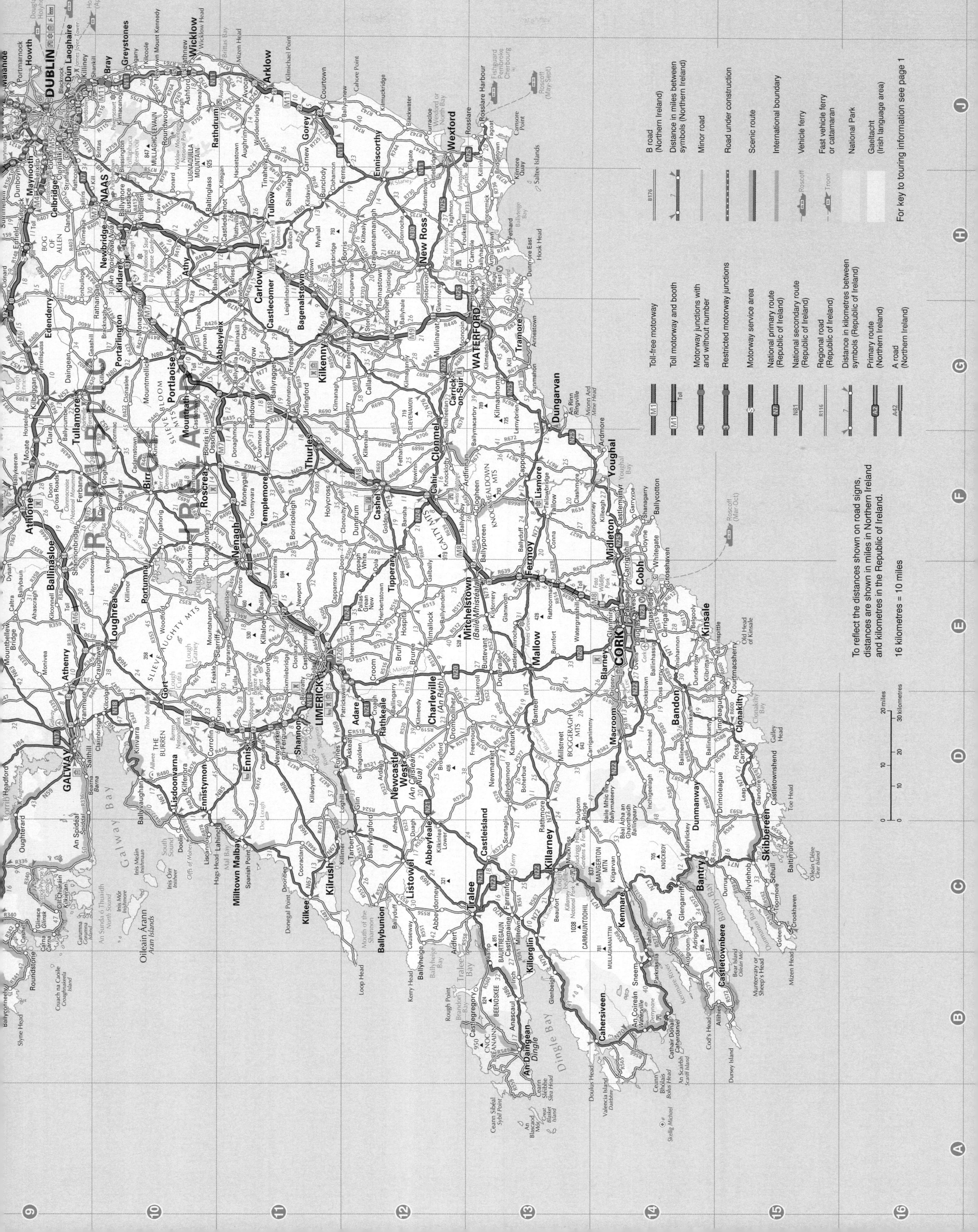
Toll-free motorway
Toll motorway and booth
Motorway junctions with and without number
Restricted motorway junctions
Motorway service area
National primary route (Republic of Ireland)
National secondary route (Republic of Ireland)
Regional road (Republic of Ireland)
Distance in kilometres between symbols (Republic of Ireland)
Primary route (Northern Ireland)
A road (Northern Ireland)
B road (Northern Ireland)
Distance in miles between symbols (Northern Ireland)
Minor road
Road under construction
Scenic route
International boundary
Vehicle ferry
Fast vehicle ferry or catamaran
National Park
Gaeltacht (Irish language area)
For key to touring information see page 1
To reflect the distances shown on road signs, distances are shown in miles in Northern Ireland and kilometres in the Republic of Ireland.
16 kilometres = 10 miles
REPUBLIC OF IRELAND
DUBLIN
CORK
LIMERICK
GALWAY
WATERFORD

Index to place names

This index lists places appearing in the main-map section of the atlas in alphabetical order. The reference following each name gives the atlas page number and grid reference of the square in which the place appears. The map shows counties, unitary authorities and administrative areas, together with a list of the abbreviated name forms used in the index. In addition airports are indexed in blue *italic*.

ORKNEY ISLANDS · SHETLAND ISLANDS

Scotland

Abbr	Name
Abers	Aberdeenshire
Ag & B	Argyll and Bute
Angus	Angus
Border	Scottish Borders
C Aber	City of Aberdeen
C Dund	City of Dundee
C Edin	City of Edinburgh
C Glas	City of Glasgow
Clacks	Clackmannanshire (1)
D & G	Dumfries & Galloway
E Ayrs	East Ayrshire
E Duns	East Dunbartonshire (2)
E Loth	East Lothian
E Rens	East Renfrewshire (3)
Falk	Falkirk
Fife	Fife
Highld	Highland
Inver	Inverclyde (4)
Mdloth	Midlothian (5)
Moray	Moray
N Ayrs	North Ayrshire
N Lans	North Lanarkshire (6)
Ork	Orkney Islands
P & K	Perth & Kinross
Rens	Renfrewshire (7)
S Ayrs	South Ayrshire
Shet	Shetland Islands
S Lans	South Lanarkshire
Stirlg	Stirling
W Duns	West Dunbartonshire (8)
W Isls	Western Isles (Na h-Eileanan an Iar)
W Loth	West Lothian

Wales

Abbr	Name
Blae G	Blaenau Gwent (9)
Brdgnd	Bridgend (10)
Caerph	Caerphilly (11)
Cardif	Cardiff
Carmth	Carmarthenshire
Cerdgn	Ceredigion
Conwy	Conwy
Denbgs	Denbighshire
Flints	Flintshire
Gwynd	Gwynedd
IoA	Isle of Anglesey
Mons	Monmouthshire
Myr Td	Merthyr Tydfil (12)
Neath	Neath Port Talbot (13)
Newpt	Newport (14)
Pembks	Pembrokeshire
Powys	Powys
Rhondd	Rhondda Cynon Taff (15)
Swans	Swansea
Torfn	Torfaen (16)
V Glam	Vale of Glamorgan (17)
Wrexhm	Wrexham

Channel Islands & Isle of Man

Abbr	Name
Guern	Guernsey
Jersey	Jersey
IoM	Isle of Man

England

Abbr	Name
BaNES	Bath & N E Somerset (18)
Barns	Barnsley (19)
Bed	Bedford
Birm	Birmingham
Bl w D	Blackburn with Darwen (20)
Bmouth	Bournemouth
Bolton	Bolton (21)
Bpool	Blackpool
Br & H	Brighton & Hove (22)
Br For	Bracknell Forest (23)
Bristl	City of Bristol
Bucks	Buckinghamshire
Bury	Bury (24)
C Beds	Central Bedfordshire
C Brad	City of Bradford
C Derb	City of Derby
C KuH	City of Kingston upon Hull
C Leic	City of Leicester
C Nott	City of Nottingham
C Pete	City of Peterborough
C Plym	City of Plymouth
C Port	City of Portsmouth
C Sotn	City of Southampton
C Stke	City of Stoke-on-Trent
C York	City of York
Calder	Calderdale (25)
Cambs	Cambridgeshire
Ches E	Cheshire East
Ches W	Cheshire West and Chester
Cnwll	Cornwall
Covtry	Coventry
Cumb	Cumbria
Darltn	Darlington (26)
Derbys	Derbyshire
Devon	Devon
Donc	Doncaster (27)
Dorset	Dorset
Dudley	Dudley (28)
Dur	Durham
E R Yk	East Riding of Yorkshire
E Susx	East Sussex
Essex	Essex
Gatesd	Gateshead (29)
Gloucs	Gloucestershire
Gt Lon	Greater London
Halton	Halton (30)
Hants	Hampshire
Hartpl	Hartlepool (31)
Herefs	Herefordshire
Herts	Hertfordshire
IoS	Isles of Scilly
IoW	Isle of Wight
Kent	Kent
Kirk	Kirklees (32)
Knows	Knowsley (33)
Lancs	Lancashire
Leeds	Leeds
Leics	Leicestershire
Lincs	Lincolnshire
Lpool	Liverpool
Luton	Luton
M Keyn	Milton Keynes
Manch	Manchester
Medway	Medway
Middsb	Middlesbrough
NE Lin	North East Lincolnshire
N Linc	North Lincolnshire
N Som	North Somerset (34)
N Tyne	North Tyneside (35)
N u Ty	Newcastle upon Tyne
N York	North Yorkshire
Nhants	Northamptonshire
Norfk	Norfolk
Notts	Nottinghamshire
Nthumb	Northumberland
Oldham	Oldham (36)
Oxon	Oxfordshire
Poole	Poole
R & Cl	Redcar & Cleveland
Readg	Reading
Rochd	Rochdale (37)
Rothm	Rotherham (38)
Rutlnd	Rutland
S Glos	South Gloucestershire (39)
S on T	Stockton-on-Tees (40)
S Tyne	South Tyneside (41)
Salfd	Salford (42)
Sandw	Sandwell (43)
Sefton	Sefton (44)
Sheff	Sheffield
Shrops	Shropshire
Slough	Slough (45)
Solhll	Solihull (46)
Somset	Somerset
St Hel	St Helens (47)
Staffs	Staffordshire
Sthend	Southend-on-Sea
Stockp	Stockport (48)
Suffk	Suffolk
Sundld	Sunderland
Surrey	Surrey
Swindn	Swindon
Tamesd	Tameside (49)
Thurr	Thurrock (50)
Torbay	Torbay
Traffd	Trafford (51)
W & M	Windsor and Maidenhead (52)
W Berk	West Berkshire
W Susx	West Sussex
Wakefd	Wakefield (53)
Warrtn	Warrington (54)
Warwks	Warwickshire
Wigan	Wigan (55)
Wilts	Wiltshire
Wirral	Wirral (56)
Wokham	Wokingham (57)
Wolves	Wolverhampton (58)
Worcs	Worcestershire
Wrekin	Telford & Wrekin (59)
Wsall	Walsall (60)

Bonnington Angus 51 Q9
Bonnington Kent 11 P9
Bonnybank Fife 51 M15
Bonnybridge Falk 44 K3
Bonnykelly Abers 55 R6
Bonnyrigg Mdloth 45 N6
Bonnyton Angus 51 L9
Bonsall Derbys 31 T14
Bonshaw Tower D & G 39 U6
Bont-Dolgadfan Powys 20 J4
Bont-goch or Elerch Cerdgn 20 F6
Bontnewydd Cerdgn 20 E9
Bontnewydd Gwynd 28 F8
Bontuchel Denbgs 29 P9
Bonvilston V Glam 14 C14
Boode Devon 4 K4
Booker Bucks 16 K11
Boon Border 46 H9
Boosbeck R & Cl 37 M4
Boose's Green Essex 18 K8
Boot Cumb 34 J7
Booth Calder 31 Q3
Boothby Graffoe Lincs 33 L14
Boothby Pagnell Lincs 25 L4
Boothferry E R Yk 32 H3
Boothstown Salfd 31 L7
Bootle Cumb 34 H9
Bootle Sefton 30 E8
Boraston Shrops 22 F14
Bordeaux Guern 2 e2
Borden Kent 11 M5
Boreham Essex 18 J12
Boreham Wilts 7 Q3
Boreham Street E Susx 10 J13
Borehamwood Herts 17 Q11
Boreland D & G 39 S4
Boreraig Highld 59 b8
Borgh W Isls 56 b18
Borgh W Isls 58 e1
Borgie Highld 57 R4
Borgue D & G 39 L10
Borgue Highld 58 E9
Borley Essex 18 K6
Borneskitaig Highld 59 b5
Borness D & G 39 L10
Boroughbridge N York 36 H12
Borough Green Kent 10 H5
Borrowash Derbys 23 S3
Borrowby N York 36 H9
Borrowstoun Falk 45 M3
Borstal Medway 10 K4
Borth Cerdgn 20 E5
Borthwickbrae Border 46 E14
Borthwickshiels Border 46 F14
Borth-y-Gest Gwynd 28 G12
Borve Highld 59 e8
Borve W Isls 56 a8
Borve W Isls 56 c4
Borve W Isls 56 e1
Borwick Lancs 35 N11
Bosbury Herefs 15 M3
Boscastle Cnwll 4 D12
Boscombe Bmouth 8 C13
Boscombe Wilts 8 D5
Bosham W Susx 9 N11
Bosherston Pembks 12 F11
Bosley Ches E 31 N13
Bossall N York 37 M13
Bossiney Cnwll 4 D12
Bossingham Kent 11 R7
Bossington Somset 5 R3
Bostock Green Ches W 30 K13
Boston Lincs 25 J15
Boston Spa Leeds 36 H16
Boswinger Cnwll 2 C9
Botallack Cnwll 2 B11
Botany Bay Gt Lon 17 R10
Botesdale Suffk 27 N13
Bothal Nthumb 41 P4
Bothamsall Notts 32 G12
Bothel Cumb 39 T12
Bothenhampton Dorset 6 J12
Bothwell S Lans 44 H7
Botley Bucks 17 M10
Botley Hants 8 J9
Botley Oxon 16 E9
Botolph Claydon Bucks 16 H6
Botolphs W Susx 9 T11
Bottesford Leics 24 J2
Bottesford N Linc 32 K6
Bottisham Cambs 18 F3
Bottomcraig Fife 51 M12
Bottoms Calder 31 P4
Botusfleming Cnwll 2 J6
Botwnnog Gwynd 28 C13
Bough Beech Kent 10 F7
Boughrood Powys 14 D3
Boughton Nhants 24 H14
Boughton Norfk 26 G9
Boughton Notts 32 G13
Boughton Aluph Kent 11 P7
Boughton Green Kent 10 K6
Boughton Monchelsea Kent 10 K7
Boughton Street Kent 11 P5
Bouldon Shrops 22 E11
Boulmer Nthumb 47 S14
Boultham Lincs 33 L13
Bourn Cambs 25 R16
Bourne Lincs 25 N5
Bournebridge Essex 18 E14
Bournebrook Birm 23 M11
Bourne End Bucks 17 L12
Bourne End C Beds 17 M3
Bourne End Herts 17 N9
Bournemouth Bmouth 7 T12
Bournemouth Airport Dorset 8 C12
Bournes Green Sthend 19 L15
Bournheath Worcs 23 L13
Bournmoor Dur 41 Q10
Bournville Birm 23 M12
Bourton Dorset 7 P6
Bourton Oxon 15 V12
Bourton Shrops 22 E10
Bourton Wilts 15 S16
Bourton on Dunsmore Warwks 23 T14
Bourton-on-the-Hill Gloucs 15 U5
Bourton-on-the-Water Gloucs 15 U7
Bousd Ag & B 42 f1
Bouth Cumb 35 L9
Bouthwaite N York 36 D11
Boveridge Dorset 7 T8
Bovey Tracey Devon 5 P14
Bovingdon Herts 17 M9
Bow Devon 5 N12
Bow Gt Lon 17 S13
Bow Ork 58 b5
Bow Brickhill M Keyn 17 L4
Bowbridge Gloucs 15 P9
Bowburn Dur 41 Q12
Bowcombe IoW 8 H14
Bowd Devon 6 D12
Bowden Border 46 G12
Bowden Hill Wilts 15 Q15
Bowdon Traffd 31 L10
Bower Highld 58 G3
Bowerchalke Wilts 7 S7
Bowermadden Highld 58 G3
Bowers Staffs 22 J3
Bowers Gifford Essex 18 J15
Bowershall Fife 45 M2
Bower's Row Leeds 32 C3
Bowes Dur 36 B5
Bowgreave Lancs 35 N16
Bowhouse D & G 39 R9
Bowland Border 46 F10
Bowley Herefs 14 K1
Bowlhead Green Surrey 9 P4
Bowling C Brad 31 S2
Bowling W Duns 44 D4
Bowmanstead Cumb 34 K7
Bowmore Ag & B 42 C7
Bowness-on-Solway Cumb 39 U8
Bowness-on-Windermere Cumb 35 M7
Bow of Fife Fife 51 L14
Bowriefauld Angus 51 P8
Bowsden Nthumb 47 N10
Bow Street Cerdgn 20 E6
Box Gloucs 15 P10
Box Wilts 15 P15
Boxford Suffk 19 M7
Boxford W Berk 16 D15
Boxgrove W Susx 9 P11
Boxley Kent 10 K5
Boxmoor Herts 17 N9
Boxted Essex 19 N8
Boxted Essex 19 M8
Boxted Suffk 18 K5
Boxted Cross Essex 19 M8
Boxworth Cambs 25 R15
Boyden Gate Kent 11 S4
Boylestone Derbys 23 P3
Boyndie Abers 55 P4
Boyndlie Abers 55 S4
Boynton E R Yk 37 T12
Boysack Angus 51 Q8
Boyton Cnwll 4 G13
Boyton Suffk 19 S5
Boyton Wilts 7 R4
Boyton Cross Essex 18 G12
Boyton End Suffk 18 H6
Bozeat Nhants 24 K15
Brabourne Kent 11 Q8
Brabourne Lees Kent 11 Q8
Brabstermire Highld 58 H2
Bracadale Highld 59 d10
Braceborough Lincs 25 M7
Bracebridge Heath Lincs 33 L13
Bracebridge Low Fields Lincs 33 L13
Braceby Lincs 25 M3
Bracewell Lancs 35 T15
Brackenfield Derbys 32 B14
Brackenhirst N Lans 44 J5
Bracklesham W Susx 9 N12
Brackletter Highld 49 P2
Brackley Nhants 16 F4
Bracknell Br For 16 K15
Braco P & K 50 D14
Bracobrae Moray 55 L6
Bracon Ash Norfk 27 Q9
Bracora Highld 52 C16
Bracorina Highld 52 D16
Bradbourne Derbys 31 S15
Bradbury Dur 41 Q14
Bradden Nhants 16 G2
Bradenham Bucks 16 K10
Bradenstoke Wilts 15 R13
Bradfield Devon 5 P7
Bradfield Essex 19 P8
Bradfield Norfk 27 R3
Bradfield Sheff 31 T9
Bradfield W Berk 16 G14
Bradfield Combust Suffk 19 L4
Bradfield Green Ches E 30 K14
Bradfield Heath Essex 19 P8
Bradfield St Clare Suffk 19 L4
Bradfield St George Suffk 19 L3
Bradford C Brad 31 S2
Bradford Devon 4 J9
Bradford Abbas Dorset 7 L8
Bradford Leigh Wilts 15 P16
Bradford-on-Avon Wilts 15 P16
Bradford-on-Tone Somset 6 E7
Bradford Peverell Dorset 7 M12
Bradiford Devon 5 L5
Brading IoW 8 K14
Bradley Derbys 23 Q1
Bradley Hants 8 K3
Bradley NE Lin 33 Q6
Bradley Staffs 22 K6
Bradley Wolves 23 L10
Bradley Worcs 23 L15
Bradley Green Worcs 23 L15
Bradley in the Moors Staffs 23 M2
Bradley Stoke S Glos 15 L13
Bradmore Notts 24 E4
Bradninch Devon 5 S10
Bradnop Staffs 31 Q15
Bradpole Dorset 6 K12
Bradshaw Calder 31 Q3
Bradstone Devon 4 H14
Bradwall Green Ches E 31 L14
Bradwell Derbys 31 S11
Bradwell Essex 19 L8
Bradwell M Keyn 16 K3
Bradwell Norfk 27 U8
Bradwell-on-Sea Essex 19 M12
Bradwell Waterside Essex 19 M12
Bradworthy Devon 4 H8
Brae Highld 53 S4
Brae Shet 59 q4
Braefacie Falk 44 J3
Braehead Angus 51 R7
Braehead D & G 38 H10
Braehead S Lans 45 L8
Braemar Abers 54 F16
Braemore Highld 52 K2
Braemore Highld 58 E9
Brae Roy Lodge Highld 53 M16
Braeside Inver 43 S4
Braes of Coul Angus 50 K6
Braes of Enzie Moray 54 J5
Braeswick Ork 58 e3
Braevallich Ag & B 49 L14
Brafferton Darltn 36 F3
Brafferton N York 36 H12
Brafield-on-the-Green Nhants 24 J15
Bragar W Isls 56 e1
Bragbury End Herts 17 R6
Braidwood S Lans 44 K9
Brailsford Derbys 23 Q2
Braintree Essex 18 J9
Braiseworth Suffk 27 P13
Braishfield Hants 8 G7
Braithwaite Cumb 34 J3
Braithwell Donc 32 E9
Bramber W Susx 9 T10
Bramcote Warwks 23 S11
Bramdean Hants 8 K7
Bramerton Norfk 27 R8
Bramfield Herts 17 R7
Bramfield Suffk 27 T13
Bramford Suffk 19 P6
Bramhall Stockp 31 N10
Bramham Leeds 36 H16
Bramhope Leeds 36 F16
Bramley Hants 16 G16
Bramley Leeds 31 S1
Bramley Rothm 32 D9
Bramley Surrey 9 R4
Bramley Corner Hants 8 K2
Bramling Kent 11 R6
Brampford Speke Devon 5 R11
Brampton Cambs 25 P14
Brampton Cumb 35 R3
Brampton Cumb 40 D8
Brampton Lincs 32 J11
Brampton Norfk 27 Q5
Brampton Rothm 32 C7
Brampton Suffk 27 U12
Brampton Abbotts Herefs 15 L6
Brampton Ash Nhants 24 H11
Brampton Bryan Herefs 21 R8
Brampton-en-le-Morthen Rothm 32 D10
Bramshall Staffs 23 M3
Bramshaw Hants 8 E9
Bramshott Hants 9 N5
Bramwell Somset 6 J6
Branault Highld 48 E4
Brancaster Norfk 26 J2
Brancaster Staithe Norfk 26 J1
Brancepeth Dur 41 P12
Branchill Moray 54 E6
Branderburgh Moray 54 G3
Brandesburton E R Yk 37 T15
Brandeston Suffk 19 R3
Brandiston Norfk 27 P5
Brandon Dur 41 P12
Brandon Lincs 32 K16
Brandon Suffk 26 J11
Brandon Warwks 23 S13
Brandon Parva Norfk 27 N7
Brandsby N York 36 K12
Brandy Wharf Lincs 33 L8
Bran End Essex 18 G9
Branksome Poole 7 S12
Branksome Park Poole 7 S12
Bransbury Hants 8 G5
Bransby Lincs 32 K11
Branscombe Devon 6 F13
Bransford Worcs 15 N1
Bransgore Hants 8 D12
Branshoime C KuH 33 N2
Bransley Shrops 22 G13
Branston Leics 24 J4
Branston Lincs 33 M13
Branston Staffs 23 P5
Branston Booths Lincs 33 M13
Branstone IoW 8 K14
Brant Broughton Lincs 32 K15
Brantham Suffk 19 P7
Branthwaite Cumb 39 S14
Branthwaite Cumb 40 A12
Brantingham E R Yk 32 K2
Branton Donc 32 F7
Branton Nthumb 47 M15
Branton Green N York 36 H13
Branxton Nthumb 47 M10
Brassington Derbys 23 Q1
Brasted Kent 10 F6
Brasted Chart Kent 10 F6
Brathens Abers 55 N15
Bratoft Lincs 33 S13
Brattleby Lincs 33 L11
Bratton Wilts 7 R2
Bratton Wrekin 22 F7
Bratton Clovelly Devon 4 K13
Bratton Fleming Devon 5 M4
Bratton Seymour Somset 7 M6
Braughing Herts 18 D9
Braunston Nhants 24 E14
Braunston Rutlnd 24 J8
Braunstone Leics 24 F8
Braunton Devon 4 K5
Brawby N York 37 N10
Brawl Highld 58 D3
Bray W & M 17 L13
Braybrooke Nhants 24 H11
Brayford Devon 5 N5
Bray Shop Cnwll 2 H4
Brayton N York 32 F1
Braywick W & M 17 L14
Breachwood Green Herts 17 P6
Breadsall Derbys 23 R2
Breadstone Gloucs 15 M10
Breage Cnwll 1 Q13
Breakachy Highld 53 P7
Brealangwell Lodge Highld 57 N15
Bream Gloucs 15 L9
Breamore Hants 8 D9
Brean Somset 6 F2
Breanais W Isls 56 c2
Brearton N York 36 G13
Breascleit W Isls 56 f2
Breasclete W Isls 56 d2
Breaston Derbys 24 E3
Brechfa Carmth 13 P5
Brechin Angus 51 Q5
Breckles Norfk 27 L10
Brecon Powys 14 C5
Bredbury Stockp 31 N10
Brede E Susx 11 L12
Bredenbury Herefs 22 F16
Bredfield Suffk 19 R4
Bredgar Kent 11 M5
Bredhurst Kent 10 K5
Bredon Worcs 15 Q4
Bredon's Hardwick Worcs 15 Q4
Bredon's Norton Worcs 15 Q3
Bredwardine Herefs 14 G3
Breedon on the Hill Leics 23 S5
Breich W Loth 45 L6
Breightmet Bolton 31 L6
Breighton E R Yk 32 G2
Breinton Herefs 14 J3
Bremhill Wilts 15 R14
Brenchley Kent 10 J8
Brendon Devon 5 P3
Brenfield Ag & B 43 L3
Brenish W Isls 56 c2
Brent Eleigh Suffk 19 L5
Brentford Gt Lon 17 Q14
Brentingby Leics 24 H6
Brent Knoll Somset 6 G2
Brent Mill Devon 3 N6
Brent Pelham Herts 18 D8
Brentwood Essex 18 F14
Brenzett Kent 11 N10
Brenzett Green Kent 11 P10
Brereton Staffs 23 M6
Brereton Green Ches E 31 L13
Bressingham Norfk 27 N12
Bretby Derbys 23 Q5
Bretford Warwks 23 S12
Bretforton Worcs 15 T3
Bretherton Lancs 30 G4
Brettabister Shet 59 q5
Brettenham Norfk 27 L11
Brettenham Suffk 19 M4
Bretton Flints 30 E13
Brewood Staffs 22 K7
Briantspuddle Dorset 7 P12
Brickendon Herts 17 S9
Bricket Wood Herts 17 P10
Brick Houses Sheff 31 U11
Bricklehampton Worcs 15 R3
Bride IoM 34 e2
Bridekirk Cumb 39 T13
Bridestowe Devon 4 K12
Brideswell Abers 55 M8
Bridford Devon 5 P13
Bridge Kent 11 R6
Bridgehampton Somset 7 L7
Bridge Hewick N York 36 G12
Bridgehill Dur 41 M10
Bridgemary Hants 8 K11
Bridgend Abers 55 L9
Bridgend Ag & B 42 D6
Bridgend Ag & B 43 L2
Bridgend Angus 51 P4
Bridgend Brdgnd 13 U13
Bridgend D & G 45 N15
Bridgend Devon 3 L8
Bridgend Fife 51 M14
Bridgend Moray 54 J9
Bridgend P & K 50 H12
Bridgend W Loth 45 N4
Bridgend of Lintrathen Angus 51 L7
Bridge of Alford Abers 55 M12
Bridge of Allan Stirlg 50 D16
Bridge of Avon Moray 54 F11
Bridge of Avon Moray 54 F9
Bridge of Balgie P & K 49 V8
Bridge of Brewlands Angus 50 J6
Bridge of Brown Highld 54 E11
Bridge of Cally P & K 50 H7
Bridge of Canny Abers 55 N15
Bridge of Craigisla Angus 50 K7
Bridge of Dee D & G 39 M8
Bridge of Don C Aber 55 S13
Bridge of Dulsie Highld 54 C8
Bridge of Dye Abers 51 R2
Bridge of Earn P & K 50 H13
Bridge of Ericht P & K 49 U6
Bridge of Feugh Abers 55 P15
Bridge of Forss Highld 58 D3
Bridge of Gairn Abers 54 J15
Bridge of Gaur P & K 49 U6
Bridge of Marnoch Abers 55 M6
Bridge of Orchy Ag & B 49 R9
Bridge of Tilt P & K 50 E5
Bridge of Tynet Moray 54 J5
Bridge of Walls Shet 59 p5
Bridge of Weir Rens 44 D6
Bridgerule Devon 4 G10
Bridge Sollers Herefs 21 R13
Bridge Street Suffk 18 K5
Bridgetown Somset 5 R5
Bridge Trafford Ches W 30 G12
Bridgham Norfk 27 L11
Bridgnorth Shrops 22 G10
Bridgwater Somset 6 G5
Bridlington E R Yk 37 U12
Bridport Dorset 6 J12
Bridstow Herefs 14 K6
Brierfield Lancs 31 M2
Brierley Barns 32 C6
Brierley Gloucs 15 L7
Brierley Hill Dudley 22 K11
Brigg N Linc 33 L6
Briggate Norfk 27 R4
Briggswath N York 37 Q6
Brigham Cumb 39 S13
Brigham E R Yk 37 S14
Brighouse Calder 31 R4
Brighstone IoW 8 H14
Brighthampton Oxon 16 C9
Brightley Devon 5 L11
Brightling E Susx 10 J11
Brightlingsea Essex 19 N10
Brighton Br & H 10 C14
Brighton le Sands Sefton 30 E8
Brightons Falk 45 L4
Brightwalton W Berk 16 D13
Brightwell Suffk 19 Q6
Brightwell Baldwin Oxon 16 G11
Brightwell-cum-Sotwell Oxon 16 F11
Brightwell Upperton Oxon 16 G11
Brignall Dur 36 C5
Brig o'Turk Stirlg 49 U15
Brigsley NE Lin 33 Q7
Brigsteer Cumb 35 M8
Brigstock Nhants 25 L11
Brill Bucks 16 G8
Brill Cnwll 2 E13
Brilley Herefs 21 P16
Brimfield Herefs 22 E14
Brimfield Cross Herefs 22 E14
Brimington Derbys 32 C12
Brimley Devon 5 P14
Brimpsfield Gloucs 15 Q8
Brimpton W Berk 16 E16
Brimscombe Gloucs 15 P9
Brimstage Wirral 30 E10
Brincliffe Sheff 31 U10
Brind E R Yk 32 H2
Brindister Shet 59 p5
Brindle Lancs 30 J4
Brineton Staffs 22 J7
Bringhurst Leics 24 J10
Bringsty Common Herefs 22 G16
Brington Cambs 25 M13
Briningham Norfk 27 N3
Brinkhill Lincs 33 R12
Brinkley Cambs 18 G4
Brinklow Warwks 23 T12
Brinkworth Wilts 15 R12
Brinscall Lancs 30 J4
Brinsley Notts 32 D16
Brinsworth Rothm 32 C9
Brinton Norfk 27 N3
Brinyan Ork 58 c3
Brisley Norfk 27 L5
Brislington Bristl 15 L15
Brissenden Green Kent 11 N8
Bristol Bristl 15 L14
Bristol Airport N Som 14 J16
Briston Norfk 27 N4
Britford Wilts 8 D7
Brithdir Caerph 14 D10
Brithdir Gwynd 28 K15
British Legion Village Kent 10 K5
Briton Ferry Neath 13 R11
Britwell Salome Oxon 16 G11
Brixham Torbay 3 R7
Brixton Devon 3 L7
Brixton Gt Lon 17 R14
Brixton Deverill Wilts 7 Q4
Brixworth Nhants 24 H13
Brize Norton Oxon 16 B9
Brize Norton Airport Oxon 16 B9
Broad Alley Worcs 22 K14
Broad Blunsdon Swindn 15 T11
Broadbottom Tamesd 31 P9
Broadbridge W Susx 9 N11
Broadbridge Heath W Susx 9 T6
Broad Campden Gloucs 15 U4
Broad Carr Calder 31 R4
Broad Chalke Wilts 7 S6
Broadclyst Devon 5 S11
Broadfield Inver 43 T4
Broadford Highld 52 B11
Broadford Bridge W Susx 9 S8
Broadgairhill Border 45 Q15
Broad Green Worcs 22 H16
Broadhaugh Border 47 L7
Broad Haven Pembks 12 D8
Broadheath Traffd 31 L10
Broadhembury Devon 6 D10
Broadhempston Devon 3 N5
Broad Hinton Wilts 15 T14
Broadland Row E Susx 11 L12
Broad Layings Hants 8 H1
Broadley Moray 54 J5
Broad Marston Worcs 15 T3
Broadmayne Dorset 7 N13
Broadmoor Pembks 12 G8
Broadoak Dorset 6 J12
Broad Oak E Susx 10 H11
Broad Oak E Susx 11 L12
Broad Oak Herefs 14 K6
Broad Oak Kent 11 R5
Broad Oak St Hel 30 H9
Broad's Green Essex 18 H11
Broadstairs Kent 11 U4
Broadstone Poole 7 S11
Broadstone Shrops 22 E10
Broad Street E Susx 11 M12
Broad Street Kent 11 L6
Broad Town Wilts 15 T14
Broadwas Worcs 22 H16
Broadwater Herts 17 R6
Broadwater W Susx 9 T11
Broadwaters Worcs 22 J13
Broadway Pembks 12 D8
Broadway Somset 6 G8
Broadway Worcs 15 T4
Broadwell Gloucs 15 L8
Broadwell Gloucs 15 U5
Broadwell Oxon 16 B9
Broadwell Warwks 24 D14
Broadwindsor Dorset 6 J10
Broadwood Kelly Devon 5 M10
Broadwoodwidger Devon 4 J12
Brochel Highld 59 g9
Brochroy Ag & B 49 M11
Brockamin Worcs 15 N1
Brockbridge Hants 8 K9
Brockdish Norfk 27 Q12
Brockenhurst Hants 8 F11
Brocketsbrae S Lans 44 K10
Brockford Street Suffk 27 P14
Brockhall Nhants 24 F15
Brockham Surrey 9 T3
Brockhampton Gloucs 15 S6
Brockhampton Hants 9 M11
Brockhampton Herefs 15 L5
Brockholes Kirk 31 S6
Brocklesby Lincs 33 N6
Brockley N Som 14 J15
Brockley Suffk 26 K13
Brockley Green Suffk 18 H5
Brockley Green Suffk 18 K5
Brockton Shrops 21 Q6
Brockton Shrops 21 Q9
Brockton Shrops 22 E10
Brockton Shrops 22 H8
Brockweir Gloucs 14 K10
Brockworth Gloucs 15 P7
Brocton Staffs 23 L6
Brodick N Ayrs 43 N11
Brodie Moray 54 C5
Brodsworth Donc 32 D6
Brogaig Highld 59 f6
Brokenborough Wilts 15 Q12
Broken Cross Ches E 31 N12
Brokerswood Wilts 7 P2
Bromborough Wirral 30 E11
Brome Suffk 27 P13
Brome Street Suffk 27 P13
Bromeswell Suffk 19 R5
Bromfield Cumb 39 T11
Bromfield Shrops 22 D12
Bromham Bed 17 M2
Bromham Wilts 15 R16
Bromley Dudley 22 K11
Bromley Gt Lon 10 E3
Bromley Shrops 22 H10
Brompton Medway 10 K4
Brompton N York 36 H7
Brompton-by-Sawdon N York 37 Q10
Brompton-on-Swale N York 36 E7
Brompton Ralph Somset 6 D5
Brompton Regis Somset 5 R5
Bromsberrow Gloucs 15 N4
Bromsberrow Heath Gloucs 15 N5
Bromsgrove Worcs 23 L14
Bromyard Herefs 15 L1
Bronant Cerdgn 20 F9
Brongest Cerdgn 13 L2
Bronington Wrexhm 22 D3
Bronllys Powys 14 D4
Bronwydd Carmth 13 M6
Bronygarth Shrops 29 S12
Brook Hants 8 E9
Brook IoW 8 G14
Brook Kent 11 P8
Brook Surrey 9 Q4
Brooke Norfk 27 R9
Brooke Rutlnd 24 J8
Brookenby Lincs 33 P8
Brookfield Rens 44 D6
Brookhampton Somset 7 M6
Brook Hill Hants 8 F9
Brookhouse Lancs 35 P13
Brookhouse Rothm 32 D9
Brookhouse Green Ches E 31 M14
Brookhouses Derbys 31 Q10
Brookland Kent 11 N11
Brooklands Traffd 31 M9
Brookmans Park Herts 17 Q10
Brook Street Essex 18 F14
Brook Street Kent 11 N9
Brookthorpe Gloucs 15 P8
Brookwood Surrey 9 Q2
Broom C Beds 17 P3
Broom Rothm 32 D9
Broom Warwks 15 T1
Broome Norfk 27 S10
Broome Shrops 21 R7
Broome Worcs 22 K12
Broomedge Warrtn 30 K10
Broomfield Essex 18 H11
Broomfield Kent 11 L6
Broomfield Kent 11 R4
Broomfield Somset 6 F5
Broomfleet E R Yk 32 K3
Broomhaugh Nthumb 41 L8
Broom Hill Barns 32 C7
Broom Hill Notts 32 E16
Broomhill Nthumb 41 P2
Broompark Dur 41 P11
Brora Highld 58 B13
Broseley Shrops 22 G9
Brotherlee Dur 40 K12
Brotherton N York 32 D3
Brotton R & Cl 37 M3
Broubster Highld 58 D4
Brough Cumb 35 T5
Brough E R Yk 32 K3
Brough Highld 58 G2
Brough Notts 32 J14
Brough Shet 59 r4
Broughall Shrops 22 E3
Brough Lodge Shet 59 s3
Brough Sowerby Cumb 35 S5
Broughton Border 45 P11
Broughton Cambs 25 Q12
Broughton Flints 30 E14
Broughton Hants 8 F6
Broughton Lancs 30 H2
Broughton M Keyn 17 L3
Broughton N Linc 33 L6
Broughton N York 35 U15
Broughton N York 37 N11
Broughton Nhants 24 J13
Broughton Oxon 16 D4
Broughton Salfd 31 M7
Broughton V Glam 13 U15
Broughton Astley Leics 24 E10
Broughton Gifford Wilts 15 Q16
Broughton Green Worcs 23 L15
Broughton Hackett Worcs 15 Q1
Broughton-in-Furness Cumb 34 J9
Broughton Mains D & G 38 K11
Broughton Mills Cumb 34 J8
Broughton Moor Cumb 39 S13
Broughton Poggs Oxon 15 V10
Broughty Ferry C Dund 51 N10
Brown Candover Hants 8 K5
Brown Edge Staffs 31 N15
Brownhill Abers 55 R8
Brownhills Fife 51 P13
Brownhills Wsall 23 M8
Browninghill Green Hants 8 K2
Brown Lees Staffs 31 N15
Brownsham Devon 4 H6
Browns Hill Gloucs 15 Q9
Brownston Devon 3 M7
Broxa N York 37 R8
Broxbourne Herts 17 S9
Broxburn E Loth 46 J4
Broxburn W Loth 45 M5
Broxted Essex 18 F8
Bruan Highld 58 H7
Bruar P & K 50 D5
Brucefield Highld 58 C16
Bruchag Ag & B 43 M7
Bruichladdich Ag & B 42 B6
Bruisyard Suffk 27 S14
Bruisyard Street Suffk 27 S14
Brumby N Linc 32 K6
Brund Staffs 31 R14
Brundall Norfk 27 S7
Brundish Suffk 27 R14
Brundish Street Suffk 27 R13
Brunery Highld 48 H3
Brunswick Village N u Ty 41 P6
Bruntcliffe Leeds 31 T3
Brunthwaite C Brad 36 C16
Bruntingthorpe Leics 24 F10
Brunton Fife 51 L11
Brunton Wilts 8 E2
Brushford Devon 5 M9
Brushford Somset 5 R6
Bruton Somset 7 M5
Bryan's Green Worcs 22 K14
Bryanston Dorset 7 Q9
Brydekirk D & G 39 T7
Brympton Somset 6 K8
Bryn Carmth 13 Q10
Bryn Neath 13 T11
Brynamman Carmth 13 S8
Brynberian Pembks 12 H4
Bryncir Gwynd 28 F11
Bryn-coch Neath 13 R11
Bryncroes Gwynd 28 B13
Bryncrug Gwynd 20 F2
Bryneglwys Denbgs 29 Q10
Brynford Flints 29 S6
Bryn Gates Wigan 30 J7
Bryngwran IoA 28 D6
Bryngwyn Mons 14 H8
Bryngwyn Powys 21 N12
Bryn-Henllan Pembks 12 F3
Brynhoffnant Cerdgn 12 U1
Bryning Lancs 30 G3
Brynmawr Blae G 14 E8
Bryn-mawr Gwynd 28 C13
Brynmenyn Brdgnd 13 U13
Brynmill Swans 13 Q11
Brynna Rhondd 14 B13
Brynrefail Gwynd 28 G8
Brynsadler Rhondd 14 C13
Bryn Saith Marchog Denbgs 29 P10
Brynsiencyn IoA 28 F7
Brynteg IoA 28 F5
Bryn-y-Maen Conwy 29 L6
Bualintur Highld 59 e12
Bubbenhall Warwks 23 R13
Bubwith E R Yk 32 H1
Buccleuch Border 45 S14
Buchanan Smithy Stirlg 44 E2
Buchanhaven Abers 55 U7
Buchanty P & K 50 F11
Buchany Stirlg 50 C15
Buchlyvie Stirlg 44 F1
Buckabank Cumb 40 B10
Buckden Cambs 25 P14
Buckden N York 35 U10
Buckenham Norfk 27 S8
Buckerell Devon 6 E11
Buckfast Devon 3 N5
Buckfastleigh Devon 3 N5
Buckhaven Fife 51 M16
Buckholt Mons 14 J7
Buckhorn Weston Dorset 7 N7
Buckhurst Hill Essex 18 D14
Buckie Moray 54 K4
Buckingham Bucks 16 H4
Buckland Bucks 17 L8
Buckland Devon 3 M9
Buckland Gloucs 15 S4
Buckland Herts 17 S4
Buckland Kent 11 T8
Buckland Oxon 16 C10
Buckland Surrey 10 C7
Buckland Brewer Devon 4 J7
Buckland Common Bucks 17 L9
Buckland Dinham Somset 7 N2
Buckland Filleigh Devon 4 K9
Buckland in the Moor Devon 3 N4
Buckland Monachorum Devon 2 K5
Buckland Newton Dorset 7 M10
Buckland Ripers Dorset 7 M13
Buckland St Mary Somset 6 G8
Buckland-Tout-Saints Devon 3 P8
Bucklebury W Berk 16 F15
Bucklers Hard Hants 8 G12
Bucklesham Suffk 19 R6
Buckley Flints 30 D14
Buckley Hill Ches E 31 L10
Bucklow Hill Ches E 31 L10
Buckminster Leics 24 K5
Bucknall C Stke 22 K1
Bucknall Lincs 33 P13
Bucknell Oxon 16 F6
Bucknell Shrops 21 Q8
Buckpool Moray 54 K4
Bucksburn C Aber 55 R13
Buck's Cross Devon 4 H7
Bucks Green W Susx 9 S5
Buckshaw Village Lancs 30 H4
Bucks Horn Oak Hants 9 N5
Buck's Mills Devon 4 H7
Buckton E R Yk 37 U11
Buckton Nthumb 47 Q10
Buckworth Cambs 25 N13
Budby Notts 32 F13
Bude Cnwll 4 F10
Budge's Shop Cnwll 2 H6
Budleigh Salterton Devon 6 D14
Budock Water Cnwll 1 S10
Buerton Ches E 22 G2
Bugbrooke Nhants 24 G16
Bugle Cnwll 2 C7
Bugley Dorset 7 P7
Bugthorpe E R Yk 37 N14
Buildwas Shrops 22 F9
Builth Wells Powys 21 L12
Bulbridge Wilts 7 T6
Bulford Wilts 8 D4
Bulkeley Ches E 30 H15
Bulkington Warwks 23 S11
Bulkington Wilts 7 R1
Bulkworthy Devon 4 J8
Bullbridge Derbys 32 B16
Bullbrook Br For 16 K15
Bullington Hants 8 H4
Bullington Lincs 33 N11
Bulmer Essex 18 K6
Bulmer N York 37 M12
Bulmer Tye Essex 18 K7
Bulphan Thurr 18 G15
Bulwark Abers 55 R7
Bulwell C Nott 24 E1
Bulwick Nhants 25 L10
Bumble's Green Essex 18 D12
Bunacaimb Highld 48 G1
Bunarkaig Highld 49 Q1
Bunbury Ches E 30 H14
Bunchrew Highld 53 R7
Bundalloch Highld 52 F10
Bunessan Ag & B 48 F12
Bungay Suffk 27 S10
Bunnahabhain Ag & B 42 E4
Bunny Notts 24 E4
Buntait Highld 53 N10
Buntingford Herts 17 S5
Bunwell Norfk 27 P10
Burbage Leics 24 D10
Burbage Wilts 15 U16
Burchett's Green W & M 16 K13
Burcombe Wilts 7 T6
Burcott Bucks 16 K6
Bures Essex 19 L8
Burford Oxon 16 B8
Burford Shrops 22 F14
Burg Ag & B 48 G9
Burgates Hants 9 M7
Burgess Hill W Susx 10 D12
Burgh Suffk 19 Q4
Burgh by Sands Cumb 40 A9
Burgh Castle Norfk 27 U8
Burghclere Hants 8 H1
Burghead Moray 54 F4
Burghfield W Berk 16 G15
Burghfield Common W Berk 16 G15
Burgh Heath Surrey 10 C6
Burghill Herefs 14 J3
Burgh le Marsh Lincs 33 T13
Burgh next Aylsham Norfk 27 Q5
Burgh on Bain Lincs 33 P10
Burgh St Margaret Norfk 27 T6
Burgh St Peter Norfk 27 U10
Burghwallis Donc 32 E6
Burham Kent 10 K5
Buriton Hants 9 M8
Burland Ches E 30 J15
Burlawn Cnwll 2 C4
Burleigh Gloucs 15 P9
Burlescombe Devon 6 D8
Burleston Dorset 7 P12
Burley Hants 8 E11
Burley Rutlnd 24 K7
Burleydam Ches E 22 F2
Burley Gate Herefs 15 L2
Burley in Wharfedale C Brad 36 D16
Burley Street Hants 8 E11
Burley Wood Head C Brad 36 D16
Burlton Shrops 22 D5
Burmarsh Kent 11 Q10
Burmington Warwks 16 B4
Burn N York 32 F3
Burnage Manch 31 N9
Burnaston Derbys 23 Q4
Burnbrae N Lans 44 K7
Burnby E R Yk 37 P16
Burneside Cumb 35 N7
Burneston N York 36 G9
Burnett BaNES 15 M16
Burnfoot Border 46 E15
Burnfoot Border 46 F15
Burnfoot D & G 39 R6
Burnfoot D & G 40 B2
Burnfoot D & G 40 B4
Burnfoot P & K 50 F15
Burnham Bucks 17 L13
Burnham Deepdale Norfk 26 J1
Burnham Market Norfk 26 K2
Burnham Norton Norfk 26 K2
Burnham-on-Crouch Essex 19 L14
Burnham-on-Sea Somset 6 G3
Burnham Overy Norfk 26 K2
Burnham Overy Staithe Norfk 26 K1
Burnham Thorpe Norfk 26 K2
Burnhaven Abers 55 U7
Burnhead D & G 39 P3
Burnhervie Abers 55 P12
Burnhill Green Staffs 22 H9
Burnhope Dur 41 P10
Burnhouse N Ayrs 44 C8
Burniston N York 37 S8
Burnley Lancs 31 M2
Burnmouth Border 47 P6
Burn of Cambus Stirlg 50 C15
Burnopfield Dur 41 N9
Burnsall N York 36 B13
Burnside Angus 51 N6
Burnside Angus 51 P8
Burnside Fife 50 J14
Burnside Moray 54 F3
Burnside W Loth 45 M4
Burnside of Duntrune Angus 51 N10
Burntisland Fife 45 Q3
Burnt Oak E Susx 10 G11
Burnton E Ayrs 44 E16
Burntwood Staffs 23 M8
Burntwood Green Staffs 23 M8
Burnt Yates N York 36 F13
Burnworthy Somset 6 E8
Burpham Surrey 9 R2
Burpham W Susx 9 R10
Burradon Nthumb 47 N16
Burrafirth Shet 59 r1
Burravoe Shet 59 r3
Burrells Cumb 35 R4
Burrelton P & K 50 J10
Burridge Devon 6 G10
Burridge Hants 8 J10
Burrill N York 36 F9
Burringham N Linc 32 J6
Burrington Devon 5 M8
Burrington Herefs 21 S8
Burrington N Som 6 K1
Burrough Green Cambs 18 G4
Burrough on the Hill Leics 24 H7
Burrow Lancs 35 Q11
Burrow Somset 5 R4
Burrow Bridge Somset 6 H6
Burrowhill Surrey 9 Q1
Burry Green Swans 13 N11
Burry Port Carmth 13 M10
Burscough Lancs 30 G6
Burscough Bridge Lancs 30 G6
Bursea E R Yk 32 J2
Bursledon Hants 8 H10
Burslem C Stke 31 N16
Burstall Suffk 19 N6
Burstock Dorset 6 J10
Burston Norfk 27 P11
Burstow Surrey 10 D8
Burstwick E R Yk 33 P3
Burtersett N York 35 U8
Burtholme Cumb 40 D8
Burthorpe Green Suffk 18 J3
Burtoft Lincs 25 Q3
Burton Ches W 30 E12
Burton Ches W 30 H14
Burton Dorset 8 D12
Burton Lincs 33 L12
Burton Pembks 12 F9
Burton Somset 6 E3
Burton Wilts 15 P13
Burton Agnes E R Yk 37 T13
Burton Bradstock Dorset 6 K12
Burton Coggles Lincs 25 L5
Burton End Essex 18 F9
Burton Fleming E R Yk 37 S11
Burton Hastings Warwks 23 S10
Burton-in-Kendal Cumb 35 N11
Burton in Lonsdale N York 35 Q11
Burton Joyce Notts 24 F1
Burton Latimer Nhants 24 K13
Burton Lazars Leics 24 H6
Burton Leonard N York 36 G13
Burton on the Wolds Leics 24 F5
Burton Overy Leics 24 G9
Burton Pedwardine Lincs 25 N2
Burton Pidsea E R Yk 33 Q2
Burton Salmon N York 32 D3
Burton's Green Essex 18 K9
Burton upon Stather N Linc 32 J5
Burton upon Trent Staffs 23 Q5
Burton Waters Lincs 32 K12
Burtonwood Warrtn 30 J9
Burwardsley Ches W 30 H15
Burwarton Shrops 22 F11
Burwash E Susx 10 J11
Burwash Common E Susx 10 H11
Burwash Weald E Susx 10 J11
Burwell Cambs 26 F14
Burwell Lincs 33 R11
Burwen IoA 28 E3
Burwick Ork 58 c6
Bury Bury 31 M5
Bury Cambs 25 Q11
Bury Somset 5 R6
Bury W Susx 9 R9
Bury Green Herts 18 D10
Bury St Edmunds Suffk 18 K3
Burythorpe N York 37 N13
Busby E Rens 44 F7
Buscot Oxon 15 U10
Bush Abers 51 S5
Bush Bank Herefs 21 S16
Bushbury Wolves 22 K8
Bushey Herts 17 P11
Bushey Heath Herts 17 P11
Bush Hill Park Gt Lon 17 S11
Bushley Worcs 15 Q4
Bushmoor Shrops 21 S6
Bushton Wilts 15 S14
Bussage Gloucs 15 Q9
Bussex Somset 6 H5
Butcombe N Som 6 K1
Butleigh Somset 6 K5
Butleigh Wootton Somset 6 K5
Butlers Marston Warwks 16 C2
Butley Suffk 19 S5
Buttercrambe N York 37 N14
Butterdean Border 47 L6
Butterknowle Dur 41 M14
Butterleigh Devon 5 S9
Buttermere Cumb 34 J4
Buttershaw C Brad 31 R3
Butterstone P & K 50 G8
Butterton Staffs 31 R15
Butterton Staffs 22 J2
Butterwick Lincs 25 R2
Butterwick N York 37 M10
Butterwick N York 37 R11
Buttington Powys 21 P2
Buttonoak Shrops 22 H12
Buxhall Suffk 19 M4
Buxted E Susx 10 F11
Buxton Derbys 31 Q12
Buxton Norfk 27 Q5
Buxton Heath Norfk 27 P5
Bwlch Powys 14 E7
Bwlchgwyn Wrexhm 30 D15
Bwlchllan Cerdgn 20 F11
Bwlchtocyn Gwynd 28 C14
Bwlch-y-cibau Powys 29 R15
Bwlch-y-ffridd Powys 21 L4
Bwlch-y-groes Pembks 12 K4
Bwlch-y-sarnau Powys 21 L8
Byers Green Dur 41 P13
Byfield Nhants 16 E1
Byfleet Surrey 9 R1
Byford Herefs 21 R13
Byker N u Ty 41 Q8
Bylchau Conwy 29 N8
Byley Ches W 31 L13
Byrness Nthumb 40 H1
Bystock Devon 6 C13
Bythorn Cambs 25 M13
Byton Herefs 21 R9
Bywell Nthumb 41 M8
Byworth W Susx 9 Q8

C

Cabourne Lincs 33 N7
Cabrach Ag & B 42 F6
Cabrach Moray 54 H10
Cabus Lancs 35 N15
Cadbury Devon 5 R10
Cadder E Duns 44 G5
Caddington C Beds 17 N7
Caddonfoot Border 46 F11
Cadeby Donc 32 E7
Cadeby Leics 23 S9
Cadeleigh Devon 5 R9
Cade Street E Susx 10 H11
Cadgwith Cnwll 1 S14
Cadham Fife 50 K15
Cadishead Salfd 30 K9
Cadle Swans 13 Q11
Cadley Lancs 30 H2
Cadley Wilts 8 D2
Cadley Wilts 15 U15
Cadmore End Bucks 16 J11
Cadnam Hants 8 F9
Cadney N Linc 33 M7
Cadoxton V Glam 14 D16
Cadoxton Juxta-Neath Neath 13 S10
Caeathro Gwynd 28 F8
Caenby Lincs 33 L10
Caeo Carmth 13 R4
Caerau Brdgnd 13 T12
Caerau Cardif 14 D15
Caer Farchell Pembks 12 C5
Caergeiliog IoA 28 C5
Caergwrle Flints 30 E15
Caerlanrig Border 46 E16
Caerleon Newpt 14 G11
Caernarfon Gwynd 28 F8
Caerphilly Caerph 14 D12
Caersws Powys 21 L5
Caerwedros Cerdgn 20 B11
Caerwent Mons 14 J11
Caerwys Flints 29 Q6
Cairinis W Isls 56 d10
Cairnbaan Ag & B 43 M1
Cairnbulg Abers 55 T4
Cairncross Border 47 M6
Cairncurran Inver 44 C5
Cairndow Ag & B 49 P15
Cairneyhill Fife 45 M3
Cairngarroch D & G 38 D10
Cairngorms National Park 54 E14
Cairnie Abers 55 L8
Cairnorrie Abers 55 R8
Cairnryan D & G 38 D6
Cairnty Moray 54 H6
Caister-on-Sea Norfk 27 U6
Caistor Lincs 33 N7
Caistor St Edmund Norfk 27 Q8
Calanais W Isls 56 f2
Calbourne IoW 8 H13
Calcot Flints 29 R6
Calcot Gloucs 15 S8
Calcot Row W Berk 16 G14
Calcots Moray 54 G4
Caldbeck Cumb 40 B12
Caldecote Cambs 25 M11
Caldecote Cambs 25 R16
Caldecote Highfields Cambs 25 R15
Caldecott Nhants 25 L14
Caldecott Oxon 16 E10
Caldecott Rutlnd 24 J10
Calderbank N Lans 44 J6
Calder Bridge Cumb 34 G6
Calder Vale Lancs 35 P15
Caldercruix N Lans 44 J6
Calder Grove Wakefd 31 U5
Caldermill S Lans 44 G10
Calderwood S Lans 44 G7
Caldicot Mons 14 J12
Caldmore Wsall 23 M9
Caldwell N York 36 E5
Calfsound Ork 58 d2
Calgary Ag & B 48 C7
Califer Moray 54 E5
California Falk 45 L4
California Norfk 27 U6
Calke Derbys 23 S5
Callakille Highld 52 C6
Callander Stirlg 50 A14
Callanish W Isls 56 f2
Callestick Cnwll 1 S9
Calligarry Highld 59 h14
Callington Cnwll 2 J5
Callow Herefs 14 J4
Callow End Worcs 15 P2
Callow Hill Wilts 15 S13
Calmore Hants 8 F9
Calmsden Gloucs 15 S8
Calne Wilts 15 R15
Calshot Hants 8 H11
Calstock Cnwll 2 J5
Calstone Wellington Wilts 15 S15
Calthorpe Norfk 27 Q3
Calthorpe Street Norfk 27 T5
Calthwaite Cumb 40 C12
Calton Staffs 31 R16
Calveley Ches E 30 J14
Calver Derbys 31 T12
Calverhall Shrops 22 F3
Calverleigh Devon 5 R8
Calverton M Keyn 16 J4
Calverton Notts 32 F16
Calvine P & K 50 D5
Calzeat Border 45 P11
Cam Gloucs 15 N10
Camasachoirce Highld 48 H6
Camasine Highld 48 H6
Camas Luinie Highld 52 G10
Camastianavaig Highld 59 f10
Camault Muir Highld 53 Q8
Camber E Susx 11 N12
Camberley Surrey 9 Q2
Camberwell Gt Lon 17 S14
Camblesforth N York 32 F3
Cambo Nthumb 41 L4
Camborne Cnwll 1 Q11
Camborne Cambs 25 R15
Cambridge Cambs 18 D4
Cambridge Gloucs 15 N9
Cambridge Airport Cambs 18 E4
Cambrose Cnwll 1 R10
Cambus Clacks 44 K1
Cambusavie Platform Highld 57 S14
Cambusbarron Stirlg 44 J1
Cambuskenneth Stirlg 44 J1
Cambuslang S Lans 44 G7
Cambus o' May Abers 54 K15
Cambuswallace S Lans 45 N10
Camden Town Gt Lon 17 R13
Cameley BaNES 7 L1
Camelford Cnwll 4 D13
Camelon Falk 44 K3
Camerory Highld 54 D9
Camerton BaNES 7 M1
Camerton Cumb 39 R13
Camghouran P & K 49 V6
Camieston Border 46 G12
Cammachmore Abers 55 R15
Cammeringham Lincs 33 L11
Camore Highld 57 S15
Campbeltown Ag & B 42 H13
Campbeltown Airport Ag & B 42 H13
Cample D & G 39 P3
Campmuir P & K 50 K9
Camps W Loth 45 N5
Campsall Donc 32 E5
Campsea Ash Suffk 19 S4
Campton C Beds 17 P4
Camptown Border 46 J14
Camrose Pembks 12 E7
Camserney P & K 50 D8
Camusnagaul Highld 49 N3
Camusnagaul Highld 56 G15
Camusteel Highld 52 C8
Camusterrach Highld 52 C8
Canada Hants 8 F9
Candacraig Abers 54 H15
Candlesby Lincs 33 S13
Candle Street Suffk 27 M13
Candy Mill Border 45 N10
Cane End Oxon 16 H14
Canewdon Essex 19 L14
Canford Cliffs Poole 7 T12
Canford Heath Poole 7 S12
Canisbay Highld 58 H2
Canley Covtry 23 R13
Cann Dorset 7 Q7
Canna Highld 59 b15
Cannich Highld 53 M9
Cannington Somset 6 F4
Canning Town Gt Lon 18 D16
Cannock Staffs 23 L7
Cannon Bridge Herefs 14 J3
Canonbie D & G 40 B6
Canon Frome Herefs 15 L2
Canon Pyon Herefs 21 S12
Canons Ashby Nhants 16 F2
Canonstown Cnwll 1 P11
Canterbury Kent 11 R5
Cantley Norfk 27 S8
Cantlop Shrops 22 E8
Canton Cardif 14 E14
Cantraywood Highld 53 S8
Cantsfield Lancs 35 Q11
Canvey Island Essex 11 L1
Canwick Lincs 33 L13
Canworthy Water Cnwll 4 F12
Caol Highld 49 N3
Caolas Scalpaigh W Isls 56 g6
Caoles Ag & B 48 C9
Caonich Highld 52 H16
Capel Kent 10 H8
Capel Surrey 9 T4
Capel Bangor Cerdgn 20 F6
Capel Coch IoA 28 E5
Capel Curig Conwy 28 K9
Capel Cynon Cerdgn 13 L2
Capel Dewi Carmth 13 M6
Capel Dewi Cerdgn 20 C13
Capel-Dewi Cerdgn 20 F6
Capel Garmon Conwy 29 L9
Capel Hendre Carmth 13 P8
Capel Iwan Carmth 12 K4
Capel-le-Ferne Kent 11 S8
Capelles Guern 2 e1
Capel Parc IoA 28 E4
Capel St Andrew Suffk 19 S5
Capel St Mary Suffk 19 N7
Capel Seion Cerdgn 20 E7
Capelulo Conwy 29 L6
Capenhurst Ches W 30 F12
Capheaton Nthumb 41 L5
Caplaw E Rens 44 D7
Capperсleuch Border 45 R13
Capton Devon 3 P7
Caputh P & K 50 G9
Carbeth Inn Stirlg 44 E4
Carbis Bay Cnwll 1 P11
Carbost Highld 59 d11
Carbost Highld 59 e9
Carbrook Sheff 32 C9
Carbrooke Norfk 27 L8
Car Colston Notts 32 G16
Carcroft Donc 32 E6
Cardenden Fife 51 L16
Cardhu Moray 54 F8
Cardiff Cardif 14 E15
Cardiff Airport V Glam 14 C15
Cardigan Cerdgn 12 J3
Cardington Bed 17 N3
Cardington Shrops 22 D9
Cardinham Cnwll 2 D5
Cardrain D & G 38 E13
Cardrona Border 45 S11
Cardross Ag & B 44 C4
Cardryne D & G 38 E13
Cardurnock Cumb 39 T9
Careby Lincs 25 M6
Careston Angus 51 P6
Carew Pembks 12 G9
Carew Cheriton Pembks 12 G9
Carew Newton Pembks 12 G9
Carey Herefs 14 K4
Carfin N Lans 44 J7
Carfraemill Border 46 F8
Cargate Green Norfk 27 S7
Cargenbridge D & G 39 P6
Cargill P & K 50 J10
Cargo Cumb 40 B9
Cargreen Cnwll 2 K6
Carham Nthumb 47 L10
Carhampton Somset 5 S3
Carharrack Cnwll 1 S10
Carie P & K 50 B7
Carinish W Isls 56 d10
Carisbrooke IoW 8 H13
Cark Cumb 35 L10
Carkeel Cnwll 2 K5
Carlabhagh W Isls 56 e1
Carlbury Darltn 36 E4
Carlby Lincs 25 M7
Carleen Cnwll 1 Q13
Carleton N York 35 V15
Carleton Forehoe Norfk 27 N8
Carleton Rode Norfk 27 P10
Carleton St Peter Norfk 27 S8
Carlincraig Abers 55 N7
Carlingcott BaNES 7 M1
Carlisle Cumb 40 B9
Carlisle Airport Cumb 40 C8
Carloggas Cnwll 1 U6
Carlops Border 45 N7
Carloway W Isls 56 e1
Carlton Barns 32 C6
Carlton Bed 25 L16
Carlton Cambs 18 G4
Carlton Leeds 32 B3
Carlton Leics 23 S8
Carlton N York 32 F4
Carlton N York 36 C9
Carlton N York 37 L9
Carlton Notts 24 F2
Carlton S on T 36 H3
Carlton Suffk 19 S3
Carlton Colville Suffk 27 U10
Carlton Curlieu Leics 24 G9
Carlton Green Cambs 18 G5
Carlton Husthwaite N York 36 J11
Carlton-in-Cleveland N York 36 J6
Carlton in Lindrick Notts 32 F10
Carlton-le-Moorland Lincs 32 K14
Carlton Miniott N York 36 H10
Carlton-on-Trent Notts 32 H14
Carlton Scroop Lincs 25 L1
Carluke S Lans 44 K8
Carmacoup S Lans 44 J12
Carmarthen Carmth 13 M7
Carmel Carmth 13 P7
Carmel Flints 29 Q6
Carmel Gwynd 28 F9
Carmichael S Lans 45 L10
Carmunnock C Glas 44 F7
Carmyle C Glas 44 G6
Carmyllie Angus 51 P9
Carnaby E R Yk 37 T12
Carnbee Fife 51 P15
Carnbo P & K 50 G15
Carn Brea Cnwll 1 R11
Carnbrogie Abers 55 R10
Carndu Highld 52 F10
Carnduff S Lans 44 G9
Carnell E Ayrs 44 E11
Carnforth Lancs 35 N12
Carn-gorm Highld 52 G11
Carnhell Green Cnwll 1 Q11
Carnie Abers 55 Q14
Carnkie Cnwll 1 R11
Carnkie Cnwll 1 R12
Carno Powys 20 K4
Carnock Fife 45 M2
Carnon Downs Cnwll 1 S11
Carnousie Abers 55 N6
Carnoustie Angus 51 P10
Carnwath S Lans 45 M9
Carol Green Solhll 23 Q12
Carperby N York 36 B8
Carradale Ag & B 43 L10
Carrbridge Highld 54 B11
Carrefour Jersey 3 c2
Carreglefn IoA 28 D3
Carr Gate Wakefd 31 U4
Carrhouse N Linc 32 H6
Carrick Ag & B 43 M2
Carrick Castle Ag & B 43 R1
Carriden Falk 45 M3
Carrington Mdloth 45 S7
Carrington Traffd 31 L9
Carrog Denbgs 29 Q11
Carron Falk 44 K3
Carron Moray 54 G8
Carronbridge D & G 39 P2
Carron Bridge Stirlg 44 H3
Carronshore Falk 44 K3
Carr Shield Nthumb 40 H10
Carrutherstown D & G 39 S7
Carruth House Inver 44 C6
Carrville Dur 41 Q11
Carsaig Ag & B 48 E12
Carseriggan D & G 38 J7
Carsethorn D & G 39 R8
Carshalton Gt Lon 10 C4
Carsington Derbys 31 T16
Carskey Ag & B 42 H15
Carsluith D & G 38 J9
Carsphairn D & G 39 K3
Carstairs S Lans 45 L9
Carstairs Junction S Lans 45 L9
Carterton Oxon 16 B9
Carthew Cnwll 2 C7
Carthorpe N York 36 G9
Cartland S Lans 44 K9
Cartmel Cumb 35 L10
Carway Carmth 13 N9
Cashe's Green Gloucs 15 P9
Cassington Oxon 16 D8
Cassop Colliery Dur 41 R12
Castel Guern 2 c3
Casterton Cumb 35 Q10
Castle Acre Norfk 26 J6
Castle Ashby Nhants 24 J16
Castlebay W Isls 56 a9
Castle Bolton N York 36 B8
Castle Bromwich Solhll 23 N10
Castle Bytham Lincs 25 L6
Castlebythe Pembks 12 F5
Castle Caereinion Powys 21 N3
Castle Camps Cambs 18 G6
Castle Carrock Cumb 40 D9
Castle Cary Somset 7 M5
Castle Combe Wilts 15 P14
Castle Donington Leics 24 D4
Castle Douglas D & G 39 N8
Castle Eaton Swindn 15 T11
Castle Eden Dur 41 S12
Castleford Wakefd 32 C3
Castle Frome Herefs 15 M2
Castle Gresley Derbys 23 Q6
Castle Hedingham Essex 18 J7
Castlehill Border 45 S11
Castlehill Highld 58 F2
Castle Hill Suffk 19 P6
Castlehill W Duns 44 C4
Castle Kennedy D & G 38 E8
Castle Lachlan Ag & B 43 N1
Castlemartin Pembks 12 E10
Castlemilk C Glas 44 G7
Castlemorton Worcs 15 N4
Castlemorton Common Worcs 15 N4
Castle O'er D & G 39 U3
Castle Pulverbatch Shrops 21 R3
Castle Rising Norfk 26 G5
Castleside Dur 41 M10
Castle Stuart Highld 53 S7
Castlethorpe M Keyn 16 J3
Castleton Border 40 D3
Castleton Derbys 31 S10
Castleton N York 37 M5
Castleton Newpt 14 F13
Castleton Rochdl 31 N6
Castletown Highld 58 F3
Castletown IoM 34 c8
Castletown Sundld 41 R9
Castley N York 36 F16
Caston Norfk 27 L9
Castor C Pete 25 N9
Catacol N Ayrs 43 M8
Catcliffe Rothm 32 C9
Catcomb Wilts 15 R14
Catcott Somset 6 H4
Catcott Burtle Somset 6 H4
Caterham Surrey 10 D6
Catfield Norfk 27 T5
Catfirth Shet 59 q5
Catford Gt Lon 10 E3
Catforth Lancs 30 G2
Cathcart C Glas 44 F7
Cathedine Powys 14 D6
Catherington Hants 9 L9
Catherston Leweston Dorset 6 H12
Catisfield Hants 8 J11
Catlodge Highld 53 R16
Catmere End Essex 18 E7
Catmore W Berk 16 D13
Caton Lancs 35 P13
Caton Green Lancs 35 P12
Catrine E Ayrs 44 F12
Catsfield E Susx 10 K12
Catsgore Somset 6 K6
Catshill Worcs 23 L13
Cattadale Ag & B 42 J15
Cattal N York 36 H14
Cattawade Suffk 19 P7
Catterall Lancs 35 N16
Catterick N York 36 E7
Catterick Bridge N York 36 E7
Catterlen Cumb 40 D13
Catterline Abers 51 T3
Catterton N York 36 J15
Catteshall Surrey 9 Q4
Catthorpe Leics 24 E12
Cattistock Dorset 7 L11
Catton N York 36 G10
Catton Nthumb 40 H9
Catwick E R Yk 37 T15
Catworth Cambs 25 M13
Caudle Green Gloucs 15 Q8
Caulcott Oxon 16 E6
Cauldcots Angus 51 Q8
Cauldhame Stirlg 44 G2
Cauldmill Border 46 G14
Cauldon Staffs 23 M1
Cauldwell Derbys 23 Q6
Caulkerbush D & G 39 Q9
Caulside D & G 40 C5
Caundle Marsh Dorset 7 M8
Caunton Notts 32 H15
Causeway End D & G 38 J8
Causeway End Essex 18 H11
Causewayend S Lans 45 N10
Causewayhead Stirlg 44 J1
Causeyend Abers 55 S11
Causey Park Bridge Nthumb 41 N3
Cavendish Suffk 18 J6
Cavenham Suffk 26 J14
Caversfield Oxon 16 F6
Caversham Readg 16 H14
Caverswall Staffs 23 L2
Caverton Mill Border 46 K13
Cawdor Highld 54 B6
Cawood N York 32 E1
Cawsand Cnwll 2 K7
Cawston Norfk 27 P5
Cawthorne Barns 31 U6
Caxton Cambs 25 Q16
Caynham Shrops 22 E13
Caythorpe Lincs 25 L1
Caythorpe Notts 24 G1

66
Cushnie - Farndish

Cushnie Abers 55 L13
Cutcloy D & G 38 H13
Cutcombe Somset 5 R4
Cuthill Highld 57 S16
Cutnall Green Worcs 22 K14
Cutsdean Gloucs 15 T5
Cutthorpe Derbys 32 B12
Cuxham Oxon 16 G11
Cuxton Medway 10 J4
Cuxwold Lincs 33 P7
Cwm Denbgs 29 P5
Cwmafan Neath 13 S11
Cwmaman Rhondd 14 B10
Cwmbach Carmth 12 K6
Cwmbach Powys 14 E3
Cwmbach Rhondd 14 C10
Cwmbach Llechrhyd Powys 21 L11
Cwmbran Torfn 14 F11
Cwmcarn Caerph 14 E11
Cwmcarvan Mons 14 J9
Cwm-cou Cerdgn 12 K3
Cwm Crawnon Powys 14 D7
Cwmdare Rhondd 14 B9
Cwmdu Powys 14 E6
Cwmdu Swans 13 Q11
Cwmduad Carmth 13 L5
Cwmfelin Brdgnd 13 T12
Cwmfelin Myr Td 14 D10
Cwmfelin Boeth Carmth 12 J7
Cwmfelinfach Caerph 14 E11
Cwmffrwd Carmth 13 M7
Cwmgiedd Powys 13 S8
Cwmgorse Carmth 13 R8
Cwmgwili Carmth 13 P8
Cwmhiraeth Carmth 13 L4
Cwm Llinau Powys 20 H2
Cwmllynfell Neath 13 S8
Cwmmawr Carmth 13 P8
Cwmparc Rhondd 13 U11
Cwmpengraig Carmth 13 L4
Cwmtillery Blae G 14 E9
Cwm-twrch Isaf Powys 13 S8
Cwm-twrch Uchaf Powys 13 S8
Cwm-y-glo Gwynd 28 G8
Cwmystwyth Cerdgn 20 G8
Cwrt-newydd Cerdgn 20 C12
Cylibebyll Neath 13 S9
Cymer Neath 13 T11
Cymmer Rhondd 14 C11
Cynghordy Carmth 20 H14
Cynonville Neath 13 T11
Cynwyd Denbgs 29 P11
Cynwyl Elfed Carmth 13 L5

D

Daccombe Devon 3 R5
Dacre Cumb 40 C14
Dacre N York 36 E13
Dacre Banks N York 36 E13
Daddry Shield Dur 40 J12
Dadford Bucks 16 G4
Dadlington Leics 23 S9
Dagenham Gt Lon 18 E16
Daglingworth Gloucs 15 R9
Dagnall Bucks 17 M7
Dailly S Ayrs 38 F2
Dairsie Fife 51 M13
Dalabrog W Isls 56 b7
Dalavich Ag & B 49 L14
Dalbeattie D & G 39 P8
Dalby IoM 34 b6
Dalby N York 37 L11
Dalcapon P & K 50 F7
Dalchalm Highld 58 B13
Dalchreichart Highld 53 M13
Dalchruin P & K 50 C13
Dalcrue P & K 50 G11
Dalditch Devon 6 C13
Dale Derbys 23 S2
Dale Pembks 12 C9
Dalelia Highld 48 H4
Dalgarven N Ayrs 43 S9
Dalgety Bay Fife 45 P3
Dalgig E Ayrs 44 F14
Dalginross P & K 50 C12
Dalguise P & K 50 F8
Dalhalvaig Highld 57 U5
Dalham Suffk 18 H3
Daliburgh W Isls 56 b7
Dalkeith Mdloth 46 D6
Dallas Moray 54 E6
Dallinghoo Suffk 19 R4
Dallington E Susx 10 J12
Dallington Nhants 24 H15
Dalmally Ag & B 49 P11
Dalmary Stirlg 44 E1
Dalmellington E Ayrs 44 E16
Dalmeny C Edin 45 P4
Dalmore Highld 53 S3
Dalmuir W Duns 44 E5
Dalnabreck Highld 48 G4
Dalnacardoch P & K 50 C4
Dalnahaitnach Highld 54 B11
Dalnaspidal P & K 50 B4
Dalnawillan Lodge Highld 58 D7
Daloist P & K 50 C6
Dalqueich P & K 50 H15
Dalquhairn S Ayrs 38 F3
Dalreavoch Lodge Highld 57 S12
Dalry N Ayrs 43 S8
Dalrymple E Ayrs 44 C14
Dalserf S Lans 44 J8
Dalsmeran Ag & B 42 H14
Dalston Cumb 40 B10
Dalston Gt Lon 17 S12
Dalswinton D & G 39 Q4
Dalton D & G 39 S6
Dalton N York 36 D5
Dalton N York 36 H11
Dalton Nthumb 41 M6
Dalton-in-Furness Cumb 34 J11
Dalton-le-Dale Dur 41 S10
Dalton-on-Tees N York 36 F5
Dalton Piercy Hartpl 41 S13
Dalveich Stirlg 50 A12
Dalwhinnie Highld 50 A2
Dalwood Devon 6 F11
Damerham Hants 8 C9
Damgate Norfk 27 T7
Danbury Essex 18 J12
Danby N York 37 M5
Danby Wiske N York 36 G7
Dandaleith Moray 54 H7
Danderhall Mdloth 45 R5
Danebridge Ches E 31 P13
Dane End Herts 17 S6
Danehill E Susx 10 E10
Dane Hills C Leic 24 E8
Dane Street Kent 11 P6
Danshillock Abers 55 P5
Danskine E Loth 46 G6
Darenth Kent 10 G3
Daresbury Halton 30 J10
Darfield Barns 32 C7
Dargate Kent 11 Q5
Darite Cnwll 2 G5
Darlaston Wsall 23 L9
Darlaston Green Wsall 23 L9
Darley N York 36 E13
Darley Abbey C Derb 23 R2
Darley Bridge Derbys 31 T14
Darley Dale Derbys 31 T14
Darley Green Solhll 23 P13
Darleyhall Herts 17 P6
Darley Head N York 36 E13
Darlingscott Warwks 15 V3
Darlington Darltn 36 F4
Darlton Notts 32 H12
Darnick Border 46 G11
Darowen Powys 20 H3
Darra Abers 55 P7
Darracott Devon 4 F8
Darracott Devon 4 K4
Darras Hall Nthumb 41 N7
Darrington Wakefd 32 D4
Darsham Suffk 27 T14
Darshill Somset 7 L3
Dartford Kent 10 G3
Dartington Devon 3 P6
Dartmouth Devon 3 Q7
Darton Barns 31 U6
Darvel E Ayrs 44 F10
Darwen Bl w D 30 K4
Datchet W & M 17 M14
Datchworth Herts 17 R7
Daubhill Bolton 30 K6
Daugh of Kinermony Moray 54 G8
Dauntsey Wilts 15 R13
Dava Highld 54 D8
Davenham Ches W 30 K12
Daventry Nhants 24 E15
Davidson's Mains C Edin 45 Q4
Davidstow Cnwll 4 E13
Davington D & G 39 U2
Davington Hill Kent 11 P5
Daviot Abers 55 P10
Daviot Highld 53 T8
Daviot House Highld 53 T8
Davoch of Grange Moray 54 K6
Dawesgreen Surrey 10 C7
Dawley Wrekin 22 G7
Dawlish Devon 3 R3
Dawlish Warren Devon 3 S3
Daybrook Notts 24 E1
Daylesford Gloucs 16 A6
Deal Kent 11 U6
Dean Cumb 39 S14
Dean Devon 3 N5
Dean Devon 5 N3
Dean Hants 8 J8
Dean Oxon 16 C6
Dean Somset 7 M3
Dean Bottom Kent 10 H4
Deanburnhaugh Border 46 E15
Deancombe Devon 3 N5
Dean Court Oxon 16 E9
Deane Bolton 30 K6
Deane Hants 8 J3
Deanhead Kirk 31 Q5
Deanland Dorset 7 S8
Dean Prior Devon 3 N5
Deanraw Nthumb 40 H8
Deans W Loth 45 N5
Deanscales Cumb 39 S14
Deanshanger Nhants 16 J3
Deanshaugh Moray 54 J6
Deanston Stirlg 50 C15
Dearham Cumb 39 S12
Debach Suffk 19 R4
Debden Essex 18 D14
Debden Essex 18 F8
Debenham Suffk 19 Q3
Deblin's Green Worcs 15 P2
Dechmont W Loth 45 N5
Dechmont Road W Loth 45 M5
Deddington Oxon 16 E5
Dedham Essex 19 N8
Dedworth W & M 17 L14
Deene Nhants 25 L10
Deenethorpe Nhants 25 L10
Deepcar Sheff 31 U8
Deeping Gate C Pete 25 N7
Deeping St James Lincs 25 P7
Deeping St Nicholas Lincs 25 P6
Deerhurst Gloucs 15 P5
Defford Worcs 15 Q3
Defynnog Powys 13 U5
Deganwy Conwy 28 K5
Degnish Ag & B 48 J14
Deighton C York 37 L16
Deighton N York 36 H6
Deiniolen Gwynd 28 G8
Delabole Cnwll 4 D13
Delamere Ches W 30 H13
Delfrigs Abers 55 S11
Delliefure Highld 54 E10
Dell Quay W Susx 9 N11
Delnabo Moray 54 F12
Delnashaugh Inn Moray 54 F9
Delny Highld 53 T3
Delph Oldham 31 P6
Delves Dur 41 N10
Dembleby Lincs 25 M3
Denaby Donc 32 D8
Denbigh Denbgs 29 P7
Denbrae Fife 51 M13
Denbury Devon 3 Q5
Denby Derbys 23 S1
Denby Dale Kirk 31 T6
Denchworth Oxon 16 C11
Dendron Cumb 34 K12
Denfield P & K 50 F13
Denford Nhants 25 L13
Dengie Essex 19 M13
Denham Bucks 17 N12
Denham Suffk 18 J3
Denham Suffk 27 Q13
Denham Green Bucks 17 N12
Denhead Abers 55 T6
Denhead Fife 51 N13
Denhead of Gray C Dund 51 L10
Denholm Border 46 H14
Denholme C Brad 31 R2
Denmead Hants 9 L10
Denmore C Aber 55 S13
Dennington Suffk 27 R14
Denny Falk 44 J3
Dennyloanhead Falk 44 J3
Den of Lindores Fife 50 K13
Denshaw Oldham 31 P6
Denside Abers 55 Q15
Densole Kent 11 R8
Denston Suffk 18 J5
Denstone Staffs 23 N2
Denstroude Kent 11 Q5
Dent Cumb 35 R9
Denton Cambs 25 N11
Denton Darltn 36 E4
Denton E Susx 10 F14
Denton Kent 11 R7
Denton Lincs 24 J3
Denton N York 36 D15
Denton Nhants 24 J16
Denton Norfk 27 R11
Denton Tamesd 31 P8
Denver Norfk 26 G8
Denwick Nthumb 47 R14
Deopham Norfk 27 N9
Deopham Green Norfk 27 N9
Depden Suffk 18 J4
Deptford Gt Lon 17 S14
Deptford Wilts 7 S4
Derby C Derb 23 R3
Derby Devon 5 L5
Derbyhaven IoM 34 c7
Derculich P & K 50 E7
Dereham Norfk 27 M7
Deri Caerph 14 D10
Derringstone Kent 11 R7
Derrington Staffs 22 K5
Derry Hill Wilts 15 R15
Derrythorpe N Linc 32 J6
Dersingham Norfk 26 H4
Dervaig Ag & B 48 D7
Derwen Denbgs 29 P10
Derwenlas Powys 20 F4
Desborough Nhants 24 J11
Desford Leics 24 D8
Deskford Moray 55 L4
Detling Kent 11 L5
Devauden Mons 14 J10
Devil's Bridge Cerdgn 20 G8
Devizes Wilts 15 R16
Devonport C Plym 2 J7
Devonside Clacks 45 L1
Devoran Cnwll 1 S11
Dewarton Mdloth 46 E6
Dewlish Dorset 7 P11
Dewsbury Kirk 31 T4
Deytheur Powys 29 R15
Dial Post W Susx 9 T8
Dibden Hants 8 G10
Dibden Purlieu Hants 8 G11
Dickleburgh Norfk 27 P12
Didbrook Gloucs 15 S5
Didcot Oxon 16 E12
Diddington Cambs 25 P14
Diddlebury Shrops 22 D11
Didling W Susx 9 N9
Didmarton Gloucs 15 P12
Didsbury Manch 31 M9
Digby Lincs 33 M15
Digg Highld 59 f6
Diggle Oldham 31 Q6
Digmoor Lancs 30 G7
Dihewyd Cerdgn 20 C11
Dilham Norfk 27 S5
Dilhorne Staffs 23 L2
Dill Hall Lancs 31 L3
Dillington Cambs 25 N14
Dilston Nthumb 41 L8
Dilton Wilts 7 Q3
Dilton Marsh Wilts 7 Q2
Dilwyn Herefs 21 R11
Dinas Gwynd 28 C12
Dinas Pembks 12 F4
Dinas-Mawddwy Gwynd 29 L16
Dinas Powys V Glam 14 D15
Dinder Somset 7 L3
Dinedor Herefs 14 K4
Dingestow Mons 14 J8
Dingle Lpool 30 F10
Dingley Nhants 24 H11
Dingwall Highld 53 Q5
Dinnet Abers 54 K15
Dinnington N u Ty 41 P6
Dinnington Rothm 32 E10
Dinnington Somset 6 H9
Dinorwic Gwynd 28 G8
Dinton Bucks 16 J8
Dinton Wilts 7 S5
Dinwoodie D & G 39 S3
Dinworthy Devon 4 G8
Dipford Somset 6 F7
Dippen Ag & B 42 K10
Dippen N Ayrs 43 P13
Dippertown Devon 4 J13
Dipple Moray 54 H5
Dipple S Ayrs 38 E1
Diptford Devon 3 N7
Dipton Dur 41 N9
Dirleton E Loth 46 G3
Dirt Pot Nthumb 40 J11
Diseworth Leics 24 D5
Dishforth N York 36 H11
Disley Ches E 31 P10
Diss Norfk 27 P12
Distington Cumb 34 F3
Ditchampton Wilts 7 T5
Ditcheat Somset 7 M5
Ditchingham Norfk 27 S10
Ditchling E Susx 10 D12
Ditherington Shrops 22 D6
Ditteridge Wilts 15 P15
Dittisham Devon 3 Q7
Ditton Kent 10 J5
Ditton Green Cambs 18 G4
Ditton Priors Shrops 22 F10
Dixton Mons 14 K8
Dobcross Oldham 31 P6
Dobwalls Cnwll 2 F5
Doccombe Devon 5 P13
Dochgarroch Highld 53 R8
Docking Norfk 26 J3
Docklow Herefs 22 E16
Dockray Cumb 35 M3
Doddinghurst Essex 18 F13
Doddington Cambs 25 S10
Doddington Kent 11 N5
Doddington Lincs 32 K12
Doddington Nthumb 47 P11
Doddington Shrops 22 F13
Doddiscombsleigh Devon 5 Q13
Dodd's Green Ches E 22 F2
Dodford Nhants 24 F15
Dodford Worcs 23 L13
Dodington S Glos 15 N13
Dodington Somset 6 E4
Dodleston Ches W 30 F14
Dodside E Rens 44 E8
Dod's Leigh Staffs 23 M3
Dodworth Barns 31 U7
Dogdyke Lincs 33 P15
Dogmersfield Hants 9 N3
Dolanog Powys 21 L2
Dolbenmaen Gwynd 28 F11
Dolfach Powys 20 J3
Dolfor Powys 21 M6
Dolgarrog Conwy 28 K7
Dolgellau Gwynd 28 J15
Doll Highld 57 U13
Dollar Clacks 50 F16
Dollarfield Clacks 50 F16
Dolphin Flints 29 R6
Dolphinholme Lancs 35 N14
Dolphinton S Lans 45 P9
Dolton Devon 5 L9
Dolwen Conwy 29 L6
Dolwyddelan Conwy 28 J10
Domgay Powys 29 S15
Doncaster Donc 32 E7
Donhead St Andrew Wilts 7 R7
Donhead St Mary Wilts 7 R7
Donibristle Fife 45 P2
Doniford Somset 6 D4
Donington Lincs 25 P3
Donington on Bain Lincs 33 Q10
Donisthorpe Leics 23 R6
Donnington Gloucs 15 U5
Donnington Shrops 22 E7
Donnington W Berk 16 E15
Donnington W Susx 9 P11
Donnington Wrekin 22 G6
Donnington Wood Wrekin 22 G7
Donyatt Somset 6 H8
Doonfoot S Ayrs 43 T13
Dorback Lodge Highld 54 E12
Dorchester Dorset 7 N12
Dorchester Oxon 16 F11
Dordon Warwks 23 Q9
Dore Sheff 31 U11
Dores Highld 53 R9
Dorking Surrey 9 T3
Dormans Land Surrey 10 E8
Dormington Herefs 14 K3
Dormston Worcs 23 L16
Dorney Bucks 17 L13
Dornie Highld 52 F10
Dornoch Highld 57 S15
Dornock D & G 39 U7
Dorrery Highld 58 E5
Dorridge Solhll 23 P13
Dorrington Lincs 33 M15
Dorrington Shrops 22 D8
Dorrington Shrops 22 H2
Dorsington Warwks 15 T2
Dorstone Herefs 21 Q13
Dorton Bucks 16 H8
Douglas IoM 34 d6
Douglas S Lans 44 K12
Douglas and Angus C Dund 51 M10
Douglas Pier Ag & B 49 P16
Douglastown Angus 51 M8
Douglas Water S Lans 44 K11
Douglas West S Lans 44 K11
Doulting Somset 7 M4
Dounby Ork 58 b3
Doune Highld 57 M13
Doune Stirlg 50 C15
Dounepark S Ayrs 38 D2
Dounie Highld 57 P15
Dousland Devon 2 K5
Dove Holes Derbys 31 R11
Dovenby Cumb 39 S13
Dover Kent 11 T8
Dovercourt Essex 19 R8
Doverdale Worcs 22 J14
Doveridge Derbys 23 N3
Doversgreen Surrey 10 C7
Dowally P & K 50 G8
Dowdeswell Gloucs 15 R7
Dowlais Myr Td 14 C9
Dowland Devon 5 L9
Dowlish Wake Somset 6 H9
Down Ampney Gloucs 15 T10
Downderry Cnwll 2 G7
Downe Gt Lon 10 E5
Downend Gloucs 15 P10
Downend S Glos 15 L14
Downfield C Dund 51 M10
Downgate Cnwll 2 H4
Downham Essex 18 H14
Downham Gt Lon 10 E3
Downham Lancs 35 S16
Downham Market Norfk 26 G8
Down Hatherley Gloucs 15 P6
Downhead Somset 7 L6
Downhead Somset 7 N3
Downhill P & K 50 H11
Downholme N York 36 D7
Downies Abers 55 S15
Downley Bucks 16 K11
Down St Mary Devon 5 N10
Downside Surrey 9 S2
Down Thomas Devon 2 K8
Downton Wilts 8 D8
Dowsby Lincs 25 N4
Doynton S Glos 15 M14
Draethen Caerph 14 E12
Draffan S Lans 44 J9
Drakeholes Notts 32 G9
Drakemyre N Ayrs 43 S8
Drakes Broughton Worcs 15 Q2
Draughton N York 36 C15
Draughton Nhants 24 H13
Drax N York 32 G3
Draycote Warwks 24 D14
Draycott Derbys 24 C3
Draycott Gloucs 15 U4
Draycott Somset 6 J2
Draycott in the Clay Staffs 23 P4
Draycott in the Moors Staffs 23 L2
Drayton C Port 9 L11
Drayton Leics 24 J10
Drayton Norfk 27 Q6
Drayton Oxon 16 D3
Drayton Oxon 16 E11
Drayton Somset 6 H7
Drayton Worcs 22 K13
Drayton Bassett Staffs 23 P9
Drayton Beauchamp Bucks 17 L8
Drayton Parslow Bucks 16 K5
Drayton St Leonard Oxon 16 F11
Dreen Hill Pembks 12 E8
Drefach Carmth 13 L4
Drefach Carmth 13 P8
Drefach Cerdgn 20 C13
Dreghorn N Ayrs 44 C10
Drellingore Kent 11 S8
Drem E Loth 46 G4
Drewsteignton Devon 5 N12
Driffield E R Yk 37 S14
Driffield Gloucs 15 S10
Drift Cnwll 1 M13
Drigg Cumb 34 G7
Drighlington Leeds 31 T3
Drimnin Highld 48 E7
Drimpton Dorset 6 J10
Drimsallie Highld 49 L3
Dringhouses C York 36 K15
Drinkstone Suffk 19 M3
Drinkstone Green Suffk 19 M3
Drointon Staffs 23 M4
Droitwich Worcs 22 K15
Dron P & K 50 H13
Dronfield Derbys 32 B11
Drongan E Ayrs 44 D14
Dronley Angus 51 L10
Droop Dorset 7 N9
Droxford Hants 8 K9
Droylsden Tamesd 31 N8
Druid Denbgs 29 P11
Druidston Pembks 12 D7
Druimarbin Highld 49 N4
Druimavuic Ag & B 49 M8
Druimdrishaig Ag & B 42 J5
Druimindarroch Highld 48 G2
Drum Ag & B 43 M4
Drum P & K 50 G16
Drumalbin S Lans 45 L10
Drumbeg Highld 56 H8
Drumblade Abers 55 M8
Drumbreddon D & G 38 C11
Drumbuie Highld 52 D10
Drumburgh Cumb 39 V9
Drumburn D & G 39 P9
Drumchapel C Glas 44 E5
Drumchastle P & K 50 B6
Drumclog S Lans 44 G10
Drumeldrie Fife 51 N15
Drumelzier Border 45 P11
Drumfearn Highld 52 C12
Drumfrennie Abers 55 P15
Drumgley Angus 51 M7
Drumguish Highld 53 U15
Drumin Moray 54 F10
Drumjohn D & G 38 J2
Drumlamford S Ayrs 38 F6
Drumlasie Abers 55 N14
Drumleaning Cumb 39 V10
Drumlemble Ag & B 42 H13
Drumlithie Abers 51 T2
Drummoddie D & G 38 G11
Drummore D & G 38 D12
Drummuir Moray 54 J7
Drumnadrochit Highld 53 Q10
Drumnaglaur D & G 38 D12
Drumnagorrach Moray 55 L6
Drumpark D & G 39 P5
Drumrunie Lodge Highld 56 H13
Drumshang S Ayrs 43 S14
Drumuie Highld 59 e9
Drumuillie Highld 54 C11
Drumvaich Stirlg 50 B15
Drunzie P & K 50 H14
Drybeck Cumb 35 Q4
Drybridge Moray 54 K4
Drybridge N Ayrs 44 C11
Drybrook Gloucs 15 L7
Dryburgh Border 46 H11
Dry Doddington Lincs 24 J1
Dry Drayton Cambs 25 S15
Drymen Stirlg 44 E2
Drymuir Abers 55 R7
Drynoch Highld 59 e11
Dubford Abers 55 Q4
Duchally Highld 57 M11
Ducklington Oxon 16 C9
Duddenhoe End Essex 18 D7
Duddingston C Edin 45 R5
Duddington Nhants 25 L9
Duddlestone Somset 6 F7
Duddo Nthumb 47 N10
Duddon Ches W 30 H13
Dudleston Shrops 29 T12
Dudleston Heath Shrops 29 T12
Dudley Dudley 23 L10
Dudley N Tyne 41 P6
Dudley Port Sandw 23 L10
Dudsbury Dorset 7 T11
Duffield Derbys 23 R2
Duffryn Neath 13 T11
Dufftown Moray 54 H8
Duffus Moray 54 F3
Dufton Cumb 40 F14
Duggleby N York 37 Q12
Duirinish Highld 52 D9
Duisdalemore Highld 52 C12
Duisky Highld 49 M3
Duke Street Suffk 19 N6
Dukinfield Tamesd 31 P8
Dulcote Somset 7 L3
Dulford Devon 6 D10
Dull P & K 50 D8
Dullatur N Lans 44 J4
Dullingham Cambs 18 G4
Dulnain Bridge Highld 54 D11
Duloe Bed 25 P15
Duloe Cnwll 2 F6
Dulverton Somset 5 R6
Dulwich Gt Lon 17 S14
Dumbarton W Duns 44 D4
Dumbleton Gloucs 15 S4
Dumfries D & G 39 R6
Dumgoyne Stirlg 44 E3
Dummer Hants 8 K4
Dumpton Kent 11 U4
Dun Angus 51 R6
Dunalastair P & K 50 B6
Dunan Ag & B 43 Q5
Dunan Highld 59 g11
Dunan P & K 49 T6
Dunaverty Ag & B 42 J15
Dunball Somset 6 G4
Dunbar E Loth 46 J4
Dunbeath Highld 58 F9
Dunbeg Ag & B 48 K10
Dunblane Stirlg 50 C15
Dunbog Fife 51 L13
Duncanston Highld 53 R5
Duncanstone Abers 55 M10
Dunchideock Devon 5 Q13
Dunchurch Warwks 24 D13
Duncow D & G 39 Q5
Duncrievie P & K 50 H14
Duncton W Susx 9 Q9
Dundee C Dund 51 M11
Dundee Airport C Dund 51 M11
Dundon Somset 6 K5
Dundonald S Ayrs 44 C11
Dundonnell Highld 56 G16
Dundraw Cumb 39 U10
Dundreggan Highld 53 M12
Dundrennan D & G 39 M10
Dundry N Som 14 K15
Dunecht Abers 55 P13
Dunfermline Fife 45 P2
Dunfield Gloucs 15 T10
Dungavel S Lans 44 G10
Dunham Notts 32 J12
Dunham-on-the-Hill Ches W 30 G12
Dunhampton Worcs 22 J14
Dunham Town Traffd 31 L10
Dunham Woodhouses Traffd 31 L10
Dunholme Lincs 33 M11
Dunino Fife 51 P14
Dunipace Falk 44 J3
Dunkeld P & K 50 G9
Dunkerton BaNES 7 N1
Dunkeswell Devon 6 E9
Dunkeswick N York 36 G15
Dunkirk Kent 11 Q5
Dunkirk S Glos 15 N12
Dunk's Green Kent 10 H6
Dunlappie Angus 51 Q5
Dunley Worcs 22 H14
Dunlop E Ayrs 44 D8
Dunmaglass Highld 53 R11
Dunmore Falk 45 L2
Dunnet Highld 58 G2
Dunnichen Angus 51 P8
Dunning P & K 50 G13
Dunnington C York 37 M14
Dunnington E R Yk 37 T15
Dunnington Warwks 15 S1
Dunoon Ag & B 43 Q4
Dunphail Moray 54 D7
Dunragit D & G 38 D9
Duns Border 47 L8
Dunsby Lincs 25 N4
Dunscore D & G 39 P4
Dunscroft Donc 32 F6
Dunsdale R & Cl 37 L4
Dunsden Green Oxon 16 H14
Dunsdon Devon 4 G9
Dunsfold Surrey 9 R6
Dunsford Devon 5 P12
Dunshalt Fife 50 K14
Dunshillock Abers 55 T7
Dunsill Notts 32 D14
Dunsley N York 37 P5
Dunsley Staffs 22 J11
Dunsmore Bucks 16 K9
Dunsop Bridge Lancs 35 Q15
Dunstable C Beds 17 M6
Dunstall Staffs 23 P5
Dunstan Nthumb 47 S13
Dunster Somset 5 S3
Duns Tew Oxon 16 D5
Dunston Gatesd 41 P8
Dunston Lincs 33 M14
Dunston Norfk 27 Q8
Dunston Staffs 22 K6
Dunstone Devon 3 L7
Dunstone Devon 3 N3
Dunsville Donc 32 F6
Dunswell E R Yk 33 M2
Dunsyre S Lans 45 N9
Dunterton Devon 4 H14
Duntisbourne Abbots Gloucs 15 R9
Duntisbourne Rouse Gloucs 15 R9
Duntish Dorset 7 N10
Duntocher W Duns 44 E5
Dunton Bucks 16 K6
Dunton C Beds 17 Q3
Dunton Norfk 26 K4
Dunton Bassett Leics 24 E10
Dunton Green Kent 10 G5
Duntulm Highld 59 e5
Dunure S Ayrs 43 S14
Dunvant Swans 13 P11
Dunvegan Highld 59 c8
Dunwich Suffk 27 U14
Durgan Cnwll 1 S13
Durham Dur 41 Q11
Durham Tees Valley Airport S on T 36 H5
Durisdeer D & G 39 P1
Durisdeermill D & G 39 P1
Durleigh Somset 6 G5
Durley Hants 8 J9
Durley Wilts 15 V16
Durley Street Hants 8 J9
Durlock Kent 11 S5
Durlock Kent 11 T4
Durness Highld 57 M2
Durno Abers 55 P10
Duror Highld 49 M7
Durran Ag & B 49 L14
Durrington W Susx 9 S11
Durrington Wilts 8 D4
Durris Abers 55 Q15
Dursley Gloucs 15 N10
Dursley Cross Gloucs 15 M7
Durston Somset 6 G6
Durweston Dorset 7 Q9
Duston Nhants 24 G15
Duthil Highld 54 C11
Dutton Ches W 30 J11
Duxford Cambs 18 E6
Duxford Oxon 16 C10
Dwygyfylchi Conwy 28 J6
Dwyran IoA 28 E7
Dyce C Aber 55 R12
Dyffryn Ardudwy Gwynd 28 G14
Dyffryn Cellwen Neath 13 T8
Dyke Lincs 25 N5
Dyke Moray 54 D5
Dykehead Angus 50 K7
Dykehead Angus 51 M6
Dykehead N Lans 44 K7
Dykehead Stirlg 49 V16
Dykelands Abers 51 R4
Dykends Angus 50 K6
Dykeside Abers 55 P7
Dymchurch Kent 11 Q10
Dymock Gloucs 15 M5
Dyrham S Glos 15 N14
Dysart Fife 45 R1
Dyserth Denbgs 29 P5

E

Eagland Hill Lancs 35 M16
Eagle Lincs 32 K13
Eaglescliffe S on T 36 H4
Eaglesfield Cumb 39 S14
Eaglesfield D & G 39 U6
Eaglesham E Rens 44 F8
Eagley Bolton 31 L5
Eakring Notts 32 G14
Ealand N Linc 32 H6
Ealing Gt Lon 17 Q13
Eals Nthumb 40 F9
Eamont Bridge Cumb 40 D14
Earby Lancs 35 U15
Eardington Shrops 22 G10
Eardisland Herefs 21 R11
Eardisley Herefs 21 Q12
Eardiston Shrops 29 T14
Eardiston Worcs 22 G14
Earith Cambs 25 S13
Earlestown St Hel 30 J8
Earley Wokham 16 J14
Earlham Norfk 27 Q7
Earlish Highld 59 d7
Earls Barton Nhants 24 J15
Earls Colne Essex 18 K8
Earls Common Worcs 23 L15
Earl's Croome Worcs 15 Q3
Earlsdon Covtry 23 R12
Earlsferry Fife 51 N16
Earlsfield Gt Lon 10 C3
Earlsford Abers 55 Q9
Earlsheaton Kirk 31 T4
Earl Shilton Leics 24 D9
Earl Soham Suffk 19 Q3
Earl Sterndale Derbys 31 R13
Earlston Border 46 H10
Earlston E Ayrs 44 D11
Earlswood Surrey 10 C7
Earlswood Warwks 23 N13
Earnley W Susx 9 N12
Earsdon N Tyne 41 Q6
Earsham Norfk 27 S11
Eartham W Susx 9 Q10
Easby N York 36 K5
Easdale Ag & B 48 H13
Easebourne W Susx 9 P8
Easenhall Warwks 24 D12
Eashing Surrey 9 Q4
Easington Bucks 16 H8
Easington Dur 41 S11
Easington E R Yk 33 S4
Easington R & Cl 37 N4
Easington Colliery Dur 41 S11
Easington Lane Sundld 41 R11
Easingwold N York 36 K12
Eassie and Nevay Angus 51 L8
East Aberthaw V Glam 14 C15
East Allington Devon 3 P8
East Anstey Devon 5 Q6
East Ashey IoW 8 K13
East Ashling W Susx 9 N10
East Ayton N York 37 R9
East Barkwith Lincs 33 P11
East Barming Kent 10 K6
East Barnby N York 37 P5
East Barnet Gt Lon 17 R11
East Barns E Loth 46 K4
East Barsham Norfk 27 L3
East Beckham Norfk 27 P2
East Bedfont Gt Lon 17 N14
East Bergholt Suffk 19 N8
East Bilney Norfk 27 L6
East Blatchington E Susx 10 F15
East Boldon S Tyne 41 R8
East Boldre Hants 8 G12
Eastbourne Darltn 36 G4
Eastbourne E Susx 10 H15
East Bradenham Norfk 27 L7
East Brent Somset 6 H2
Eastbridge Suffk 27 T14
East Bridgford Notts 24 G2
East Buckland Devon 5 N5
East Budleigh Devon 6 D13
Eastburn C Brad 36 C16
Eastbury Herts 17 N11
Eastbury W Berk 16 C14
East Butterwick N Linc 32 J7
Eastby N York 36 C14
East Calder W Loth 45 N5
East Carleton Norfk 27 Q8
East Carlton Leeds 36 E16
East Carlton Nhants 24 J10
East Chaldon (Chaldon Herring) Dorset 7 P13
East Challow Oxon 16 C12
East Charleton Devon 3 P9
East Chelborough Dorset 7 L10
East Chiltington E Susx 10 E12
East Chinnock Somset 6 K8
East Chisenbury Wilts 8 D3
Eastchurch Kent 11 N3
East Clandon Surrey 9 R3
East Claydon Bucks 16 H6
East Coker Somset 6 K9
Eastcombe Gloucs 15 Q9
East Compton Somset 7 L4
East Cornworthy Devon 3 Q7
Eastcote Gt Lon 17 P12
Eastcote Nhants 16 H1
Eastcote Solhll 23 P12
Eastcott Wilts 7 S2
East Cottingwith E R Yk 37 M16
Eastcourt Wilts 15 V16
East Cowes IoW 8 J12
East Cowick E R Yk 32 G4
East Cowton N York 36 G6
East Cranmore Somset 7 M3
East Dean E Susx 10 G15
East Dean Gloucs 15 L7
East Dean Hants 8 E7
East Dean W Susx 9 P9
East Drayton Notts 32 H12
East Dulwich Gt Lon 17 S14
East Dundry N Som 14 K15
East Ella C KuH 33 M3
Eastend Essex 19 L14
East End Hants 8 G12
East End Hants 8 G2
East End Kent 11 L9
East End Oxon 16 D7
East End Somset 7 M3
Easter Balmoral Abers 54 G16
Easter Compton S Glos 14 K13
Easter Dalziel Highld 53 T6
Eastergate W Susx 9 Q11
Easterhouse C Glas 44 H6
Easter Howgate Mdloth 45 Q6
Easter Kinkell Highld 53 R5
Easter Moniack Highld 53 Q7
Eastern Green Covtry 23 Q12
Easter Ord Abers 55 Q14
Easter Pitkierie Fife 51 P15
Easter Skeld Shet 59 p6
Easter Softlaw Border 46 K11
Easterton Wilts 7 S2
East Everleigh Wilts 8 D3
East Farleigh Kent 10 K6
East Farndon Nhants 24 G11
East Ferry Lincs 32 J8
Eastfield N Lans 45 L6
Eastfield N York 37 S9
East Fortune E Loth 46 G4
East Garston W Berk 16 C14
Eastgate Dur 40 K12
Eastgate Norfk 27 P5
East Goscote Leics 24 F7
East Grafton Wilts 8 E2
East Grimstead Wilts 8 E7
East Grinstead W Susx 10 E9
East Guldeford E Susx 11 N11
East Haddon Nhants 24 G14
East Hagbourne Oxon 16 E12
East Halton N Linc 33 N4
East Ham Gt Lon 10 E1
Easthampton Herefs 21 R10
East Hanney Oxon 16 D11
East Hanningfield Essex 18 J13
East Hardwick Wakefd 32 D5
East Harling Norfk 27 M11
East Harlsey N York 36 H7
East Harnham Wilts 8 D7
East Harptree BaNES 7 L1
East Hartburn S on T 36 H4
East Harting W Susx 9 N8
East Hatch Wilts 7 R6
East Hatley Cambs 17 R2
East Hauxwell N York 36 E8
East Haven Angus 51 Q10
East Heckington Lincs 25 P1
East Hedleyhope Dur 41 N12
East Helmsdale Highld 58 D11
East Hendred Oxon 16 D12
East Heslerton N York 37 Q11
East Hoathly E Susx 10 G12
East Holme Dorset 7 Q13
Easthope Shrops 22 E9
Easthorpe Essex 19 L10
East Horrington Somset 7 L3
East Horsley Surrey 9 S3
East Howe Bmouth 7 T11
East Huntspill Somset 6 H3
East Ilsley W Berk 16 E13
Eastington Devon 5 N9
Eastington Gloucs 15 N9
Eastington Gloucs 15 T8
East Keal Lincs 33 S13
East Kennett Wilts 15 T15
East Keswick Leeds 36 G16
East Kilbride S Lans 44 G8
East Kirkby Lincs 33 R14
East Knighton Dorset 7 P13
East Knoyle Wilts 7 Q6
East Lambrook Somset 6 J8
Eastlands D & G 39 N6
East Langdon Kent 11 T7
East Langton Leics 24 G10
East Lavant W Susx 9 P10
East Lavington W Susx 9 Q9
East Layton N York 36 E5
Eastleach Martin Gloucs 15 U9
Eastleach Turville Gloucs 15 U9
East Leake Notts 24 E4
Eastleigh Devon 4 K6
Eastleigh Hants 8 H8
East Lexham Norfk 26 K6
Eastling Kent 11 N6
East Linton E Loth 46 H4
East Lockinge Oxon 16 D12
East Lound N Linc 32 H8
East Lulworth Dorset 7 Q14
East Lutton N York 37 Q12
East Lydford Somset 7 L6
East Malling Kent 10 J6
East Marden W Susx 9 N9
East Markham Notts 32 H12
East Martin Hants 7 T7
East Marton N York 35 U15
East Meon Hants 9 L8
East Mersea Essex 19 N11
East Midlands Airport Leics 24 D4
East Molesey Surrey 17 P15
East Morden Dorset 7 R11
East Morton C Brad 36 D16
East Morton D & G 39 P2
East Ness N York 37 M10
Eastney C Port 9 L12
Eastnor Herefs 15 M4
East Norton Leics 24 H9
Eastoft N Linc 32 J5
East Ogwell Devon 3 Q4
Easton Cambs 25 N13
Easton Devon 5 N12
Easton Dorset 7 N15
Easton Hants 8 J6
Easton Lincs 24 K4
Easton Norfk 27 P7
Easton Somset 6 K3
Easton Suffk 19 R4
Easton Wilts 15 Q15
Easton Grey Wilts 15 Q12
Easton-in-Gordano N Som 14 K14
Easton Maudit Nhants 24 K15
Easton-on-the-Hill Nhants 25 L8
Easton Royal Wilts 8 D2
East Orchard Dorset 7 P8
East Peckham Kent 10 J7
East Pennar Pembks 12 F10
East Pennard Somset 7 L4
East Perry Cambs 25 N14
East Portlemouth Devon 3 N10
East Prawle Devon 3 P10
East Preston W Susx 9 S11
East Putford Devon 4 H8
East Quantoxhead Somset 6 E4
East Rainton Sundld 41 R10
East Ravendale NE Lin 33 Q8
East Raynham Norfk 27 L5
Eastrea Cambs 25 Q9
Eastriggs D & G 39 U7
East Rigton Leeds 36 G16
Eastrington E R Yk 32 H3
Eastrop Swindn 15 U11
East Rounton N York 36 H6
East Rudham Norfk 26 K4
East Runton Norfk 27 Q2
East Ruston Norfk 27 S4
Eastry Kent 11 T6
East Saltoun E Loth 46 F5
East Sheen Gt Lon 17 Q14
East Shefford W Berk 16 C14
East Stockwith Lincs 32 H8
East Stoke Dorset 7 Q13
East Stoke Notts 32 H16
East Stour Dorset 7 P7
East Stourmouth Kent 11 S5
East Stowford Devon 5 M6
East Stratton Hants 8 J5
East Studdal Kent 11 T7
East Taphouse Cnwll 2 F5
East-the-Water Devon 4 J6
East Thirston Nthumb 41 P2
East Tilbury Thurr 10 J2
East Tisted Hants 9 L6
East Torrington Lincs 33 N10
East Tuddenham Norfk 27 N7
East Tytherley Hants 8 F7
East Tytherton Wilts 15 R14
East Village Devon 5 Q10
Eastville Bristl 15 L14
Eastville Lincs 33 S15
East Walton Norfk 26 H6
East Week Devon 5 M12
Eastwell Leics 24 H4
East Wellow Hants 8 F8
East Wemyss Fife 51 L16
East Whitburn W Loth 45 M6
Eastwick Herts 18 D11
East Wickham Gt Lon 10 F2
East Williamston Pembks 12 G9
East Winch Norfk 26 H6
East Winterslow Wilts 8 E6
East Wittering W Susx 9 N12
East Witton N York 36 D9
Eastwood Notts 24 D1
Eastwood Sthend 18 K15
East Woodburn Nthumb 40 K4
East Woodhay Hants 8 G2
East Worldham Hants 9 M5
East Wretham Norfk 27 L10
East Youlstone Devon 4 G8
Eathorpe Warwks 23 S14
Eaton Ches E 31 N13
Eaton Ches W 30 J14
Eaton Leics 24 H4
Eaton Norfk 27 Q8
Eaton Notts 32 G11
Eaton Oxon 16 D9
Eaton Shrops 22 D10
Eaton Bray C Beds 17 M7
Eaton Constantine Shrops 22 F8
Eaton Green C Beds 17 M6
Eaton Hastings Oxon 16 B10
Eaton Mascott Shrops 22 E8
Eaton Socon Cambs 25 P15
Eaton upon Tern Shrops 22 G5
Ebberston N York 37 Q10
Ebbesborne Wake Wilts 7 S7
Ebbw Vale Blae G 14 E8
Ebchester Dur 41 M9
Ebford Devon 5 S13
Ebley Gloucs 15 P9
Ebnal Ches W 30 G16
Ebrington Gloucs 15 U3
Ecchinswell Hants 8 J2
Ecclaw Border 46 K5
Ecclefechan D & G 39 U6
Eccles Border 46 K10
Eccles Kent 10 K5
Eccles Salfd 31 L8
Ecclesall Sheff 31 U10
Ecclesfield Sheff 32 B9
Eccleshall Staffs 22 J4
Eccleshill C Brad 31 S2
Ecclesmachan W Loth 45 N4
Eccles Road Norfk 27 M10
Eccleston Ches W 30 F14
Eccleston Lancs 30 H5
Eccleston St Hel 30 G8
Echt Abers 55 P14
Eckford Border 46 J12
Eckington Derbys 32 C11
Eckington Worcs 15 Q3
Ecton Nhants 24 J15
Edale Derbys 31 R10
Eday Airport Ork 58 d2
Edburton W Susx 10 C13
Edderton Highld 57 R16
Eddleston Border 45 R9
Eddlewood S Lans 44 H8
Edenbridge Kent 10 F7
Edenfield Lancs 31 M4
Edenhall Cumb 40 E13
Edenham Lincs 25 M5
Eden Park Gt Lon 10 E4
Edensor Derbys 31 T13
Edentaggart Ag & B 43 T1
Edenthorpe Donc 32 F6
Edern Gwynd 28 C12
Edgbaston Birm 23 M11
Edgcott Bucks 16 H6
Edgcott Somset 5 Q4
Edge Gloucs 15 P8
Edgefield Norfk 27 N3
Edgefield Green Norfk 27 N3
Edgerton Kirk 31 R5
Edgeworth Gloucs 15 R9
Edgmond Wrekin 22 G6
Edgton Shrops 21 R6
Edgware Gt Lon 17 Q11
Edgworth Bl w D 31 L5
Edinbane Highld 59 d8
Edinburgh C Edin 45 R5
Edinburgh Airport C Edin 45 P5
Edingale Staffs 23 P7
Edingham D & G 39 P8
Edingley Notts 32 G15
Edingthorpe Norfk 27 R3
Edingthorpe Green Norfk 27 R3
Edington Border 47 M8
Edington Nthumb 41 N5
Edington Somset 6 H4
Edington Wilts 7 R2
Edington Burtle Somset 6 H4
Edingworth Somset 6 H2
Edithmead Somset 6 G3
Edith Weston Rutlnd 24 K8
Edlesborough Bucks 17 M7
Edlingham Nthumb 47 Q15
Edlington Lincs 33 Q12
Edmondsham Dorset 7 T9
Edmondsley Dur 41 P10
Edmondthorpe Leics 24 J6
Edmonton Gt Lon 17 S11
Edmundbyers Dur 41 L10
Ednam Border 46 K10
Edradynate P & K 50 E7
Edrom Border 47 L7
Edstaston Shrops 22 E3
Edstone Warwks 23 P15
Edwalton Notts 24 F3
Edwinstowe Notts 32 F13
Edworth C Beds 17 Q3
Edwyn Ralph Herefs 22 F16
Edzell Angus 51 Q4
Edzell Woods Abers 51 Q4
Efail-fach Neath 13 S11
Efail Isaf Rhondd 14 C12
Efailnewydd Gwynd 28 D12
Efailwen Carmth 12 H6
Efenechtyd Denbgs 29 Q9
Effgill D & G 40 A3
Effingham Surrey 9 S3
Egerton Bolton 30 K5
Egerton Kent 11 M7
Eggborough N York 32 E4
Eggbuckland C Plym 2 K6
Eggesford Devon 5 N9
Eggington C Beds 17 L6
Egginton Derbys 23 Q4
Egglescliffe S on T 36 H4
Eggleston Dur 36 B3
Egham Surrey 17 M15
Egleton Rutlnd 24 K7
Eglingham Nthumb 47 Q13
Egloshayle Cnwll 2 C4
Egloskerry Cnwll 4 G13
Eglwysbach Conwy 28 K7
Eglwys Cross Wrexhm 22 D2
Eglwyswrw Pembks 12 H4
Egmanton Notts 32 H13
Egremont Cumb 34 F5
Egremont Wirral 30 E9
Egton N York 37 P6
Egton Bridge N York 37 P6
Egypt Bucks 17 L12
Eight Ash Green Essex 19 L9
Eilanreach Highld 52 E12
Elan Village Powys 20 J10
Elberton S Glos 15 L12
Elburton C Plym 2 K7
Elcombe Swindn 15 T13
Eldersfield Worcs 15 N5
Elderslie Rens 44 D6
Eldon Dur 41 P14
Elfhill Abers 51 T2
Elford Staffs 23 P7
Elgin Moray 54 G4
Elgol Highld 59 f13
Elham Kent 11 R8
Elie Fife 51 N16
Elim IoA 28 D4
Eling Hants 8 G10
Elkesley Notts 32 G12
Elkstone Gloucs 15 R8
Ella Abers 55 N5
Ellacombe Torbay 3 R5
Elland Calder 31 R4
Ellary Ag & B 42 J4
Ellastone Staffs 23 N2
Ellel Lancs 35 N14
Ellemford Border 46 K7
Ellenabeich Ag & B 48 H13
Ellenhall Staffs 22 J4
Ellen's Green Surrey 9 S6
Ellerbeck N York 36 H7
Ellerby N York 37 N4
Ellerdine Heath Wrekin 22 F5
Elleric Ag & B 49 M8
Ellerker E R Yk 32 K3
Ellerton E R Yk 32 G1
Ellerton N York 36 F7
Ellesborough Bucks 16 K9
Ellesmere Shrops 22 C3
Ellesmere Port Ches W 30 F11
Ellingham Norfk 27 S10
Ellingham Nthumb 47 R12
Ellingstring N York 36 E9
Ellington Cambs 25 P13
Ellington Nthumb 41 Q3
Elliots Green Somset 7 P3
Ellisfield Hants 9 L4
Ellishader Highld 59 f6
Ellistown Leics 23 S7
Ellon Abers 55 S10
Ellonby Cumb 40 C12
Elloughton E R Yk 33 L3
Ellwood Gloucs 15 L9
Elm Cambs 26 E8
Elmbridge Worcs 22 K14
Elmdon Essex 18 E7
Elmdon Solhll 23 P11
Elmers End Gt Lon 10 E4
Elmer's Green Lancs 30 H6
Elmesthorpe Leics 24 D9
Elmhurst Staffs 23 N7
Elmley Castle Worcs 15 R3
Elmley Lovett Worcs 22 K14
Elmore Gloucs 15 N7
Elmore Back Gloucs 15 N7
Elm Park Gt Lon 18 F16
Elmsett Suffk 19 N6
Elmstead Market Essex 19 N9
Elmsted Kent 11 Q7
Elmstone Kent 11 S5
Elmstone Hardwicke Gloucs 15 Q6
Elmswell E R Yk 37 R14
Elmswell Suffk 19 M3
Elmton Derbys 32 D12
Elphin Highld 56 J12
Elphinstone E Loth 46 E5
Elrick Abers 55 Q13
Elrig D & G 38 F10
Elrington Nthumb 40 J8
Elsdon Nthumb 40 K3
Elsenham Essex 18 F9
Elsfield Oxon 16 F8
Elsham N Linc 33 M6
Elsing Norfk 27 N6
Elslack N York 35 U15
Elson Hants 8 K11
Elsrickle S Lans 45 N9
Elstead Surrey 9 P4
Elsted W Susx 9 N8
Elsthorpe Lincs 25 M5
Elston Notts 32 H16
Elstow Bed 17 N2
Elstree Herts 17 Q11
Elstronwick E R Yk 33 Q2
Elswick Lancs 30 F1
Elswick N u Ty 41 P8
Elsworth Cambs 25 R15
Elterwater Cumb 35 L6
Eltham Gt Lon 10 E3
Eltisley Cambs 25 Q15
Elton Cambs 25 N10
Elton Ches W 30 G12
Elton Derbys 31 T14
Elton Herefs 21 S9
Elton Notts 24 H2
Elton S on T 36 H4
Eltringham Nthumb 41 M8
Elvanfoot S Lans 45 L14
Elvaston Derbys 23 S3
Elveden Suffk 26 K12
Elvetham Heath Hants 9 N3
Elvingston E Loth 46 F4
Elvington C York 37 M15
Elvington Kent 11 S7
Elwick Hartpl 41 S13
Elworth Ches E 31 L14
Elworthy Somset 6 D5
Ely Cambs 26 F12
Ely Cardif 14 D14
Emberton M Keyn 17 L2
Embleton Cumb 39 T13
Embleton Nthumb 47 S13
Embo Highld 57 T15
Emborough Somset 7 L2
Embo Street Highld 57 S15
Embsay N York 36 B14
Emery Down Hants 8 F10
Emley Kirk 31 T5
Emmington Oxon 16 H10
Emneth Norfk 26 E7
Emneth Hungate Norfk 26 E7
Empingham Rutlnd 25 L7
Empshott Hants 9 M6
Emsworth Hants 9 M11
Enborne W Berk 16 D16
Enborne Row W Berk 8 H1
Enderby Leics 24 E9
Endmoor Cumb 35 P9
Endon Staffs 31 P15
Endon Bank Staffs 31 P15
Enfield Gt Lon 17 S10
Enfield Lock Gt Lon 17 S10
Enfield Wash Gt Lon 17 S10
Enford Wilts 8 C3
Engine Common S Glos 15 M13
Englefield W Berk 16 G15
Englefield Green Surrey 17 M15
English Bicknor Gloucs 14 K7
Englishcombe BaNES 15 M16
English Frankton Shrops 22 D4
Enham-Alamein Hants 8 G4
Enmore Somset 6 F5
Enmore Green Dorset 7 Q7
Ennerdale Bridge Cumb 34 G4
Enochdhu P & K 50 G5
Ensay Ag & B 48 C8
Ensbury Bmouth 7 T11
Ensdon Shrops 22 C6
Enstone Oxon 16 C6
Enterkinfoot D & G 39 P1
Enville Staffs 22 J11
Eolaigearraidh W Isls 56 b8
Epney Gloucs 15 N8
Epperstone Notts 32 F16
Epping Essex 18 D13
Epping Green Essex 18 D12
Epping Upland Essex 18 D12
Eppleby N York 36 E5
Epsom Surrey 9 U2
Epwell Oxon 16 C3
Epworth N Linc 32 H7
Erbistock Wrexhm 29 T11
Erdington Birm 23 N10
Eridge Green E Susx 10 G9
Erines Ag & B 43 L4
Eriska Ag & B 48 K9
Eriswell Suffk 26 H12
Erith Gt Lon 10 G2
Erlestoke Wilts 7 R2
Ermington Devon 3 M7
Erpingham Norfk 27 Q3
Errogie Highld 53 Q11
Errol P & K 50 K12
Erskine Rens 44 E5
Ervie D & G 38 B7
Erwarton Suffk 19 Q8
Erwood Powys 21 M13
Eryholme N York 36 G5
Eryrys Denbgs 29 R9
Escomb Dur 41 N13
Escrick N York 37 L16
Esgairgeiliog Powys 20 G3
Esh Dur 41 P11
Esher Surrey 17 P16
Eshott Nthumb 41 P2
Esh Winning Dur 41 P11
Eskadale Highld 53 P8
Eskbank Mdloth 45 S6
Eskdale Green Cumb 34 H7
Eskdalemuir D & G 39 U2
Esprick Lancs 30 F2
Essendine Rutlnd 25 M7
Essendon Herts 17 R8
Essich Highld 53 S8
Essington Staffs 23 L8
Esslemont Abers 55 S10
Eston R & Cl 36 K4
Etal Nthumb 47 N10
Etchilhampton Wilts 7 S1
Etchingham E Susx 10 J11
Etchinghill Kent 11 R8
Etchinghill Staffs 23 M6
Eton W & M 17 M14
Eton Wick W & M 17 L13
Etruria C Stke 22 J1
Etteridge Highld 53 S16
Ettersgill Dur 40 J13
Ettiley Heath Ches E 31 L14
Ettingshall Wolves 22 K9
Ettington Warwks 16 B2
Etton C Pete 25 N8
Etton E R Yk 37 R16
Ettrick Border 45 R14
Ettrickbridge Border 46 E13
Ettrickhill Border 45 R14
Etwall Derbys 23 Q3
Euston Suffk 27 L12
Euxton Lancs 30 H4
Evanton Highld 53 R4
Evedon Lincs 25 N1
Evelix Highld 57 S15
Evenjobb Powys 21 P10
Evenley Nhants 16 F4
Evenlode Gloucs 15 U5
Evenwood Dur 41 N14
Evercreech Somset 7 M4
Everingham E R Yk 37 P16
Everleigh Wilts 8 D3
Eversholt C Beds 17 M5
Evershot Dorset 7 L10
Eversley Hants 9 M1
Eversley Cross Hants 9 N1
Everthorpe E R Yk 32 K2
Everton C Beds 17 Q2
Everton Hants 8 F13
Everton Lpool 30 E9
Everton Notts 32 G9
Evertown D & G 40 B6
Evesbatch Herefs 15 M2
Evesham Worcs 15 S3
Evington C Leic 24 F8
Ewden Village Sheff 31 T8
Ewell Surrey 10 C5
Ewell Minnis Kent 11 S8
Ewelme Oxon 16 G11
Ewen Gloucs 15 R10
Ewenny V Glam 13 U14
Ewerby Lincs 25 N1
Ewhurst Surrey 9 S5
Ewhurst Green E Susx 11 L11
Ewhurst Green Surrey 9 S5
Ewloe Flints 30 E13
Eworthy Devon 4 J11
Ewshot Hants 9 N3
Ewyas Harold Herefs 14 H5
Exbourne Devon 5 L10
Exbridge Somset 5 R7
Exbury Hants 8 H12
Exelby N York 36 F9
Exeter Devon 5 R12
Exeter Airport Devon 5 S12
Exford Somset 5 Q4
Exfordsgreen Shrops 21 S3
Exhall Warwks 23 N16
Exhall Warwks 23 R11
Exlade Street Oxon 16 G13
Exminster Devon 5 R13
Exmouth Devon 5 S14
Exning Suffk 26 G14
Exton Devon 5 S13
Exton Hants 8 K8
Exton Rutlnd 24 K7
Exton Somset 5 R5
Exwick Devon 5 R12
Eyam Derbys 31 T11
Eydon Nhants 16 F2
Eye C Pete 25 P8
Eye Herefs 22 D15
Eye Suffk 27 P13
Eyemouth Border 47 N6
Eyeworth C Beds 17 R2
Eyhorne Street Kent 11 L6
Eyke Suffk 19 S5
Eynesbury Cambs 25 P15
Eynsford Kent 10 G4
Eynsham Oxon 16 D8
Eype Dorset 6 J12
Eyre Highld 59 e8
Eythorne Kent 11 S7
Eyton Herefs 22 D15
Eyton Shrops 22 D5
Eyton on Severn Shrops 22 E8
Eyton upon the Weald Moors Wrekin 22 F6

F

Faccombe Hants 8 G2
Faceby N York 36 J6
Fachwen Powys 29 P16
Faddiley Ches E 30 J15
Fadmoor N York 37 M8
Faerdre Swans 13 R10
Faifley W Duns 44 E5
Failand N Som 14 K15
Failford S Ayrs 44 E12
Failsworth Oldham 31 N7
Fairbourne Gwynd 20 E2
Fairburn N York 32 D3
Fairfield Derbys 31 Q12
Fairfield Worcs 23 L13
Fairford Gloucs 15 T10
Fairgirth D & G 39 P9
Fair Green Norfk 26 G6
Fairhaven Lancs 30 E3
Fairlands Surrey 9 Q3
Fairlie N Ayrs 43 R8
Fairlight E Susx 11 L13
Fairmile Devon 6 D11
Fairmile Surrey 9 S2
Fairnilee Border 46 F11
Fair Oak Hants 8 J9
Fairoak Staffs 22 H3
Fair Oak Green Hants 9 L2
Fairseat Kent 10 H5
Fairstead Essex 18 J10
Fairstead Norfk 26 G5
Fairwarp E Susx 10 F11
Fairwater Cardif 14 D14
Fairy Cross Devon 4 J7
Fakenham Norfk 27 L4
Fakenham Magna Suffk 27 L13
Fala Mdloth 46 F7
Fala Dam Mdloth 46 F6
Faldingworth Lincs 33 M10
Faldouet Jersey 3 e2
Falfield S Glos 15 M11
Falkenham Suffk 19 R7
Falkirk Falk 45 L3
Falkland Fife 50 K14
Fallburn S Lans 45 M10
Fallin Stirlg 44 K1
Fallodon Nthumb 47 R13
Fallowfield Manch 31 N9
Fallowfield Nthumb 40 K7
Falls of Blarghour Ag & B 49 M13
Falmer E Susx 10 D13
Falmouth Cnwll 1 T12
Falnash Border 46 E16
Falsgrave N York 37 S9
Falstone Nthumb 40 G4
Fanagmore Highld 56 J5
Fancott C Beds 17 M5
Fanellan Highld 53 P8
Fangdale Beck N York 36 K8
Fangfoss E R Yk 37 N14
Fanmore Ag & B 48 C8
Fannich Lodge Highld 53 L4
Fans Border 46 H10
Far Bletchley M Keyn 16 K4
Farcet Cambs 25 P10
Far Cotton Nhants 24 H15
Fareham Hants 8 K11
Far End Cumb 34 K7
Farewell Staffs 23 N7
Faringdon Oxon 16 B11
Farington Lancs 30 H3
Farlam Cumb 40 E9
Farleigh N Som 14 J15
Farleigh Surrey 10 E5
Farleigh Hungerford Somset 7 P1
Farleigh Wallop Hants 8 K4
Farlesthorpe Lincs 33 T12
Farleton Cumb 35 P10
Farleton Lancs 35 P12
Farley Staffs 23 M1
Farley Wilts 8 E7
Farley Green Surrey 9 R4
Farley Hill Wokham 16 J16
Farleys End Gloucs 15 N7
Farlington C Port 9 L11
Farlington N York 37 L12
Farlow Shrops 22 F12
Farmborough BaNES 7 M1
Farmcote Gloucs 15 S5
Farmers Carmth 20 E13
Farmington Gloucs 15 T7
Farmoor Oxon 16 D9
Far Moor Wigan 30 H7
Farmtown Moray 55 L6
Farnborough Gt Lon 10 F4
Farnborough Hants 9 P3
Farnborough W Berk 16 D13
Farnborough Warwks 16 D2
Farnborough Park Hants 9 P3
Farnborough Street Hants 9 P2
Farncombe Surrey 9 Q4
Farndish Bed 24 K15

(The full page continues with many further columns of index entries in the same format, covering place names alphabetically from Farndon through Hallaton, including the section break letter headings "G" and "H".)

70 Little Scatwell - Milton

Little Scatwell Highld 53 N5
Little Shelford Cambs 18 D5
Little Singleton Lancs 30 F1
Little Skipwith N York 32 F1
Little Smeaton N York 32 E5
Little Snoring Norfk 27 L3
Little Sodbury S Glos 15 N13
Little Somborne Hants 8 G6
Little Somerford Wilts 15 R13
Little Soudley Shrops 22 G4
Little Stainton Darltn 36 G3
Little Stanney Ches W 30 F12
Little Staughton Bed 25 N15
Little Steeping Lincs 33 S14
Little Stoke Staffs 22 K3
Littlestone-on-Sea Kent 11 Q11
Little Stonham Suffk 19 P3
Little Stretton Leics 24 G9
Little Stretton Shrops 21 S5
Little Strickland Cumb 35 P3
Little Stukeley Cambs 25 P13
Little Sugnall Staffs 22 J3
Little Swinburne Nthumb 40 K6
Little Sypland D & G 39 M10
Little Tew Oxon 16 C5
Little Tey Essex 19 L9
Little Thetford Cambs 26 F13
Little Thorpe Dur 41 S11
Littlethorpe Leics 24 E9
Littlethorpe N York 36 G12
Little Thurlow Suffk 18 H5
Little Thurrock Thurr 10 H2
Littleton Angus 51 L7
Littleton Ches W 30 G13
Littleton D & G 39 L9
Littleton Hants 8 H6
Littleton Somset 6 K6
Littleton Surrey 17 N15
Littleton Drew Wilts 15 P13
Littleton-on-Severn S Glos 15 L12
Littleton Pannell Wilts 7 S2
Little Torrington Devon 4 K8
Littletown Dur 41 R11
Little Town Lancs 30 K2
Little Urswick Cumb 34 K11
Little Wakering Essex 19 L15
Little Walden Essex 18 F6
Little Waldingfield Suffk 19 L6
Little Walsingham Norfk 27 L3
Little Waltham Essex 18 H11
Little Weighton E R Yk 33 L2
Little Weldon Nhants 24 K10
Little Wenlock Wrekin 22 F8
Little Weston Somset 7 M6
Little Whitefield IoW 8 K13
Littlewick Green W & M 16 K13
Little Wilbraham Cambs 18 F4
Little Witcombe Gloucs 15 Q7
Little Witley Worcs 22 H15
Little Wittenham Oxon 16 F11
Little Wolford Warwks 16 B4
Little Woodcote Gt Lon 10 C5
Littleworth Oxon 16 B10
Littleworth Staffs 22 K5
Littleworth Worcs 15 Q2
Little Wymington Bed 25 L14
Little Wymondley Herts 17 Q5
Little Wyrley Staffs 23 M8
Little Yeldham Essex 18 J7
Littley Green Essex 18 H10
Litton Derbys 31 S12
Litton N York 35 U11
Litton Somset 7 L2
Litton Cheney Dorset 6 K12
Liurbost W Isls 56 e2
Liverpool Lpool 30 E9
Liversedge Kirk 31 S4
Liverton Devon 3 P4
Liverton R & Cl 37 M4
Livingston W Loth 45 N5
Livingston Village W Loth 45 N6
Lixwm Flints 29 R6
Lizard Cnwll 1 R16
Llanaelhaearn Gwynd 28 E11
Llanafan Cerdgn 20 F8
Llanafan-Fawr Powys 20 K11
Llanallgo IoA 28 F4
Llanarmon Dyffryn Ceiriog Wrexhm 29 Q13
Llanarmon-yn-Ial Denbgs 29 R9
Llanarth Cerdgn 20 B11
Llanarth Mons 14 H8
Llanarthne Carmth 13 P7
Llanasa Flints 29 Q5
Llanbadarn Fawr Cerdgn 20 E7
Llanbadarn Fynydd Powys 21 M7
Llanbadoc Mons 14 H10
Llanbeder Newpt 14 H11
Llanbedr Gwynd 28 G14
Llanbedr Powys 14 F7
Llanbedr-Dyffryn-Clwyd Denbgs 29 Q8
Llanbedrgoch IoA 28 F5
Llanbedrog Gwynd 28 D13
Llanbedr-y-Cennin Conwy 28 K7
Llanberis Gwynd 28 G8
Llanbethery V Glam 14 C15
Llanbister Powys 21 M8
Llanblethian V Glam 14 B14
Llanboidy Carmth 12 J6
Llanbradach Caerph 14 D12
Llanbrynmair Powys 20 J3
Llancadle V Glam 14 C15
Llancarfan V Glam 14 C15
Llancloudy Herefs 14 J6
Llandaff Cardif 14 D14
Llandanwg Gwynd 28 G14
Llanddaniel Fab IoA 28 F7
Llanddarog Carmth 13 N7
Llanddeiniol Cerdgn 20 D8
Llanddeiniolen Gwynd 28 G7
Llandderfel Gwynd 29 N12
Llanddeusant IoA 28 D4
Llanddew Powys 14 C5
Llanddewi Swans 13 N12
Llanddewi Brefi Cerdgn 20 F11
Llanddewi Rhydderch Mons 14 G8
Llanddewi Velfrey Pembks 12 H7
Llanddewi Ystradenni Powys 21 M9
Llanddoget Conwy 28 K8
Llanddona IoA 28 G5
Llanddowror Carmth 12 K8
Llanddulas Conwy 29 M5
Llanddwywe Gwynd 28 G15
Llanddyfnan IoA 28 F5
Llandefaelog-Tre'r-Graig Powys 14 D5
Llandefalle Powys 14 D4
Llandegfan IoA 28 G6
Llandegla Denbgs 29 R10
Llandegley Powys 21 M10
Llandegveth Mons 14 G11
Llandeilo Carmth 13 Q6
Llandeilo Graban Powys 21 M13
Llandeloy Pembks 12 D6
Llandenny Mons 14 H9
Llandevaud Newpt 14 H12
Llandevenny Mons 14 H12
Llandinam Powys 21 L6
Llandissilio Pembks 12 H6
Llandogo Mons 14 K9
Llandough V Glam 14 B14
Llandough V Glam 14 E14
Llandovery Carmth 13 S4
Llandow V Glam 13 U14
Llandre Carmth 20 F13
Llandre Cerdgn 20 E6
Llandre Isaf Pembks 12 H5
Llandrillo Denbgs 29 P12
Llandrillo-yn-Rhos Conwy 29 L5
Llandrindod Wells Powys 21 L10
Llandrinio Powys 29 S15
Llandudno Conwy 28 K5
Llandudno Junction Conwy 28 K5
Llandulas Powys 20 J13
Llandwrog Gwynd 28 E9
Llandybie Carmth 13 Q7
Llandyfaelog Carmth 13 M8
Llandyfriog Cerdgn 13 L3
Llandygai Gwynd 28 H6
Llandygwydd Cerdgn 12 J3
Llandyrnog Denbgs 29 Q7
Llandyssil Powys 21 N5
Llandysul Cerdgn 20 B14
Llanedeyrn Cardif 14 E13
Llaneglwys Powys 14 C4
Llanegryn Gwynd 20 E3
Llanegwad Carmth 13 N6
Llaneilian IoA 28 F3
Llanelian-yn-Rhôs Conwy 29 L6
Llanelidan Denbgs 29 Q10
Llanelieu Powys 14 E4
Llanellen Mons 14 G8
Llanelli Carmth 13 N10
Llanelltyd Gwynd 28 J15
Llanelwedd Powys 21 L12
Llanenddwyn Gwynd 28 G14
Llanengan Gwynd 28 C14
Llanerchymedd IoA 28 E4
Llanerfyl Powys 21 L2
Llanfachraeth IoA 28 D5
Llanfachreth Gwynd 28 K14
Llanfaelog IoA 28 D6
Llanfaelrhys Gwynd 28 B14
Llanfaethlu IoA 28 C4
Llanfair Gwynd 28 G13
Llanfair Caereinion Powys 21 M3
Llanfair Clydogau Cerdgn 20 E12
Llanfair Dyffryn Clwyd Denbgs 29 Q9
Llanfairfechan Conwy 28 J6
Llanfair P G IoA 28 G6
Llanfair Talhaiarn Conwy 29 M7
Llanfair Waterdine Shrops 21 P8
Llanfairynghornwy IoA 28 D3
Llanfair-yn-Neubwll IoA 28 C6
Llanfallteg Carmth 12 H7
Llanfallteg West Carmth 12 H7
Llanfarian Cerdgn 20 E7
Llanfechain Powys 29 R15
Llanfechell IoA 28 D3
Llanferres Denbgs 29 R8
Llanfihangel-ar-arth Carmth 13 N3
Llanfihangel Glyn Myfyr Conwy 29 N10
Llanfihangel Nant Bran Powys 13 U4
Llanfihangel Rhydithon Powys 21 M9
Llanfihangel Rogiet Mons 14 J12
Llanfihangel-y-Creuddyn Cerdgn 20 F8
Llanfihangel-yng-Ngwynfa Powys 29 P15
Llanfihangel yn Nhowyn IoA 28 D5
Llanfihangel-y-traethau Gwynd 28 G12
Llanfilo Powys 14 D5
Llanfoist Mons 14 F8
Llanfor Gwynd 29 M12
Llanfrechfa Torfn 14 G11
Llanfrynach Powys 14 C6
Llanfwrog Denbgs 29 Q9
Llanfwrog IoA 28 C4
Llanfyllin Powys 29 Q15
Llanfynydd Carmth 13 P5
Llanfynydd Flints 30 D15
Llanfyrnach Pembks 12 J5
Llangadfan Powys 20 K2
Llangadog Carmth 13 R5
Llangadwaladr IoA 28 D7
Llangaffo IoA 28 E7
Llangammarch Wells Powys 20 J12
Llangan V Glam 14 B14
Llangarron Herefs 14 K6
Llangathen Carmth 13 P6
Llangattock Powys 14 E7
Llangattock Lingoed Mons 14 G7
Llangedwyn Powys 29 R14
Llangefni IoA 28 F6
Llangeinor Brdgnd 13 U12
Llangeitho Cerdgn 20 E10
Llangeler Carmth 13 L3
Llangelynin Gwynd 20 D3
Llangendeirne Carmth 13 M8
Llangennech Carmth 13 P10
Llangennith Swans 13 M11
Llangernyw Conwy 29 L7
Llangian Gwynd 28 C13
Llangloffan Pembks 12 E5
Llanglydwen Carmth 12 J6
Llangoed IoA 28 H5
Llangollen Denbgs 29 R11
Llangolman Pembks 12 H5
Llangors Powys 14 D5
Llangower Gwynd 29 M13
Llangrannog Cerdgn 13 L1
Llangristiolus IoA 28 E6
Llangrove Herefs 14 K7
Llangunllo Powys 21 N8
Llangunnor Carmth 13 M7
Llangurig Powys 20 J7
Llangwm Conwy 29 N11
Llangwm Mons 14 H10
Llangwm Pembks 12 F8
Llangwnnadl Gwynd 28 B13
Llangwyryfon Cerdgn 20 E9
Llangybi Cerdgn 20 E11
Llangybi Gwynd 28 E11
Llangybi Mons 14 H10
Llangynhafal Denbgs 29 Q8
Llangynidr Powys 14 D7
Llangynin Carmth 12 K7
Llangynog Carmth 13 L7
Llangynog Powys 29 P14
Llangynwyd Brdgnd 13 T12
Llanhamlach Powys 14 D6
Llanharan Rhondd 14 B13
Llanharry Rhondd 14 B13
Llanhennock Mons 14 G11
Llanhilleth Blae G 14 E10
Llanidloes Powys 20 K6
Llaniestyn Gwynd 28 C13
Llanigon Powys 14 E3
Llanilar Cerdgn 20 E8
Llanilid Rhondd 14 B13
Llanina Cerdgn 20 B10
Llanishen Cardif 14 E13
Llanishen Mons 14 J9
Llanllechid Gwynd 28 H7
Llanllowell Mons 14 H10
Llanllugan Powys 21 L3
Llanllwch Carmth 13 M7
Llanllwchaiarn Powys 21 M5
Llanllwni Carmth 13 N4
Llanllyfni Gwynd 28 F10
Llanmadoc Swans 13 M11
Llanmaes V Glam 14 B15
Llanmartin Newpt 14 H12
Llanmiloe Carmth 12 K9
Llannefydd Conwy 29 N7
Llannon Carmth 13 P9
Llannor Gwynd 28 D12
Llanon Cerdgn 20 D9
Llanover Mons 14 G8
Llanpumsaint Carmth 13 M5
Llanrhaeadr-ym-Mochnant Powys 29 Q14
Llanrhian Pembks 12 D5
Llanrhidian Swans 13 N11
Llanrhychwyn Conwy 28 K8
Llanrhyddlad IoA 28 D4
Llanrhystud Cerdgn 20 D9
Llanrug Gwynd 28 G8
Llanrumney Cardif 14 E13
Llanrwst Conwy 28 K8
Llansadurnen Carmth 12 K8
Llansadwrn Carmth 13 R5
Llansadwrn IoA 28 G6
Llansaint Carmth 13 M9
Llansamlet Swans 13 R10
Llansanffraid Glan Conwy Conwy 28 K6
Llansannan Conwy 29 M7
Llansantffraed Powys 14 D6
Llansantffraed-Cwmdeuddwr Powys 20 K9
Llansantffraed-in-Elvel Powys 21 M11
Llansantffraid Cerdgn 20 D9
Llansantffraid-ym-Mechain Powys 29 R15
Llansawel Carmth 13 Q4
Llansilin Powys 29 R14
Llansoy Mons 14 H10
Llanspyddid Powys 14 B5
Llanstadwell Pembks 12 E9
Llansteffan Carmth 13 L8
Llantarnam Torfn 14 G11
Llanteg Pembks 12 J8
Llanthewy Skirrid Mons 14 G7
Llanthony Mons 14 F5
Llantilio-Crossenny Mons 14 H8
Llantilio Pertholey Mons 14 G7
Llantrisant Mons 14 H10
Llantrisant Rhondd 14 C13
Llantrithyd V Glam 14 C14
Llantwit Fardre Rhondd 14 C12
Llantwit Major V Glam 14 B15
Llanuwchllyn Gwynd 29 L13
Llanvaches Newpt 14 H11
Llanvair Discoed Mons 14 J11
Llanvapley Mons 14 G8
Llanvetherine Mons 14 G7
Llanvihangel Crucorney Mons 14 G7
Llanwddyn Powys 29 N15
Llanwenog Cerdgn 20 C13
Llanwern Newpt 14 G12
Llanwinio Carmth 12 K6
Llanwnda Gwynd 28 F9
Llanwnda Pembks 12 E3
Llanwnnen Cerdgn 20 D12
Llanwnog Powys 21 L5
Llanwrda Carmth 13 R5
Llanwrin Powys 20 G3
Llanwrthwl Powys 20 K10
Llanwrtyd Wells Powys 20 J13
Llanwyddelan Powys 21 L4
Llanyblodwel Shrops 29 R14
Llanybri Carmth 13 L8
Llanybydder Carmth 20 D13
Llanycefn Pembks 12 G6
Llanychaer Bridge Pembks 12 F4
Llanymawddwy Gwynd 29 M15
Llanymynech Powys 29 S15
Llanynghenedl IoA 28 D5
Llanynys Denbgs 29 Q8
Llanyre Powys 21 L10
Llanystumdwy Gwynd 28 F12
Llanywern Powys 14 D5
Llawhaden Pembks 12 G7
Llawryglyn Powys 20 J5
Llay Wrexhm 30 E15
Llechrhyd Caerph 14 D8
Llechryd Cerdgn 12 J3
Lledrod Cerdgn 20 E9
Llithfaen Gwynd 28 D11
Lloc Flints 29 Q6
Llowes Powys 21 N13
Llwydcoed Rhondd 14 B9
Llwydiarth Powys 29 P16
Llwyncelyn Cerdgn 20 B10
Llwyndafydd Cerdgn 20 B11
Llwyngwril Gwynd 20 E2
Llwynmawr Wrexhm 29 R12
Llwynypia Rhondd 14 B11
Llynclys Shrops 29 S14
Llynfaes IoA 28 E5
Llysfaen Conwy 29 M5
Llyswen Powys 14 D4
Llysworney V Glam 14 B14
Llys-y-frân Pembks 12 G6
Llywel Powys 13 T5
Loan Falk 45 M4
Loanhead Mdloth 45 R6
Loaningfoot D & G 39 Q9
Loans S Ayrs 43 T11
Lobhillcross Devon 4 K13
Lochailort Highld 48 H2
Lochaline Highld 48 G8
Lochans D & G 38 C9
Locharbriggs D & G 39 R5
Lochavich Ag & B 49 L13
Lochawe Ag & B 49 N11
Loch Baghasdail W Isls 56 b8
Lochboisdale W Isls 56 b8
Lochbuie Ag & B 48 F12
Lochcarron Highld 52 F8
Lochdon Ag & B 48 H10
Lochdonhead Ag & B 48 H10
Lochead Ag & B 42 K4
Lochearnhead Stirlg 49 V12
Lochee C Dund 51 M11
Locheilside Station Highld 49 M3
Lochend Highld 53 R8
Locheport W Isls 56 b5
Loch Euphoirt W Isls 56 b5
Lochfoot D & G 39 P6
Lochgair Ag & B 43 M2
Lochgelly Fife 45 Q1
Lochgilphead Ag & B 43 L2
Lochgoilhead Ag & B 49 P15
Lochieheads Fife 50 K14
Lochill Moray 54 H4
Lochindorb Lodge Highld 54 C9
Lochinver Highld 56 G10
Lochluichart Highld 53 M4
Lochmaben D & G 39 S5
Lochmaddy W Isls 56 c5
Loch Maree Hotel Highld 52 F3
Loch nam Madadh W Isls 56 c5
Lochore Fife 50 J16
Lochranza N Ayrs 43 M8
Lochside Abers 51 S5
Lochside D & G 39 Q6
Lochside Highld 53 U6
Lochslin Highld 53 U1
Lochton S Ayrs 38 E5
Lochty Angus 51 P5
Lochty Fife 51 P14
Lochuisge Highld 48 J6
Lochwinnoch Rens 44 C7
Lochwood D & G 39 S2
Lockengate Cnwll 2 C6
Lockerbie D & G 39 T5
Lockeridge Wilts 15 T15
Lockerley Hants 8 F7
Locking N Som 6 H1
Locking Stumps Warrtn 30 K9
Lockington E R Yk 37 R15
Lockleywood Shrops 22 G4
Locksbottom Gt Lon 10 E4
Locks Heath Hants 8 J10
Lockton N York 37 P8
Loddington Leics 24 H8
Loddington Nhants 24 J12
Loddiswell Devon 3 N8
Loddon Norfk 27 S9
Lode Cambs 18 F3
Lode Heath Solhll 23 P12
Loders Dorset 6 K12
Lodsworth W Susx 9 Q8
Lofthouse Leeds 32 B3
Lofthouse N York 36 D11
Lofthouse Gate Wakefd 32 B4
Loftus R & Cl 37 M4
Logan E Ayrs 44 F13
Loganlea W Loth 45 M6
Loggerheads Staffs 22 H3
Logie Angus 51 R5
Logie Fife 51 M12
Logie Moray 54 D6
Logie Coldstone Abers 54 K14
Logie Newton Abers 55 N8
Logie Pert Angus 51 R5
Logierait P & K 50 F7
Logierieve Abers 55 S10
Login Carmth 12 H6
Lolworth Cambs 25 R15
Lonbain Highld 52 C6
Londesborough E R Yk 37 P16
London Gt Lon 17 R13
London Apprentice Cnwll 2 C8
London Colney Herts 17 Q9
Londonderry N York 36 G9
Londonthorpe Lincs 25 L2
Londubh Highld 52 F1
Lonemore Highld 52 D2
Long Ashton N Som 14 K15
Long Bank Worcs 22 H13
Long Bennington Lincs 24 J1
Longbenton N Tyne 41 Q7
Longborough Gloucs 15 U5
Long Bredy Dorset 7 L12
Longbridge Birm 23 M12
Longbridge Deverill Wilts 7 Q4
Long Buckby Nhants 24 F14
Longburton Dorset 7 M9
Long Clawson Leics 24 G4
Longcliffe Derbys 31 T15
Longcombe Devon 3 Q6
Long Compton Staffs 22 J5
Long Compton Warwks 16 B5
Longcot Oxon 16 B11
Long Crendon Bucks 16 H9
Long Crichel Dorset 7 S9
Longden Shrops 21 S3
Long Ditton Surrey 17 Q15
Longdon Staffs 23 M6
Longdon Worcs 15 P4
Longdon Green Staffs 23 N7
Longdon upon Tern Wrekin 22 F6
Longdown Devon 5 Q12
Longdowns Cnwll 1 S12
Long Duckmanton Derbys 32 C12
Long Eaton Derbys 24 D3
Longfield Kent 10 H4
Longford Covtry 23 R11
Longford Derbys 23 P3
Longford Gloucs 15 P7
Longford Shrops 22 F3
Longford Wrekin 22 H6
Longforgan P & K 51 L11
Longformacus Border 46 J7
Longframlington Nthumb 41 N2
Long Green Ches W 30 G12
Longham Dorset 7 T11
Longham Norfk 27 L6
Long Hanborough Oxon 16 D8
Longhaven Abers 55 U8
Longhirst Nthumb 41 P4
Longhope Gloucs 15 M7
Longhope Ork 58 b5
Longhorsley Nthumb 41 N3
Longhoughton Nthumb 47 S14
Long Itchington Warwks 23 S14
Longlane Derbys 23 Q2
Long Lawford Warwks 24 D13
Longlevens Gloucs 15 P7
Longleys P & K 50 K9
Long Load Somset 6 J7
Longmanhill Abers 55 P4
Long Marston Herts 17 L7
Long Marston N York 36 J15
Long Marston Warwks 15 T2
Long Marton Cumb 40 F14
Long Melford Suffk 18 K6
Longmoor Camp Hants 9 N6
Longmorn Moray 54 G5
Longmoss Ches E 31 N12
Long Newnton Gloucs 15 Q11
Longnewton Border 46 H12
Long Newton E Loth 46 G6
Longnewton S on T 36 H4
Longney Gloucs 15 N8
Longniddry E Loth 46 F4
Longnor Shrops 22 D9
Longnor Staffs 31 R13
Longparish Hants 8 H4
Long Preston N York 35 T14
Longridge Lancs 30 J1
Longridge W Loth 45 L6
Longriggend N Lans 44 K5
Long Riston E R Yk 37 T16
Longrock Cnwll 1 N13
Longsdon Staffs 31 P15
Longside Abers 55 T7
Longstanton Cambs 25 S14
Longstock Hants 8 G5
Longstowe Cambs 17 R1
Long Stratton Norfk 27 Q10
Long Street M Keyn 16 J2
Longstreet Wilts 8 D3
Long Sutton Hants 9 M4
Long Sutton Lincs 26 D5
Long Sutton Somset 6 J6
Longthorpe C Pete 25 P9
Long Thurlow Suffk 27 M14
Longthwaite Cumb 35 M3
Longton C Stke 22 K2
Longton Lancs 30 G3
Longtown Cumb 40 B7
Longtown Herefs 14 G5
Longueville Jersey 3 d3
Longville in the Dale Shrops 22 E10
Long Waste Wrekin 22 F6
Long Whatton Leics 24 D5
Longwick Bucks 16 J9
Long Wittenham Oxon 16 F11
Longwitton Nthumb 41 M4
Longwood D & G 39 M8
Longworth Oxon 16 C10
Longyester E Loth 46 G6
Lonmay Abers 55 T5
Lonmore Highld 59 c9
Looe Cnwll 2 G7
Loose Kent 10 K6
Loosley Row Bucks 16 K10
Lootcherbrae Abers 55 M6
Lopen Somset 6 J8
Loppington Shrops 22 D4
Lords Wood Medway 10 K5
Lornty P & K 50 J8
Loscoe Derbys 23 S1
Lossiemouth Moray 54 G3
Lostock Gralam Ches W 30 K12
Lostock Green Ches W 30 K12
Lostwithiel Cnwll 2 D6
Lothbeg Highld 58 C12
Lothersdale N York 36 B16
Lothmore Highld 58 C12
Loudwater Bucks 17 L11
Loughborough Leics 24 E5
Loughor Swans 13 P10
Loughton Essex 18 D14
Loughton M Keyn 16 K4
Lound Lincs 25 M6
Lound Notts 32 G10
Lound Suffk 27 U9
Lount Leics 23 S6
Louth Lincs 33 R10
Lovedean Hants 9 L9
Lover Wilts 8 E8
Loversall Donc 32 E8
Loves Green Essex 18 G12
Loveston Pembks 12 G9
Lovington Somset 7 L6
Low Ackworth Wakefd 32 D5
Low Barbeth D & G 38 B7
Low Bentham N York 35 Q12
Low Biggins Cumb 35 Q10
Low Borrowbridge Cumb 35 Q7
Low Bradfield Sheff 31 T9
Low Bradley N York 36 B15
Low Burnham N Linc 32 H7
Lowca Cumb 34 F3
Low Catton E R Yk 37 M14
Low Crosby Cumb 40 C9
Lowdham Notts 24 G1
Low Dinsdale Darltn 36 G5
Lower Aisholt Somset 6 F5
Lower Ansty Dorset 7 P10
Lower Apperley Gloucs 15 P5
Lower Ashton Devon 5 Q13
Lower Assendon Oxon 16 H12
Lower Bartle Lancs 30 G2
Lower Basildon W Berk 16 G13
Lower Beeding W Susx 10 C10
Lower Benefield Nhants 25 L11
Lower Bentley Worcs 23 L14
Lower Boddington Nhants 16 E1
Lower Bourne Surrey 9 N4
Lower Brailes Warwks 16 B3
Lower Breakish Highld 52 C11
Lower Broadheath Worcs 22 J16
Lower Broxwood Herefs 21 Q11
Lower Bullingham Herefs 14 K4
Lower Burgate Hants 8 D9
Lower Caldecote C Beds 17 Q2
Lower Chapel Powys 14 C4
Lower Chicksgrove Wilts 7 R6
Lower Chute Wilts 8 F3
Lower Clapton Gt Lon 17 S12
Lower Clent Worcs 22 K12
Lower Cumberworth Kirk 31 T6
Lower Dean Bed 25 M14
Lower Diabaig Highld 52 E5
Lower Dicker E Susx 10 G13
Lower Down Shrops 21 Q6
Lower Dunsforth N York 36 H13
Lower Egleton Herefs 15 L2
Lower End M Keyn 17 L4
Lower Eythorne Kent 11 S7
Lower Failand N Som 14 J14
Lower Farringdon Hants 9 L6
Lower Feltham Gt Lon 17 N15
Lower Froyle Hants 9 M4
Lower Gabwell Devon 3 R4
Lower Gledfield Highld 57 P15
Lower Godney Somset 6 J4
Lower Gravenhurst C Beds 17 P4
Lower Green Kent 10 G8
Lower Green Kent 10 H8
Lower Halliford Surrey 17 N15
Lower Halstow Kent 11 L4
Lower Hamworthy Poole 7 S12
Lower Hardres Kent 11 R6
Lower Hartwell Bucks 16 J8
Lower Hergest Herefs 21 P11
Lower Heyford Oxon 16 E6
Lower Houses Kirk 31 S5
Lower Irlam Salfd 31 L9
Lower Killeyan Ag & B 42 C10
Lower Langford N Som 6 J1
Lower Largo Fife 51 M15
Lower Leigh Staffs 23 M3
Lower Loxhore Devon 5 M4
Lower Lydbrook Gloucs 15 L7
Lower Lye Herefs 21 R9
Lower Machen Newpt 14 E12
Lower Merridge Somset 6 F5
Lower Middleton Cheney Nhants 16 E3
Lower Moor Worcs 15 R2
Lower Morton S Glos 15 L11
Lower Nazeing Essex 18 D12
Lower Penarth V Glam 14 E15
Lower Penn Staffs 22 K9
Lower Peover Ches E 31 L12
Lower Quinton Warwks 15 U2
Lower Raydon Suffk 19 N7
Lower Roadwater Somset 5 S4
Lower Seagry Wilts 15 R13
Lower Shelton C Beds 17 M3
Lower Shiplake Oxon 16 J13
Lower Shuckburgh Warwks 24 D15
Lower Slaughter Gloucs 15 U6
Lower Standen Kent 11 S8
Lower Stanton St Quintin Wilts 15 Q13
Lower Stoke Medway 11 L2
Lower Stone Gloucs 15 M11
Lower Stow Bedon Norfk 27 M10
Lower Street Norfk 27 R3
Lower Street Suffk 19 P5
Lower Swanwick Hants 8 J10
Lower Swell Gloucs 15 U6
Lower Tean Staffs 23 M2
Lower Town Devon 3 N4
Lower Town Pembks 12 F4
Lower Upcott Devon 5 Q14
Lower Upham Hants 8 J8
Lower Weare Somset 6 H2
Lower Welson Herefs 21 P12
Lower Westmancote Worcs 15 Q4
Lower Whatley Somset 7 N3
Lower Whitley Ches W 30 J11
Lower Wield Hants 8 K5
Lower Willingdon E Susx 10 H14
Lower Withington Ches E 31 M13
Lower Woodford Wilts 8 C6
Lower Wraxhall Dorset 7 L10
Lowesby Leics 24 G7
Lowestoft Suffk 27 V10
Loweswater Cumb 34 H3
Low Fell Gatesd 41 P8
Lowfield Heath W Susx 10 C8
Low Gartachorrans Stirlg 44 E3
Low Grantley N York 36 F12
Low Ham Somset 6 J6
Low Harrogate N York 36 F14
Low Hesket Cumb 40 C11
Low Hutton N York 37 N12
Lowick Nhants 25 L12
Lowick Nthumb 47 P10
Lowick Green Cumb 34 K9
Low Lorton Cumb 39 T14
Low Marnham Notts 32 J13
Low Mill N York 37 M8
Low Moorsley Sundld 41 R11
Low Moresby Cumb 34 F3
Low Newton Cumb 35 M10
Low Row Cumb 40 E8
Low Row N York 36 B7
Low Salchrie D & G 38 B8
Low Santon N Linc 32 K5
Lowsonford Warwks 23 P14
Low Tharston Norfk 27 Q9
Lowther Cumb 35 P3
Lowthorpe E R Yk 37 S13
Lowton Somset 6 F8
Low Torry Fife 45 M2
Low Worsall N York 36 H5
Low Wray Cumb 35 L7
Loxbeare Devon 5 R8
Loxhill Surrey 9 R5
Loxhore Devon 5 M4
Loxley Warwks 16 B1
Loxton N Som 6 H1
Loxwood W Susx 9 R6
Loyal Lodge Highld 57 Q6
Lubenham Leics 24 G11
Luccombe Somset 5 R3
Luccombe Village IoW 8 K15
Lucker Nthumb 47 R12
Luckett Cnwll 2 H4
Lucking Street Essex 18 J8
Luckington Wilts 15 P13
Lucklawhill Fife 51 M12
Luckwell Bridge Somset 5 R4
Lucton Herefs 21 R10
Ludag W Isls 56 b8
Ludborough Lincs 33 Q8
Ludbrook Devon 3 M7
Ludchurch Pembks 12 H8
Luddenden Calder 31 Q3
Luddenden Foot Calder 31 Q3
Luddesdown Kent 10 J4
Luddington N Linc 32 J5
Luddington Warwks 15 U1
Luddington in the Brook Nhants 25 N11
Ludford Lincs 33 P9
Ludford Shrops 22 E13
Ludgershall Bucks 16 G7
Ludgershall Wilts 8 E3
Ludgvan Cnwll 1 N12
Ludham Norfk 27 T6
Ludlow Shrops 22 E13
Ludney Somset 6 H9
Ludwell Wilts 7 R7
Ludworth Dur 41 R12
Luffness E Loth 46 F3
Lugar E Ayrs 44 F13
Luggate Burn E Loth 46 H4
Luggiebank N Lans 44 J5
Lugton E Ayrs 44 D8
Lugwardine Herefs 14 K3
Luib Highld 59 g11
Lulham Herefs 21 R13
Lullington Derbys 23 Q7
Lullington Somset 7 P2
Lulsgate Bottom N Som 14 J16
Lulsley Worcs 22 H16
Lumb Calder 31 Q4
Lumby N York 32 D3
Lumloch E Duns 44 G5
Lumphanan Abers 55 M14
Lumphinnans Fife 45 Q1
Lumsden Abers 54 K11
Lunan Angus 51 R7
Lunanhead Angus 51 N7
Luncarty P & K 50 H11
Lund E R Yk 37 R15
Lund N York 32 F2
Lundie Angus 51 L10
Lundin Links Fife 51 M15
Lundin Mill Fife 51 M15
Lunna Shet 59 q4
Lunsford Kent 10 J5
Lunsford's Cross E Susx 10 K13
Lunt Sefton 30 E7
Luppitt Devon 6 E10
Lupset Wakefd 31 U4
Lupton Cumb 35 P10
Lurgashall W Susx 9 Q7
Lurley Devon 5 R8
Luscombe Devon 3 P7
Luss Ag & B 44 C1
Lussagiven Ag & B 42 H2
Lusta Highld 59 c7
Lustleigh Devon 5 P14
Luston Herefs 22 D15
Luthermuir Abers 51 R4
Luthrie Fife 51 L12
Luton Devon 3 R3
Luton Devon 6 D10
Luton Luton 17 N6
Luton Medway 10 K4
Luton Airport Luton 17 P7
Lutterworth Leics 24 E11
Lutton Devon 3 L6
Lutton Devon 3 N6
Lutton Lincs 26 D4
Lutton Nhants 25 N11
Luxborough Somset 5 S4
Luxulyan Cnwll 2 D6
Lybster Highld 58 G8
Lydbury North Shrops 21 Q6
Lydd Kent 11 P11
Lydd Airport Kent 11 P11
Lydden Kent 11 S7
Lydden Kent 11 T4
Lyddington Rutlnd 24 K9
Lydeard St Lawrence Somset 6 E5
Lydford Devon 4 K13
Lydford on Fosse Somset 7 L6
Lydgate Calder 31 N3
Lydham Shrops 21 Q5
Lydiard Millicent Wilts 15 T12
Lydiard Tregoze Swindn 15 T12
Lydiate Sefton 30 F7
Lydiate Ash Worcs 23 L13
Lydlinch Dorset 7 N8
Lydney Gloucs 15 L9
Lydstep Pembks 12 G10
Lye Dudley 22 K11
Lye Green E Susx 10 G9
Lye Green Warwks 23 P14
Lye's Green Wilts 7 P3
Lyford Oxon 16 D11
Lymbridge Green Kent 11 Q8
Lyme Regis Dorset 6 H12
Lyminge Kent 11 R8
Lymington Hants 8 F12
Lyminster W Susx 9 R11
Lymm Warrtn 30 K10
Lympne Kent 11 Q9
Lympsham Somset 6 H2
Lympstone Devon 5 S13
Lynchat Highld 53 T14
Lynch Green Norfk 27 P8
Lyndhurst Hants 8 F10
Lyndon Rutlnd 24 K8
Lyne Border 45 Q10
Lyne Surrey 17 M15
Lyneal Shrops 22 D3
Lyneham Oxon 16 B7
Lyneham Wilts 15 S13
Lynemouth Nthumb 41 Q3
Lyne of Skene Abers 55 P13
Lyness Ork 58 b5
Lyng Norfk 27 N6
Lyng Somset 6 G6
Lynmouth Devon 5 N3
Lynsted Kent 11 N5
Lynton Devon 5 N3
Lyon's Gate Dorset 7 M10
Lyonshall Herefs 21 Q11
Lytchett Matravers Dorset 7 R11
Lytchett Minster Dorset 7 R12
Lyth Highld 58 G3
Lytham Lancs 30 F3
Lytham St Anne's Lancs 30 E3
Lythe N York 37 P5
Lythmore Highld 58 D3

M

Mabe Burnthouse Cnwll 1 S12
Mablethorpe Lincs 33 T10
Macclesfield Ches E 31 N12
Macduff Abers 55 P4
Macharioch Ag & B 42 J15
Machen Caerph 14 E12
Machrie N Ayrs 43 M11
Machrihanish Ag & B 42 H13
Machrins Ag & B 42 D1
Machynlleth Powys 20 G4
Machynys Carmth 13 N10
Mackworth Derbys 23 R3
Macmerry E Loth 46 F5
Madderty P & K 50 F12
Maddiston Falk 45 L4
Madeley Staffs 22 H1
Madeley Wrekin 22 G8
Madingley Cambs 25 S15
Madley Herefs 14 H4
Madresfield Worcs 15 P2
Madron Cnwll 1 N12
Maenclochog Pembks 12 G5
Maendy V Glam 14 B14
Maentwrog Gwynd 28 H11
Maen-y-groes Cerdgn 20 B11
Maer Staffs 22 H2
Maerdy Rhondd 14 B10
Maesbrook Shrops 29 S15
Maesbury Shrops 29 S14
Maesbury Marsh Shrops 29 T14
Maesllyn Cerdgn 20 A13
Maesteg Brdgnd 13 T11
Maesybont Carmth 13 P7
Maesycwmmer Caerph 14 D11
Maggieknockater Moray 54 H7
Magham Down E Susx 10 H13
Maghull Sefton 30 F7
Magna Park Leics 24 D11
Magor Mons 14 H12
Maidenbower W Susx 10 D9
Maiden Bradley Wilts 7 P4
Maidencombe Torbay 3 R5
Maidenhayne Devon 6 G11
Maiden Head N Som 14 K15
Maidenhead W & M 17 L13
Maiden Newton Dorset 7 L11
Maidens S Ayrs 43 R15
Maiden's Green Br For 17 L14
Maiden Wells Pembks 12 F10
Maidford Nhants 16 G1
Maids Moreton Bucks 16 H4
Maidstone Kent 10 K6
Maidwell Nhants 24 H13
Mail Shet 59 q6
Maindee Newpt 14 G12
Mainsforth Dur 41 Q13
Mains of Balhall Angus 51 P5
Mains of Balnakettle Abers 51 Q3
Mains of Dalvey Highld 54 E9
Mains of Haulkerton Abers 51 S4
Mains of Lesmoir Abers 54 K10
Mains of Melgunds Angus 51 P7
Mainsriddle D & G 39 Q9
Mainstone Shrops 21 P6
Maisemore Gloucs 15 P6
Malborough Devon 3 N9
Maldon Essex 18 K12
Malham N York 35 U13
Maligar Highld 59 f6
Mallaig Highld 52 C15
Mallaigvaig Highld 52 C15
Malleny Mills C Edin 45 P6
Malltraeth IoA 28 E7
Mallwyd Gwynd 20 H2
Malmesbury Wilts 15 Q12
Malmsmead Devon 5 P3
Malpas Ches W 22 D1
Malpas Cnwll 1 T11
Malpas Newpt 14 G12
Maltby Rothm 32 E9
Maltby S on T 36 J5
Maltby le Marsh Lincs 33 T11
Maltman's Hill Kent 11 M8
Malton N York 37 N11
Malvern Link Worcs 15 N2
Malvern Wells Worcs 15 N3
Mamble Worcs 22 G13
Mamhilad Mons 14 G9
Manaccan Cnwll 1 S14
Manafon Powys 21 M3
Manais W Isls 56 d4
Manaton Devon 5 N14
Manby Lincs 33 S10
Mancetter Warwks 23 R9
Manchester Manch 31 M8
Manchester Airport Manch 31 M10
Mancot Flints 30 E13
Mandally Highld 53 M15
Manea Cambs 26 E10
Maney Birm 23 N9
Manfield N York 36 E5
Mangotsfield S Glos 15 M14
Manish W Isls 56 d4
Manley Ches W 30 H12
Manmoel Caerph 14 E9
Mannel Ag & B 42 b5
Manningford Bohune Wilts 8 C2
Manningford Bruce Wilts 8 C2
Manningham C Brad 31 S2
Manning's Heath W Susx 9 T7
Mannington Dorset 7 T10
Manningtree Essex 19 P8
Mannofield C Aber 55 S14
Manorbier Pembks 12 G10
Manorbier Newton Pembks 12 G10
Manorhill Border 46 J11
Manorowen Pembks 12 E4
Manor Park Gt Lon 18 D16
Mansell Gamage Herefs 21 R13
Mansell Lacy Herefs 21 R13
Mansfield E Ayrs 44 G14
Mansfield Notts 32 E14
Mansfield Woodhouse Notts 32 E14
Manston Dorset 7 P8
Manston Kent 11 T4
Manston Leeds 32 B2
Manswood Dorset 7 S9
Manthorpe Lincs 25 M6
Manton N Linc 32 K7
Manton Rutlnd 24 K8
Manton Wilts 15 U15
Manuden Essex 18 E9
Maperton Somset 7 M6
Maplebeck Notts 32 G14
Mapledurham Oxon 16 G14
Mapledurwell Hants 9 L3
Maplehurst W Susx 9 T8
Maplescombe Kent 10 G4
Mapleton Derbys 31 S16
Mapperley Derbys 23 S2
Mapperley Park C Nott 24 E2
Mapperton Dorset 6 K11
Mappleborough Green Warwks 23 N14
Mappleton E R Yk 37 U16
Mapplewell Barns 31 U6
Mappowder Dorset 7 N10
Marazanvose Cnwll 1 S9
Marazion Cnwll 1 P13
Marbury Ches E 22 E1
March Cambs 26 D9
March S Lans 45 M14
Marcham Oxon 16 D10
Marchamley Shrops 22 F4
Marchington Staffs 23 N4
Marchros Gwynd 28 D14
Marchwiel Wrexhm 29 T10
Marchwood Hants 8 G10
Marcross V Glam 13 U15
Marden Herefs 14 K2
Marden Kent 10 K8
Marden Wilts 7 T1
Marden Thorn Kent 10 K8
Mardy Mons 14 G7
Mareham le Fen Lincs 33 Q14
Mareham on the Hill Lincs 33 Q13
Marehill W Susx 9 R9
Maresfield E Susx 10 F11
Marfleet C KuH 33 N3
Marford Wrexhm 30 F15
Margam Neath 13 S12
Margaret Marsh Dorset 7 P8
Margaretting Essex 18 G13
Margaretting Tye Essex 18 H13
Margate Kent 11 U3
Margnaheglish N Ayrs 43 P11
Margrie D & G 38 K10
Margrove Park R & Cl 37 L4
Marham Norfk 26 H7
Marhamchurch Cnwll 4 F10
Marholm C Pete 25 N8
Mariansleigh Devon 5 N7
Marine Town Kent 11 M3
Marionburgh Abers 55 P14
Marishader Highld 59 f6
Maristow Devon 2 K5
Marjoriebanks D & G 39 S5
Mark Somset 6 H3
Markbeech Kent 10 F8
Markby Lincs 33 T11
Mark Cross E Susx 10 H10
Market Bosworth Leics 23 S8
Market Deeping Lincs 25 N7
Market Drayton Shrops 22 G3
Market Harborough Leics 24 H11
Market Lavington Wilts 7 S2
Market Overton Rutlnd 24 K6
Market Rasen Lincs 33 N9
Market Stainton Lincs 33 Q11
Market Warsop Notts 32 E13
Market Weighton E R Yk 32 K1
Market Weston Suffk 27 M12
Markfield Leics 24 D7
Markham Caerph 14 E10
Markham Moor Notts 32 G12
Markinch Fife 51 L15
Markington N York 36 F12
Markle E Loth 46 H4
Marksbury BaNES 15 M16
Marks Tey Essex 19 L9
Markyate Herts 17 N7
Marlborough Wilts 15 U15
Marlcliff Warwks 15 T2
Marldon Devon 3 Q5
Marlesford Suffk 19 S4
Marlingford Norfk 27 P7
Marloes Pembks 12 C9
Marlow Bucks 16 K12
Marlow Bottom Bucks 16 K12
Marlpit Hill Kent 10 F7
Marnhull Dorset 7 P8
Marple Stockp 31 P9
Marr Donc 32 D7
Marrick N York 36 C7
Marsden Kirk 31 Q6
Marsden S Tyne 41 R8
Marshalswick Herts 17 P9
Marsham Norfk 27 Q5
Marsh Baldon Oxon 16 F10
Marshborough Kent 11 T5
Marshbrook Shrops 21 S5
Marshchapel Lincs 33 R8
Marsh Farm Luton 17 N6
Marshfield Newpt 14 F13
Marshfield S Glos 15 N14
Marshgate Cnwll 4 E12
Marsh Gibbon Bucks 16 G6
Marsh Green Devon 5 T12
Marsh Green Kent 10 F8
Marshland St James Norfk 26 E7
Marsh Lane Derbys 32 C11
Marsh Street Somset 5 S3
Marshwood Dorset 6 H11
Marske N York 36 D7
Marske-by-the-Sea R & Cl 37 L3
Marston Herefs 21 Q11
Marston Lincs 24 K2
Marston Oxon 16 E8
Marston Staffs 22 K4
Marston Wilts 7 R1
Marston Green Solhll 23 P11
Marston Magna Somset 7 L7
Marston Meysey Wilts 15 T10
Marston Montgomery Derbys 23 N3
Marston Moretaine C Beds 17 M3
Marston on Dove Derbys 23 Q4
Marston St Lawrence Nhants 16 F3
Marston Trussell Nhants 24 G11
Marstow Herefs 14 K7
Marsworth Bucks 17 L8
Marten Wilts 8 F2
Martham Norfk 27 T6
Martin Hants 7 T7
Martin Kent 11 T7
Martin Lincs 33 N14
Martinhoe Devon 5 M3
Martin Hussingtree Worcs 22 K15
Martinstown Dorset 7 M12
Martlesham Suffk 19 R6
Martlesham Heath Suffk 19 R6
Martletwy Pembks 12 G8
Martley Worcs 22 H15
Martock Somset 6 J7
Marton Ches E 31 M13
Marton E R Yk 33 P1
Marton Lincs 32 J11
Marton Middsb 36 J4
Marton N York 36 H13
Marton N York 37 N9
Marton Shrops 21 P3
Marton Warwks 23 S14
Marton-le-Moor N York 36 G12
Martyr Worthy Hants 8 J6
Marwick Ork 58 a3
Marwood Devon 5 L4
Marybank Highld 53 P6
Maryburgh Highld 53 Q5
Maryculter Abers 55 R15
Marygold Border 47 L7
Maryhill C Glas 44 F5
Marykirk Abers 51 R5
Marylebone Gt Lon 17 R13
Marylebone Wigan 30 J6
Marypark Moray 54 F8
Maryport Cumb 39 R12
Maryport D & G 38 D13
Marystow Devon 4 J13
Mary Tavy Devon 4 K14
Maryton Angus 51 R6
Marywell Abers 55 M15
Marywell Abers 55 S15
Marywell Angus 51 R8
Masham N York 36 E10
Masongill N York 35 Q11
Mastin Moor Derbys 32 D12
Matching Green Essex 18 F11
Matching Tye Essex 18 E11
Matfen Nthumb 41 L7
Matfield Kent 10 J8
Mathern Mons 14 K11
Mathon Herefs 15 N2
Mathry Pembks 12 D5
Matlask Norfk 27 P3
Matlock Derbys 31 U14
Matlock Bath Derbys 31 U14
Matson Gloucs 15 P7
Mattersey Notts 32 G9
Mattingley Hants 9 M2
Mattishall Norfk 27 N7
Mattishall Burgh Norfk 27 N7
Mauchline E Ayrs 44 E12
Maud Abers 55 S7
Maufant Jersey 3 d2
Maugersbury Gloucs 15 U6
Maughold IoM 34 f3
Mauld Highld 53 N8
Maulden C Beds 17 N4
Maulds Meaburn Cumb 35 Q4
Maunby N York 36 G9
Maundown Somset 6 D6
Mautby Norfk 27 U7
Mavesyn Ridware Staffs 23 N6
Mavis Enderby Lincs 33 R13
Mawbray Cumb 39 S11
Mawdesley Lancs 30 G5
Mawdlam Brdgnd 13 S13
Mawgan Cnwll 1 R14
Mawgan Porth Cnwll 1 T7
Mawla Cnwll 1 R10
Mawnan Cnwll 1 S13
Mawnan Smith Cnwll 1 S13
Mawsley Nhants 24 J13
Maxey C Pete 25 N7
Maxstoke Warwks 23 Q11
Maxton Border 46 H12
Maxton Kent 11 T8
Maxwell Town D & G 39 Q6
Maxworthy Cnwll 4 G12
May Bank Staffs 22 J1
Maybole S Ayrs 43 S15
Maybury Surrey 9 R2
Mayfield E Susx 10 H10
Mayfield Mdloth 46 D6
Mayfield Staffs 23 P1
Mayford Surrey 9 R2
May Hill Gloucs 15 M7
Mayland Essex 19 L13
Maylandsea Essex 19 L13
Maynard's Green E Susx 10 H12
Maypole Green Norfk 27 T9
Maypole Green Suffk 19 L4
Meadgate BaNES 7 M1
Meadle Bucks 16 J9
Meadowfield Dur 41 P12
Meadwell Devon 4 J14
Meanwood Leeds 31 U1
Meare Somset 6 J4
Meare Green Somset 6 G7
Meare Green Somset 6 H6
Mearns E Rens 44 F8
Mears Ashby Nhants 24 J14
Measham Leics 23 R7
Meathop Cumb 35 M10
Meavy Devon 3 L5
Medbourne Leics 24 H10
Meddon Devon 4 G8
Meden Vale Notts 32 E13
Medmenham Bucks 16 J12
Medomsley Dur 41 N9
Medstead Hants 9 L5
Meerbrook Staffs 31 P14
Meesden Herts 18 D8
Meeth Devon 5 L9
Meeting House Hill Norfk 27 R4
Meidrim Carmth 12 K7
Meifod Powys 21 M2
Meigle P & K 51 L8
Meikle Carco D & G 44 J14
Meikle Earnock S Lans 44 H8
Meikle Kilmory Ag & B 43 P7
Meikle Obney P & K 50 G10
Meikleour P & K 50 J9
Meikle Wartle Abers 55 P10
Meinciau Carmth 13 N8
Meir C Stke 22 K2
Melbourn Cambs 17 S3
Melbourne Derbys 23 S5
Melbourne E R Yk 37 N16
Melbury Abbas Dorset 7 Q7
Melbury Bubb Dorset 7 L10
Melbury Osmond Dorset 7 L9
Melchbourne Bed 25 M14
Melcombe Bingham Dorset 7 N10
Meldon Devon 5 L12
Meldon Nthumb 41 N5
Meldreth Cambs 17 S2
Meldrum Stirlg 50 C16
Melfort Ag & B 48 J13
Meliden Denbgs 29 P5
Melin-y-wig Denbgs 29 P10
Melkinthorpe Cumb 40 E14
Melkridge Nthumb 40 G8
Melksham Wilts 15 Q16
Melling Lancs 35 P11
Melling Sefton 30 F8
Mellis Suffk 27 N13
Mellon Charles Highld 56 D15
Mellon Udrigle Highld 56 E14
Mellor Lancs 30 K3
Mellor Stockp 31 P9
Mellor Brook Lancs 30 J2
Mells Somset 7 N3
Melmerby Cumb 40 E12
Melmerby N York 36 C9
Melmerby N York 36 G11
Melness Highld 57 P3
Melplash Dorset 6 K11
Melrose Border 46 G11
Melsetter Ork 58 b5
Melsonby N York 36 E5
Meltham Kirk 31 R6
Melton E R Yk 33 L3
Melton Suffk 19 R5
Melton Constable Norfk 27 N3
Melton Mowbray Leics 24 H6
Melton Ross N Linc 33 M6
Melvaig Highld 56 B16
Melverley Shrops 29 T15
Melvich Highld 57 T3
Membury Devon 6 G10
Memsie Abers 55 S4
Memus Angus 51 N6
Menai Bridge IoA 28 G6
Mendham Suffk 27 R12
Mendlesham Suffk 27 P14
Mendlesham Green Suffk 19 N3
Menheniot Cnwll 2 G6
Mennock D & G 44 J15
Menston C Brad 36 E16
Menstrie Clacks 50 D16
Mentmore Bucks 17 L7
Meoble Highld 48 J1
Meole Brace Shrops 22 D7
Meonstoke Hants 8 K8
Meopham Kent 10 H4
Mepal Cambs 26 D12
Meppershall C Beds 17 P4
Mere Ches E 31 L11
Mere Wilts 7 P5
Mere Brow Lancs 30 F5
Mereclough Lancs 31 N3
Mereworth Kent 10 J6
Meriden Solhll 23 Q12
Merkadale Highld 59 d11
Merley Poole 7 S11
Merrion Pembks 12 E10
Merriott Somset 6 J9
Merrow Surrey 9 R3
Merry Hill Herts 17 P11
Merryhill Wolves 22 K9
Merrymeet Cnwll 2 G5
Mersham Kent 11 P8
Merstham Surrey 10 C6
Merston W Susx 9 P11
Merstone IoW 8 J14
Merthyr Cynog Powys 14 B4
Merthyr Mawr Brdgnd 13 U14
Merthyr Tydfil Myr Td 14 C9
Merthyr Vale Myr Td 14 C10
Merton Devon 4 K9
Merton Gt Lon 10 C3
Merton Norfk 27 L9
Merton Oxon 16 F7
Meshaw Devon 5 P7
Messing Essex 19 L10
Messingham N Linc 32 K7
Metfield Suffk 27 R12
Metherell Cnwll 2 J4
Metheringham Lincs 33 M14
Methil Fife 51 M16
Methilhill Fife 51 M16
Methlick Abers 55 R8
Methven P & K 50 G11
Methwold Norfk 26 H10
Methwold Hythe Norfk 26 H10
Mettingham Suffk 27 S10
Metton Norfk 27 Q3
Mevagissey Cnwll 2 C9
Mexborough Donc 32 D8
Mey Highld 58 H2
Meyllteyrn Gwynd 28 B13
Meysey Hampton Gloucs 15 T10
Miabhig W Isls 56 d2
Miavaig W Isls 56 d2
Michaelchurch Herefs 14 K6
Michaelchurch Escley Herefs 14 G4
Michaelstone-y-Fedw Newpt 14 F13
Michaelston-le-Pit V Glam 14 D14
Michaelstow Cnwll 2 D3
Micheldever Hants 8 J5
Micheldever Station Hants 8 J5
Michelmersh Hants 8 F7
Mickfield Suffk 19 P3
Micklebring Donc 32 E8
Mickleby N York 37 P5
Micklefield Leeds 32 C2
Mickleham Surrey 9 T3
Mickleover C Derb 23 R3
Mickleton Dur 36 B3
Mickleton Gloucs 15 U3
Mickletown Leeds 32 C3
Mickle Trafford Ches W 30 G13
Mickley N York 36 F10
Mickley Square Nthumb 41 M8
Mid Ardlaw Abers 55 S4
Midbea Ork 58 c2
Mid Beltie Abers 55 N14
Mid Calder W Loth 45 N5
Mid Clyth Highld 58 H7
Mid Culbeuchly Abers 55 N4
Middle Aston Oxon 16 E6
Middle Barton Oxon 16 D6
Middlebie D & G 39 U6
Middlebridge P & K 50 E5
Middle Chinnock Somset 6 J8
Middle Claydon Bucks 16 H6
Middleham N York 36 D9
Middle Handley Derbys 32 C11
Middlehill Wilts 15 P15
Middlehope Shrops 22 D11
Middle Kames Ag & B 43 M2
Middle Littleton Worcs 15 T2
Middlemarsh Dorset 7 M9
Middle Mayfield Staffs 23 N1
Middle Rasen Lincs 33 N9
Middle Rocombe Devon 3 R4
Middlesbrough Middsb 36 J4
Middleshaw Cumb 35 P9
Middlesmoor N York 36 D11
Middle Stoke Medway 11 L2
Middlestone Dur 41 P13
Middlestown Wakefd 31 T5
Middlethird Border 46 J9
Middleton Ag & B 42 a4
Middleton Derbys 31 S14
Middleton Derbys 31 T15
Middleton Essex 18 K7
Middleton Hants 8 H4
Middleton Herefs 22 E14
Middleton Leeds 31 U3
Middleton N York 36 D15
Middleton N York 37 N9
Middleton Nhants 24 J10
Middleton Norfk 26 G6
Middleton Nthumb 41 M4
Middleton P & K 50 H15
Middleton Rochdl 31 N7
Middleton Shrops 22 E12
Middleton Suffk 27 T14
Middleton Swans 13 M12
Middleton Warwks 23 P9
Middleton Cheney Nhants 16 E3
Middleton-in-Teesdale Dur 40 K14
Middleton Moor Suffk 27 T14
Middleton One Row Darltn 36 G5
Middleton-on-Sea W Susx 9 Q12
Middleton on the Hill Herefs 22 E14
Middleton on the Wolds E R Yk 37 R15
Middleton Park C Aber 55 S13
Middleton Quernhow N York 36 G10
Middleton St George Darltn 36 G5
Middleton Scriven Shrops 22 G11
Middleton Stoney Oxon 16 F6
Middleton Tyas N York 36 E6
Middle Town IoS 1 b2
Middletown Powys 21 Q2
Middle Tysoe Warwks 16 C3
Middle Wallop Hants 8 F5
Middlewich Ches E 30 K13
Middle Winterslow Wilts 8 E6
Middlewood Cnwll 2 G4
Middle Woodford Wilts 8 C6
Middlewood Green Suffk 19 N3
Middleyard E Ayrs 44 E11
Middlezoy Somset 6 H5
Midford BaNES 15 N16
Midgham W Berk 16 F15
Midgley Calder 31 Q3
Midgley Wakefd 31 T5
Midhopestones Sheff 31 T8
Midhurst W Susx 9 P8
Mid Lavant W Susx 9 P10
Midlem Border 46 G12
Mid Mains Highld 53 N8
Midpark Ag & B 43 N7
Midsomer Norton BaNES 7 M2
Midtown Highld 57 P3
Mid Yell Shet 59 r3
Migvie Abers 54 K14
Milborne Port Somset 7 M8
Milborne St Andrew Dorset 7 P11
Milborne Wick Somset 7 M7
Milbourne Nthumb 41 N6
Milbourne Wilts 15 R12
Milburn Cumb 40 F13
Milbury Heath S Glos 15 M12
Milby N York 36 H12
Milcombe Oxon 16 D4
Milden Suffk 19 L6
Mildenhall Suffk 26 H13
Mildenhall Wilts 15 U15
Mileham Norfk 27 L5
Mile Oak Br & H 10 C14
Milesmark Fife 45 N2
Miles Platting Manch 31 N8
Mile Town Kent 11 M3
Milfield Nthumb 47 N11
Milford Derbys 23 R1
Milford Devon 4 F7
Milford Staffs 23 L5
Milford Surrey 9 Q5
Milford Haven Pembks 12 E9
Milford on Sea Hants 8 F13
Milkwall Gloucs 14 K8
Milland W Susx 9 N7
Mill Bank Calder 31 Q4
Millbreck Abers 55 T7
Millbridge Surrey 9 N5
Millbrook C Beds 17 M4
Millbrook C Sotn 8 G9
Millbrook Cnwll 2 J7
Millbrook Jersey 3 c3
Mill Brow Stockp 31 P9
Millbuie Abers 55 Q13
Millbuie Highld 53 Q6
Millcorner E Susx 11 L11
Millcraig Highld 53 S3
Milldale Staffs 31 R15
Mill End Bucks 16 J12
Mill End Herts 17 S5
Millerhill Mdloth 45 S5
Miller's Dale Derbys 31 S12
Millerston C Glas 44 G5
Mill Green Cambs 18 G6
Mill Green Essex 18 G13
Mill Green Lincs 25 P5
Mill Green Suffk 19 L6
Mill Green Suffk 19 M4
Mill Green Suffk 19 P3
Millhalf Herefs 21 P12
Millheugh S Lans 44 J8
Mill Hill Gt Lon 17 Q11
Millhouse Ag & B 43 M5
Millhousebridge D & G 39 S4
Millhouse Green Barns 31 T7
Millhouses Sheff 32 B10
Milliken Park Rens 44 D6
Millington E R Yk 37 P15
Millmeece Staffs 22 J3
Mill of Drummond P & K 50 D13
Mill of Haldane W Duns 44 D3
Millom Cumb 34 H10
Millport N Ayrs 43 Q8
Mill Street Suffk 27 N13
Millthrop Cumb 35 Q8
Milltimber C Aber 55 R14
Milltown Abers 54 G13
Milltown Abers 54 K12
Milltown D & G 40 B6
Milltown Devon 5 L4
Milltown of Campfield Abers 55 N15
Milltown of Edinvillie Moray 54 G8
Milltown of Learney Abers 55 N14
Milnathort P & K 50 H15
Milngavie E Duns 44 F4
Milnrow Rochdl 31 N5
Milnthorpe Cumb 35 N10
Milovaig Highld 59 a8
Milson Shrops 22 F13
Milstead Kent 11 M5
Milston Wilts 8 D4
Milthorpe Nhants 16 F2
Milton Cambs 18 E3
Milton Cumb 40 E8
Milton D & G 38 E9
Milton D & G 39 P7
Milton Derbys 23 R4
Milton Highld 52 C7
Milton Highld 53 P10
Milton Highld 53 R6
Milton Highld 53 T2

Milton Highld 58 H5
Milton Inver 44 C5
Milton Kent 10 J3
Milton Moray 54 F11
Milton Moray 55 L4
Milton N Som 14 G16
Milton Notts 32 G12
Milton Oxon 16 D4
Milton Oxon 16 E11
Milton P & K 50 H6
Milton Pembks 12 G9
Milton Somset 6 J7
Milton Stirlg 49 U15
Milton W Duns 44 D4
Milton Abbas Dorset 7 P10
Milton Abbot Devon 4 J14
Milton Bridge Mdloth 45 R6
Milton Bryan C Beds 17 M5
Milton Clevedon Somset 7 M5
Milton Combe Devon 2 K5
Milton Damerel Devon 4 H9
Milton Ernest Bed 25 L16
Milton Green Ches W 30 G14
Milton Hill Oxon 16 E12
Milton Keynes M Keyn 16 K4
Milton Lilbourne Wilts 8 D2
Milton Malsor Nhants 24 H16
Milton Morenish P & K 50 A10
Milton of Auchinhove Abers 55 L14
Milton of Balgonie Fife 51 L16
Milton of Buchanan Stirlg 44 D2
Milton of Campsie E Duns 44 G4
Milton of Leys Highld 53 S8
Milton of Murtle C Aber 55 R14
Milton of Tullich Abers 54 J15
Milton on Stour Dorset 7 P6
Milton Regis Kent 11 M4
Milton-under-Wychwood Oxon 16 B7
Milverton Somset 6 E6
Milverton Warwks 23 R14
Milwich Staffs 23 L3
Minard Ag & B 43 N1
Minchinhampton Gloucs 15 Q10
Minehead Somset 5 S3
Minera Wrexhm 30 D15
Minety Wilts 15 S11
Minffordd Gwynd 28 G12
Mingarrypark Highld 48 G4
Miningsby Lincs 33 R13
Minions Cnwll 2 G4
Minishant S Ayrs 43 T14
Minllyn Gwynd 20 H1
Minnigaff D & G 38 H7
Minnonie Abers 55 Q5
Minskip N York 36 H13
Minstead Hants 8 E10
Minsted W Susx 9 P8
Minster Kent 11 N3
Minster Kent 11 T4
Minsterley Shrops 21 R3
Minster Lovell Oxon 16 C8
Minsterworth Gloucs 15 N7
Minterne Magna Dorset 7 M10
Minting Lincs 33 P12
Mintlaw Abers 55 T7
Minto Border 46 G13
Minton Shrops 21 R5
Mirehouse Cumb 34 F4
Mireland Highld 58 H4
Mirfield Kirk 31 S4
Miserden Gloucs 15 Q8
Miskin Rhondd 14 C13
Misson Notts 32 G8
Misterton Leics 24 E11
Misterton Notts 32 H8
Misterton Somset 6 J9
Mistley Essex 19 P8
Mitcham Gt Lon 10 C4
Mitcheldean Gloucs 15 M7
Mitchell Cnwll 1 T9
Mitchellslacks D & G 39 Q3
Mitchel Troy Mons 14 J8
Mitford Nthumb 41 N4
Mithian Cnwll 1 S9
Mixbury Oxon 16 G4
Mobberley Ches E 31 M11
Mobberley Staffs 23 L2
Mochdre Powys 21 L6
Mochrum D & G 38 G11
Mockbeggar Kent 10 J7
Mockerkin Cumb 34 G3
Modbury Devon 3 M7
Moddershall Staffs 22 K3
Moelfre IoA 28 F4
Moelfre Powys 29 R14
Moffat D & G 45 N16
Moggerhanger C Beds 17 P2
Moira Leics 23 R6
Molash Kent 11 P6
Mol-chlach Highld 59 e13
Mold Flints 29 R8
Moldgreen Kirk 31 S5
Molehill Green Essex 18 F9
Molescroft E R Yk 33 M1
Molesworth Cambs 25 M13
Molland Devon 5 P6
Mollington Ches W 30 F12
Mollington Oxon 16 D2
Mollinsburn N Lans 44 H5
Mondynes Abers 51 S3
Monewden Suffk 19 Q4
Moneydie P & K 50 G11
Moniaive D & G 39 N3
Monifieth Angus 51 N10
Monikie Angus 51 P9
Monimail Fife 51 L13
Monken Hadley Gt Lon 17 R10
Monk Fryston N York 32 D3
Monkhide Herefs 15 L3
Monkhill Cumb 40 B9
Monkhopton Shrops 22 F10
Monkland Herefs 21 S11
Monkleigh Devon 4 J7
Monknash V Glam 13 U15
Monkokehampton Devon 5 L10
Monkseaton N Tyne 41 R6
Monks Eleigh Suffk 19 M5
Monk's Gate W Susx 9 T7
Monks Heath Ches E 31 M12
Monk Sherborne Hants 8 K2
Monksilver Somset 6 D4
Monks Kirby Warwks 24 D11
Monk Soham Suffk 27 Q14
Monks Risborough Bucks 16 J9
Monksthorpe Lincs 33 T13
Monk Street Essex 18 G8
Monkswood Mons 14 G9
Monkton Devon 6 E10
Monkton Kent 11 T4
Monkton S Ayrs 44 C12
Monkton S Tyne 41 Q8
Monkton Combe BaNES 15 N16
Monkton Deverill Wilts 7 Q5
Monkton Farleigh Wilts 15 P16
Monkton Heathfield Somset 6 F6
Monkton Wyld Dorset 6 H11
Monkwearmouth Sundld 41 R9
Monkwood Hants 9 L7
Monmore Green Wolves 22 K9
Monmouth Mons 14 J8
Monnington on Wye Herefs 21 R13
Monreith D & G 38 G12
Montacute Somset 6 K8
Montford Shrops 21 R1
Montford Bridge Shrops 22 C6
Montgarrie Abers 55 M12
Montgomery Powys 21 N4
Montrose Angus 51 S6
Mont Saint Guern 2 b3
Monxton Hants 8 F4
Monyash Derbys 31 S13
Monymusk Abers 55 N12
Monzie P & K 50 E12
Moodiesburn N Lans 44 H5
Moonzie Fife 51 L13
Moor Allerton Leeds 31 U1
Moorby Lincs 33 Q13
Moor Crichel Dorset 7 S9
Moordown Bmouth 7 T11
Moore Halton 30 J10
Moor End Calder 31 Q3
Moorends Donc 32 G5
Moorhead C Brad 31 R1
Moorhouse Cumb 40 A9
Moorhouse Notts 32 H13
Moorhouse Bank Surrey 10 E6
Moorlinch Somset 6 H5
Moor Monkton N York 36 J14
Moorsholm R & Cl 37 M4
Moorside Dorset 7 P7
Moorswater Cnwll 2 F5
Moorthorpe Wakefd 32 D6
Moortown Leeds 31 U1
Moortown Lincs 33 M8
Morangie Highld 53 T1
Morar Highld 52 C16
Morborne Cambs 25 N10
Morchard Bishop Devon 5 P9
Morcombelake Dorset 6 H12
Morcott Rutlnd 24 K9
Morda Shrops 29 S14
Morden Dorset 7 R11
Morden Gt Lon 10 C4
Mordiford Herefs 14 K4
Mordon Dur 41 Q14
More Shrops 21 Q5
Morebath Devon 5 R7
Morebattle Border 46 K12
Morecambe Lancs 35 M13
Moredon Swindn 15 T12
Morefield Highld 56 H14
Morehall Kent 11 R9
Moreleigh Devon 3 P7
Morenish P & K 50 A10
Morestead Hants 8 J7
Moreton Dorset 7 P12
Moreton Essex 18 F12
Moreton Herefs 22 D15
Moreton Oxon 16 H9
Moreton Wirral 29 S3
Moreton Corbet Shrops 22 E5
Moretonhampstead Devon 5 P13
Moreton-in-Marsh Gloucs 15 U5
Moreton Jeffries Herefs 15 L2
Moreton Morrell Warwks 23 R16
Moreton on Lugg Herefs 14 J2
Moreton Pinkney Nhants 16 F2
Moreton Say Shrops 22 F3
Moreton Valence Gloucs 15 N8
Morfa Nefyn Gwynd 28 C12
Morham E Loth 46 G5
Morland Cumb 35 P3
Morley Ches E 31 M10
Morley Derbys 23 S2
Morley Leeds 31 T3
Morley Green Ches E 31 M11
Morley St Botolph Norfk 27 N9
Morningside C Edin 45 R5
Morningside N Lans 44 K7
Morningthorpe Norfk 27 Q10
Morpeth Nthumb 41 P4
Morphie Abers 51 S5
Morrey Staffs 23 N6
Morriston Swans 13 Q10
Morston Norfk 27 M2
Mortehoe Devon 4 J3
Morthen Rothm 32 D9
Mortimer W Berk 16 G16
Mortimer West End Hants 8 K1
Mortlake Gt Lon 17 Q14
Morton Cumb 40 B9
Morton Derbys 32 C14
Morton Lincs 25 N5
Morton Lincs 32 J9
Morton Notts 32 G16
Morton Shrops 29 S14
Morton-on-Swale N York 36 G8
Morton on the Hill Norfk 27 P6
Morvah Cnwll 1 M12
Morvich Highld 52 G11
Morville Shrops 22 G10
Morwenstow Cnwll 4 F8
Mosborough Sheff 32 C11
Moscow E Ayrs 44 E10
Moseley Birm 23 M11
Moseley Wolves 23 L9
Moseley Worcs 22 J15
Moss Ag & B 42 b4
Moss Donc 32 F5
Mossat Abers 54 K11
Mossbank Shet 59 q4
Moss Bank St Hel 30 H8
Mossbay Cumb 39 R14
Mossblown S Ayrs 44 D12
Mossburnford Border 46 J14
Mossdale D & G 39 L7
Mossdale E Ayrs 38 J1
Moss Edge Lancs 35 M16
Mossend N Lans 44 J7
Mossley Tamesd 31 P7
Mosspaul Hotel Border 40 B2
Moss-side Highld 54 B6
Mosstodloch Moray 54 H5
Mossyard D & G 38 K10
Mossy Lea Lancs 30 H6
Mosterton Dorset 6 J10
Moston Manch 31 N7
Mostyn Flints 29 Q5
Motcombe Dorset 7 Q6
Mothecombe Devon 3 M8
Motherby Cumb 40 C14
Motherwell N Lans 44 J7
Motspur Park Gt Lon 10 C4
Mottingham Gt Lon 10 E3
Mottisfont Hants 8 F7
Mottistone IoW 8 G14
Mottram in Longdendale Tamesd 31 P8
Mottram St Andrew Ches E 31 N11
Mouldsworth Ches W 30 H12
Moulin P & K 50 F6
Moulsecoomb Br & H 10 D14
Moulsford Oxon 16 F13
Moulsoe M Keyn 17 L3
Moultavie Highld 53 R3
Moulton Ches W 30 K13
Moulton Lincs 25 R5
Moulton N York 36 F6
Moulton Nhants 24 H14
Moulton Suffk 18 H3
Moulton V Glam 14 C15
Moulton Chapel Lincs 25 Q6
Moulton St Mary Norfk 27 T7
Moulton Seas End Lincs 25 R4
Mount Cnwll 2 E5
Mountain C Brad 31 R2
Mountain Ash Rhondd 14 C10
Mountain Cross Border 45 P9
Mount Ambrose Cnwll 1 R11
Mount Bures Essex 19 L8
Mountfield E Susx 10 K12
Mountgerald House Highld 53 Q5
Mount Hawke Cnwll 1 R10
Mountjoy Cnwll 1 U8
Mount Lothian Mdloth 45 R7
Mountnessing Essex 18 G14
Mounton Mons 14 J11
Mount Pleasant Derbys 32 B16
Mount Pleasant Suffk 18 H5
Mountsorrel Leics 24 E6
Mount Tabor Calder 31 Q3
Mousehill Surrey 9 Q5
Mousehole Cnwll 1 N13
Mouswald D & G 39 S6
Mow Cop Ches E 31 M15
Mowhaugh Border 47 L13
Mowsley Leics 24 F11
Moy Highld 49 T2
Moy Highld 53 T9
Moyle Highld 52 F12
Moylegrove Pembks 12 H3
Muasdale Ag & B 42 J10
Muchalls Abers 55 R16
Much Birch Herefs 14 J5
Much Cowarne Herefs 15 L2
Much Dewchurch Herefs 14 J5
Muchelney Somset 6 J7
Muchelney Ham Somset 6 J7
Much Hadham Herts 18 D10
Much Hoole Lancs 30 G4
Muchlarnick Cnwll 2 F7
Much Marcle Herefs 15 L5
Much Wenlock Shrops 22 F9
Mucklestone Staffs 22 G3
Muckton Lincs 33 S11
Muddiford Devon 5 L4
Muddles Green E Susx 10 G13
Mudeford Dorset 8 D13
Mudford Somset 7 L7
Mudford Sock Somset 7 L8
Mugdock Stirlg 44 F4
Mugeary Highld 59 e10
Mugginton Derbys 23 Q2
Muirden Abers 55 P6
Muirdrum Angus 51 P10
Muiresk Abers 55 N7
Muirhead Angus 51 L10
Muirhead Fife 51 L15
Muirhead N Lans 44 H5
Muirkirk E Ayrs 44 H12
Muirmill Stirlg 44 H3
Muir of Fowlis Abers 55 M13
Muir of Miltonduff Moray 54 F5
Muir of Ord Highld 53 Q6
Muirshearlich Highld 49 P2
Muirtack Abers 55 T8
Muirton P & K 50 E14
Muirton Mains Highld 53 P6
Muirton of Ardblair P & K 50 J9
Muker N York 35 U7
Mulbarton Norfk 27 Q9
Mulben Moray 54 J6
Mullion Cnwll 1 R15
Mullion Cove Cnwll 1 R15
Mumby Lincs 33 U12
Munderfield Row Herefs 15 L1
Munderfield Stocks Herefs 15 L2
Mundesley Norfk 27 R3
Mundford Norfk 26 J10
Mundham Norfk 27 S9
Mundon Hill Essex 18 K13
Mungrisdale Cumb 40 B13
Munlochy Highld 53 S6
Munnoch N Ayrs 43 S9
Munsley Herefs 15 M3
Munslow Shrops 22 E11
Murchington Devon 5 N13
Murcott Oxon 16 F7
Murkle Highld 58 F2
Murlaggan Highld 52 H16
Murroes Angus 51 N10
Murrow Cambs 25 S7
Mursley Bucks 16 K5
Murthill Angus 51 N6
Murthly P & K 50 H9
Murton C York 37 L14
Murton Cumb 35 R3
Murton Dur 41 R11
Murton Nthumb 47 N9
Musbury Devon 6 G11
Musselburgh E Loth 46 D5
Muston Leics 24 J2
Muston N York 37 T10
Muswell Hill Gt Lon 17 R12
Mutehill D & G 39 M10
Mutford Suffk 27 U11
Muthill P & K 50 E13
Mybster Highld 58 F5
Myddfai Carmth 13 S5
Myddle Shrops 22 D5
Mydroilyn Cerdgn 20 C11
Mylor Cnwll 1 T12
Mylor Bridge Cnwll 1 T12
Mynachlog ddu Pembks 12 H5
Mynydd-bach Mons 14 J11
Mynydd-Bach Swans 13 Q10
Mynyddgarreg Carmth 13 M9
Mynydd Isa Flints 29 S8
Myrebird Abers 55 P15
Myredykes Border 40 E2
Mytchett Surrey 9 P3
Mytholm Calder 31 P3
Mytholmroyd Calder 31 Q3
Myton-on-Swale N York 36 H12

N

Naast Highld 52 E1
Na Buirgh W Isls 56 c4
Naburn C York 37 L16
Nackington Kent 11 R6
Nacton Suffk 19 Q7
Nafferton E R Yk 37 S13
Nailsbourne Somset 6 F6
Nailsea N Som 14 J15
Nailstone Leics 23 S8
Nailsworth Gloucs 15 P10
Nairn Highld 54 B5
Nannerch Flints 29 Q7
Nanpantan Leics 24 D6
Nanpean Cnwll 2 B7
Nanstallon Cnwll 2 D5
Nanternis Cerdgn 20 B11
Nantgaredig Carmth 13 N6
Nantglyn Denbgs 29 N8
Nantmel Powys 21 L9
Nantmor Gwynd 28 H11
Nant Peris Gwynd 28 H9
Nantwich Ches E 30 K15
Nantyglo Blae G 14 E8
Nant-y-moel Brdgnd 13 U11
Naphill Bucks 16 K10
Napton on the Hill Warwks 24 D15
Narberth Pembks 12 H7
Narborough Leics 24 E9
Narborough Norfk 26 J7
Nasareth Gwynd 28 F10
Naseby Nhants 24 G12
Nash Bucks 16 J4
Nash Newpt 14 G13
Nash Shrops 22 F13
Nassington Nhants 25 M9
Nateby Cumb 35 S6
Nateby Lancs 35 N16
Natland Cumb 35 N9
Naughton Suffk 19 M5
Naunton Gloucs 15 T6
Naunton Worcs 15 Q3
Naunton Beauchamp Worcs 15 R1
Navenby Lincs 33 L14
Navestock Essex 18 F14
Navestock Side Essex 18 F14
Navidale House Hotel Highld 58 D11
Navity Highld 53 T4
Nawton N York 37 L9
Nayland Suffk 19 M8
Nazeing Essex 18 D12
Neap Shet 59 r5
Near Cotton Staffs 23 M1
Near Sawrey Cumb 35 L7
Neasden Gt Lon 17 Q12
Neasham Darltn 36 G5
Neath Neath 13 S10
Neatham Hants 9 M5
Neatishead Norfk 27 S5
Nebo Cerdgn 20 D10
Nebo Conwy 29 L9
Nebo Gwynd 28 F10
Nebo IoA 28 F3
Necton Norfk 26 K7
Nedd Highld 56 H8
Nedging Suffk 19 M5
Nedging Tye Suffk 19 M5
Needham Norfk 27 Q12
Needham Market Suffk 19 N4
Needingworth Cambs 25 R13
Neen Savage Shrops 22 G12
Neen Sollars Shrops 22 G13
Neenton Shrops 22 F11
Nefyn Gwynd 28 C12
Neilston E Rens 44 E7
Nelson Caerph 14 D11
Nelson Lancs 31 N1
Nemphlar S Lans 44 K9
Nempnett Thrubwell BaNES 6 K1
Nenthead Cumb 40 H11
Nenthorn Border 46 J10
Nercwys Flints 29 R8
Nereabolls Ag & B 42 B7
Nerston S Lans 44 G7
Nesbit Nthumb 47 N11
Nesfield N York 36 D15
Nesscliffe Shrops 22 C6
Neston Ches W 30 E11
Neston Wilts 15 P15
Netchwood Shrops 22 F10
Nether Alderley Ches E 31 M11
Netheravon Wilts 8 D4
Nether Blainslie Border 46 G9
Netherbrae Abers 55 Q5
Nether Broughton Leics 24 G4
Netherburn S Lans 44 J9
Netherbury Dorset 6 J11
Netherby N York 36 G15
Nether Cerne Dorset 7 M11
Nethercleuch D & G 39 T4
Nether Compton Dorset 7 L8
Nether Crimond Abers 55 Q11
Nether Dallachy Moray 54 J4
Netherend Gloucs 15 L10
Netherfield E Susx 10 J12
Nether Fingland S Lans 45 L15
Netherhampton Wilts 8 C7
Nether Handwick Angus 51 M9
Nether Haugh Rothm 32 C8
Netherhay Dorset 6 J10
Nether Headon Notts 32 H11
Nether Heage Derbys 32 B16
Nether Heyford Nhants 24 G16
Nether Howcleugh S Lans 45 N14
Nether Kellet Lancs 35 N12
Nether Kinmundy Abers 55 T7
Nether Langwith Notts 32 E12
Netherlaw D & G 39 M11
Netherley Abers 55 R16
Nethermill D & G 39 S4
Nethermuir Abers 55 R7
Netherne-on-the-Hill Surrey 10 D6
Netheroyd Hill Kirk 31 S4
Nether Padley Derbys 31 T11
Netherplace E Rens 44 E7
Nether Poppleton C York 36 K14
Netherseal Derbys 23 Q7
Nether Silton N York 36 J8
Nether Stowey Somset 6 E4
Netherthong Kirk 31 R6
Netherton Angus 51 P6
Netherton Devon 3 Q4
Netherton Dudley 23 L11
Netherton Kirk 31 R5
Netherton N Lans 44 J8
Netherton Nthumb 47 N15
Netherton P & K 50 J7
Netherton Stirlg 44 F3
Netherton Wakefd 31 U5
Nethertown Cumb 34 F6
Nethertown Highld 58 H1
Nethertown Staffs 23 N6
Netherurd Border 45 P9
Nether Wallop Hants 8 F6
Nether Wasdale Cumb 34 H6
Nether Westcote Gloucs 15 U7
Nether Whitacre Warwks 23 Q10
Nether Whitecleuch S Lans 44 K13
Nether Winchendon Bucks 16 H8
Netherwitton Nthumb 41 M3
Nethy Bridge Highld 54 D11
Netley Hants 8 H10
Netley Marsh Hants 8 F9
Nettlebed Oxon 16 H12
Nettlebridge Somset 7 M3
Nettlecombe Dorset 6 K11
Nettleden Herts 17 M8
Nettleham Lincs 33 L12
Nettlestead Kent 10 J6
Nettlestead Green Kent 10 J7
Nettlestone IoW 8 K13
Nettlesworth Dur 41 P10
Nettleton Lincs 33 N8
Nettleton Wilts 15 P13
Netton Wilts 8 C6
Nevern Pembks 12 G3
Nevill Holt Leics 24 J10
New Abbey D & G 39 Q7
New Aberdour Abers 55 R4
New Addington Gt Lon 10 E5
Newall Leeds 36 E16
New Alresford Hants 8 K6
New Alyth P & K 50 K8
Newark Ork 58 e2
Newark-on-Trent Notts 32 H15
Newarthill N Lans 44 J7
New Ash Green Kent 10 H4
New Balderton Notts 32 J15
New Barn Kent 10 H4
New Barnet Gt Lon 17 R11
Newbattle Mdloth 45 S6
New Bewick Nthumb 47 P13
Newbie D & G 39 T8
Newbiggin Cumb 40 C14
Newbiggin Cumb 40 E10
Newbiggin Cumb 40 F14
Newbiggin Dur 40 K14
Newbiggin N York 36 B9
Newbiggin-by-the-Sea Nthumb 41 Q4
Newbigging Angus 51 L9
Newbigging Angus 51 M10
Newbigging Angus 51 P10
Newbigging S Lans 45 M9
Newbiggin-on-Lune Cumb 35 R6
New Bilton Warwks 24 D13
Newbold Derbys 32 B12
Newbold on Avon Warwks 24 D12
Newbold on Stour Warwks 16 B2
Newbold Pacey Warwks 23 R16
Newbold Verdon Leics 24 D8
New Bolingbroke Lincs 33 R15
Newborough C Pete 25 P8
Newborough IoA 28 E7
Newborough Staffs 23 N5
New Boultham Lincs 33 L12
Newbourne Suffk 19 R6
New Bradwell M Keyn 16 K3
New Brampton Derbys 32 B12
New Brancepeth Dur 41 P12
Newbridge C Edin 45 P5
Newbridge Caerph 14 E10
Newbridge Cnwll 1 M13
Newbridge D & G 39 Q5
Newbridge Hants 8 F9
Newbridge IoW 8 G14
Newbridge Green Worcs 15 P3
Newbridge on Wye Powys 21 L11
New Brighton Wirral 30 E9
Newbrough Nthumb 40 J7
New Buckenham Norfk 27 N10
Newbuildings Devon 5 P10
Newburgh Abers 55 S5
Newburgh Abers 55 T10
Newburgh Fife 50 K13
Newburgh Lancs 30 G6
Newburgh Priory N York 36 K11
Newburn N u Ty 41 N8
Newbury Somset 7 N2
Newbury W Berk 16 E15
Newbury Park Gt Lon 18 D15
Newby Cumb 35 P3
Newby Lancs 35 T16
Newby N York 35 R12
Newby N York 36 J5
Newby Bridge Cumb 35 L9
Newby East Cumb 40 D9
New Byth Abers 55 Q6
Newby West Cumb 40 B9
Newcastle Mons 14 J7
Newcastle Shrops 21 P7
Newcastle Airport Nthumb 41 N7
Newcastle Emlyn Carmth 12 K3
Newcastleton Border 40 D4
Newcastle-under-Lyme Staffs 22 J1
Newcastle upon Tyne N u Ty 41 P8
Newchapel Pembks 12 J3
Newchapel Surrey 10 E8
Newchurch IoW 8 J14
Newchurch Kent 11 P10
Newchurch Mons 14 J10
Newchurch Powys 21 N12
Newchurch Staffs 23 N5
New Costessey Norfk 27 Q7
Newcraighall C Edin 45 S5
New Crofton Wakefd 32 C5
New Cross Gt Lon 17 S14
New Cross Somset 6 J7
New Cumnock E Ayrs 44 G14
New Deer Abers 55 R7
New Denham Bucks 17 N12
Newdigate Surrey 9 T5
New Duston Nhants 24 G15
New Earswick C York 37 L14
New Edlington Donc 32 E8
New Elgin Moray 54 G5
New Ellerby E R Yk 33 P1
Newell Green Br For 16 K15
New Eltham Gt Lon 10 F3
New End Worcs 23 M15
Newenden Kent 11 L10
New England C Pete 25 P9
Newent Gloucs 15 M6
Newfield Dur 41 P13
Newfield Highld 53 T2
New Fletton C Pete 25 P9
Newgale Pembks 12 D6
New Galloway D & G 39 L6
Newgate Street Herts 17 R9
New Gilston Fife 51 N14
New Grimsby IoS 1 b1
Newhall Ches E 22 F1
New Hartley Nthumb 41 Q6
Newhaven C Edin 45 R4
Newhaven E Susx 10 F15
New Haw Surrey 9 R1
New Hedges Pembks 12 H10
New Holland N Linc 33 M4
Newholm N York 37 P5
New Houghton Derbys 32 D13
New Houghton Norfk 26 J4
Newhouse N Lans 44 J6
New Hutton Cumb 35 P8
Newick E Susx 10 E11
Newington Kent 11 M4
Newington Kent 11 R9
Newington Oxon 16 G10
New Inn Carmth 13 N4
New Inn Torfn 14 G10
New Invention Shrops 21 P8
New Lakenham Norfk 27 Q8
New Lanark S Lans 44 K10
Newland C KuH 33 M2
Newland Gloucs 14 K8
Newland N York 32 G3
Newland Somset 5 Q4
Newland Worcs 15 N2
Newlandrig Mdloth 46 E6
Newlands Border 40 D3
Newlands Nthumb 41 M9
Newlands of Dundurcas Moray 54 H6
New Langholm D & G 40 B4
New Leake Lincs 33 S15
New Leeds Abers 55 T6
New Lodge Barns 32 B6
New Longton Lancs 30 H3
New Luce D & G 38 D8
Newlyn Cnwll 1 N13
Newlyn East Cnwll 1 T8
Newmachar Abers 55 R11
Newmains N Lans 44 K7
New Malden Gt Lon 10 B4
Newman's Green Suffk 18 K6
Newmarket Suffk 18 G3
Newmarket W Isls 56 e2
New Marske R & Cl 37 L3
New Marston Oxon 16 E9
New Mill Abers 51 T2
Newmill Border 46 F15
New Mill Cnwll 1 N12
New Mill Kirk 31 S6
Newmill Moray 54 K6
Newmillerdam Wakefd 32 B5
Newmill of Inshewan Angus 51 M6
Newmills C Edin 45 P6
New Mills Derbys 31 Q10
Newmills Fife 45 M2
Newmills Mons 14 J9
New Mills Powys 21 M4
Newmiln P & K 50 H11
Newmilns E Ayrs 44 F10
New Milton Hants 8 E12
New Mistley Essex 19 P8
New Moat Pembks 12 G6
Newney Green Essex 18 G12
Newnham Gloucs 15 M8
Newnham Hants 9 L3
Newnham Herts 17 R4
Newnham Kent 11 N5
Newnham Nhants 24 E15
Newnham Worcs 22 F14
New Ollerton Notts 32 G13
New Pitsligo Abers 55 R5
Newport Cnwll 4 H13
Newport E R Yk 32 J3
Newport Essex 18 E8
Newport Gloucs 15 M10
Newport Highld 58 E10
Newport IoW 8 J13
Newport Newpt 14 G12
Newport Pembks 12 G3
Newport Wrekin 22 H6
Newport-on-Tay Fife 51 M11
Newport Pagnell M Keyn 16 K3
New Prestwick S Ayrs 43 T13
New Quay Cerdgn 20 B10
Newquay Cnwll 1 T8
Newquay Airport Cnwll 1 U7
New Rackheath Norfk 27 R7
New Radnor Powys 21 N10
New Ridley Nthumb 41 M9
New Romney Kent 11 P11
New Rossington Donc 32 F8
New Sauchie Clacks 45 L1
Newseat Abers 55 P9
Newsham Lancs 30 H2
Newsham N York 36 D5
Newsham N York 36 H9
Newsham Nthumb 41 Q5
New Sharlston Wakefd 32 C4
Newsholme E R Yk 32 G3
New Silksworth Sundld 41 R10
Newsome Kirk 31 S5
New Somerby Lincs 24 K3
Newstead Border 46 G11
Newstead Notts 32 E15
Newstead Nthumb 47 R12
New Stevenston N Lans 44 J7
Newthorpe Notts 24 D1
Newton Ag & B 49 M16
Newton Border 46 H13
Newton Brdgnd 13 T14
Newton C Beds 17 Q3
Newton Cambs 18 D5
Newton Cambs 26 D6
Newton Ches W 30 F13
Newton Ches W 30 H14
Newton Cumb 34 J11
Newton Derbys 32 C14
Newton Herefs 14 G5
Newton Herefs 14 J1
Newton Highld 53 R6
Newton Highld 53 T4
Newton Highld 53 T7
Newton Highld 58 H5
Newton Lincs 25 M3
Newton Mdloth 45 S5
Newton Moray 54 F4
Newton Moray 54 H4
Newton Nhants 24 K11
Newton Norfk 26 K6
Newton Notts 24 G2
Newton Nthumb 41 L8
Newton S Lans 44 H7
Newton S Lans 45 L11
Newton Staffs 23 M5
Newton Suffk 19 L7
Newton W Loth 45 N4
Newton Warwks 24 E12
Newton Abbot Devon 3 Q4
Newton Arlosh Cumb 39 U9
Newton Aycliffe Dur 41 Q14
Newton Bewley Hartpl 41 S14
Newton Blossomville M Keyn 17 L1
Newton Bromswold Nhants 25 L14
Newton Burgoland Leics 23 S7
Newton-by-the-Sea Nthumb 47 S12
Newton by Toft Lincs 33 M10
Newton Ferrers Cnwll 2 H5
Newton Ferrers Devon 3 L8
Newton Ferry W Isls 56 c5
Newton Flotman Norfk 27 Q9
Newtongrange Mdloth 46 D6
Newton Green Mons 14 K11
Newton Harcourt Leics 24 F9
Newton Heath Manch 31 N7
Newtonhill Abers 55 R16
Newton-in-Bowland Lancs 35 R15
Newton Kyme N York 36 J16
Newton-le-Willows N York 36 E8
Newton-le-Willows St Hel 30 J8
Newtonloan Mdloth 46 D6
Newton Longville Bucks 16 K5
Newton Mearns E Rens 44 F7
Newtonmill Angus 51 Q5
Newtonmore Highld 53 S15
Newton Morrell N York 36 F5
Newton of Balcanquhal P & K 50 J14
Newton of Balcormo Fife 51 P15
Newton on Ouse N York 36 J13
Newton-on-Rawcliffe N York 37 P8
Newton-on-the-Moor Nthumb 47 R16
Newton on Trent Lincs 32 J12
Newton Poppleford Devon 6 D12
Newton Purcell Oxon 16 G5
Newton Regis Warwks 23 Q8
Newton Reigny Cumb 40 D13
Newton St Cyres Devon 5 Q11
Newton St Faith Norfk 27 Q6
Newton St Loe BaNES 15 M16
Newton St Petrock Devon 4 J9
Newton Solney Derbys 23 Q4
Newton Stacey Hants 8 G5
Newton Stewart D & G 38 H8
Newton Tony Wilts 8 E5
Newton Tracey Devon 4 K6
Newton under Roseberry R & Cl 36 K5
Newton upon Derwent E R Yk 37 M15
Newton Valence Hants 9 M6
Newton Wamphray D & G 39 S3
Newton with Scales Lancs 30 G3
Newtown Cumb 39 S10
Newtown Cumb 40 D8
Newtown D & G 44 J15
Newtown Devon 5 P7
Newtown Devon 6 D11
New Town Dorset 7 R8
New Town Dorset 7 S8
New Town E Susx 10 F11
Newtown Gloucs 15 M10
Newtown Hants 8 K9
Newtown Herefs 15 L3
Newtown Herefs 15 M4
Newtown Highld 53 M14
Newtown IoW 8 G13
Newtown Nthumb 47 P12
Newtown Poole 7 S12
Newtown Powys 21 M5
Newtown Shrops 22 C5
Newtown Shrops 22 D4
Newtown Somset 6 G9
Newtown Staffs 31 N14
Newtown Wigan 30 H7
Newtown Worcs 22 K16
Newtown Linford Leics 24 E7
Newtown of Beltrees Rens 44 C7
Newtown St Boswells Border 46 H11
New Tredegar Caerph 14 D9
New Trows S Lans 44 J10
Newtyle Angus 51 L9
New Walsoken Cambs 26 E7
New Waltham NE Lin 33 Q7
New Winton E Loth 46 E5
Newyork Ag & B 49 L14
New York Lincs 33 Q15
Neyland Pembks 12 F9
Nicholashayne Devon 6 D8
Nicholaston Swans 13 N12
Nidd N York 36 G13
Nigg C Aber 55 S14
Nigg Highld 53 U3
Nigg Ferry Highld 53 U3
Ninebanks Nthumb 40 H10
Nine Elms Swindn 15 T12
Ninfield E Susx 10 J13
Ningwood IoW 8 G13
Nisbet Border 46 J12
Nisbet Hill Border 47 L8
Niton IoW 8 J15
Nitshill C Glas 44 E7
Nocton Lincs 33 M13
Noke Oxon 16 F8
Nolton Pembks 12 D7
Nolton Haven Pembks 12 D7
No Man's Heath Ches W 30 H16
No Man's Heath Warwks 23 Q7
Nomansland Devon 5 Q8
Nomansland Wilts 8 E9
Noneley Shrops 22 D4
Nonington Kent 11 S6
Nook Cumb 35 P10
Norbiton Gt Lon 17 Q15
Norbury Ches E 22 E1
Norbury Derbys 23 N2
Norbury Gt Lon 10 D3
Norbury Shrops 21 Q5
Norbury Staffs 22 H5
Norchard Worcs 22 J14
Nordelph Norfk 26 F9
Nordley Shrops 22 G9
Norham Nthumb 47 M9
Norley Ches W 30 J12
Norleywood Hants 8 G12
Normanby Lincs 33 L10
Normanby N Linc 32 K5
Normanby N York 37 N10
Normanby R & Cl 36 K4
Normanby le Wold Lincs 33 N8
Normandy Surrey 9 Q3
Norman's Green Devon 6 D10
Normanton C Derb 23 R3
Normanton Leics 24 J2
Normanton Lincs 25 L1
Normanton Notts 32 G15
Normanton Wakefd 32 C4
Normanton le Heath Leics 23 S7
Normanton on Soar Notts 24 E5
Normanton on the Wolds Notts 24 F3
Normanton on Trent Notts 32 H13
Norris Green Lpool 30 F8
Norris Hill Leics 23 R6
Norristhorpe Kirk 31 T4
Northall Bucks 17 L7
Northallerton N York 36 G8
Northam C Sotn 8 H10
Northam Devon 4 J6
Northampton Nhants 24 H15
Northampton Worcs 22 J14
North Anston Rothm 32 E10
North Ascot Br For 17 L15
North Aston Oxon 16 E5
Northaw Herts 17 R10
Northay Somset 6 G9
North Baddesley Hants 8 G8
North Ballachulish Highld 49 M6
North Barrow Somset 7 L6
North Barsham Norfk 27 L3
North Benfleet Essex 18 J15
North Bersted W Susx 9 Q11
North Berwick E Loth 46 G3
North Boarhunt Hants 8 K10
Northborough C Pete 25 N7
Northbourne Kent 11 T6
North Bovey Devon 5 N13
North Bradley Wilts 7 Q2
North Brentor Devon 4 K14
North Brewham Somset 7 N5
Northbrook Hants 8 J5
North Buckland Devon 4 K4
North Burlingham Norfk 27 S7
North Cadbury Somset 7 M6
North Carlton Lincs 33 L11
North Carlton Notts 32 F10
North Cave E R Yk 32 K2
North Cerney Gloucs 15 S9
North Chailey E Susx 10 E11
Northchapel W Susx 9 Q7
North Charford Hants 8 D8
North Charlton Nthumb 47 R13
North Cheam Gt Lon 10 C4
North Cheriton Somset 7 M6
North Chideock Dorset 6 J12
Northchurch Herts 17 M8
North Cliffe E R Yk 32 K2
North Clifton Notts 32 J12
North Cockerington Lincs 33 S9
North Connel Ag & B 48 K10
North Cornelly Brdgnd 13 T13
North Cotes Lincs 33 R8
Northcott Devon 4 H12
Northcourt Oxon 16 E10
North Cove Suffk 27 U10
North Cowton N York 36 F6
North Crawley M Keyn 17 L3
North Creake Norfk 26 K2
North Curry Somset 6 G6
North Dalton E R Yk 37 Q15
North Deighton N York 36 H15
Northdown Kent 11 U3
North Duffield N York 32 G1
North Duntulm Highld 59 e5
North Elmham Norfk 27 M5
North Elmsall Wakefd 32 D6
North End C Port 9 L11
North End Essex 18 G10
North End Hants 8 C9
North End Nhants 25 L14
North End W Susx 9 Q11
Northend Warwks 16 D1
Northenden Manch 31 M9
North Erradale Highld 52 D1
North Evington C Leic 24 F8
North Fambridge Essex 18 K14
North Ferriby E R Yk 33 L3
Northfield Birm 23 M12
Northfield C Aber 55 R13
Northfield E R Yk 33 M3
Northfields Lincs 25 M7
Northfleet Kent 10 H3
North Frodingham E R Yk 37 T14
North Gorley Hants 8 D10
North Green Suffk 19 R3
North Greetwell Lincs 33 L12
North Grimston N York 37 P12
North Hayling Hants 9 M11
North Hill Cnwll 2 G3
North Hillingdon Gt Lon 17 N12
North Hinksey Village Oxon 16 E9
North Holmwood Surrey 9 T4
North Huish Devon 3 N7
North Hykeham Lincs 32 K13
Northiam E Susx 11 L11
Northill C Beds 17 P2
Northington Hants 8 K5
North Kelsey Lincs 33 M7
North Kessock Highld 53 S7
North Killingholme N Linc 33 N5
North Kilvington N York 36 H9
North Kilworth Leics 24 F11
North Kyme Lincs 33 N15
North Landing E R Yk 37 V11
Northlands Lincs 33 R15
Northleach Gloucs 15 T8
North Lee Bucks 16 K8
Northleigh Devon 6 F11
North Leigh Oxon 16 D8
North Leverton with Habblesthorpe Notts 32 H11
Northlew Devon 4 K11
North Littleton Worcs 15 S2
North Lopham Norfk 27 N12
North Luffenham Rutlnd 24 K8
North Marden W Susx 9 N9
North Marston Bucks 16 J6
North Middleton Mdloth 46 E7
North Millbrex Abers 55 Q7
North Milmain D & G 38 C10
North Molton Devon 5 N6
Northmoor Oxon 16 D9
North Moreton Oxon 16 F12
Northmuir Angus 51 M7
North Mundham W Susx 9 P11
North Muskham Notts 32 H14
North Newbald E R Yk 32 K2
North Newington Oxon 16 D3
North Newnton Wilts 8 C2
North Newton Somset 6 G6
Northney Hants 9 M11
North Nibley Gloucs 15 N11
Northolt Gt Lon 17 P13
Northop Flints 29 S7
Northop Hall Flints 30 D13
North Ormesby Middsb 36 J3
North Ormsby Lincs 33 Q9
Northorpe Kirk 31 T4
Northorpe Lincs 25 P3
Northorpe Lincs 32 K8
North Otterington N York 36 G8
North Owersby Lincs 33 M8
Northowram Calder 31 R3
North Perrott Somset 6 J9
North Petherton Somset 6 G5
North Petherwin Cnwll 4 G12
North Pickenham Norfk 26 K8
North Piddle Worcs 15 R1
North Poorton Dorset 6 K11
Northport Dorset 7 R13
North Queensferry Fife 45 P3
North Rauceby Lincs 25 M1
Northrepps Norfk 27 R2
North Reston Lincs 33 S10
North Rigton N York 36 F15
North Rode Ches E 31 N13
North Ronaldsay Airport Ork 58 e1
North Runcton Norfk 26 G6
North Scarle Lincs 32 J13
North Shian Ag & B 48 K9
North Shields N Tyne 41 R7
North Shoebury Sthend 19 L15
North Shore Bpool 30 E1
North Side C Pete 25 Q9
North Somercotes Lincs 33 S8
North Stainley N York 36 F11
North Stifford Thurr 10 H2
North Stoke BaNES 15 M15
North Stoke Oxon 16 G12
North Stoke W Susx 9 R10
North Street Kent 11 P5
North Street W Berk 16 G15
North Sunderland Nthumb 47 R11
North Tamerton Cnwll 4 G11
North Tawton Devon 5 M10
North Third Stirlg 44 J2
North Thoresby Lincs 33 Q8
Northton W Isls 56 c4
North Town Devon 4 K9
North Town Somset 7 L4
North Town W & M 17 L13
North Tuddenham Norfk 27 N6
North Walsham Norfk 27 R4
North Waltham Hants 8 J4
North Warnborough Hants 9 M3
North Weald Bassett Essex 18 E13
North Wheatley Notts 32 H10
Northwich Ches W 30 K12
Northwick Worcs 22 J16
North Widcombe BaNES 7 L1
North Willingham Lincs 33 P9
North Wingfield Derbys 32 C13
North Witham Lincs 24 K5
Northwold Norfk 26 J9
Northwood Gt Lon 17 N11
Northwood IoW 8 H13
Northwood Shrops 22 D3
Northwood Green Gloucs 15 M7
North Wootton Dorset 7 M8
North Wootton Norfk 26 G5
North Wootton Somset 7 L4
North Wraxall Wilts 15 P14
Norton Donc 32 E5
Norton E Susx 10 F15
Norton Gloucs 15 P6
Norton Halton 30 H11
Norton N York 37 N11
Norton Nhants 24 F15
Norton Notts 32 E12
Norton Powys 21 Q9
Norton S on T 36 J3
Norton Shrops 22 H9
Norton Suffk 27 L14
Norton W Susx 9 Q11
Norton Wilts 15 Q13
Norton Worcs 15 Q2
Norton Worcs 15 S2
Norton Bavant Wilts 7 R4
Norton Bridge Staffs 22 K4
Norton Canes Staffs 23 M7
Norton Canon Herefs 21 R12
Norton Disney Lincs 32 K14
Norton Fitzwarren Somset 6 F6
Norton Green IoW 8 F14
Norton Hawkfield BaNES 15 L16
Norton Heath Essex 18 F12
Norton in Hales Shrops 22 G2
Norton-Juxta-Twycross Leics 23 R8
Norton-le-Clay N York 36 H11
Norton Lindsey Warwks 23 Q15
Norton Little Green Suffk 27 M14
Norton Malreward BaNES 15 L16
Norton St Philip Somset 7 P1
Norton Subcourse Norfk 27 T9
Norton sub Hamdon Somset 6 J8
Norwell Notts 32 H14
Norwell Woodhouse Notts 32 H14
Norwich Norfk 27 Q7
Norwich Airport Norfk 27 Q7
Norwick Shet 59 s1
Norwood Clacks 44 K1
Norwood Green Gt Lon 17 P13
Norwood Hill Surrey 10 C8
Noss Mayo Devon 3 L8
Nosterfield N York 36 F10
Nostie Highld 52 E10
Notgrove Gloucs 15 T7
Nottage Brdgnd 13 T14
Nottingham C Nott 24 E2
Notton Wakefd 32 B5
Notton Wilts 15 Q15
Noutard's Green Worcs 22 J14
Nuffield Oxon 16 G12
Nunburnholme E R Yk 37 P15
Nuneaton Warwks 23 R10
Nunhead Gt Lon 17 S14
Nun Monkton N York 36 J14
Nunney Somset 7 N3
Nunnington N York 37 M10
Nunsthorpe NE Lin 33 Q6
Nunthorpe C York 37 L15
Nunthorpe Middsb 36 K4
Nunthorpe Village Middsb 36 K5
Nunton Wilts 8 D7
Nunwick N York 36 G11
Nursling Hants 8 G9
Nutbourne W Susx 9 M11
Nutbourne W Susx 9 S8
Nutfield Surrey 10 D7
Nuthall Notts 24 E2
Nuthampstead Herts 18 D8
Nuthurst W Susx 9 T7
Nutley E Susx 10 F10
Nuttall Bury 31 M5
Nybster Highld 58 J3
Nyetimber W Susx 9 P12
Nyewood W Susx 9 N8
Nymet Rowland Devon 5 N9
Nymet Tracey Devon 5 N11
Nympsfield Gloucs 15 N10
Nynehead Somset 6 E7
Nyton W Susx 9 Q11

O

Oadby Leics 24 F9
Oad Street Kent 11 M5
Oakamoor Staffs 23 M1
Oakbank W Loth 45 N6
Oak Cross Devon 5 L11
Oakdale Caerph 14 E10
Oake Somset 6 E7
Oaken Staffs 22 J8
Oakenclough Lancs 35 P15
Oakengates Wrekin 22 G7
Oakenshaw Dur 41 P12
Oakenshaw Kirk 31 S3
Oakford Cerdgn 20 C11
Oakford Devon 5 R7
Oakham Rutlnd 24 J7
Oakhanger Hants 9 M6
Oakhill Somset 7 M3
Oakington Cambs 25 S15
Oakle Street Gloucs 15 N7
Oakley Bed 17 M1
Oakley Bucks 16 G8
Oakley Fife 45 M2
Oakley Hants 8 K3
Oakley Suffk 27 P12
Oakridge Gloucs 15 Q9
Oaksey Wilts 15 R11
Oakthorpe Leics 23 R7
Oakwood C Derb 23 S2
Oakworth C Brad 31 Q1
Oare Kent 11 P4
Oare Somset 5 P3
Oare Wilts 15 U16
Oasby Lincs 25 L2
Oath Somset 6 H6
Oathlaw Angus 51 N6
Oatlands Park Surrey 17 N16
Oban Ag & B 48 K11
Oban Airport Ag & B 48 K10
Obley Shrops 21 Q7
Obney P & K 50 G10
Oborne Dorset 7 M8
Occold Suffk 27 P13
Occumster Highld 58 G8
Ochiltree E Ayrs 44 E13
Ockbrook Derbys 23 S3
Ockham Surrey 9 S2
Ockle Highld 48 E4
Ockley Surrey 9 T5
Ocle Pychard Herefs 15 L2
Odcombe Somset 6 K8
Odd Down BaNES 15 N16
Oddingley Worcs 22 K15
Oddington Gloucs 15 U6
Oddington Oxon 16 F7
Odell Bed 25 L16
Odiham Hants 9 M3
Odsal C Brad 31 S3
Odsey Cambs 17 R4
Odstock Wilts 8 D7
Odstone Leics 23 S7
Offchurch Warwks 23 R14
Offenham Worcs 15 S2
Offerton Stockp 31 N9
Offham E Susx 10 E13
Offham Kent 10 J5
Offham W Susx 9 R10
Offord Cluny Cambs 25 P14
Offord D'Arcy Cambs 25 P14
Offton Suffk 19 N5
Offwell Devon 6 F11
Ogbourne Maizey Wilts 15 U15
Ogbourne St Andrew Wilts 15 U14
Ogbourne St George Wilts 15 U14
Ogle Nthumb 41 N5
Oglet Lpool 30 G11
Ogmore V Glam 13 U14
Ogmore-by-Sea V Glam 13 T14
Ogmore Vale Brdgnd 13 U12
Okeford Fitzpaine Dorset 7 P9
Okehampton Devon 5 L11
Oker Side Derbys 31 T14
Okewood Hill Surrey 9 S5
Old Nhants 24 H13
Old Aberdeen C Aber 55 S13
Old Alresford Hants 8 K6
Oldany Highld 56 G8
Old Auchenbrack D & G 39 M2
Old Basford C Nott 24 E2
Old Basing Hants 9 L3
Old Beetley Norfk 27 M6
Oldberrow Warwks 23 N14
Old Bewick Nthumb 47 P13
Old Bolingbroke Lincs 33 R13
Old Bramhope Leeds 36 F16
Old Brampton Derbys 32 B12
Old Bridge of Urr D & G 39 N7
Old Buckenham Norfk 27 N10
Old Burghclere Hants 8 H2
Oldbury Sandw 23 L11
Oldbury Shrops 22 G10
Oldbury Warwks 23 R10
Oldbury-on-Severn S Glos 15 L11
Oldbury on the Hill Gloucs 15 P12
Old Byland N York 36 K9
Old Cantley Donc 32 F7
Oldcastle Mons 14 G6
Old Catton Norfk 27 Q7
Old Clee NE Lin 33 Q6
Old Cleeve Somset 5 T4
Old Clipstone Notts 32 F13
Old Colwyn Conwy 29 L5
Oldcotes Notts 32 F9
Old Dailly S Ayrs 38 E2
Old Dalby Leics 24 G5
Old Deer Abers 55 S7
Old Edlington Donc 32 E8
Old Ellerby E R Yk 33 P1
Old Felixstowe Suffk 19 S7
Oldfield Worcs 22 J14
Old Fletton C Pete 25 P9
Oldford Somset 7 P2
Old Forge Herefs 14 K7
Old Grimsby IoS 1 b1
Old Hall Green Herts 17 S6
Oldham Oldham 31 N7
Oldhamstocks E Loth 46 K5
Old Harlow Essex 18 E11
Old Hunstanton Norfk 26 H2
Old Hurst Cambs 25 R12
Old Hutton Cumb 35 P9
Old Kilpatrick W Duns 44 E5
Old Knebworth Herts 17 Q7
Old Lakenham Norfk 27 Q8
Oldland S Glos 15 M15
Old Langho Lancs 30 K2
Old Leake Lincs 33 S16
Old Malton N York 37 N11
Oldmeldrum Abers 55 Q10
Oldmill Cnwll 2 H4
Old Milverton Warwks 23 R14
Oldmixon N Som 6 H1
Old Newton Suffk 19 N3
Old Radnor Powys 21 P11
Old Rayne Abers 55 N10
Old Romney Kent 11 P11
Old Shoreham W Susx 9 U11
Oldshoremore Highld 56 J4
Old Sodbury S Glos 15 N13
Old Somerby Lincs 25 L3
Oldstead N York 36 K10
Old Stratford Nhants 16 J3
Old Struan P & K 50 D5
Old Swinford Dudley 22 K11
Old Thirsk N York 36 H10
Old Town Cumb 35 P10
Old Town E Susx 10 H15
Old Town IoS 1 b2
Old Trafford Traffd 31 M8
Oldwall Cumb 40 D8
Oldwalls Swans 13 N11
Old Warden C Beds 17 P3
Old Weston Cambs 25 N12
Old Wick Highld 58 J5
Old Windsor W & M 17 M14
Old Wives Lees Kent 11 Q6
Old Woking Surrey 9 R2
Olgrinmore Highld 58 E5
Olive Green Staffs 23 N6
Oliver's Battery Hants 8 H7
Ollaberry Shet 59 q3
Ollach Highld 59 f10
Ollerton Ches E 31 L11
Ollerton Notts 32 F13
Ollerton Shrops 22 F5
Olney M Keyn 17 L1
Olrig House Highld 58 F3
Olton Solhll 23 N12
Olveston S Glos 15 L12
Ombersley Worcs 22 J15
Ompton Notts 32 G13
Onchan IoM 34 e6
Onecote Staffs 31 Q15
Onibury Shrops 21 S7
Onich Highld 49 M6
Onllwyn Neath 13 T8
Onneley Staffs 22 H2
Onslow Green Essex 18 G10
Onslow Village Surrey 9 Q3
Onston Ches W 30 J12
Opinan Highld 52 D3
Orbliston Moray 54 H5
Orbost Highld 59 c9
Orby Lincs 33 T13
Orchard Portman Somset 6 F7
Orcheston Wilts 7 T3
Orcop Herefs 14 J6
Orcop Hill Herefs 14 J5
Ord Abers 55 M5
Ordhead Abers 55 N13
Ordie Abers 54 K14
Ordiequish Moray 54 H5
Ordsall Notts 32 G11
Ore E Susx 11 L13
Orford Suffk 19 T5
Orford Warrtn 30 J9
Organford Dorset 7 R12
Orkney Islands Ork 58 c4
Orlestone Kent 11 N9
Orleton Herefs 22 D14
Orleton Worcs 22 G14
Orlingbury Nhants 24 J13
Ormesby R & Cl 36 K4
Ormesby St Margaret Norfk 27 U6
Ormesby St Michael Norfk 27 U6
Ormiscaig Highld 56 D15
Ormiston E Loth 46 E5
Ormsaigmore Highld 48 D5
Ormsary Ag & B 42 J5
Ormskirk Lancs 30 F6
Oronsay Ag & B 42 D2
Orphir Ork 58 b4
Orpington Gt Lon 10 F4
Orrell Sefton 30 E8
Orrell Wigan 30 H7
Orroland D & G 39 N11
Orsett Thurr 10 H1
Orslow Staffs 22 J6
Orston Notts 24 H2
Orton Cumb 35 Q5
Orton Nhants 24 J12
Orton Staffs 22 K9
Orton Longueville C Pete 25 P9
Orton-on-the-Hill Leics 23 R8
Orton Waterville C Pete 25 N9
Orwell Cambs 17 S2
Osbaldeston Lancs 30 K2
Osbaldwick C York 37 L15
Osbaston Leics 23 S8
Osbaston Shrops 29 T14
Osbournby Lincs 25 M2
Oscroft Ches W 30 H13
Ose Highld 59 c9
Osgathorpe Leics 23 S6
Osgodby Lincs 33 M9
Osgodby N York 32 F2
Osgodby N York 37 S9
Oskaig Highld 59 g10
Oskamull Ag & B 48 D9
Osmaston Derbys 23 P2
Osmington Dorset 7 N13
Osmington Mills Dorset 7 N14
Osmondthorpe Leeds 32 B2
Osmotherley N York 36 J7
Osney Oxon 16 E9
Ospringe Kent 11 P5
Ossett Wakefd 31 T4
Ossington Notts 32 H13
Osterley Gt Lon 17 P14
Oswaldkirk N York 37 L10
Oswaldtwistle Lancs 31 L3
Oswestry Shrops 29 S13
Otford Kent 10 G5
Otham Kent 11 L6
Othery Somset 6 H5
Otley Leeds 36 E16
Otley Suffk 19 Q4
Otterbourne Hants 8 H8
Otterburn N York 35 T14
Otterburn Nthumb 40 J3
Otter Ferry Ag & B 43 M3
Otterham Cnwll 4 E12
Otterhampton Somset 6 F4
Otternish W Isls 56 c5
Ottershaw Surrey 17 M16
Otterswick Shet 59 r3
Otterton Devon 6 D13
Ottery St Mary Devon 6 D11
Ottinge Kent 11 R8
Ottringham E R Yk 33 Q4
Oughterside Cumb 39 T12
Oughtibridge Sheff 31 U9
Oughtrington Warrtn 30 K10
Oulston N York 36 K11
Oulton Cumb 39 U10
Oulton Norfk 27 P4
Oulton Staffs 22 K3
Oulton Suffk 27 U10
Oulton Broad Suffk 27 U10
Oulton Street Norfk 27 P4
Oundle Nhants 25 M11
Ounsdale Staffs 22 K10
Ousby Cumb 40 E13
Ousden Suffk 18 H3
Ousefleet E R Yk 32 J4
Ouston Dur 41 P9
Outgate Cumb 35 L7
Outhgill Cumb 35 S6
Outhill Warwks 23 N14
Outlane Kirk 31 R5
Out Rawcliffe Lancs 30 F1
Outwell Norfk 26 E8
Outwood Surrey 10 D7
Outwoods Staffs 22 H6
Ouzlewell Green Leeds 32 B3
Over Cambs 25 S14
Overbury Worcs 15 R4
Overcombe Dorset 7 N14
Over Compton Dorset 7 L8
Over Haddon Derbys 31 S13
Over Kellet Lancs 35 N12
Over Kiddington Oxon 16 D6
Overleigh Somset 6 K5
Over Norton Oxon 16 B5
Over Peover Ches E 31 L12
Overpool Ches W 30 F11
Overscaig Hotel Highld 57 M10
Overseal Derbys 23 R6
Over Silton N York 36 J8
Oversland Kent 11 P5
Overstone Nhants 24 H14
Over Stowey Somset 6 E4
Overstrand Norfk 27 R2
Over Stratton Somset 6 J8
Overthorpe Nhants 16 E3
Overton C Aber 55 R12
Overton Hants 8 J3
Overton Lancs 35 M14
Overton N York 36 K14
Overton Shrops 22 D13
Overton Swans 13 N12
Overton Wakefd 31 T5
Overton Wrexhm 29 T11
Overtown N Lans 44 J8
Over Wallop Hants 8 F5
Over Whitacre Warwks 23 Q10
Over Worton Oxon 16 D5
Oving Bucks 16 J6
Oving W Susx 9 P11
Ovingdean Br & H 10 D14
Ovingham Nthumb 41 M8
Ovington Dur 36 D4
Ovington Essex 18 J6
Ovington Hants 8 J6
Ovington Norfk 27 L8
Ovington Nthumb 41 M8
Ower Hants 8 F9
Owermoigne Dorset 7 P13
Owlerton Sheff 32 B9
Owlsmoor Br For 9 N1
Owlswick Bucks 16 J9
Owmby Lincs 33 L10
Owmby Lincs 33 M7
Owslebury Hants 8 J8
Owston Donc 32 E6
Owston Leics 24 H7
Owston Ferry N Linc 32 J8
Owstwick E R Yk 33 Q2
Owthorne E R Yk 33 R3
Owthorpe Notts 24 G3
Owton Manor Hartpl 41 T13
Oxborough Norfk 26 H8
Oxcombe Lincs 33 R11
Oxenholme Cumb 35 P8
Oxenhope C Brad 31 Q2
Oxen Park Cumb 35 L9
Oxenpill Somset 6 J4
Oxenton Gloucs 15 R5
Oxenwood Wilts 8 F2
Oxford Oxon 16 E9
Oxford Airport Oxon 16 E7
Oxhey Herts 17 P11
Oxhill Warwks 16 B2
Oxley Wolves 22 K8
Oxley Green Essex 19 L11
Oxlode Cambs 26 E11
Oxnam Border 46 J14
Oxnead Norfk 27 Q5

72
Oxshott - Rusper

Oxshott Surrey 9 T2
Oxspring Barns 31 T7
Oxted Surrey 10 E6
Oxton Border 46 F8
Oxton N York 36 J16
Oxton Notts 32 F16
Oxwich Swans 13 N12
Oxwich Green Swans 13 N12
Oykel Bridge Hotel Highld 57 L13
Oyne Abers 55 N10
Oystermouth Swans 13 Q12

P

Pabail W Isls 56 f2
Packington Leics 23 R6
Padanaram Angus 51 M7
Padbury Bucks 16 H5
Paddington Gt Lon 17 R13
Paddlesworth Kent 10 J5
Paddlesworth Kent 11 R8
Paddock Wood Kent 10 J8
Padiham Lancs 31 M2
Padside N York 36 E13
Padstow Cnwll 2 B4
Padworth W Berk 16 G15
Pagham W Susx 9 P12
Paglesham Essex 19 L14
Paignton Torbay 3 Q6
Pailton Warwks 24 D12
Painscastle Powys 21 N13
Painshawfield Nthumb 41 M8
Painsthorpe E R Yk 37 P14
Painswick Gloucs 15 P8
Painter's Forstal Kent 11 N5
Paisley Rens 44 E6
Pakefield Suffk 27 V10
Pakenham Suffk 27 L14
Paley Street W & M 16 K14
Palfrey Wsall 23 M9
Palgrave Suffk 27 P12
Pallington Dorset 7 P12
Palmerston E Ayrs 44 E13
Palnackie D & G 39 N9
Palnure D & G 38 H8
Palterton Derbys 32 D13
Pamber End Hants 8 K2
Pamber Green Hants 8 K2
Pamber Heath Hants 8 K1
Pamington Gloucs 15 Q4
Pamphill Dorset 7 S11
Pampisford Cambs 18 E5
Panbride Angus 51 P10
Pancrasweek Devon 4 G10
Pandy Mons 14 G6
Pandy Tudur Conwy 29 L8
Panfield Essex 18 H9
Pangbourne W Berk 16 G14
Pangdean W Susx 10 D13
Pannal N York 36 G15
Pannal Ash N York 36 F14
Pannanich Wells Hotel Abers 54 J15
Pant Shrops 29 S14
Pantasaph Flints 29 Q6
Pant-ffrwyth Brdgnd 13 U13
Pant Glas Gwynd 28 F10
Pantglas Powys 20 G4
Panton Lincs 33 P11
Pant-y-dwr Powys 20 K8
Pant-y-mwyn Flints 29 R8
Panxworth Norfk 27 S7
Papa Westray Airport Ork 58 c1
Papcastle Cumb 39 S13
Papigoe Highld 58 J5
Papple E Loth 46 H5
Papplewick Notts 32 E16
Papworth Everard Cambs 25 Q15
Papworth St Agnes Cambs 25 Q15
Par Cnwll 2 D7
Parbold Lancs 30 G6
Parbrook Somset 7 L5
Parc Gwynd 29 L13
Parc Seymour Newpt 14 H11
Pardshaw Cumb 39 S14
Parham Suffk 19 R3
Park D & G 39 Q3
Park Nthumb 40 F8
Park Corner Oxon 16 H12
Parkend Gloucs 15 L9
Parkers Green Kent 10 H7
Park Farm Kent 11 P8
Parkgate Ches W 30 D11
Parkgate D & G 39 R4
Park Gate Hants 8 J10
Park Gate Leeds 31 S1
Parkgate Surrey 9 T4
Parkhall W Duns 44 E5
Parkham Devon 4 H7
Parkmill Swans 13 P12
Park Royal Gt Lon 17 Q13
Parkside Dur 41 S10
Parkside N Lans 44 J7
Parkstone Poole 7 S12
Park Street Herts 17 P9
Parndon Essex 18 D12
Parracombe Devon 5 M3
Parson Drove Cambs 25 S7
Parson's Heath Essex 19 M9
Partick C Glas 44 F5
Partington Traffd 31 L9
Partney Lincs 33 S13
Parton Cumb 34 F3
Partridge Green W Susx 9 T8
Parwich Derbys 31 S15
Passenham Nhants 16 J3
Paston Norfk 27 S3
Patcham Br & H 10 D13
Patching W Susx 9 S10
Patchway S Glos 15 L13
Pateley Bridge N York 36 D12
Pathhead Fife 45 R1
Pathhead Mdloth 46 E6
Path of Condie P & K 50 H14
Patna E Ayrs 44 D15
Patney Wilts 7 T1
Patrick IoM 34 b5
Patrick Brompton N York 36 E8
Patricroft Salfd 31 L8
Patrington E R Yk 33 R4
Patrington Haven E R Yk 33 R4
Patrixbourne Kent 11 R6
Patterdale Cumb 35 M4
Pattingham Staffs 22 J9
Pattishall Nhants 16 G1
Pattiswick Green Essex 18 K9
Paul Cnwll 1 N13
Paulerspury Nhants 16 H2
Paull E R Yk 33 P3
Paul's Dene Wilts 8 D6
Paulton BaNES 7 M1
Pauperhaugh Nthumb 41 M2
Pavenham Bed 25 L16
Pawlett Somset 6 G4
Paxford Gloucs 15 U4
Paxton Border 47 N8
Payhembury Devon 6 D10
Paythorne Lancs 35 T15
Peacehaven E Susx 10 E15
Peak Forest Derbys 31 R11
Peakirk C Pete 25 P8
Peasedown St John BaNES 7 N1
Peaseland Green Norfk 27 N6
Peasemore W Berk 16 D14
Peasenhall Suffk 27 S14
Pease Pottage W Susx 10 C9
Peaslake Surrey 9 S4
Peasley Cross St Hel 30 H9
Peasmarsh E Susx 11 M11
Peathill Abers 55 S4
Peat Inn Fife 51 N14
Peatling Magna Leics 24 F10
Peatling Parva Leics 24 F10
Pebmarsh Essex 18 K8
Pebworth Worcs 15 T2
Pecket Well Calder 31 P3
Peckforton Ches E 30 H15
Peckham Gt Lon 17 S14
Peckleton Leics 24 D9
Pedlinge Kent 11 Q9
Pedmore Dudley 22 K12
Pedwell Somset 6 J5
Peebles Border 45 R10
Peel IoM 34 b5
Peene Kent 11 R9
Pegsdon C Beds 17 P5
Pegswood Nthumb 41 P4
Pegwell Kent 11 U4
Peinchorran Highld 59 f10
Peinlich Highld 59 e7
Peldon Essex 19 M10
Pelsall Wsall 23 M8
Pelton Dur 41 P10
Pelynt Cnwll 2 F7
Pemberton Carmth 13 P10
Pemberton Wigan 30 H7
Pembrey Carmth 13 M10
Pembridge Herefs 21 R11
Pembroke Pembks 12 F10
Pembroke Dock Pembks 12 F9
Pembury Kent 10 H8
Pen-allt Herefs 14 K5
Penallt Mons 14 K8
Penally Pembks 12 H10
Penarth V Glam 14 E15
Pen-bont Rhydybeddau Cerdgn 20 F6
Penbryn Cerdgn 12 K1
Pencader Carmth 13 M4
Pencaitland E Loth 46 F5
Pencarnisiog IoA 28 D6
Pencarreg Carmth 20 D13
Pencelli Powys 14 D6
Penclawdd Swans 13 P11
Pencoed Brdgnd 14 B13
Pencombe Herefs 15 L1
Pencraig Herefs 14 K7
Pencraig Powys 29 P14
Pendeen Cnwll 1 M12
Penderyn Rhondd 13 U9
Pendine Carmth 12 J9
Pendlebury Salfd 31 M7
Pendleton Lancs 31 L1
Pendock Worcs 15 N5
Pendoggett Cnwll 4 C14
Pendomer Somset 6 K9
Pendoylan V Glam 14 C14
Penegoes Powys 20 G4
Pen-ffordd Pembks 12 G6
Pengam Caerph 14 D10
Pengam Cardif 14 E14
Penge Gt Lon 10 D3
Pengelly Cnwll 4 D13
Penhallow Cnwll 1 S9
Penhalvean Cnwll 1 R11
Penhill Swindn 15 T12
Penhow Newpt 14 H11
Penicuik Mdloth 45 Q7
Penifiler Highld 59 f9
Peninver Ag & B 42 K13
Penistone Barns 31 T7
Penkill S Ayrs 38 E2
Penkridge Staffs 22 K6
Penley Wrexhm 22 C2
Penllyn V Glam 14 B14
Penmachno Conwy 28 K10
Penmaen Caerph 14 E10
Penmaen Swans 13 P12
Penmaenmawr Conwy 28 J6
Penmaenpool Gwynd 28 J15
Penmark V Glam 14 C15
Penmynydd IoA 28 F6
Penn Bucks 17 L11
Pennal Gwynd 20 F4
Pennan Abers 55 R4
Pennant Powys 20 J4
Pennerley Shrops 21 Q4
Pennington Cumb 34 K10
Pennorth Powys 14 D6
Penn Street Bucks 17 L11
Penny Bridge Cumb 34 K10
Pennycross Ag & B 48 E11
Pennyghael Ag & B 48 E11
Pennyglen S Ayrs 43 S15
Pennymoor Devon 5 Q9
Pennywell Sundld 41 R9
Penparc Cerdgn 12 J2
Penperlleni Mons 14 G9
Penpoll Cnwll 2 E7
Penponds Cnwll 1 Q11
Penpont D & G 39 P3
Pen-rhiw Pembks 12 K3
Penrhiwceiber Rhondd 14 C10
Pen Rhiwfawr Neath 13 S8
Penrhiw-llan Cerdgn 20 A13
Penrhiw-pal Cerdgn 20 A13
Penrhos Gwynd 28 D13
Penrhos Mons 14 H8
Penrhyn Bay Conwy 29 L5
Penrhyndeudraeth Gwynd 28 H12
Penrice Swans 13 N12
Penrioch N Ayrs 43 L9
Penrith Cumb 40 D13
Penrose Cnwll 1 U6
Penruddock Cumb 40 C14
Penryn Cnwll 1 S12
Pensarn Conwy 29 M5
Pensax Worcs 22 G14
Penselwood Somset 7 N5
Pensford BaNES 15 L16
Pensham Worcs 15 Q3
Penshaw Sundld 41 Q10
Penshurst Kent 10 G8
Pensilva Cnwll 2 G4
Pentewan Cnwll 2 C8
Pentir Gwynd 28 G7
Pentire Cnwll 1 S8
Pentlow Essex 18 J6
Pentney Norfk 26 H6
Pentonbridge Cumb 40 C6
Penton Mewsey Hants 8 F4
Pentraeth IoA 28 F5
Pentre Mons 14 H10
Pentre Rhondd 14 B11
Pentre Shrops 29 T15
Pentrebach Myr Td 14 C9
Pentre-bach Powys 13 U5
Pentre Berw IoA 28 F6
Pentre-celyn Denbgs 29 Q9
Pentre-celyn Powys 20 J3
Pentre-chwyth Swans 13 R11
Pentre-cwrt Carmth 13 M4
Pentredwr Denbgs 29 R10
Pentrefelin Gwynd 28 G12
Pentrefoelas Conwy 29 L10
Pentregat Cerdgn 20 A12
Pentre-Gwenlais Carmth 13 Q7
Pentre Hodrey Shrops 21 Q8
Pentre Llanrhaeadr Denbgs 29 P8
Pentre Meyrick V Glam 14 B14
Pentre-tafarn-y-fedw Conwy 29 L8
Pentrich Derbys 32 C15
Pentridge Dorset 7 S8
Pen-twyn Mons 14 K8
Pentwynmaur Caerph 14 E11
Pentyrch Cardif 14 D13
Penwithick Cnwll 2 C7
Penybanc Carmth 13 Q6
Penybont Powys 21 M10
Pen-y-bont Powys 29 R14
Pen-y-bont-fawr Powys 29 P14
Pen-y-bryn Pembks 12 J3
Penycae Wrexhm 29 S11
Pen-y-clawdd Mons 14 J9
Pen-y-coedcae Rhondd 14 C12
Pen-y-cwn Pembks 12 D6
Pen-y-felin Flints 29 Q7
Penyffordd Flints 30 E14
Pen-y-Garnedd Powys 29 Q14
Pen-y-graig Gwynd 28 B13
Penygraig Rhondd 14 B11
Penygroes Carmth 13 P8
Penygroes Gwynd 28 F9
Pen-y-Mynydd Carmth 13 N9
Penymynydd Flints 30 E14
Penysarn IoA 28 F3
Pen-y-stryt Denbgs 29 R10
Penywaun Rhondd 14 B9
Penzance Cnwll 1 N13
Peopleton Worcs 15 Q2
Peplow Shrops 22 F5
Perceton N Ayrs 44 C10
Percyhorner Abers 55 S4
Perham Down Wilts 8 E4
Periton Somset 5 R3
Perivale Gt Lon 17 P13
Perkins Village Devon 5 S12
Perlethorpe Notts 32 F12
Perranarworthal Cnwll 1 S11
Perranporth Cnwll 1 S9
Perranuthnoe Cnwll 1 P13
Perranwell Cnwll 1 S11
Perranzabuloe Cnwll 1 S9
Perry Barr Birm 23 M10
Perry Green Wilts 15 R12
Pershall Staffs 22 J4
Pershore Worcs 15 R2
Pertenhall Bed 25 M14
Perth P & K 50 H12
Perthy Shrops 29 T13
Perton Herefs 15 L3
Perton Staffs 22 J9
Peterborough C Pete 25 P9
Peterchurch Herefs 14 G4
Peterculter C Aber 55 R14
Peterhead Abers 55 V7
Peterlee Dur 41 S12
Petersfield Hants 9 M8
Peter's Green Herts 17 P7
Petersham Gt Lon 17 Q14
Peters Marland Devon 4 K8
Peterstone Wentlooge Newpt 14 F13
Peterston-super-Ely V Glam 14 C14
Peterstow Herefs 14 K6
Peter Tavy Devon 2 K3
Petham Kent 11 Q6
Petherwin Gate Cnwll 4 G12
Petrockstow Devon 4 K9
Pett E Susx 11 M13
Pettaugh Suffk 19 P3
Petterden Angus 51 M9
Pettinain S Lans 45 L10
Pettistree Suffk 19 R4
Petton Devon 5 S7
Petts Wood Gt Lon 10 F4
Pettycur Fife 45 R2
Pettymuk Abers 55 R11
Petworth W Susx 9 Q8
Pevensey E Susx 10 J14
Pevensey Bay E Susx 10 J14
Pewsey Wilts 8 D2
Phepson Worcs 23 L15
Philham Devon 4 G7
Philiphaugh Border 46 F12
Phillack Cnwll 1 P11
Philleigh Cnwll 1 T11
Philpstoun W Loth 45 N4
Phoenix Green Hants 9 M2
Phones Highld 53 S16
Pibsbury Somset 6 J6
Pickburn Donc 32 D6
Pickering N York 37 N9
Pickford Covtry 23 Q12
Pickhill N York 36 G9
Picklescott Shrops 21 R4
Pickmere Ches E 30 K11
Pickney Somset 6 F6
Pickwell Leics 24 H7
Pickworth Lincs 25 M3
Pickworth Rutlnd 25 L6
Picton Ches W 30 G12
Picton N York 36 H6
Piddinghoe E Susx 10 F14
Piddington Nhants 16 J1
Piddington Oxon 16 G7
Piddlehinton Dorset 7 N11
Piddletrenthide Dorset 7 N11
Pidley Cambs 25 R12
Piercebridge Darltn 36 E4
Pierowall Ork 58 C1
Pilgrims Hatch Essex 18 F14
Pilham Lincs 32 J9
Pillaton Cnwll 2 H5
Pillerton Hersey Warwks 16 B2
Pillerton Priors Warwks 16 B2
Pilley Barns 32 B7
Pilley Hants 8 F12
Pilling Lancs 35 M15
Pilning S Glos 14 K12
Pilsbury Derbys 31 R14
Pilsdon Dorset 6 J11
Pilsley Derbys 31 T12
Pilsley Derbys 32 C14
Pilson Green Norfk 27 S6
Piltdown E Susx 10 F11
Pilton Devon 5 L5
Pilton Nhants 25 M11
Pilton Rutlnd 24 K8
Pilton Somset 7 L4
Pimperne Dorset 7 R9
Pinchbeck Lincs 25 Q4
Pin Green Herts 17 R6
Pinhoe Devon 5 R12
Pinley Green Warwks 23 P14
Pinminnoch S Ayrs 38 E3
Pinmore S Ayrs 38 E3
Pinn Devon 6 D13
Pinner Gt Lon 17 P12
Pinner Green Gt Lon 17 P12
Pinvin Worcs 15 R2
Pinwherry S Ayrs 38 E4
Pinxton Derbys 32 D15
Pipe and Lyde Herefs 14 J3
Pipe Aston Herefs 21 S8
Pipe Gate Shrops 22 H2
Piperhill Highld 54 B6
Pipewell Nhants 24 J11
Pirbright Surrey 9 Q2
Pirnie Border 46 J12
Pirnmill N Ayrs 43 L9
Pirton Herts 17 P5
Pishill Oxon 16 H12
Pistyll Gwynd 28 D11
Pitagowan P & K 50 D5
Pitblae Abers 55 S4
Pitcairngreen P & K 50 G11
Pitcalnie Highld 53 U3
Pitcaple Abers 55 P10
Pitcarity Angus 51 L5
Pitchcombe Gloucs 15 P9
Pitchcott Bucks 16 J7
Pitchford Shrops 22 E8
Pitch Green Bucks 16 J9
Pitchroy Moray 54 F8
Pitcombe Somset 7 M5
Pitcox E Loth 46 J4
Pitfichie Abers 55 N12
Pitglassie Abers 55 N7
Pitgrudy Highld 57 S15
Pitlessie Fife 51 L14
Pitlochry P & K 50 F6
Pitmachie Abers 55 N10
Pitmain Highld 53 T15
Pitmedden Abers 55 R10
Pitminster Somset 6 F7
Pitmuies Angus 51 P8
Pitmunie Abers 55 N12
Pitney Somset 6 J6
Pitroddie P & K 50 K12
Pitscottie Fife 51 M14
Pitsea Essex 18 H15
Pitsford Nhants 24 H14
Pitstone Bucks 17 L7
Pittarrow Abers 51 S3
Pittenweem Fife 51 P15
Pitteuchar Fife 51 L16
Pittington Dur 41 Q11
Pittodrie House Hotel Abers 55 N11
Pitton Wilts 8 E6
Pittulie Abers 55 S4
Pity Me Dur 41 Q11
Pixham Surrey 9 T3
Plains N Lans 44 J6
Plaish Shrops 22 E9
Plaistow Gt Lon 10 E1
Plaistow W Susx 9 R7
Plaitford Hants 8 E8
Platt Kent 10 H5
Plawsworth Dur 41 Q10
Plaxtol Kent 10 H6
Playden E Susx 11 M11
Playford Suffk 19 Q5
Play Hatch Oxon 16 H14
Playing Place Cnwll 1 T11
Playley Green Gloucs 15 N5
Plealey Shrops 21 R3
Plean Stirlg 44 K2
Pleasance Fife 50 K14
Pleasington Bl w D 30 K3
Pleasley Derbys 32 D13
Plemstall Ches W 30 G12
Pleshey Essex 18 G11
Plockton Highld 52 E9
Plowden Shrops 21 R6
Pluckley Kent 11 M7
Pluckley Thorne Kent 11 M8
Plumbland Cumb 39 T12
Plumley Ches E 31 L12
Plumpton Cumb 40 D12
Plumpton E Susx 10 E13
Plumpton Nhants 16 F2
Plumpton Green E Susx 10 E12
Plumstead Gt Lon 10 F2
Plumstead Norfk 27 P3
Plumtree Notts 24 F3
Plungar Leics 24 H3
Plurenden Kent 11 N9
Plush Dorset 7 N10
Plwmp Cerdgn 20 A12
Plymouth C Plym 2 K7
Plymouth Airport C Plym 2 K6
Plympton C Plym 3 L7
Plymstock C Plym 2 K7
Plymtree Devon 6 D10
Pockley N York 37 L9
Pocklington E R Yk 37 P15
Podimore Somset 6 K7
Podington Bed 24 K15
Podmore Staffs 22 H3
Pointon Lincs 25 N3
Pokesdown Bmouth 8 C13
Polbain Highld 56 F12
Polbathic Cnwll 2 H7
Polbeth W Loth 45 M6
Polebrook Nhants 25 M11
Polegate E Susx 10 H14
Polesworth Warwks 23 Q8
Polglass Highld 56 G12
Polgooth Cnwll 2 C8
Polgown D & G 39 M1
Poling W Susx 9 R11
Poling Corner W Susx 9 R11
Polkerris Cnwll 2 D7
Pollington E R Yk 32 F4
Polloch Highld 48 J4
Pollokshaws C Glas 44 F7
Pollokshields C Glas 44 F6
Polmassick Cnwll 2 C8
Polmont Falk 45 L4
Polnish Highld 48 H2
Polperro Cnwll 2 F7
Polruan Cnwll 2 E8
Polstead Suffk 19 M7
Poltalloch Ag & B 48 J16
Poltimore Devon 5 S11
Polton Mdloth 45 R6
Polwarth Border 46 K8
Polyphant Cnwll 4 G14
Polzeath Cnwll 2 B3
Pomathorn Mdloth 45 R7
Pondersbridge Cambs 25 Q10
Ponders End Gt Lon 17 S11
Ponsanooth Cnwll 1 S12
Ponsworthy Devon 3 N4
Pontantwn Carmth 13 M8
Pontardawe Neath 13 R9
Pontarddulais Swans 13 P9
Pont-ar-gothi Carmth 13 N6
Pontarsais Carmth 13 M5
Pontblyddyn Flints 30 D14
Pontefract Wakefd 32 D4
Ponteland Nthumb 41 N6
Ponterwyd Cerdgn 20 G7
Pontesbury Shrops 21 R3
Pontesford Shrops 21 R3
Pontfadog Wrexhm 29 R12
Pontfaen Pembks 12 F4
Pont-faen Powys 14 B4
Pontgarreg Cerdgn 20 A11
Ponthenry Carmth 13 N8
Ponthir Torfn 14 G11
Ponthirwaun Cerdgn 12 K3
Pontllanfraith Caerph 14 E11
Pontlliw Swans 13 Q10
Pontlottyn Caerph 14 D9
Pontlyfni Gwynd 28 E10
Pontneddfechan Neath 13 U9
Pontnewydd Torfn 14 F11
Pontrhydfendigaid Cerdgn 20 G9
Pont-rhyd-y-fen Neath 13 S11
Pontrhydygroes Cerdgn 20 G8
Pontrilas Herefs 14 H5
Pont Robert Powys 21 M2
Pontshaen Cerdgn 20 B13
Pontsticill Myr Td 14 C8
Pontwelly Carmth 20 B14
Pontyates Carmth 13 N9
Pontyberem Carmth 13 N8
Pontybodkin Flints 30 D14
Pontyclun Rhondd 14 C13
Pontycymer Brdgnd 13 U11
Pont-y-pant Conwy 28 K9
Pontypool Torfn 14 F10
Pontypridd Rhondd 14 C12
Pontywaun Caerph 14 E11
Pool Cnwll 1 R11
Pool Leeds 36 F16
Poole Poole 7 S12
Poole Keynes Gloucs 15 R11
Poolewe Highld 52 E1
Pooley Bridge Cumb 40 C14
Poolfold Staffs 31 N14
Poolhill Gloucs 15 M5
Pool of Muckhart Clacks 50 G16
Pool Street Essex 18 J7
Poplar Gt Lon 17 S13
Porchfield IoW 8 H13
Poringland Norfk 27 R8
Porkellis Cnwll 1 R12
Porlock Somset 5 Q3
Porlock Weir Somset 5 Q3
Portachoillan Ag & B 42 K7
Port-an-Eorna Highld 52 D9
Port Appin Ag & B 48 K8
Port Askaig Ag & B 42 E5
Portavadie Ag & B 43 M5
Port Bannatyne Ag & B 43 P6
Portbury N Som 14 J14
Port Carlisle Cumb 39 U8
Port Charlotte Ag & B 42 C7
Portchester Hants 8 K11
Port Driseach Ag & B 43 N4
Port Ellen Ag & B 42 D9
Port Elphinstone Abers 55 Q11
Portencalzie D & G 38 B7
Portencross N Ayrs 43 R9
Port Erin IoM 34 b7
Portesham Dorset 7 L13
Portessie Moray 54 K4
Port Eynon Swans 13 N12
Portfield Gate Pembks 12 E7
Portgate Devon 4 J13
Port Gaverne Cnwll 4 C14
Port Glasgow Inver 43 T4
Portgordon Moray 54 J4
Portgower Highld 58 D11
Porth Cnwll 1 T7
Porth Rhondd 14 C11
Porthallow Cnwll 1 S14
Porthallow Cnwll 2 F7
Porthcawl Brdgnd 13 T14
Porthcothan Cnwll 1 T6
Porthcurno Cnwll 1 M14
Port Henderson Highld 52 D3
Porthgain Pembks 12 D5
Porthgwarra Cnwll 1 L14
Porthkerry V Glam 14 C15
Porthleven Cnwll 1 Q13
Porthmadog Gwynd 28 G12
Porth Navas Cnwll 1 S13
Porthoustock Cnwll 1 T14
Porthpean Cnwll 2 C8
Porthtowan Cnwll 1 R10
Porthyrhyd Carmth 13 N7
Portincaple Ag & B 43 R1
Portington E R Yk 32 H2
Portinnisherrich Ag & B 49 L14
Portinscale Cumb 34 K3
Port Isaac Cnwll 4 C14
Portishead N Som 14 J14
Portknockie Moray 55 L3
Portland Dorset 7 M15
Portlethen Abers 55 S15
Portling D & G 39 P9
Portloe Cnwll 2 B9
Port Logan D & G 38 C12
Portmahomack Highld 58 B16
Portmellon Cnwll 2 C9
Port Mor Highld 48 D3
Portnacroish Ag & B 49 L8
Portnaguran W Isls 56 f2
Portnahaven Ag & B 42 A8
Portnalong Highld 59 d10
Port nan Giuran W Isls 56 f2
Port nan Long W Isls 56 c5
Port Nis W Isls 56 f1
Portobello C Edin 45 R4
Portobello Wolves 23 L9
Port of Menteith Stirlg 49 V15
Port of Ness W Isls 56 f1
Porton Wilts 8 D6
Portpatrick D & G 38 B9
Port Quin Cnwll 4 C14
Port Ramsay Ag & B 48 K8
Portreath Cnwll 1 Q10
Portree Highld 59 f9
Port St Mary IoM 34 b7
Portscatho Cnwll 1 U12
Portsea C Port 8 K12
Portskerra Highld 57 T3
Portskewett Mons 14 J12
Portslade Br & H 10 C14
Portslade-by-Sea Br & H 10 C14
Portslogan D & G 38 B9
Portsmouth C Port 9 L12
Portsmouth Calder 31 N3
Port Soderick IoM 34 d6
Portsonachan Hotel Ag & B 49 M12
Portsoy Abers 55 M4
Port Sunlight Wirral 30 E10
Portswood C Sotn 8 H9
Port Talbot Neath 13 S12
Portuairk Highld 48 D4
Portway Worcs 23 N13
Port Wemyss Ag & B 42 A8
Port William D & G 38 G11
Portwrinkle Cnwll 2 H7
Portyerrock D & G 38 J12
Poslingford Suffk 18 J5
Posso Border 45 Q11
Postbridge Devon 5 M14
Postcombe Oxon 16 H10
Postling Kent 11 R8
Postwick Norfk 27 R7
Potarch Abers 55 M15
Potten End Herts 17 M8
Potter Brompton N York 37 R10
Potterhanworth Lincs 33 M13
Potterhanworth Booths Lincs 33 M13
Potter Heigham Norfk 27 T5
Potterne Wilts 7 S1
Potterne Wick Wilts 7 S1
Potters Bar Herts 17 R10
Potters Crouch Herts 17 P9
Potters Green Covtry 23 S12
Potters Marston Leics 24 D9
Potterspury Nhants 16 J3
Potterton Abers 55 S12
Potto N York 36 J6
Potton C Beds 17 Q2
Pott Shrigley Ches E 31 P11
Poughill Cnwll 4 F9
Poughill Devon 5 Q9
Poulner Hants 8 D11
Poulshot Wilts 7 R1
Poulton Gloucs 15 T10
Poulton-le-Fylde Lancs 30 E1
Poundbury Dorset 7 M12
Poundffald Swans 13 P11
Pound Green E Susx 10 G11
Pound Green Suffk 18 H4
Pound Hill W Susx 10 D9
Poundon Bucks 16 G6
Poundsgate Devon 3 N4
Poundstock Cnwll 4 F11
Pouton D & G 38 H11
Povey Cross Surrey 10 C8
Powburn Nthumb 47 P14
Powderham Devon 5 S13
Powerstock Dorset 6 K11
Powfoot D & G 39 T8
Powick Worcs 15 P1
Powmill P & K 50 G16
Poxwell Dorset 7 N13
Poyle Slough 17 N14
Poynings W Susx 10 C13
Poyntington Dorset 7 M7
Poynton Ches E 31 N10
Poynton Green Wrekin 22 E6
Praa Sands Cnwll 1 P13
Pratt's Bottom Gt Lon 10 F5
Praze-an-Beeble Cnwll 1 Q12
Prees Shrops 22 E3
Preesall Lancs 35 L15
Prees Green Shrops 22 E4
Prees Heath Shrops 22 E2
Prees Higher Heath Shrops 22 E3
Pren-gwyn Cerdgn 20 B13
Prenteg Gwynd 28 G11
Prescot Knows 30 G9
Prescott Devon 6 D8
Presnerb Angus 50 J5
Prestatyn Denbgs 29 P5
Prestbury Ches E 31 N11
Prestbury Gloucs 15 R6
Presteigne Powys 21 Q10
Prestleigh Somset 7 M4
Preston Border 47 L7
Preston Br & H 10 D14
Preston Devon 3 Q4
Preston Dorset 7 N13
Preston E R Yk 33 P3
Preston Gloucs 15 S10
Preston Herts 17 Q6
Preston Kent 11 P5
Preston Kent 11 S5
Preston Lancs 30 H3
Preston Nthumb 47 R12
Preston Rutlnd 24 J8
Preston Somset 6 D5
Preston Suffk 19 L5
Preston Torbay 3 Q6
Preston Wilts 15 S14
Preston Bagot Warwks 23 P14
Preston Bissett Bucks 16 G5
Preston Bowyer Somset 6 E6
Preston Brockhurst Shrops 22 E5
Preston Brook Halton 30 H11
Preston Candover Hants 8 K5
Preston Capes Nhants 16 F1
Preston Green Warwks 23 P14
Preston Gubbals Shrops 22 D5
Preston on Stour Warwks 15 U2
Preston on the Hill Halton 30 J11
Preston on Wye Herefs 21 R13
Prestonpans E Loth 46 E4
Preston Patrick Cumb 35 P9
Preston Plucknett Somset 6 K8
Preston-under-Scar N York 36 C8
Preston upon the Weald Moors Wrekin 22 G6
Preston Wynne Herefs 14 K2
Prestwich Bury 31 M7
Prestwick S Ayrs 44 C12
Prestwick Airport S Ayrs 44 C12
Prestwood Bucks 16 K10
Prickwillow Cambs 26 F12
Priddy Somset 6 K2
Priest Hutton Lancs 35 N11
Priestland E Ayrs 44 F10
Priest Weston Shrops 21 P4
Primrosehill Border 46 K7
Primsidemill Border 47 L12
Princes Risborough Bucks 16 J9
Princethorpe Warwks 23 S14
Princetown Devon 3 L4
Priors Hardwick Warwks 24 D16
Priorslee Wrekin 22 G7
Priors Marston Warwks 24 D16
Priors Norton Gloucs 15 P6
Priory Vale Swindn 15 T12
Priston BaNES 7 N1
Prittlewell Sthend 18 K15
Privett Hants 9 L7
Prixford Devon 5 L5
Probus Cnwll 1 U10
Prora E Loth 46 G3
Prospect Cumb 39 T12
Prospidnick Cnwll 1 Q13
Protstonhill Abers 55 Q4
Prudhoe Nthumb 41 M8
Publow BaNES 15 L16
Puckeridge Herts 17 T6
Puckington Somset 6 H8
Pucklechurch S Glos 15 M14
Puddington Ches W 30 E12
Puddington Devon 5 Q9
Puddletown Dorset 7 N12
Pudsey Leeds 31 T2
Pulborough W Susx 9 R8
Pulford Ches W 30 F14
Pulham Dorset 7 N9
Pulham Market Norfk 27 Q11
Pulham St Mary Norfk 27 Q11
Pulloxhill C Beds 17 N4
Pumpherston W Loth 45 N5
Pumsaint Carmth 20 F14
Puncheston Pembks 12 F5
Puncknowle Dorset 6 K13
Punnett's Town E Susx 10 H11
Purbrook Hants 9 L10
Purfleet Thurr 10 G2
Puriton Somset 6 G4
Purleigh Essex 18 K13
Purley Gt Lon 10 D5
Purley W Berk 16 G14
Purse Caundle Dorset 7 N8
Purtington Somset 6 H9
Purton Gloucs 15 M9
Purton Gloucs 15 M9
Purton Wilts 15 T12
Purton Stoke Wilts 15 T11
Pury End Nhants 16 H3
Pusey Oxon 16 C10
Putley Herefs 15 L4
Putley Green Herefs 15 L4
Putney Gt Lon 17 Q14
Puttenham Surrey 9 Q4
Puxley Nhants 16 J3
Puxton N Som 14 H16
Pwll Carmth 13 N10
Pwll-glâs Denbgs 29 Q9
Pwllgloyw Powys 14 C4
Pwllheli Gwynd 28 D12
Pwllmeyric Mons 14 K11
Pwll Trap Carmth 12 K7
Pwll-y-glaw Neath 13 S11
Pye Bridge Derbys 32 C15
Pyecombe W Susx 10 C13
Pyle Brdgnd 13 T13
Pyleigh Somset 6 E6
Pylle Somset 7 L4
Pymoor Cambs 26 E11
Pymore Dorset 6 J12
Pyrford Surrey 9 R2
Pyrton Oxon 16 H11
Pytchley Nhants 24 J13
Pyworthy Devon 4 G10

Q

Quadring Lincs 25 P3
Quadring Eaudike Lincs 25 Q3
Quainton Bucks 16 J7
Quarff Shet 59 q6
Quarley Hants 8 E4
Quarndon Derbys 23 R2
Quarrier's Village Inver 44 C6
Quarrington Lincs 25 M1
Quarrington Hill Dur 41 R12
Quarry Bank Dudley 22 K11
Quarrywood Moray 54 F4
Quarter N Ayrs 43 R6
Quarter S Lans 44 H8
Quatford Shrops 22 H10
Quatt Shrops 22 H11
Quebec Dur 41 N11
Quedgeley Gloucs 15 P8
Queen Adelaide Cambs 26 F12
Queenborough Kent 11 M3
Queen Camel Somset 7 L7
Queen Charlton BaNES 15 L15
Queenhill Worcs 15 P4
Queen Oak Dorset 7 P6
Queen's Bower IoW 8 K14
Queensbury C Brad 31 R3
Queensferry Flints 30 E13
Queenslie C Glas 44 G6
Queenzieburn N Lans 44 H4
Quendon Essex 18 E8
Queniborough Leics 24 F7
Quenington Gloucs 15 T9
Queslett Birm 23 M10
Quethiock Cnwll 2 G5
Quidenham Norfk 27 M11
Quidhampton Wilts 8 C7
Quinton Nhants 16 J1
Quintrell Downs Cnwll 1 T8
Quixwood Border 47 L6
Quoig P & K 50 D12
Quorn Leics 24 E6
Quothquan S Lans 45 M10
Quoyburray Ork 58 c4
Quoyloo Ork 58 a3

R

Rachan Mill Border 45 P11
Rachub Gwynd 28 H7
Rackenford Devon 5 Q8
Rackham W Susx 9 R9
Rackheath Norfk 27 R6
Racks D & G 39 R6
Rackwick Ork 58 a5
Radbourne Derbys 23 Q3
Radcliffe Bury 31 M6
Radcliffe on Trent Notts 24 F2
Radclive Bucks 16 H4
Raddery Highld 53 S5
Radernie Fife 51 N14
Radford Covtry 23 R12
Radford Semele Warwks 23 R15
Radlett Herts 17 P10
Radley Oxon 16 F10
Radley Green Essex 18 G12
Radnage Bucks 16 J10
Radstock BaNES 7 M2
Radstone Nhants 16 F3
Radway Warwks 16 C2
Radwell Bed 25 L16
Radwell Herts 17 Q4
Radwinter Essex 18 G7
Radyr Cardif 14 D13
Rafford Moray 54 E5
Ragdale Leics 24 G5
Raglan Mons 14 H9
Ragnall Notts 32 J12
Raigbeg Highld 53 U10
Rainbow Hill Worcs 22 J16
Rainford St Hel 30 G7
Rainham Gt Lon 10 G1
Rainham Medway 11 L4
Rainhill St Hel 30 G9
Rainhill Stoops St Hel 30 H9
Rainow Ches E 31 P12
Rainton N York 36 G11
Rainworth Notts 32 F14
Rait P & K 50 K11
Raithby Lincs 33 R10
Raithby Lincs 33 S13
Rake Hants 9 N7
Ralia Highld 53 S15
Ramasaig Highld 59 a9
Rame Cnwll 1 R12
Rame Cnwll 2 J8
Rampisham Dorset 7 L10
Rampside Cumb 34 J12
Rampton Cambs 26 D14
Rampton Notts 32 H11
Ramsbottom Bury 31 M5
Ramsbury Wilts 16 B15
Ramscraigs Highld 58 F9
Ramsdean Hants 9 L8
Ramsdell Hants 8 K2
Ramsden Oxon 16 C7
Ramsden Bellhouse Essex 18 H14
Ramsey Cambs 25 Q11
Ramsey Essex 19 Q8
Ramsey IoM 34 e3
Ramsey Forty Foot Cambs 25 R11
Ramsey Heights Cambs 25 Q11
Ramsey Island Essex 19 L12
Ramsey Mereside Cambs 25 Q10
Ramsey St Mary's Cambs 25 Q11
Ramsgate Kent 11 U4
Ramsgill N York 36 D11
Ramshope Nthumb 40 G1
Ramshorn Staffs 23 N1
Ramsnest Common Surrey 9 Q6
Ranby Lincs 33 P11
Ranby Notts 32 F11
Rand Lincs 33 N11
Randwick Gloucs 15 P9
Ranfurly Rens 44 D6
Rangemore Staffs 23 P5
Rangeworthy S Glos 15 M12
Rankinston E Ayrs 44 D14
Rannoch Station P & K 49 T6
Ranscombe Somset 5 R4
Ranskill Notts 32 F10
Ranton Staffs 22 J5
Ranton Green Staffs 22 J5
Ranworth Norfk 27 S6
Raploch Stirlg 44 J1
Rapness Ork 58 c2
Rascarrel D & G 39 N10
Rashfield Ag & B 43 Q3
Rashwood Worcs 22 K14
Raskelf N York 36 J11
Rastrick Calder 31 S4
Ratagan Highld 52 F11
Ratby Leics 24 D8
Ratcliffe Culey Leics 23 R9
Ratcliffe on Soar Notts 24 D4
Ratcliffe on the Wreake Leics 24 F6
Rathen Abers 55 T5
Rathillet Fife 51 M12
Rathmell N York 35 S13
Ratho C Edin 45 P5
Ratho Station C Edin 45 P5
Rathven Moray 54 K4
Ratley Warwks 16 C2
Ratling Kent 11 S6
Ratlinghope Shrops 21 R4
Rattar Highld 58 G2
Rattery Devon 3 N6
Rattlesden Suffk 19 M4
Ratton Village E Susx 10 H15
Rattray P & K 50 J8
Raunds Nhants 25 L13
Ravenfield Rothm 32 D8
Ravenglass Cumb 34 G7
Raveningham Norfk 27 T9
Ravenscar N York 37 R6
Ravenscraig N Lans 44 J7
Ravensden Bed 17 N1
Ravenshead Notts 32 E15
Ravensthorpe Kirk 31 T4
Ravensthorpe Nhants 24 G14
Ravenstone Leics 23 S6
Ravenstone M Keyn 16 K2
Ravenstonedale Cumb 35 R6
Ravenstruther S Lans 45 L9
Ravensworth N York 36 D5
Rawcliffe C York 36 K14
Rawcliffe E R Yk 32 G4
Rawdon Leeds 31 T1
Rawling Street Kent 11 M5
Rawmarsh Rothm 32 C8
Rawreth Essex 18 J14
Rawridge Devon 6 F10
Rawtenstall Lancs 31 M4
Raydon Suffk 19 N7
Rayleigh Essex 18 J15
Rayne Essex 18 H9
Raynes Park Gt Lon 10 C4
Reach Cambs 26 F14
Read Lancs 31 L2
Reading Readg 16 H14
Reading Street Kent 11 M10
Reading Street Kent 11 U3
Reagill Cumb 35 Q4
Realwa Cnwll 1 Q12
Rearquhar Highld 57 R15
Rearsby Leics 24 F6
Reay Highld 58 C3
Reculver Kent 11 S4
Red Ball Devon 6 D8
Redberth Pembks 12 G9
Redbourn Herts 17 P8
Redbourne N Linc 33 L8
Redbrook Gloucs 14 K8
Redbrook Wrexhm 22 D2
Redbrook Street Kent 11 N9
Redburn Highld 54 C7
Redcar R & Cl 41 U14
Redcastle D & G 39 N8
Redcastle Highld 53 R6
Redding Falk 45 L4
Reddingmuirhead Falk 45 L4
Redditch Worcs 23 M14
Rede Suffk 18 J4
Redenhall Norfk 27 R11
Redesmouth Nthumb 40 J5
Redford Abers 51 S4
Redford Angus 51 P8
Redford W Susx 9 P7
Redfordgreen Border 46 E14
Redgorton P & K 50 H11
Redgrave Suffk 27 N12
Redhill Abers 55 Q14
Red Hill Bmouth 7 T11
Redhill Herts 17 R5
Redhill N Som 14 J16
Redhill Surrey 10 C7
Redisham Suffk 27 T11
Redland Bristl 14 K14
Redland Ork 58 b3
Redlingfield Suffk 27 Q14
Redlingfield Green Suffk 27 Q13
Red Lodge Suffk 26 H14
Redlynch Somset 7 N5
Redlynch Wilts 8 D8
Redmarley Worcs 22 H14
Redmarley D'Abitot Gloucs 15 N5
Redmarshall S on T 36 H3
Redmile Leics 24 H3
Redmire N York 36 C8
Redmyre Abers 51 S3
Rednal Shrops 29 T14
Redpath Border 46 H11
Redpoint Highld 52 D3
Red Roses Carmth 12 J8
Red Row Nthumb 41 P2
Redruth Cnwll 1 R11
Redstone P & K 50 J10
Red Wharf Bay IoA 28 G5
Redwick Newpt 14 H13
Redwick S Glos 14 K12
Redworth Darltn 36 F3
Reed Herts 17 S4
Reedham Norfk 27 T8
Reedness E R Yk 32 H4
Reeds Holme Lancs 31 M4
Reepham Lincs 33 M12
Reepham Norfk 27 P5
Reeth N York 36 C7
Reeves Green Solhll 23 Q12
Regil N Som 14 K16
Reiff Highld 56 F11
Reigate Surrey 10 C7
Reighton N York 37 T11
Reisque Abers 55 R11
Reiss Highld 58 H5
Relubbus Cnwll 1 P12
Relugas Moray 54 D7
Remenham Wokham 16 J13
Remenham Hill Wokham 16 J13
Rempstone Notts 24 E5
Rendcomb Gloucs 15 S8
Rendham Suffk 19 S3
Rendlesham Suffk 19 S4
Renfrew Rens 44 E5
Renhold Bed 17 N1
Renishaw Derbys 32 D11
Rennington Nthumb 47 R14
Renton W Duns 44 D4
Renwick Cumb 40 E11
Repps Norfk 27 T6
Repton Derbys 23 R4
Resaurie Highld 53 S7
Resipole Highld 48 H5
Reskadinnick Cnwll 1 Q11
Resolis Highld 53 S4
Resolven Neath 13 T10
Rest and be thankful Ag & B 49 Q14
Reston Border 47 M6
Reswallie Angus 51 P7
Retford Notts 32 G11
Rettendon Essex 18 J14
Revesby Lincs 33 Q14
Rewe Devon 5 R11
Rew Street IoW 8 H13
Reydon Suffk 27 U12
Reymerston Norfk 27 M8
Reynalton Pembks 12 G9
Reynoldston Swans 13 N12
Rezare Cnwll 2 H3
Rhandirmwyn Carmth 20 G13
Rhayader Powys 20 K9
Rheindown Highld 53 Q7
Rhes-y-cae Flints 29 R6
Rhewl Denbgs 29 Q8
Rhewl Denbgs 29 R11
Rhicarn Highld 56 G9
Rhiconich Highld 56 K5
Rhicullen Highld 53 S3
Rhigos Rhondd 13 U9
Rhireavach Highld 56 F14
Rhives Highld 57 T13
Rhiwbina Cardif 14 E13
Rhiwderyn Newpt 14 F12
Rhiwlas Gwynd 28 G7
Rhoden Green Kent 10 J7
Rhodes Minnis Kent 11 R8
Rhodiad-y-brenin Pembks 12 C5
Rhonehouse D & G 39 M8
Rhoose V Glam 14 C15
Rhos Carmth 13 L4
Rhos Neath 13 R9
Rhoscolyn IoA 28 C6
Rhoscrowther Pembks 12 E10
Rhosesmor Flints 29 R7
Rhosgoch Powys 21 N12
Rhoshill Pembks 12 J3
Rhoshirwaun Gwynd 28 B13
Rhoslefain Gwynd 20 D3
Rhosllanerchrugog Wrexhm 29 S11
Rhosmeirch IoA 28 F5
Rhosneigr IoA 28 D6
Rhosnesni Wrexhm 30 E16
Rhôs-on-Sea Conwy 29 L5
Rhossili Swans 13 M12
Rhostryfan Gwynd 28 F9
Rhostyllen Wrexhm 30 E16
Rhosybol IoA 28 E4
Rhos-y-gwaliau Gwynd 29 M12
Rhosymedre Wrexhm 29 S11
Rhu Ag & B 43 S3
Rhuallt Denbgs 29 P6
Rhubodach Ag & B 43 N4
Rhuddlan Denbgs 29 N5
Rhunahaorine Ag & B 42 J9
Rhyd Gwynd 28 H11
Rhydargaeau Carmth 13 M6
Rhydcymerau Carmth 13 P4
Rhyd-Ddu Gwynd 28 G10
Rhydlewis Cerdgn 20 A12
Rhydowen Cerdgn 20 C13
Rhyd-uchaf Gwynd 29 M12
Rhyd-y-clafdy Gwynd 28 D12
Rhyd-y-foel Conwy 29 M6
Rhydyfro Neath 13 R9
Rhyd-y-groes Gwynd 28 G7
Rhyd-y pennau Cerdgn 20 E6
Rhyl Denbgs 29 N5
Rhymney Caerph 14 D9
Rhynd P & K 50 J12
Rhynie Abers 55 L10
Rhynie Highld 53 U2
Ribbesford Worcs 22 H13
Ribbleton Lancs 30 H2
Ribchester Lancs 30 K2
Riby Lincs 33 P6
Riccall N York 32 F1
Riccarton Border 40 D3
Riccarton E Ayrs 44 D11
Richards Castle Herefs 22 D14
Richmond Gt Lon 17 Q14
Richmond N York 36 E7
Richmond Sheff 32 C10
Rickerscote Staffs 22 K5
Rickford N Som 6 K1
Rickham Devon 3 P10
Rickinghall Suffk 27 N13
Rickling Green Essex 18 E8
Rickmansworth Herts 17 N11
Riddell Border 46 G13
Riddlecombe Devon 5 M8
Riddlesden C Brad 36 C16
Ridge Dorset 7 R13
Ridge Herts 17 Q10
Ridge Wilts 7 R5
Ridge Lane Warwks 23 R10
Ridgeway Derbys 32 C11
Ridgewell Essex 18 H7
Ridgewood E Susx 10 F12
Ridgmont C Beds 17 M4
Riding Mill Nthumb 41 L8
Ridlington Norfk 27 S4
Ridlington Rutlnd 24 J8
Ridsdale Nthumb 40 K4
Rievaulx N York 36 K9
Rigg D & G 39 V7
Riggend N Lans 44 J5
Righoul Highld 54 B6
Rigsby Lincs 33 S12
Rigside S Lans 44 K11
Riley Green Lancs 30 J3
Rilla Mill Cnwll 2 G4
Rillington N York 37 P11
Rimington Lancs 35 S16
Rimpton Somset 7 L7
Rimswell E R Yk 33 R3
Rinaston Pembks 12 F6
Rindleford Shrops 22 H9
Ringford D & G 39 M9
Ringland Norfk 27 P6
Ringmer E Susx 10 F13
Ringmore Devon 3 M8
Ringmore Devon 3 R4
Ringorm Moray 54 G7
Ringsfield Suffk 27 T11
Ringsfield Corner Suffk 27 T11
Ringshall Herts 17 M8
Ringshall Suffk 19 N5
Ringshall Stocks Suffk 19 N5
Ringstead Nhants 25 L13
Ringstead Norfk 26 H2
Ringwood Hants 8 D11
Ringwould Kent 11 U7
Ripe E Susx 10 G13
Ripley Derbys 32 C16
Ripley Hants 8 D12
Ripley N York 36 F13
Ripley Surrey 9 R2
Riplington Hants 9 L8
Ripon N York 36 G11
Rippingale Lincs 25 N4
Ripple Kent 11 T7
Ripple Worcs 15 Q4
Ripponden Calder 31 Q4
Risabus Ag & B 42 C9
Risbury Herefs 22 E16
Risby Suffk 26 J14
Risca Caerph 14 F11
Rise E R Yk 37 T16
Risegate Lincs 25 P4
Riseley Bed 25 M15
Riseley Wokham 9 M1
Rishangles Suffk 27 P14
Rishton Lancs 31 L3
Rishworth Calder 31 Q5
Risley Derbys 24 D3
Risley Warrtn 30 K9
Risplith N York 36 F12
River Kent 11 T8
River W Susx 9 Q8
Riverford Highld 53 Q6
Riverhead Kent 10 G6
Rivington Lancs 30 J5
Roade Nhants 16 J1
Roadmeetings S Lans 44 K8
Roadside E Ayrs 44 F14
Roadside Highld 58 F4
Roadwater Somset 5 S4
Roag Highld 59 c9
Roan of Craigoch S Ayrs 38 F1
Roath Cardif 14 E14
Roberton Border 46 F14
Roberton S Lans 45 L12
Robertsbridge E Susx 10 K11
Roberttown Kirk 31 S4
Robeston Wathen Pembks 12 G7
Robgill Tower D & G 39 U7
Robin Hood Doncaster Sheffield Airport Donc 32 F8
Robin Hood's Bay N York 37 R6
Roborough Devon 2 K6
Roborough Devon 5 L8
Roby Knows 30 G9
Rocester Staffs 23 N2
Roch Pembks 12 D6
Rochdale Rochdl 31 N5
Roche Cnwll 2 C6
Rochester Medway 10 K4
Rochester Nthumb 40 H2
Rochford Essex 18 K15
Rochford Worcs 22 F14
Rock Cnwll 2 B3
Rock Nthumb 47 R13
Rock Worcs 22 H13
Rockbeare Devon 5 S11
Rockbourne Hants 8 C9
Rockcliffe Cumb 40 B8
Rockcliffe D & G 39 P9
Rockend Torbay 3 R6
Rock Ferry Wirral 30 E10
Rockfield Highld 54 C1
Rockfield Mons 14 J7
Rockford Devon 5 P3
Rockhampton S Glos 15 L11
Rockhill Shrops 21 P7
Rockingham Nhants 24 J10
Rockland All Saints Norfk 27 M9
Rockland St Mary Norfk 27 R8
Rockland St Peter Norfk 27 M9
Rockley Notts 32 G12
Rockville Ag & B 43 R2
Rockwell End Bucks 16 J12
Rodborough Gloucs 15 P9
Rodbourne Swindn 15 T12
Rodbourne Wilts 15 Q13
Rodden Dorset 7 L13
Rode Somset 7 P2
Rode Heath Ches E 31 M15
Rodel W Isls 56 c4
Roden Wrekin 22 E6
Rodhuish Somset 5 S4
Rodington Wrekin 22 F6
Rodington Heath Wrekin 22 F6
Rodley Gloucs 15 N8
Rodmarton Gloucs 15 Q10
Rodmell E Susx 10 E14
Rodmersham Kent 11 M5
Rodmersham Green Kent 11 M5
Rodney Stoke Somset 6 K2
Rodsley Derbys 23 P2
Roecliffe N York 36 H12
Roe Green Herts 17 Q9
Roe Green Herts 17 S4
Roehampton Gt Lon 17 Q14
Roffey W Susx 9 T6
Rogart Highld 57 R13
Rogate W Susx 9 N8
Rogerstone Newpt 14 F12
Roghadal W Isls 56 c4
Rogiet Mons 14 J12
Roke Oxon 16 G11
Roker Sundld 41 R9
Rollesby Norfk 27 T6
Rolleston Leics 24 H9
Rolleston Notts 32 H15
Rolleston on Dove Staffs 23 Q4
Rolston E R Yk 37 U16
Rolvenden Kent 11 L10
Rolvenden Layne Kent 11 L10
Romaldkirk Dur 36 B3
Romanby N York 36 G8
Romanno Bridge Border 45 P9
Romansleigh Devon 5 N7
Romesdal Highld 59 e8
Romford Dorset 7 T9
Romford Gt Lon 18 E15
Romiley Stockp 31 P9
Romsey Hants 8 G8
Romsley Shrops 22 H11
Romsley Worcs 23 L12
Ronachan Ag & B 42 K8
Rookhope Dur 40 K11
Rookley IoW 8 J14
Rooks Bridge Somset 6 H2
Rooks Nest Somset 6 D5
Rookwith N York 36 E9
Roos E R Yk 33 Q3
Roothams Green Bed 25 N16
Ropley Hants 9 L6
Ropley Dean Hants 8 K6
Ropsley Lincs 25 L3
Rora Abers 55 U6
Rorrington Shrops 21 Q4
Rosarie Moray 54 J6
Rose Cnwll 1 S9
Rose Ash Devon 5 P7
Rosebank S Lans 44 J8
Rosebush Pembks 12 G5
Rosedale Abbey N York 37 M7
Rose Green Essex 19 L9
Rose Green Suffk 19 L7
Rose Green Suffk 19 M6
Rose Green W Susx 9 P12
Rosehall Highld 57 N13
Rosehearty Abers 55 S4
Rose Hill Lancs 31 M2
Roseisle Moray 54 F4
Roselands E Susx 10 H15
Rosemarket Pembks 12 E9
Rosemarkie Highld 53 T5
Rosemary Lane Devon 6 E8
Rosemount P & K 50 J9
Rosenannon Cnwll 2 B5
Rosewell Mdloth 45 R6
Roseworth S on T 36 H3
Rosgill Cumb 35 P4
Roskhill Highld 59 c9
Rosley Cumb 40 A11
Roslin Mdloth 45 R6
Rosliston Derbys 23 Q6
Rosneath Ag & B 43 S3
Ross D & G 39 L11
Rossett Wrexhm 30 F15
Rossett Green N York 36 F14
Rossington Donc 32 F8
Rossland Rens 44 D5
Ross-on-Wye Herefs 15 L6
Roster Highld 58 G7
Rostherne Ches E 31 L10
Rosthwaite Cumb 34 K4
Roston Derbys 23 N2
Rosyth Fife 45 P3
Rothbury Nthumb 41 M2
Rotherby Leics 24 G6
Rotherfield E Susx 10 G10
Rotherfield Greys Oxon 16 H13
Rotherfield Peppard Oxon 16 H13
Rotherham Rothm 32 C9
Rothersthorpe Nhants 24 G16
Rotherwick Hants 9 M2
Rothes Moray 54 H7
Rothesay Ag & B 43 P6
Rothiebrisbane Abers 55 P8
Rothiemay Moray 55 L7
Rothiemurchus Lodge Highld 54 C13
Rothienorman Abers 55 P9
Rothley Leics 24 E7
Rothmaise Abers 55 N9
Rothwell Leeds 32 B3
Rothwell Lincs 33 N8
Rothwell Nhants 24 J12
Rottal Lodge Angus 51 M4
Rottingdean Br & H 10 E14
Rottington Cumb 34 F5
Roucan D & G 39 R6
Rougham Norfk 26 K5
Rougham Green Suffk 19 L3
Rough Common Kent 11 Q5
Roughpark Abers 54 H13
Roughton Lincs 33 Q13
Roughton Norfk 27 Q3
Roughton Shrops 22 H10
Roundbush Green Essex 18 F11
Round Green Luton 17 N6
Roundham Somset 6 J9
Roundhay Leeds 32 B1
Roundway Wilts 15 R16
Roundyhill Angus 51 M7
Rousdon Devon 6 G12
Rousham Oxon 16 E6
Rous Lench Worcs 15 R1
Routenburn N Ayrs 43 R7
Routh E R Yk 37 T16
Row Cumb 35 M9
Rowanburn D & G 40 C6
Rowardennan Stirlg 49 S16
Rowarth Derbys 31 Q9
Rowberrow Somset 6 J1
Rowde Wilts 15 R16
Rowen Conwy 28 K6
Rowfoot Nthumb 40 F8
Rowhedge Essex 19 M10
Rowington Warwks 23 P14
Rowland Derbys 31 T12
Rowland's Castle Hants 9 M10
Rowland's Gill Gatesd 41 N9
Rowledge Surrey 9 N4
Rowley Dur 41 M10
Rowley Regis Sandw 23 L11
Rowlstone Herefs 14 H5
Rowly Surrey 9 R5
Rowner Hants 8 K11
Rowney Green Worcs 23 M13
Rownhams Hants 8 G9
Rowrah Cumb 34 G4
Rowsham Bucks 16 K7
Rowsley Derbys 31 T13
Rowston Lincs 33 M15
Rowton Ches W 30 G13
Rowton Wrekin 22 F5
Roxburgh Border 46 J12
Roxby N Linc 32 K5
Roxton Bed 17 P1
Roxwell Essex 18 G12
Royal Leamington Spa Warwks 23 R14
Royal Tunbridge Wells Kent 10 H8
Royal Wootton Bassett Wilts 15 S13
Roy Bridge Highld 49 Q2
Roydon Essex 18 D12
Roydon Norfk 26 H5
Roydon Norfk 27 P12
Roydon Hamlet Essex 18 D12
Royston Barns 32 B6
Royston Herts 17 S3
Royton Oldham 31 N6
Rozel Jersey 3 e2
Ruabon Wrexhm 29 S11
Ruaig Ag & B 42 c3
Ruan Lanihorne Cnwll 1 U11
Ruan Major Cnwll 1 R15
Ruan Minor Cnwll 1 R15
Ruardean Gloucs 15 L7
Ruardean Hill Gloucs 15 L7
Ruardean Woodside Gloucs 15 L7
Rubery Birm 23 L12
Rubha Ban W Isls 56 b8
Ruckhall Herefs 14 J4
Ruckinge Kent 11 P9
Ruckley Shrops 22 E9
Rudby N York 36 J6
Rudchester Nthumb 41 M7
Ruddington Notts 24 E3
Rudge Somset 7 P2
Rudgeway S Glos 15 L12
Rudgwick W Susx 9 S6
Rudheath Ches W 30 K12
Rudley Green Essex 18 K13
Rudloe Wilts 15 P15
Rudry Caerph 14 E12
Rudston E R Yk 37 T12
Rudyard Staffs 31 P14
Ruecastle Border 46 H13
Rufford Lancs 30 G5
Rufforth C York 36 K15
Rugby Warwks 24 D13
Rugeley Staffs 23 M6
Ruishton Somset 6 G7
Ruislip Gt Lon 17 N12
Rumbach Moray 54 J6
Rumbling Bridge P & K 50 G16
Rumburgh Suffk 27 S12
Rumford Cnwll 1 U6
Rumford Falk 45 L4
Rumney Cardif 14 E13
Runcorn Halton 30 H10
Runcton W Susx 9 P11
Runcton Holme Norfk 26 G7
Runfold Surrey 9 P4
Runhall Norfk 27 N7
Runham Norfk 27 U7
Runnington Somset 6 D7
Runswick N York 37 P4
Runtaleave Angus 51 L5
Runwell Essex 18 J14
Ruscombe Wokham 16 J14
Rushall Herefs 15 L4
Rushall Norfk 27 Q12
Rushall Wilts 8 C2
Rushbrooke Suffk 19 L3
Rushbury Shrops 22 E10
Rushden Herts 17 R5
Rushden Nhants 25 L14
Rushenden Kent 11 M3
Rushford Norfk 27 L12
Rush Green Essex 19 P11
Rush Green Gt Lon 18 E15
Rush Green Warrtn 30 K10
Rushlake Green E Susx 10 H12
Rushmere Suffk 27 U11
Rushmoor Surrey 9 P5
Rushock Worcs 22 K13
Rusholme Manch 31 N8
Rushton Nhants 24 J12
Rushton Spencer Staffs 31 P14
Rushwick Worcs 15 P1
Rushyford Dur 41 Q14
Ruskie Stirlg 50 A16
Ruskington Lincs 33 N16
Rusland Cross Cumb 35 L9
Rusper W Susx 9 T5

Ruspidge Gloucs 15 M8
Russell's Water Oxon 16 H12
Russ Hill Surrey 10 C8
Rusthall Kent 10 G8
Rustington W Susx 9 R11
Ruston N York 37 R9
Ruston Parva E R Yk 37 S13
Ruswarp N York 37 Q5
Rutherford Border 46 J12
Rutherglen S Lans 44 G6
Ruthernbridge Cnwll 2 C5
Ruthin Denbgs 29 Q9
Ruthrieston C Aber 55 S14
Ruthven Abers 55 L7
Ruthven Angus 51 L8
Ruthven Highld 53 T15
Ruthvoes Cnwll 2 B6
Ruthwell D & G 39 S7
Ruyton-XI-Towns Shrops 22 C5
Ryal Nthumb 41 L6
Ryall Dorset 6 H11
Ryall Worcs 15 P3
Ryarsh Kent 10 J5
Rydal Cumb 35 L6
Ryde IoW 8 K13
Rye E Susx 11 M12
Rye Foreign E Susx 11 M11
Rye Street Worcs 15 N4
Ryhall Rutlnd 25 M7
Ryhill Wakefd 32 C5
Ryhope Sundld 41 S10
Ryland Lincs 33 M11
Rylands Notts 24 E3
Rylstone N York 36 B13
Ryme Intrinseca Dorset 7 L9
Ryther N York 32 E1
Ryton Gatesd 41 N8
Ryton Shrops 22 H8
Ryton-on-Dunsmore Warwks 23 S13

S

Sabden Lancs 31 L1
Sacombe Herts 17 S7
Sacriston Dur 41 P11
Sadberge Darltn 36 G4
Saddell Ag & B 42 K11
Saddington Leics 24 G10
Saddle Bow Norfk 26 G6
Saddlescombe W Susx 10 C13
Saffron Walden Essex 18 F7
Sageston Pembks 12 G9
Saham Hills Norfk 27 L8
Saham Toney Norfk 27 L8
Saighton Ches W 30 G14
St Abbs Border 47 M5
St Agnes Border 46 J6
St Agnes Cnwll 1 R9
St Albans Herts 17 P9
St Allen Cnwll 1 T9
St Andrew Guern 2 c3
St Andrews Fife 51 P13
St Andrew's Major V Glam 14 D15
St Andrews Well Dorset 6 J12
St Anne's Lancs 30 E3
St Ann's D & G 39 S3
St Ann's Chapel Cnwll 2 J4
St Ann's Chapel Devon 3 M8
St Anthony Cnwll 1 S14
St Anthony's Hill E Susx 10 H15
St Arvans Mons 14 K11
St Asaph Denbgs 29 P6
St Athan V Glam 14 B15
St Aubin Jersey 3 b3
St Austell Cnwll 2 C7
St Bees Cumb 34 F5
St Blazey Cnwll 2 D7
St Boswells Border 46 H12
St Brelade Jersey 3 b3
St Brelade's Bay Jersey 3 b3
St Breock Cnwll 2 C4
St Breward Cnwll 2 D3
St Briavels Gloucs 14 K9
St Bride's Major V Glam 13 U14
St Brides super-Ely V Glam 14 D14
St Brides Wentlooge Newpt 14 F13
St Budeaux C Plym 2 J6
Saintbury Gloucs 15 T3
St Buryan Cnwll 1 M14
St Catherines Ag & B 49 N14
St Chloe Gloucs 15 P10
St Clears Carmth 12 K7
St Cleer Cnwll 2 F5
St Clement Cnwll 1 T11
St Clement Jersey 3 e4
St Clether Cnwll 4 F13
St Colmac Ag & B 43 P6
St Columb Major Cnwll 1 U7
St Columb Minor Cnwll 1 T8
St Columb Road Cnwll 1 U8
St Combs Abers 55 T4
St Cross South Elmham Suffk 27 R11
St Cyrus Abers 51 S5
St David's P & K 50 F12
St Davids Pembks 12 C6
St Day Cnwll 1 R11
St Dennis Cnwll 2 B6
St Dogmaels Pembks 12 H2
St Dominick Cnwll 2 J5
St Donats V Glam 13 U15
St Endellion Cnwll 2 C3
St Enoder Cnwll 1 U8
St Erme Cnwll 1 T10
St Erney Cnwll 2 H6
St Erth Cnwll 1 P12
St Erth Praze Cnwll 1 P12
St Ervan Cnwll 1 U6
St Eval Cnwll 1 U6
St Ewe Cnwll 2 C8
St Fagans Cardif 14 D14
St Fergus Abers 55 U6
St Fillans P & K 50 B12
St Florence Pembks 12 G10
St Gennys Cnwll 4 E11
St George Conwy 29 N6
St Georges N Som 14 H16
St George's V Glam 14 D14
St Germans Cnwll 2 H6
St Giles in the Wood Devon 4 K8
St Giles-on-the-Heath Devon 4 H12
St Harmon Powys 20 K8
St Helen Auckland Dur 41 N14
St Helens IoW 8 K13
St Helens St Hel 30 H8
St Helier Gt Lon 10 C4
St Helier Jersey 3 c3
St Hilary Cnwll 1 P13
St Hilary V Glam 14 B14
St Ippollitts Herts 17 Q5
St Ishmael's Pembks 12 D9
St Issey Cnwll 2 B4
St Ive Cnwll 2 G5
St Ives Cambs 25 R13
St Ives Cnwll 1 P11
St James's End Nhants 24 H15
St James South Elmham Suffk 27 S12
St Jidgey Cnwll 2 B4
St John Cnwll 2 J7
St John Jersey 3 c1
St John's IoM 34 c5
St Johns Kent 10 G6
St Johns Surrey 9 Q2
St Johns Worcs 15 P1
St John's Chapel Devon 4 K6
St John's Chapel Dur 40 J12
St John's Fen End Norfk 26 F7
St John's Kirk S Lans 45 M11
St John's Town of Dalry D & G 39 L5
St John's Wood Gt Lon 17 R13
St Jude's IoM 34 e3
St Just Cnwll 1 L13
St Just-in-Roseland Cnwll 1 T12
St Katherines Abers 55 Q9
St Keverne Cnwll 1 S14
St Kew Cnwll 2 C3
St Kew Highway Cnwll 2 C3
St Keyne Cnwll 2 F6
St Lawrence Essex 19 M13
St Lawrence IoW 8 J15
St Lawrence Jersey 3 c2
St Lawrence Kent 11 U4
St Leonards Bucks 17 L9
St Leonards Dorset 8 C11
St Leonards E Susx 11 L13
St Levan Cnwll 1 M14
St Lythans V Glam 14 D14
St Mabyn Cnwll 2 D4
St Madoes P & K 50 J12
St Margarets Herefs 14 G4
St Margarets Herts 17 S8
St Margaret's at Cliffe Kent 11 U7
St Margaret's Hope Ork 58 c5
St Margaret South Elmham Suffk 27 R11
St Marks IoM 34 c6
St Martin Cnwll 1 S14
St Martin Cnwll 2 G7
St Martin Guern 2 d3
St Martin Jersey 3 e2
St Martin's P & K 50 J11
St Martins Shrops 29 T12
St Mary Jersey 3 b2
St Mary Bourne Hants 8 G3
St Marychurch Torbay 3 R5
St Mary Church V Glam 14 B15
St Mary Cray Gt Lon 10 F4
St Mary in the Marsh Kent 11 P10
St Mary's Ork 58 c4
St Mary's Bay Kent 11 Q10
St Mary's Hoo Medway 11 L2
St Maughans Green Mons 14 J7
St Mawes Cnwll 1 T12
St Mawgan Cnwll 1 U7
St Mellion Cnwll 2 H5
St Mellons Cardif 14 E13
St Merryn Cnwll 1 U6
St Michael Caerhays Cnwll 2 B9
St Michael Church Somset 6 G6
St Michael Penkevil Cnwll 1 T11
St Michaels Kent 11 M9
St Michaels Worcs 22 F14
St Michael's on Wyre Lancs 30 G1
St Minver Cnwll 2 B3
St Monans Fife 51 P15
St Neot Cnwll 2 F5
St Neots Cambs 25 P15
St Nicholas Pembks 12 E4
St Nicholas V Glam 14 D14
St Nicholas at Wade Kent 11 S4
St Ninians Stirlg 44 J1
St Olaves Norfk 27 U9
St Osyth Essex 19 P11
St Ouen Jersey 3 b2
St Owens Cross Herefs 14 K6
St Pauls Cray Gt Lon 10 F4
St Paul's Walden Herts 17 Q6
St Peter Jersey 3 b2
St Peter Port Guern 2 d3
St Peter's Guern 2 b3
St Peter's Kent 11 U4
St Pinnock Cnwll 2 F5
St Quivox S Ayrs 44 C13
St Sampson Guern 2 d2
St Saviour Guern 2 c3
St Saviour Jersey 3 d3
St Stephen Cnwll 2 B7
St Stephens Cnwll 2 J6
St Stephens Cnwll 4 G13
St Teath Cnwll 4 D14
St Tudy Cnwll 2 D3
St Twynnells Pembks 12 E10
St Veep Cnwll 2 E7
St Vigeans Angus 51 R9
St Wenn Cnwll 2 C5
St Weonards Herefs 14 J6
Salcombe Devon 3 N9
Salcombe Regis Devon 6 E12
Salcott-cum-Virley Essex 19 L11
Sale Traffd 31 M9
Saleby Lincs 33 T11
Sale Green Worcs 22 K16
Salehurst E Susx 10 K11
Salem Cerdgn 20 F6
Salen Ag & B 48 F9
Salen Highld 48 G5
Salford C Beds 17 L3
Salford Oxon 16 B5
Salford Salfd 31 M8
Salford Priors Warwks 15 S2
Salfords Surrey 10 C7
Salhouse Norfk 27 R6
Saline Fife 45 M1
Salisbury Wilts 8 D7
Salkeld Dykes Cumb 40 D12
Salle Norfk 27 P5
Salmonby Lincs 33 R12
Salperton Gloucs 15 S7
Salsburgh N Lans 44 K6
Salt Staffs 23 L4
Saltaire C Brad 31 S1
Saltash Cnwll 2 J6
Saltburn Highld 53 T3
Saltburn-by-the-Sea R & Cl 37 M3
Saltby Leics 24 J4
Saltcoats N Ayrs 43 S10
Saltdean Br & H 10 E14
Salterbeck Cumb 39 R14
Salterforth Lancs 35 U16
Salterton Wilts 8 C6
Saltfleet Lincs 33 T9
Saltfleetby All Saints Lincs 33 T9
Saltfleetby St Clement Lincs 33 T9
Saltfleetby St Peter Lincs 33 S9
Saltford BaNES 15 M15
Salthouse Norfk 27 N2
Saltmarshe E R Yk 32 H4
Saltney Flints 30 F13
Salton N York 37 M10
Saltrens Devon 4 J7
Saltwood Kent 11 R9
Salvington W Susx 9 S11
Salwarpe Worcs 22 K15
Salway Ash Dorset 6 J11
Sambourne Warwks 23 M15
Sambrook Wrekin 22 G5
Sampford Arundel Somset 6 D8
Sampford Brett Somset 6 D4
Sampford Courtenay Devon 5 M10
Sampford Moor Somset 6 D8
Sampford Peverell Devon 5 S8
Sampford Spiney Devon 2 K4
Samsonlane Ork 58 d3
Samuelston E Loth 46 F5
Sanaigmore Ag & B 42 B5
Sancreed Cnwll 1 M13
Sancton E R Yk 32 K1
Sandaig Highld 52 D14
Sandal Magna Wakefd 32 B5
Sandavore Highld 48 D2
Sanday Airport Ork 58 d2
Sandbach Ches E 31 L14
Sandbank Ag & B 43 Q3
Sandbanks Poole 7 S13
Sandend Abers 55 L4
Sanderstead Gt Lon 10 D5
Sandford Cumb 35 R4
Sandford Devon 5 Q10
Sandford Dorset 7 R12
Sandford Hants 8 D11
Sandford IoW 8 J15
Sandford N Som 6 J1
Sandford S Lans 44 H9
Sandford-on-Thames Oxon 16 F10
Sandford Orcas Dorset 7 M7
Sandford St Martin Oxon 16 D6
Sandgate Kent 11 R9
Sandhaven Abers 55 S4
Sandhead D & G 38 C10
Sand Hills Leeds 32 B1
Sandhills Oxon 16 F9
Sandhills Surrey 9 Q5
Sandhoe Nthumb 40 K7
Sandhole Ag & B 49 M16
Sand Hole E R Yk 32 J1
Sandholme E R Yk 32 J3
Sandhurst Br For 9 N1
Sandhurst Gloucs 15 P6
Sandhurst Kent 11 L10
Sandhutton N York 36 H10
Sand Hutton N York 37 M14
Sandiacre Derbys 24 D3
Sandilands Lincs 33 U11
Sandleheath Hants 8 C9
Sandleigh Oxon 16 E10
Sandley Dorset 7 P7
Sandness Shet 59 n5
Sandon Essex 18 H12
Sandon Herts 17 S4
Sandon Staffs 23 L4
Sandon Bank Staffs 23 L4
Sandown IoW 8 K14
Sandplace Cnwll 2 F7
Sandridge Herts 17 P8
Sandringham Norfk 26 H4
Sandsend N York 37 P5
Sandtoft N Linc 32 H6
Sandway Kent 11 M7
Sandwich Kent 11 T5
Sandwick Shet 59 q7
Sandwick W Isls 56 f2
Sandwith Cumb 34 F4
Sandy C Beds 17 P2
Sandyford D & G 39 U3
Sandygate Devon 3 Q4
Sandygate IoM 34 d3
Sandyhills D & G 39 P9
Sandylands Lancs 35 M13
Sandy Lane Wilts 15 R15
Sandy Park Devon 5 N12
Sangobeg Highld 57 M3
Sangomore Highld 57 M2
Sankyn's Green Worcs 22 H14
Sanna Bay Highld 48 D4
Sanndabhaig W Isls 56 f2
Sannox N Ayrs 43 N9
Sanquhar D & G 44 J15
Santon Bridge Cumb 34 H6
Santon Downham Suffk 26 J11
Sapcote Leics 24 D10
Sapey Common Herefs 22 G15
Sapiston Suffk 27 L13
Sapperton Gloucs 15 R9
Sapperton Lincs 25 M3
Saracen's Head Lincs 25 R4
Sarclet Highld 58 H6
Sarisbury Hants 8 J10
Sarn Gwynd 28 B13
Sarn Powys 20 K4
Sarn Powys 21 N5
Sarnau Cerdgn 13 L2
Sarnau Powys 29 R16
Saron Carmth 13 Q8
Saron Gwynd 28 G7
Sarratt Herts 17 N10
Sarre Kent 11 S4
Sarsden Oxon 16 B6
Satley Dur 41 N11
Satterleigh Devon 5 M7
Satterthwaite Cumb 35 L8
Sauchen Abers 55 P13
Saucher P & K 50 J10
Sauchieburn Abers 51 R4
Saul Gloucs 15 N8
Saundby Notts 32 H10
Saundersfoot Pembks 12 H9
Saunderton Bucks 16 J10
Saunton Devon 4 J4
Sausthorpe Lincs 33 S13
Savile Town Kirk 31 T4
Sawbridge Warwks 24 D14
Sawbridgeworth Herts 18 E11
Sawdon N York 37 Q9
Sawley Lancs 35 S15
Sawley N York 36 F12
Sawston Cambs 18 E5
Sawtry Cambs 25 P11
Saxby Leics 24 J5
Saxby Lincs 33 L10
Saxby All Saints N Linc 33 L5
Saxelbye Leics 24 G5
Saxham Street Suffk 19 N3
Saxilby Lincs 32 K12
Saxlingham Norfk 27 M2
Saxlingham Green Norfk 27 Q9
Saxlingham Nethergate Norfk 27 Q9
Saxlingham Thorpe Norfk 27 Q9
Saxmundham Suffk 19 T3
Saxondale Notts 24 G2
Saxon Street Cambs 18 H3
Saxtead Suffk 27 R14
Saxtead Green Suffk 19 R3
Saxtead Little Green Suffk 27 R14
Saxthorpe Norfk 27 P4
Saxton N York 32 D2
Sayers Common W Susx 10 C12
Scackleton N York 37 L11
Scaftworth Notts 32 G9
Scagglethorpe N York 37 P11
Scalasaig Ag & B 42 E1
Scalby E R Yk 32 J3
Scalby N York 37 R8
Scaldwell Nhants 24 H13
Scaleby Cumb 40 C8
Scalebyhill Cumb 40 C8
Scales Cumb 34 K11
Scales Cumb 40 B14
Scalford Leics 24 H5
Scaling N York 37 N5
Scalloway Shet 59 q6
Scamblesby Lincs 33 Q11
Scamodale Highld 48 J4
Scampston N York 37 P11
Scampton Lincs 33 L11
Scaniport Highld 53 R8
Scapegoat Hill Kirk 31 R5
Scarborough N York 37 S9
Scarcewater Cnwll 1 U9
Scarcliffe Derbys 32 D13
Scarcroft Leeds 32 B1
Scarfskerry Highld 58 G1
Scarinish Ag & B 42 c4
Scarisbrick Lancs 30 F5
Scarning Norfk 27 L7
Scarrington Notts 24 H2
Scartho NE Lin 33 Q7
Scatsta Airport Shet 59 q4
Scawby N Linc 33 L7
Scawsby Donc 32 E7
Scawthorpe Donc 32 E7
Scawton N York 36 K9
Scayne's Hill W Susx 10 E11
Scethrog Powys 14 D6
Scholar Green Ches E 31 M15
Scholes Kirk 31 S6
Scholes Leeds 32 C2
Scholes Rothm 32 C8
Scholes Wigan 30 J7
Scissett Kirk 31 T6
Scleddau Pembks 12 E4
Scofton Notts 32 F11
Scole Norfk 27 P12
Scone P & K 50 H11
Sconser Highld 59 f11
Scoonie Fife 51 M15
Scopwick Lincs 33 M14
Scoraig Highld 56 F14
Scorborough E R Yk 37 R16
Scorrier Cnwll 1 R10
Scorton Lancs 35 N15
Scorton N York 36 F7
Scotby Cumb 40 C9
Scotch Corner N York 36 E6
Scotforth Lancs 35 N13
Scothern Lincs 33 M11
Scotlandwell P & K 50 J15
Scotscalder Station Highld 58 E4
Scot's Gap Nthumb 41 L4
Scotsmill Abers 55 M12
Scotstoun C Glas 44 F5
Scotswood N u Ty 41 P8
Scotter Lincs 32 K7
Scotterthorpe Lincs 32 K7
Scotton Lincs 32 K8
Scotton N York 36 E7
Scotton N York 36 G13
Scoulton Norfk 27 M9
Scourie Highld 56 H6
Scourie More Highld 56 H6
Scousburgh Shet 59 q7
Scrabster Highld 58 E2
Scraesburgh Border 46 J14
Scrane End Lincs 25 S2
Scraptoft Leics 24 F8
Scratby Norfk 27 U6
Scrayingham N York 37 N13
Scredington Lincs 25 N2
Scremby Lincs 33 T13
Scremerston Nthumb 47 P8
Screveton Notts 24 H2
Scriven N York 36 G14
Scrooby Notts 32 F9
Scropton Derbys 23 P4
Scrub Hill Lincs 33 Q15
Scruton N York 36 F8
Scullomie Highld 57 Q4
Sculthorpe Norfk 27 L4
Scunthorpe N Linc 32 K6
Seaborough Dorset 6 J10
Seabrook Kent 11 R9
Seaburn Sundld 41 S8
Seacroft Leeds 32 B2
Seafield Highld 59 f9
Seafield W Loth 45 M6
Seaford E Susx 10 F15
Seaforth Sefton 30 E8
Seagrave Leics 24 F6
Seaham Dur 41 S10
Seahouses Nthumb 47 S11
Seal Kent 10 G6
Sealand Flints 30 E13
Seale Surrey 9 P4
Seamer N York 36 J5
Seamer N York 37 S9
Seamill N Ayrs 43 R9
Sea Palling Norfk 27 T4
Searby Lincs 33 M7
Seasalter Kent 11 Q4
Seascale Cumb 34 G7
Seathwaite Cumb 34 J7
Seatoller Cumb 34 J4
Seaton Cnwll 2 G7
Seaton Cumb 39 R13
Seaton Devon 6 F12
Seaton E R Yk 37 U15
Seaton Kent 11 S5
Seaton Nthumb 41 Q6
Seaton Rutlnd 24 K9
Seaton Carew Hartpl 41 T13
Seaton Delaval Nthumb 41 Q6
Seaton Ross E R Yk 32 H1
Seaton Sluice Nthumb 41 R6
Seatown Dorset 6 J12
Seave Green N York 36 K7
Seaview IoW 8 K13
Seaville Cumb 39 T10
Seavington St Mary Somset 6 H8
Seavington St Michael Somset 6 J8
Sebergham Cumb 40 B11
Seckington Warwks 23 Q8
Sedbergh Cumb 35 Q8
Sedbury Gloucs 14 K11
Sedbusk N York 35 T8
Sedgeberrow Worcs 15 S4
Sedgebrook Lincs 24 J2
Sedgefield Dur 41 R14
Sedgeford Norfk 26 H3
Sedgehill Wilts 7 Q6
Sedgley Dudley 22 K10
Sedgwick Cumb 35 N9
Sedlescombe E Susx 10 K12
Sedrup Bucks 16 J8
Seend Wilts 15 R16
Seend Cleeve Wilts 7 R1
Seer Green Bucks 17 M11
Seething Norfk 27 S9
Sefton Sefton 30 F7
Seighford Staffs 22 K5
Seion Gwynd 28 G7
Seisdon Staffs 22 J10
Selattyn Shrops 29 S13
Selborne Hants 9 M6
Selby N York 32 F2
Selham W Susx 9 Q8
Selhurst Gt Lon 10 D4
Selkirk Border 46 F12
Sellack Herefs 14 K5
Sellafirth Shet 59 r2
Sellindge Kent 11 Q9
Selling Kent 11 P6
Sells Green Wilts 15 R16
Selly Oak Birm 23 M12
Selmeston E Susx 10 G14
Selsdon Gt Lon 10 D5
Selsey Gloucs 15 P9
Selsey W Susx 9 P13
Selside N York 35 S11
Selsted Kent 11 S7
Selston Notts 32 D15
Selworthy Somset 5 R3
Semer Suffk 19 M6
Semington Wilts 7 Q1
Semley Wilts 7 Q6
Send Surrey 9 R2
Senghenydd Caerph 14 D11
Sennen Cnwll 1 L14
Sennen Cove Cnwll 1 L13
Sennybridge Powys 13 U5
Sessay N York 36 J11
Setchey Norfk 26 G6
Seton Mains E Loth 46 F4
Settle N York 35 T13
Settrington N York 37 P12
Sevenhampton Gloucs 15 S6
Sevenhampton Swindn 15 U12
Seven Kings Gt Lon 18 D15
Sevenoaks Kent 10 G6
Sevenoaks Weald Kent 10 G7
Seven Sisters Neath 13 T8
Seven Star Green Essex 19 L9
Severn Beach S Glos 14 K12
Severn Stoke Worcs 15 P3
Sevington Kent 11 P8
Sewards End Essex 18 F7
Sewell C Beds 17 M6
Sewerby E R Yk 37 U12
Seworgan Cnwll 1 R13
Sewstern Leics 24 K5
Sgiogarstaigh W Isls 56 f1
Shabbington Bucks 16 G9
Shackerstone Leics 23 S8
Shackleford Surrey 9 Q4
Shader W Isls 56 e1
Shadforth Dur 41 R12
Shadingfield Suffk 27 T11
Shadoxhurst Kent 11 N9
Shadwell Norfk 27 L11
Shaftenhoe End Herts 18 D7
Shaftesbury Dorset 7 Q7
Shafton Barns 32 C6
Shakerley Wigan 30 K7
Shalbourne Wilts 8 F1
Shalden Hants 9 L5
Shaldon Devon 3 R4
Shalfleet IoW 8 G13
Shalford Essex 18 H8
Shalford Surrey 9 R4
Shalford Green Essex 18 H9
Shalmsford Street Kent 11 Q6
Shalstone Bucks 16 G4
Shamley Green Surrey 9 R4
Shandford Angus 51 N5
Shandon Ag & B 43 S2
Shandwick Highld 54 B2
Shangton Leics 24 G9
Shanklin IoW 8 K15
Shap Cumb 35 P4
Shapwick Dorset 7 R10
Shapwick Somset 6 J4
Shardlow Derbys 23 S4
Shareshill Staffs 23 L8
Sharlston Wakefd 32 C4
Sharnbrook Bed 25 L15
Sharnford Leics 24 D10
Sharoe Green Lancs 30 H2
Sharow N York 36 G11
Sharpenhoe C Beds 17 N5
Sharperton Nthumb 40 K1
Sharpness Gloucs 15 M10
Sharrington Norfk 27 N3
Shatterford Worcs 22 H12
Shaugh Prior Devon 3 L5
Shavington Ches E 30 K15
Shaw Oldham 31 P6
Shaw W Berk 16 E15
Shaw Wilts 15 Q16
Shawbirch Wrekin 22 F6
Shawbost W Isls 56 e1
Shawbury Shrops 22 E5
Shawell Leics 24 E12
Shawford Hants 8 H7
Shawhead D & G 39 P6
Shaw Mills N York 36 F13
Shawsburn S Lans 44 J8
Shearington D & G 39 R7
Shearsby Leics 24 F10
Shearston Somset 6 G6
Shebbear Devon 4 J9
Shebdon Staffs 22 H4
Shebster Highld 58 D3
Sheddens E Rens 44 F7
Shedfield Hants 8 J9
Sheen Staffs 31 R14
Sheepridge Kirk 31 S4
Sheepscar Leeds 31 U2
Sheepscombe Gloucs 15 Q8
Sheepstor Devon 3 L5
Sheepwash Devon 4 K10
Sheepy Magna Leics 23 R8
Sheepy Parva Leics 23 R8
Sheering Essex 18 E11
Sheerness Kent 11 M3
Sheerwater Surrey 9 R2
Sheet Hants 9 M8
Sheffield Sheff 32 B10
Shefford C Beds 17 P3
Sheigra Highld 56 J4
Sheinton Shrops 22 F8
Shelderton Shrops 21 R7
Sheldon Birm 23 N11
Sheldon Derbys 31 S13
Sheldon Devon 6 E9
Sheldwich Kent 11 P6
Shelfanger Norfk 27 P11
Shelford Notts 24 G2
Shelley Kirk 31 S6
Shelley Suffk 19 M7
Shellingford Oxon 16 C11
Shellow Bowells Essex 18 G12
Shelsley Beauchamp Worcs 22 H15
Shelsley Walsh Worcs 22 G15
Shelton Bed 25 M14
Shelton Norfk 27 Q10
Shelton Notts 24 H1
Shelton Under Harley Staffs 22 J2
Shelve Shrops 21 Q4
Shelwick Herefs 14 K3
Shenfield Essex 18 G14
Shenington Oxon 16 C3
Shenley Herts 17 Q10
Shenley Brook End M Keyn 16 K4
Shenley Church End M Keyn 16 K4
Shenmore Herefs 14 H4
Shennanton D & G 38 G8
Shenstone Staffs 23 N8
Shenstone Worcs 22 J13
Shenton Leics 23 S9
Shenval Moray 54 G10
Shephall Herts 17 R6
Shepherd's Bush Gt Lon 17 Q13
Shepherdswell Kent 11 S7
Shepley Kirk 31 S6
Shepperton Surrey 17 N15
Shepreth Cambs 18 D5
Shepshed Leics 24 D5
Shepton Beauchamp Somset 6 H8
Shepton Mallet Somset 7 L3
Shepton Montague Somset 7 M5
Shepway Kent 10 K6
Sheraton Dur 41 S13
Sherborne Dorset 7 M8
Sherborne Gloucs 15 U8
Sherborne Somset 7 L2
Sherborne St John Hants 8 K2
Sherbourne Warwks 23 Q15
Sherburn Dur 41 Q11
Sherburn N York 37 R11
Sherburn Hill Dur 41 R11
Sherburn in Elmet N York 32 D2
Shere Surrey 9 S4
Shereford Norfk 27 L4
Sherfield English Hants 8 F8
Sherfield on Loddon Hants 9 L2
Sherford Devon 3 P9
Sheriffhales Shrops 22 H7
Sheriff Hutton N York 37 L12
Sheringham Norfk 27 P2
Sherington M Keyn 17 L2
Shernborne Norfk 26 H3
Sherrington Wilts 7 R4
Sherston Wilts 15 P12
Sherwood C Nott 24 E2
Shetland Islands Shet 59 q5
Shettleston C Glas 44 G6
Shevington Wigan 30 H6
Sheviock Cnwll 2 H7
Shibden Head C Brad 31 R3
Shide IoW 8 J13
Shidlaw Nthumb 47 L10
Shiel Bridge Highld 52 G12
Shieldaig Highld 52 E6
Shieldhill D & G 39 R4
Shieldhill Falk 45 L4
Shieldhill House Hotel S Lans 45 M10
Shields N Lans 44 J7
Shielfoot Highld 48 G4
Shielhill Angus 51 N6
Shielhill Inver 43 R5
Shifnal Shrops 22 H7
Shilbottle Nthumb 47 R15
Shildon Dur 41 P14
Shillford E Rens 44 D7
Shillingford Devon 5 S7
Shillingford Oxon 16 F11
Shillingford Abbot Devon 5 R12
Shillingford St George Devon 5 R13
Shillingstone Dorset 7 P9
Shillington C Beds 17 P4
Shilton Oxon 16 B9
Shilton Warwks 23 S11
Shimpling Norfk 27 P11
Shimpling Suffk 18 K5
Shimpling Street Suffk 18 K5
Shincliffe Dur 41 Q12
Shiney Row Sundld 41 Q10
Shinfield Wokham 16 H15
Shinness Highld 57 P11
Shipbourne Kent 10 H6
Shipdham Norfk 27 M7
Shipham Somset 6 J1
Shiphay Torbay 3 Q5
Shiplake Oxon 16 J14
Shipley C Brad 31 S1
Shipley W Susx 9 T8
Shipley Bridge Surrey 10 D8
Shipmeadow Suffk 27 S10
Shippon Oxon 16 E10
Shipston-on-Stour Warwks 16 B3
Shipton Gloucs 15 S7
Shipton N York 36 K13
Shipton Shrops 22 E10
Shipton Bellinger Hants 8 E4
Shipton Gorge Dorset 6 K12
Shipton Green W Susx 9 N12
Shipton Moyne Gloucs 15 Q12
Shipton-on-Cherwell Oxon 16 E7
Shiptonthorpe E R Yk 37 P16
Shipton-under-Wychwood Oxon 16 B7
Shirburn Oxon 16 H11
Shirdley Hill Lancs 30 F5
Shirebrook Derbys 32 E13
Shiregreen Sheff 32 B9
Shirehampton Bristl 14 K14
Shiremoor N Tyne 41 Q7
Shirenewton Mons 14 J11
Shireoaks Notts 32 E11
Shirland Derbys 32 C14
Shirley C Sotn 8 G9
Shirley Derbys 23 P2
Shirley Gt Lon 10 D4
Shirley Solhll 23 N12
Shirrell Heath Hants 8 K9
Shirvan Ag & B 43 L3
Shirwell Devon 5 L5
Shiskine N Ayrs 43 M12
Shobdon Herefs 21 R10
Shobrooke Devon 5 Q10
Shoby Leics 24 G5
Shocklach Ches W 30 G16
Shoeburyness Sthend 19 L16
Sholden Kent 11 U6
Sholing C Sotn 8 H10
Shop Cnwll 4 F8
Shoreditch Gt Lon 17 S13
Shoreditch Somset 6 F7
Shoreham Kent 10 G5
Shoreham Airport W Susx 9 T11
Shoreham-by-Sea W Susx 10 B14
Shorley Hants 8 K7
Shorne Kent 10 J3
Shortgate E Susx 10 F12
Shortlanesend Cnwll 1 T10
Shortlees E Ayrs 44 D11
Shortstown Bed 17 N2
Shorwell IoW 8 H14
Shoscombe BaNES 7 N1
Shotesham Norfk 27 R9
Shotgate Essex 18 J14
Shotley Suffk 19 Q7
Shotley Bridge Dur 41 M10
Shotley Gate Suffk 19 R8
Shotley Street Suffk 19 Q7
Shottenden Kent 11 P6
Shottery Warwks 15 U1
Shotteswell Warwks 16 D2
Shottisham Suffk 19 S6
Shottlegate Derbys 23 R1
Shotton Dur 41 S12
Shotton Flints 30 E13
Shotton Colliery Dur 41 R12
Shotts N Lans 44 K7
Shotwick Ches W 30 E12
Shougle Moray 54 G6
Shouldham Norfk 26 H7
Shouldham Thorpe Norfk 26 G7
Shoulton Worcs 22 J15
Shrawardine Shrops 22 C6
Shrawley Worcs 22 J14
Shrewley Warwks 23 P14
Shrewsbury Shrops 22 D7
Shrewton Wilts 7 T3
Shripney W Susx 9 Q11
Shrivenham Oxon 16 A12
Shropham Norfk 27 M10
Shucknall Herefs 15 L3
Shudy Camps Cambs 18 G6
Shurdington Gloucs 15 Q7
Shurlock Row W & M 16 K14
Shurrery Highld 58 D4
Shurrery Lodge Highld 58 D4
Shurton Somset 6 F3
Shustoke Warwks 23 Q10
Shute Devon 5 Q11
Shute Devon 6 F11
Shutford Oxon 16 C3
Shut Heath Staffs 22 J5
Shuthonger Gloucs 15 Q4
Shutlanger Nhants 16 H2
Shuttington Warwks 23 Q8
Shuttlewood Derbys 32 D12
Shuttleworth Bury 31 M5
Siabost W Isls 56 e1
Siadar W Isls 56 e1
Sibbertoft Nhants 24 G12
Sibford Ferris Oxon 16 C4
Sibford Gower Oxon 16 C4
Sible Hedingham Essex 18 J8
Sibley's Green Essex 18 G9
Sibsey Lincs 33 R16
Sibson Cambs 25 N9
Sibson Leics 23 R9
Sibster Highld 58 H5
Sibthorpe Notts 24 H1
Sibthorpe Notts 32 G12
Sibton Suffk 27 S14
Sicklesmere Suffk 18 K3
Sicklinghall N York 36 G15
Sidbury Devon 6 E12
Sidbury Shrops 22 G11
Sidcot N Som 6 J1
Sidcup Gt Lon 10 F3
Siddington Ches E 31 M12
Siddington Gloucs 15 S10
Sidestrand Norfk 27 R2
Sidford Devon 6 E12
Sidlesham W Susx 9 P12
Sidley E Susx 10 K13
Sidmouth Devon 6 E13
Sigglesthorne E R Yk 37 T16
Sigingstone V Glam 14 B15
Silchester Hants 8 K1
Sileby Leics 24 F6
Silecroft Cumb 34 H10
Silfield Norfk 27 P9
Silkstone Barns 31 U7
Silkstone Common Barns 31 U7
Silk Willoughby Lincs 25 M2
Silloth Cumb 39 S9
Silpho N York 37 R8
Silsden C Brad 36 C15
Silsoe C Beds 17 N4
Silton Dorset 7 P6
Silverburn Mdloth 45 Q7
Silverdale Lancs 35 N11
Silverdale Staffs 22 J1
Silver End Essex 18 J10
Silverford Abers 55 Q4
Silverstone Nhants 16 G3
Silverton Devon 5 R10
Silvington Shrops 22 F12
Simonburn Nthumb 40 J6
Simonsbath Somset 5 P4
Simonstone Lancs 31 L2
Simprim Border 47 L9
Simpson M Keyn 16 K4
Simpson Cross Pembks 12 E7
Sinclair's Hill Border 47 L8
Sinclairston E Ayrs 44 E14
Sinderby N York 36 G10
Sinderland Green Traffd 31 L9
Sindlesham Wokham 16 J15
Sinfin C Derb 23 R4
Singleton Kent 11 P8
Singleton Lancs 30 F1
Singleton W Susx 9 P9
Singlewell Kent 10 J3
Sinnarhard Abers 54 K12
Sinnington N York 37 N9
Sinton Worcs 22 J15
Sinton Worcs 22 J15
Sinton Green Worcs 22 J15
Sissinghurst Kent 11 L9
Siston S Glos 15 M14
Sithney Cnwll 1 Q13
Sittingbourne Kent 11 M4
Six Ashes Shrops 22 H11
Sixhills Lincs 33 P10
Six Mile Bottom Cambs 18 F4
Sixpenny Handley Dorset 7 S8
Skaill Ork 58 d4
Skares E Ayrs 44 F14
Skateraw Abers 55 S16
Skateraw E Loth 46 K4
Skeabost Highld 59 e8
Skeeby N York 36 E6
Skeffington Leics 24 H8
Skeffling E R Yk 33 S4
Skegby Notts 32 D14
Skegby Notts 32 H13
Skegness Lincs 33 U14
Skelbo Highld 57 S14
Skelbo Street Highld 57 S14
Skelbrooke Donc 32 D6
Skeldyke Lincs 25 R3
Skellingthorpe Lincs 32 K12
Skellow Donc 32 E6
Skelmanthorpe Kirk 31 T6
Skelmersdale Lancs 30 G7
Skelmorlie N Ayrs 43 R5
Skelpick Highld 57 R4
Skelston D & G 39 N4
Skelton C York 36 K14
Skelton Cumb 40 C12
Skelton E R Yk 32 H3
Skelton N York 36 G12
Skelton R & Cl 37 M4
Skelwith Bridge Cumb 35 L6
Skendleby Lincs 33 S13
Skene House Abers 55 P13
Skenfrith Mons 14 J7
Skerne E R Yk 37 S14
Skerray Highld 57 Q3
Skerricha Highld 56 J5
Skerton Lancs 35 N13
Sketchley Leics 23 S10
Sketty Swans 13 Q11
Skewen Neath 13 R11
Skewsby N York 37 L11
Skiall Highld 58 D3
Skidby E R Yk 33 L2
Skigersta W Isls 56 f1
Skilgate Somset 5 S6
Skillington Lincs 24 K5
Skinburness Cumb 39 T9
Skinflats Falk 45 L3
Skinidin Highld 59 b8
Skipness Ag & B 43 M7
Skipper's Bridge D & G 40 B5
Skipsea E R Yk 37 U14
Skipton N York 36 B15
Skipton-on-Swale N York 36 G10
Skipwith N York 32 G1
Skirlaugh E R Yk 33 N1
Skirling Border 45 N10
Skirmett Bucks 16 J12
Skirpenbeck E R Yk 37 N14
Skirwith Cumb 40 E13
Skirza Highld 58 J2
Skulamus Highld 52 C11
Skye Green Essex 18 K10
Skye of Curr Highld 54 D11
Slack Calder 31 P3
Slacks of Cairnbanno Abers 55 R7
Slad Gloucs 15 Q9
Slade Devon 4 K3
Slade Green Gt Lon 10 G2
Slade Hooton Rothm 32 E9
Slaggyford Nthumb 40 F10
Slaidburn Lancs 35 R15
Slaithwaite Kirk 31 R5
Slaley Nthumb 40 K9
Slamannan Falk 44 K5
Slapton Bucks 17 L7
Slapton Devon 3 Q8
Slapton Nhants 16 G2
Slaugham W Susx 10 C10
Slaughterford Wilts 15 P14
Slawston Leics 24 H10
Sleaford Hants 9 N5
Sleaford Lincs 25 M1
Sleagill Cumb 35 P4
Sleapford Wrekin 22 F6
Sleasdairidh Highld 57 Q14
Sledmere E R Yk 37 Q12
Sleetbeck Cumb 40 D6
Sleights N York 37 P5
Slickly Highld 58 H3
Sliddery N Ayrs 43 M13
Sligachan Highld 59 f11
Sligrachan Ag & B 43 Q2
Slimbridge Gloucs 15 N9
Slindon Staffs 22 J3
Slindon W Susx 9 Q10
Slinfold W Susx 9 S6
Slingsby N York 37 M11
Slip End C Beds 17 N7
Slip End Herts 17 R4
Slipton Nhants 25 L12
Slitting Mill Staffs 23 M6
Slockavullin Ag & B 48 J16
Sloncombe Devon 5 N13
Sloothby Lincs 33 T12
Slough Slough 17 M13
Slough Green Somset 6 G7
Slumbay Highld 52 F8
Slyne Lancs 35 N12
Smailholm Border 46 J11
Smallburgh Norfk 27 S5
Small Dole W Susx 10 B13
Smalley Derbys 23 S1
Smallfield Surrey 10 D8
Small Heath Birm 23 N11
Small Hythe Kent 11 M10
Smallridge Devon 6 G10
Smallworth Norfk 27 M12
Smannell Hants 8 G4
Smarden Kent 11 M8
Smarden Bell Kent 11 M8
Smart's Hill Kent 10 G8
Smearisary Highld 48 G3
Smeatharpe Devon 6 F9
Smeeth Kent 11 Q8
Smeeton Westerby Leics 24 G10
Smerral Highld 58 F8
Smestow Staffs 22 J10
Smethwick Sandw 23 M11
Smisby Derbys 23 R6
Smithfield Cumb 40 C8
Smith's Green Essex 18 G7
Smithstown Highld 52 E2
Smithton Highld 53 S7
Smoo Highld 57 M3
Smythe's Green Essex 19 L10
Snade D & G 39 P4
Snailbeach Shrops 21 R3
Snailwell Cambs 26 G14
Snainton N York 37 Q10
Snaith E R Yk 32 F4
Snape N York 36 F9
Snape Suffk 19 T3
Snape Street Suffk 19 T4
Snaresbrook Gt Lon 18 D15
Snarestone Leics 23 R7
Snarford Lincs 33 M10
Snargate Kent 11 N10
Snave Kent 11 P10
Sneaton N York 37 Q5
Snelland Lincs 33 M11
Snelston Derbys 23 N2
Snetterton Norfk 27 M10
Snettisham Norfk 26 H3
Snitter Nthumb 41 L1
Snitterby Lincs 33 L8
Snitterfield Warwks 23 P15
Snitton Shrops 22 E13
Snodland Kent 10 J5
Snow End Herts 18 D8
Snowshill Gloucs 15 T4
Soake Hants 9 L10
Soberton Hants 8 K9
Soberton Heath Hants 8 K9
Sockburn Darltn 36 G6
Soham Cambs 26 F13
Solas W Isls 56 b5
Soldridge Hants 9 L6
Sole Street Kent 10 J4
Sole Street Kent 11 Q7
Solihull Solhll 23 P12
Sollers Dilwyn Herefs 21 R11
Sollers Hope Herefs 15 L5
Solva Pembks 12 C6
Solwaybank D & G 40 A6
Somerby Leics 24 H7
Somerby Lincs 33 M7
Somercotes Derbys 32 C15
Somerford Dorset 8 D13
Somerford Keynes Gloucs 15 R11
Somerley W Susx 9 N12
Somerleyton Suffk 27 U9
Somersal Herbert Derbys 23 N3
Somersby Lincs 33 R12
Somersham Cambs 25 R12
Somersham Suffk 19 N5
Somerton Oxon 16 E5
Somerton Somset 6 K6
Somerton Suffk 18 J5
Sompting W Susx 9 T11
Sonning Wokham 16 J14
Sonning Common Oxon 16 H13
Sopley Hants 8 D12
Sopworth Wilts 15 P12
Sorbie D & G 38 H11
Sordale Highld 58 F3
Sorisdale Ag & B 42 f1
Sorn E Ayrs 44 F12
Sortat Highld 58 H3
Sotby Lincs 33 P11
Sotterley Suffk 27 T11
Soughton Flints 29 S7
Soulbury Bucks 16 K6
Soulby Cumb 35 S5
Souldern Oxon 16 E5
Souldrop Bed 25 L15
Sound Ches E 30 J16
Sound Muir Moray 54 J6
Soundwell S Glos 15 L14
Sourton Devon 4 K12
Soutergate Cumb 34 J10
South Acre Norfk 26 J6
South Alkham Kent 11 S8
Southall Gt Lon 17 P13
South Allington Devon 3 P10
South Alloa Falk 44 K2
Southam Gloucs 15 R6
Southam Warwks 23 S15
South Ambersham W Susx 9 P8
Southampton C Sotn 8 G10
Southampton Airport Hants 8 H9
South Anston Rothm 32 E10
South Ashford Kent 11 P8
South Baddesley Hants 8 G12
South Ballachulish Highld 49 M6
South Bank C York 37 L15
South Barrow Somset 7 L6
South Beddington Gt Lon 10 D4
South Benfleet Essex 18 J15
South Bersted W Susx 9 Q12
Southborough Gt Lon 10 E4
Southborough Kent 10 H8
Southbourne Bmouth 8 D13
Southbourne W Susx 9 M11
South Bramwith Donc 32 F6
South Brent Devon 3 N6
South Brewham Somset 7 N5
South Broomhill Nthumb 41 P2
Southburgh Norfk 27 M8
South Burlingham Norfk 27 S7
Southburn E R Yk 37 R14
South Cadbury Somset 7 M6
South Carlton Lincs 33 L11
South Carlton Notts 32 F10
South Cave E R Yk 32 K3
South Cerney Gloucs 15 S10
South Chailey E Susx 10 E12
South Charlton Nthumb 47 R13
South Cheriton Somset 7 N7
South Church Dur 41 P14
Southchurch Sthend 19 L15
South Cliffe E R Yk 32 K2
South Clifton Notts 32 J12
South Cockerington Lincs 33 S9
South Cornelly Brdgnd 13 T13
Southcott Cnwll 4 F11
Southcott Devon 5 N14
Southcourt Bucks 16 J8
South Cove Suffk 27 U12
South Creake Norfk 26 K3
South Croxton Leics 24 G7
South Dalton E R Yk 37 R16
South Darenth Kent 10 G3
South Duffield N York 32 G2
Southease E Susx 10 E14
South Elkington Lincs 33 Q9
South Elmsall Wakefd 32 D6
Southend Ag & B 42 J15
Southend Airport Essex 18 K15
Southend-on-Sea Sthend 18 K16
Southerndown V Glam 13 T14
Southerness D & G 39 R9
South Erradale Highld 52 D3
Southerton Devon 6 D12
Southery Norfk 26 G10
South Fambridge Essex 18 K14
South Ferriby N Linc 33 L4
South Field E R Yk 33 M3
Southfield Falk 44 K5
Southfleet Kent 10 H3
Southgate Gt Lon 17 R11
Southgate Swans 13 P12
South Gorley Hants 8 D10
South Gosforth N u Ty 41 P7
South Green Essex 18 H14
South Green Kent 11 L5
South Green Norfk 27 N7
South Gyle C Edin 45 Q5
South Hanningfield Essex 18 H14
South Harting W Susx 9 N8
South Hayling Hants 9 M12
South Heath Bucks 17 L10
South Heighton E Susx 10 F14
South Hetton Dur 41 R11
South Hiendley Wakefd 32 C6
South Hill Cnwll 2 H4
South Hinksey Oxon 16 E9
South Holmwood Surrey 9 T4
South Hornchurch Gt Lon 18 E16
South Huish Devon 3 N9
South Hykeham Lincs 32 K13
South Hylton Sundld 41 R9
Southill C Beds 17 P3
Southington Hants 8 J3
South Kelsey Lincs 33 M8
South Kessock Highld 53 S7
South Killingholme N Linc 33 N5
South Kilvington N York 36 H9
South Kilworth Leics 24 F12
South Kirkby Wakefd 32 D6
South Kyme Lincs 33 P16
Southleigh Devon 6 F12
South Leigh Oxon 16 D9
South Leverton Notts 32 H11
South Littleton Worcs 15 S2
South Lopham Norfk 27 N12
South Luffenham Rutlnd 24 K8
South Malling E Susx 10 E13
South Marston Swindn 15 U12
South Merstham Surrey 10 D6
South Milford N York 32 D2
South Milton Devon 3 N9
South Mimms Herts 17 Q10
Southminster Essex 19 L13
South Molton Devon 5 N6
South Moor Dur 41 P10
Southmoor Oxon 16 D10
South Moreton Oxon 16 F12
Southmuir Angus 51 M7
South Mundham W Susx 9 P12
South Newbald E R Yk 32 K2
South Newington Oxon 16 D4
South Newton Wilts 7 T5
South Normanton Derbys 32 C15
South Norwood Gt Lon 10 D4
South Ockendon Thurr 10 H1
Southoe Cambs 25 P15
Southolt Suffk 27 Q14
South Ormsby Lincs 33 R12
Southorpe C Pete 25 M8
South Otterington N York 36 G9
Southover Dorset 7 M11
South Owersby Lincs 33 M9
Southowram Calder 31 R4
South Park Surrey 10 C7
South Perrott Dorset 6 J9
South Petherton Somset 6 J8
South Petherwin Cnwll 4 G14
South Pickenham Norfk 26 K8
South Pill Cnwll 2 J6
South Pool Devon 3 P9
South Poorton Dorset 6 K11
Southport Sefton 30 E5
South Queensferry C Edin 45 P4
South Rauceby Lincs 25 M1
South Raynham Norfk 26 K5
Southrepps Norfk 27 R3
South Reston Lincs 33 S10
Southrey Lincs 33 N13
Southrop Gloucs 15 U9
Southrope Hants 9 L4
South Runcton Norfk 26 G7
South Scarle Notts 32 J13
Southsea C Port 9 L12
South Shian Ag & B 48 K9
South Shields S Tyne 41 R7
South Shore Bpool 30 E2
Southside Dur 41 M14
South Stainley N York 36 G13
South Stoke BaNES 15 N16
South Stoke Oxon 16 F13
South Stoke W Susx 9 R10
South Street Kent 11 P5
South Street Kent 11 Q4
South Tarbrax S Lans 45 N8
South Tawton Devon 5 M12
South Tehidy Cnwll 1 Q11
South Thoresby Lincs 33 S11
Southtown Norfk 27 U8
Southwaite Cumb 40 C11
South Walsham Norfk 27 S7
Southwark Gt Lon 17 S13
South Warnborough Hants 9 M4
Southwater W Susx 9 T7
South Weald Essex 18 F14
Southwell Notts 32 G15
South Weston Oxon 16 H10
Southwick Hants 8 K10
Southwick Nhants 25 M10
Southwick Sundld 41 R9
Southwick W Susx 10 C14
Southwick Wilts 7 Q2
South Widcombe BaNES 7 L1
South Wigston Leics 24 F9
South Willesborough Kent 11 P8
South Willingham Lincs 33 P10
South Wingfield Derbys 32 C15
South Witham Lincs 24 K6
Southwold Suffk 27 U13
South Woodham Ferrers Essex 18 J14
South Wootton Norfk 26 G5
South Wraxall Wilts 15 P16
South Zeal Devon 5 M12
Sowerby Calder 31 Q4
Sowerby N York 36 H10
Sowerby Bridge Calder 31 Q4
Sowood Calder 31 R5
Sowton Devon 2 K5
Sowton Devon 5 S12
Soyland Town Calder 31 Q4
Spain's End Essex 18 G7
Spalding Lincs 25 Q5
Spaldington E R Yk 32 H2
Spaldwick Cambs 25 N13
Spalford Notts 32 J13
Spanby Lincs 25 N2
Sparham Norfk 27 N5
Spark Bridge Cumb 34 K9
Sparkford Somset 7 L6
Sparkhill Birm 23 N11
Sparkwell Devon 3 L6
Sparrowpit Derbys 31 R11
Sparrows Green E Susx 10 H10
Sparsholt Hants 8 H6
Sparsholt Oxon 16 C12
Spaunton N York 37 M8
Spaxton Somset 6 F5
Spean Bridge Highld 49 Q2
Spearywell Hants 8 F7
Speen Bucks 16 K10
Speen W Berk 16 D15
Speeton N York 37 T11
Speke Lpool 30 G10
Speldhurst Kent 10 G8
Spellbrook Herts 18 E10
Spencers Wood Wokham 16 H15
Spen Green Ches E 31 M14
Spennithorne N York 36 D9
Spennymoor Dur 41 P13
Spetchley Worcs 15 Q1
Spetisbury Dorset 7 R10
Spexhall Suffk 27 S12
Spey Bay Moray 54 J4
Speybridge Highld 54 D10
Speyview Moray 54 G8
Spilsby Lincs 33 S13
Spinkhill Derbys 32 D11
Spinningdale Highld 57 R15
Spital Hill Donc 32 F9
Spittal E Loth 46 F4
Spittal Highld 58 F5
Spittal Nthumb 47 P8
Spittal Pembks 12 F6
Spittalfield P & K 50 H9
Spittal of Glenmuick Abers 51 L2
Spittal of Glenshee P & K 50 H4
Spittal-on-Rule Border 46 H13
Spixworth Norfk 27 Q6
Splatt Devon 5 L10
Splayne's Green E Susx 10 E11
Splottlands Cardif 14 E14
Spofforth N York 36 G15
Spondon C Derb 23 S3
Spooner Row Norfk 27 N9
Sporle Norfk 26 K7
Spott E Loth 46 J4
Spottiswoode Border 46 H8
Spratton Nhants 24 G14
Spreakley Surrey 9 N5
Spreyton Devon 5 N11
Spriddlestone Devon 2 K7
Spridlington Lincs 33 L10
Springburn C Glas 44 G5
Springfield D & G 40 A7
Springfield Essex 18 H12
Springfield Fife 51 L14
Springholm D & G 39 N7
Springside N Ayrs 44 C10
Springthorpe Lincs 32 K9
Springwell Sundld 41 Q9
Sproatley E R Yk 33 P2
Sproston Green Ches W 31 L13
Sprotbrough Donc 32 E7
Sproughton Suffk 19 P6
Sprouston Border 46 K11
Sprowston Norfk 27 R7
Sproxton Leics 24 J5
Sproxton N York 37 L10
Spurstow Ches E 30 H15
Spyway Dorset 6 K12
Stableford Shrops 22 H9
Stacey Bank Sheff 31 U9
Stackhouse N York 35 S12
Stackpole Pembks 12 F11
Staddiscombe C Plym 2 K7
Stadhampton Oxon 16 G10
Stadhlaigearraidh W Isls 56 b7
Staffield Cumb 40 D11
Staffin Highld 59 f6
Stafford Staffs 22 K5
Stagsden Bed 17 M2
Stainburn Cumb 39 R14
Stainby Lincs 24 K5
Staincross Barns 31 U6
Staindrop Dur 36 D3
Staines-upon-Thames Surrey 17 N15
Stainforth Donc 32 F6
Stainforth N York 35 T12
Staining Lancs 30 E2
Stainland Calder 31 R4
Stainsacre N York 37 Q5
Stainton Cumb 35 N9
Stainton Cumb 40 D14
Stainton Donc 32 E9
Stainton Dur 36 C4
Stainton Middsb 36 J4
Stainton by Langworth Lincs 33 M11
Staintondale N York 37 R7
Stainton le Vale Lincs 33 P8
Stainton with Adgarley Cumb 34 K11
Stair E Ayrs 44 D13
Stairhaven D & G 38 E9
Staithes N York 37 N4
Stakeford Nthumb 41 Q4
Stakes Hants 9 L10
Stalbridge Dorset 7 N8
Stalbridge Weston Dorset 7 N8
Stalham Norfk 27 S5
Stalisfield Green Kent 11 N6
Stallen Dorset 7 L8
Stallingborough NE Lin 33 P6
Stalmine Lancs 35 L16
Stalybridge Tamesd 31 P8
Stambourne Essex 18 H7
Stambourne Green Essex 18 H7
Stamford Lincs 25 M8
Stamford Nthumb 47 S13
Stamford Bridge Ches W 30 G13
Stamford Bridge E R Yk 37 M14
Stamfordham Nthumb 41 M6
Stamford Hill Gt Lon 17 S12
Stanbridge C Beds 17 M6
Stanbury C Brad 31 Q1
Stand N Lans 44 J5
Standburn Falk 45 L4
Standeford Staffs 22 K7
Standen Kent 11 M8
Standerwick Somset 7 P2
Standford Hants 9 N6
Standingstone Cumb 39 S13
Standish Wigan 30 H6
Standlake Oxon 16 D9
Standon Hants 8 H7
Standon Herts 18 D10
Standon Staffs 22 J3
Stane N Lans 45 L7
Stanfield Norfk 27 L5
Stanford C Beds 17 P3
Stanford Kent 11 Q9
Stanford Bishop Herefs 15 M1
Stanford Bridge Worcs 22 G14
Stanford Dingley W Berk 16 F15
Stanford in the Vale Oxon 16 C11
Stanford le Hope Thurr 10 J1
Stanford on Avon Nhants 24 F12
Stanford on Soar Notts 24 E5
Stanford on Teme Worcs 22 G14
Stanfree Derbys 32 D12
Stanghow R & Cl 37 M4
Stanground C Pete 25 P9
Stanhoe Norfk 26 J3
Stanhope Border 45 P12
Stanhope Dur 41 L12
Stanhope Kent 11 P8
Stanion Nhants 24 K11
Stanley Derbys 23 S2
Stanley Dur 41 P10
Stanley P & K 50 H10
Stanley Staffs 31 P15
Stanley Crook Dur 41 N12
Stanley Pontlarge Gloucs 15 R5
Stanmer Br & H 10 D13
Stanmore Gt Lon 17 P11
Stanmore Hants 8 H7
Stannersburn Nthumb 40 G4
Stanningfield Suffk 18 K4
Stannington Nthumb 41 P5
Stannington Sheff 31 U10
Stannington Station Nthumb 41 P5
Stansbatch Herefs 21 Q10
Stansfield Suffk 18 J5
Stanstead Suffk 18 K5
Stanstead Abbotts Herts 17 T8
Stansted Kent 10 H5
Stansted Airport Essex 18 F10
Stansted Mountfitchet Essex 18 E9
Stanton Gloucs 15 S4
Stanton Nthumb 41 N4
Stanton Staffs 23 N1
Stanton Suffk 27 M13
Stanton by Bridge Derbys 23 S4
Stanton by Dale Derbys 24 D2
Stanton Drew BaNES 15 L16
Stanton Fitzwarren Swindn 15 U12
Stanton Harcourt Oxon 16 D9
Stanton in Peak Derbys 31 T13
Stanton Lacy Shrops 22 D12
Stanton Lees Derbys 31 T14
Stanton Long Shrops 22 E10
Stanton on the Wolds Notts 24 F4
Stanton Prior BaNES 15 M16
Stanton St Bernard Wilts 15 T16
Stanton St John Oxon 16 F8
Stanton St Quintin Wilts 15 Q13
Stanton Street Suffk 27 L14
Stanton under Bardon Leics 24 D7
Stanton upon Hine Heath Shrops 22 E5
Stanton Wick BaNES 15 L16
Stanway Essex 19 L9
Stanway Gloucs 15 S5
Stanwell Surrey 17 N14
Stanwick Nhants 25 L13
Stanwix Cumb 40 B9
Staoinebrig W Isls 56 b7
Stape N York 37 N8
Stapeley Ches E 30 K16
Stapenhill Staffs 23 Q5
Staple Kent 11 S6
Staple Cross Devon 5 S7
Staplecross E Susx 10 K11
Staplefield W Susx 10 C10
Staple Fitzpaine Somset 6 F8
Stapleford Cambs 18 E5
Stapleford Herts 17 R7
Stapleford Leics 24 J6
Stapleford Lincs 32 K15
Stapleford Notts 24 D3
Stapleford Wilts 7 T5
Stapleford Abbotts Essex 18 E14
Staplegrove Somset 6 F6
Staplehay Somset 6 F7
Staplehurst Kent 10 K8
Staplestreet Kent 11 P5
Stapleton Herefs 21 Q9
Stapleton Leics 23 S9
Stapleton N York 36 F5
Stapleton Shrops 21 S3
Stapleton Somset 6 J7
Stapley Somset 6 E8
Staploe Bed 25 N15

Turvey - Winterbourne Earls 75

Turvey Bed 17 L1
Turville Bucks 16 J11
Turweston Bucks 16 F4
Tushielaw Inn Border 45 R14
Tutbury Staffs 23 P4
Tutshill Gloucs 14 K11
Tuttington Norfk 27 Q4
Tuxford Notts 32 H12
Twatt Ork 58 b3
Twatt Shet 59 p5
Twechar E Duns 44 H4
Tweedbank Border 46 G11
Tweedmouth Nthumb 47 N8
Tweedsmuir Border 45 P13
Twelveheads Cnwll 1 S11
Twemlow Green Ches E 31 L13
Twenty Lincs 25 N5
Twerton BaNES 15 M16
Twickenham Gt Lon 17 P14
Twigworth Gloucs 15 P6
Twineham W Susx 10 C12
Twinstead Essex 18 K7
Twitchen Devon 5 P6
Two Dales Derbys 31 T14
Two Gates Staffs 23 P8
Twycross Leics 23 R8
Twyford Bucks 16 G6
Twyford Hants 8 H8
Twyford Leics 24 G7
Twyford Norfk 27 M5
Twyford Wokham 16 J14
Twynholm D & G 39 L9
Twyning Green Gloucs 15 Q4
Twynllanan Carmth 13 S6
Twywell Nhants 25 L12
Tyberton Herefs 14 H3
Tycroes Carmth 13 Q8
Tycrwyn Powys 29 Q15
Tydd Gote Lincs 26 D6
Tydd St Giles Cambs 26 D6
Tydd St Mary Lincs 26 D6
Tye Green Essex 18 F7
Tyldesley Wigan 30 K7
Tyler Hill Kent 11 Q5
Tylorstown Rhondd 14 B11
Ty-nant Conwy 29 N11
Tyndrum Stirlg 49 R11
Ty'n-dwr Denbgs 29 R11
Tynemouth N Tyne 41 R7
Tyninghame E Loth 46 H4
Tynron D & G 39 N3
Tynygraig Cerdgn 20 F9
Ty'n-y-Groes Conwy 28 K6
Tyn-y-nant Rhondd 14 C12
Tyringham M Keyn 16 K2
Tythegston Brdgnd 13 T13
Tytherington Ches E 31 N12
Tytherington S Glos 15 M12
Tytherington Wilts 7 R4
Tytherleigh Devon 6 G10
Tytherton Lucas Wilts 15 R14
Tywardreath Cnwll 2 D7
Tywyn Gwynd 20 E4

U

Ubbeston Green Suffk 27 S13
Ubley BaNES 6 K1
Uckfield E Susx 10 F11
Uckinghall Worcs 15 P4
Uckington Gloucs 15 Q6
Uddingston S Lans 44 H7
Uddington S Lans 44 K11
Udimore E Susx 11 M12
Udny Green Abers 55 R10
Udny Station Abers 55 R11
Uffculme Devon 6 D9
Uffington Lincs 25 M7
Uffington Oxon 16 B12
Uffington Shrops 22 E6
Ufford C Pete 25 N8
Ufford Suffk 19 R5
Ufton Warwks 23 S15
Ufton Nervet W Berk 16 G15
Ugadale Ag & B 42 K12
Ugborough Devon 3 M7
Uggeshall Suffk 27 T12
Ugglebarnby N York 37 Q6
Ughill Sheff 31 T9
Ugley Essex 18 E9
Ugley Green Essex 18 E9
Ugthorpe N York 37 N5
Uig Ag & B 42 d2
Uig Highld 59 b8
Uig Highld 59 e6
Uig W Isls 56 d2
Uigshader Highld 59 e9
Uisken Ag & B 48 C13
Ulbster Highld 58 H7
Ulceby Lincs 33 S12
Ulceby N Linc 33 N5
Ulceby Skitter N Linc 33 N5
Ulcombe Kent 11 L7
Uldale Cumb 39 U12
Uley Gloucs 15 N10
Ulgham Nthumb 41 P3
Ullapool Highld 56 H15
Ullenhall Warwks 23 N14
Ulleskelf N York 32 E1
Ullesthorpe Leics 24 D11
Ulley Rothm 32 D10
Ullingswick Herefs 15 L2
Ullinish Lodge Hotel Highld 59 d10
Ullock Cumb 34 G3
Ulpha Cumb 34 J8
Ulrome E R Yk 37 U14
Ulsta Shet 59 q3
Ulverston Cumb 34 K10
Ulwell Dorset 7 S14
Ulzieside D & G 44 J15
Umberleigh Devon 5 L7
Unapool Highld 56 J8
Underbarrow Cumb 35 N8
Under Burnmouth Border 40 C5
Undercliffe C Brad 31 S2
Underdale Shrops 22 D6
Under River Kent 10 G6
Underwood Notts 32 D16
Undy Mons 14 H12
Union Mills IoM 34 d6
Unstone Derbys 32 B11
Upavon Wilts 8 C3
Upchurch Kent 11 L4
Upcott Devon 5 P6
Up Exe Devon 5 R10
Upgate Norfk 27 P6
Uphall Dorset 7 L10
Uphall W Loth 45 N5
Upham Devon 5 Q9
Upham Hants 8 J8
Uphampton Herefs 21 R10
Uphampton Worcs 22 J14
Uphill N Som 6 G1
Up Holland Lancs 30 H7
Uplawmoor E Rens 44 D8
Upleadon Gloucs 15 N6
Upleatham R & Cl 37 L4
Uploders Dorset 6 K12
Uplowman Devon 5 S8
Uplyme Devon 6 G12
Up Marden W Susx 9 N9
Upminster Gt Lon 18 F15
Up Mudford Somset 7 L8
Up Nately Hants 9 L3
Upottery Devon 6 F9
Upper Affcot Shrops 21 S6
Upper Ardchronie Highld 57 Q15
Upper Arley Worcs 22 H12
Upper Basildon W Berk 16 F14
Upper Beeding W Susx 9 T10
Upper Benefield Nhants 25 L10
Upper Bentley Worcs 23 L14
Upper Bighouse Highld 57 U4
Upper Boddington Nhants 16 E1
Upper Brailes Warwks 16 B3
Upper Breakish Highld 52 C11
Upper Broadheath Worcs 22 J16
Upper Broughton Notts 24 G4
Upper Bucklebury W Berk 16 F15
Upper Burgate Hants 8 D9
Upperby Cumb 40 C10
Upper Caldecote C Beds 17 P2
Upper Chapel Powys 20 K14
Upper Chicksgrove Wilts 7 R6
Upper Chute Wilts 8 F3
Upper Clapton Gt Lon 17 S12
Upper Clatford Hants 8 G4
Upper Cound Shrops 22 E8
Upper Cumberworth Kirk 31 S6
Upper Dallachy Moray 54 J4
Upper Deal Kent 11 U6
Upper Dean Bed 25 M14
Upper Denby Kirk 31 T6
Upper Dicker E Susx 10 G13
Upper Dounreay Highld 58 D3
Upper Dovercourt Essex 19 Q8
Upper Drumbane Stirlg 50 B15
Upper Dunsforth N York 36 H13
Upper Eashing Surrey 9 Q4
Upper Eathie Highld 53 T4
Upper Egleton Herefs 15 L3
Upper Elkstone Staffs 31 Q14
Upper Ellastone Staffs 23 N2
Upper Farringdon Hants 9 M6
Upper Framilode Gloucs 15 N8
Upper Froyle Hants 9 M5
Upperglen Highld 59 c8
Upper Godney Somset 6 K4
Upper Gravenhurst C Beds 17 P4
Upper Green W Berk 8 G1
Upper Grove Common Herefs 14 K6
Upper Hale Surrey 9 N4
Upper Halliford Surrey 17 N15
Upper Hambleton Rutlnd 24 K7
Upper Harbledown Kent 11 Q5
Upper Hartfield E Susx 10 F9
Upper Hatherley Gloucs 15 Q7
Upper Heaton Kirk 31 S4
Upper Helmsley N York 37 M14
Upper Hergest Herefs 21 P11
Upper Heyford Nhants 24 G15
Upper Heyford Oxon 16 E6
Upper Hill Herefs 21 S11
Upper Hopton Kirk 31 S5
Upper Hulme Staffs 31 Q14
Upper Inglesham Swindn 15 U11
Upper Killay Swans 13 P11
Upper Kinchrackine Ag & B 49 P11
Upper Lambourn W Berk 16 B13
Upper Landywood Staffs 23 L8
Upper Langford N Som 6 J1
Upper Langwith Derbys 32 E13
Upper Largo Fife 51 N15
Upper Leigh Staffs 23 M3
Upper Lochton Abers 55 N15
Upper Longdon Staffs 23 M6
Upper & Lower Stondon C Beds 17 P4
Upper Lybster Highld 58 G7
Upper Lydbrook Gloucs 15 L7
Upper Lye Herefs 21 R9
Uppermill Oldham 31 Q7
Upper Milton Worcs 22 J13
Upper Minety Wilts 15 R11
Upper Mulben Moray 54 J6
Upper Netchwood Shrops 22 F10
Upper Nobut Staffs 23 M3
Upper Norwood W Susx 9 Q9
Upper Poppleton C York 36 K14
Upper Ratley Hants 8 F8
Upper Rissington Gloucs 15 U7
Upper Rochford Worcs 22 F14
Upper Ruscoe D & G 38 K8
Upper Sapey Herefs 22 G15
Upper Seagry Wilts 15 R13
Upper Shelton C Beds 17 M3
Upper Sheringham Norfk 27 P2
Upper Skelmorlie N Ayrs 43 R5
Upper Slaughter Gloucs 15 T6
Upper Soudley Gloucs 15 L8
Upper Standen Kent 11 S8
Upper Stoke Norfk 27 R8
Upper Stowe Nhants 24 F16
Upper Street Hants 8 D9
Upper Street Norfk 27 S6
Upper Street Norfk 27 S6
Upper Street Suffk 18 J5
Upper Street Suffk 19 P5
Upper Sundon C Beds 17 N5
Upper Swell Gloucs 15 U6
Upper Tasburgh Norfk 27 Q9
Upper Tean Staffs 23 M2
Upperthong Kirk 31 R6
Upperton W Susx 9 Q8
Upper Town Herefs 14 K2
Uppertown Highld 58 H1
Upper Town N Som 14 K16
Upper Town Suffk 27 L14
Upper Tumble Carmth 13 P8
Upper Tysoe Warwks 16 C3
Upper Victoria Angus 51 P10
Upper Wardington Oxon 16 E2
Upper Welland Worcs 15 N3
Upper Wellingham E Susx 10 F13
Upper Weybread Suffk 27 Q12
Upper Wield Hants 8 K5
Upper Winchendon Bucks 16 J8
Upper Woodford Wilts 8 C5
Upper Wraxall Wilts 15 P14
Uppingham Rutlnd 24 J9
Uppington Shrops 22 F7
Upsall N York 36 J9
Upsettlington Border 47 M9
Upshire Essex 18 D13
Up Somborne Hants 8 G6
Upstreet Kent 11 S4
Upton Bucks 16 J8
Upton C Pete 25 N9
Upton Cambs 25 P12
Upton Ches W 30 F13
Upton Cnwll 2 G4
Upton Devon 3 N9
Upton Devon 6 D10
Upton Dorset 7 N13
Upton Dorset 7 S12
Upton Halton 30 G10
Upton Hants 8 G3
Upton Hants 8 G9
Upton Leics 23 S9
Upton Lincs 32 J10
Upton Norfk 27 T7
Upton Notts 32 H11
Upton Notts 32 H15
Upton Oxon 16 E12
Upton Slough 17 M13
Upton Somset 5 S6
Upton Somset 6 J6
Upton Wakefd 32 D5
Upton Wirral 30 D10
Upton Bishop Herefs 15 L5
Upton Cheyney S Glos 15 M15
Upton Cressett Shrops 22 G10
Upton Grey Hants 9 L4
Upton Hellions Devon 5 Q10
Upton Lovell Wilts 7 R4
Upton Magna Shrops 22 E7
Upton Noble Somset 7 N4
Upton Pyne Devon 5 R11
Upton St Leonards Gloucs 15 P7
Upton Scudamore Wilts 7 Q3
Upton Snodsbury Worcs 15 R1
Upton-upon-Severn Worcs 15 P3
Upton Warren Worcs 22 K14
Upwaltham W Susx 9 Q9
Upwell Norfk 26 E8
Upwood Cambs 25 Q12
Urchfont Wilts 7 S1
Urmston Traffd 31 L8
Urquhart Moray 54 H4
Urra N York 36 K6
Urray Highld 53 Q6
Usan Angus 51 S7
Ushaw Moor Dur 41 P11
Usk Mons 14 H10
Usselby Lincs 33 N9
Usworth Sundld 41 Q9
Utkinton Ches W 30 H13
Utley C Brad 36 C16
Uton Devon 5 Q11
Utterby Lincs 33 R9
Uttoxeter Staffs 23 N3
Uxbridge Gt Lon 17 N13
Uyeasound Shet 59 r2
Uzmaston Pembks 12 F8

V

Vale Guern 2 d2
Valley IoA 28 C5
Valtos Highld 59 f6
Valtos W Isls 56 d2
Vange Essex 18 H15
Vatsetter Shet 59 r3
Vatten Highld 59 c9
Vaynor Myr Td 14 C8
Veensgarth Shet 59 q6
Velindre Powys 14 E4
Venngreen Devon 4 H9
Venn Ottery Devon 6 D12
Ventnor IoW 8 J15
Venton Devon 3 L7
Vernham Dean Hants 8 F2
Vernham Street Hants 8 F2
Verwood Dorset 7 T9
Veryan Cnwll 1 U11
Vickerstown Cumb 34 J12
Victoria Cnwll 2 C6
Vidlin Shet 59 q4
Viewfield Moray 54 H4
Viewpark N Lans 44 H7
Vigo Kent 10 H5
Village de Putron Guern 2 d3
Vines Cross E Susx 10 H12
Virginia Water Surrey 17 M15
Virginstow Devon 4 H12
Vobster Somset 7 N3
Voe Shet 59 q5
Vowchurch Herefs 14 G4

W

Waberthwaite Cumb 34 H8
Wackerfield Dur 36 D3
Wacton Norfk 27 Q10
Wadborough Worcs 15 Q2
Waddesdon Bucks 16 H7
Waddeton Devon 3 Q7
Waddingham Lincs 33 L8
Waddington Lancs 35 R16
Waddington Lincs 33 L13
Wadebridge Cnwll 2 C4
Wadeford Somset 6 G9
Wadenhoe Nhants 25 L11
Wadesmill Herts 17 S7
Wadhurst E Susx 10 H10
Wadshelf Derbys 31 U12
Wadworth Donc 32 E8
Wainfleet All Saints Lincs 33 T14
Wainfleet St Mary Lincs 33 T14
Wainhouse Corner Cnwll 4 E11
Wainscott Medway 10 K3
Wainstalls Calder 31 Q3
Waitby Cumb 35 S5
Waithe Lincs 33 Q7
Wakefield Wakefd 32 B4
Wakerley Nhants 25 L9
Wakes Colne Essex 19 L9
Walberswick Suffk 27 U13
Walberton W Susx 9 Q11
Walbutt D & G 39 M7
Walcombe Somset 7 L3
Walcot Lincs 25 M3
Walcot Shrops 22 F7
Walcot Swindn 15 U12
Walcote Leics 24 E11
Walcot Green Norfk 27 P12
Walcott Lincs 33 N15
Walcott Norfk 27 S3
Walden Stubbs N York 32 E5
Walderslade Medway 10 K4
Walderton W Susx 9 N10
Walditch Dorset 6 K12
Waldridge Dur 41 P10
Waldringfield Suffk 19 R6
Waldron E Susx 10 G12
Wales Rothm 32 D10
Wales Somset 7 L7
Walesby Lincs 33 N9
Walesby Notts 32 G12
Walford Herefs 15 L7
Walford Herefs 21 R8
Walford Heath Shrops 22 D5
Walgherton Ches E 30 K16
Walgrave Nhants 24 J13
Walkden Salfd 31 L7
Walker N u Ty 41 Q8
Walkerburn Border 46 E10
Walkeringham Notts 32 H9
Walkerith Lincs 32 H9
Walkern Herts 17 R6
Walkerton Fife 50 K15
Walkford Dorset 8 E12
Walkhampton Devon 2 K4
Walkington E R Yk 33 L2
Walkley Sheff 32 B9
Walk Mill Lancs 31 N3
Walkwood Worcs 23 M14
Wall Nthumb 40 K7
Wall Staffs 23 N8
Wallacetown S Ayrs 38 F1
Wallacetown S Ayrs 43 T13
Wallands Park E Susx 10 E13
Wallasey Wirral 30 E9
Wallingford Oxon 16 G12
Wallington Gt Lon 10 C4
Wallington Hants 8 K10
Wallington Herts 17 R4
Wallisdown Poole 7 T12
Walls Shet 59 p5
Wallsend N Tyne 41 Q7
Wallyford E Loth 46 E5
Walmer Kent 11 U7
Walmer Bridge Lancs 30 G4
Walmley Birm 23 N10
Walpole Suffk 27 S13
Walpole Cross Keys Norfk 26 E5
Walpole Highway Norfk 26 E6
Walpole St Andrew Norfk 26 E6
Walpole St Peter Norfk 26 E6
Walsall Wsall 23 M9
Walsden Calder 31 P4
Walsgrave on Sowe Covtry 23 S12
Walsham le Willows Suffk 27 M13
Walshford N York 36 H14
Walsoken Norfk 26 E7
Walston S Lans 45 N9
Walsworth Herts 17 Q5
Walter's Ash Bucks 16 K10
Waltham Kent 11 Q7
Waltham NE Lin 33 Q7
Waltham Abbey Essex 18 C13
Waltham Chase Hants 8 J9
Waltham Cross Herts 17 S10
Waltham on the Wolds Leics 24 J5
Waltham St Lawrence W & M 16 K14
Walthamstow Gt Lon 17 S12
Walton Cumb 40 D8
Walton Derbys 32 B13
Walton Leeds 36 H15
Walton Leics 24 F11
Walton M Keyn 17 L4
Walton Powys 21 P10
Walton Somset 6 J5
Walton Suffk 19 R7
Walton W Susx 9 N11
Walton Wakefd 32 B5
Walton Wrekin 22 F6
Walton Cardiff Gloucs 15 Q5
Walton East Pembks 12 F6
Walton-in-Gordano N Som 14 H14
Walton-le-Dale Lancs 30 H3
Walton-on-Thames Surrey 17 P15
Walton-on-the-Hill Staffs 23 L5
Walton on the Hill Surrey 10 C6
Walton on the Naze Essex 19 R9
Walton on the Wolds Leics 24 F6
Walton-on-Trent Derbys 23 P6
Walton Park N Som 14 H14
Walton West Pembks 12 D8
Walworth Darltn 36 F4
Walworth Gt Lon 17 S14
Walwyn's Castle Pembks 12 D8
Wambrook Somset 6 G9
Wanborough Surrey 9 Q4
Wanborough Swindn 15 U13
Wandsworth Gt Lon 17 R14
Wangford Suffk 27 U12
Wanlip Leics 24 F7
Wanlockhead D & G 44 K14
Wannock E Susx 10 H14
Wansford C Pete 25 M9
Wansford E R Yk 37 S14
Wanshurst Green Kent 10 K7
Wanstead Gt Lon 18 D15
Wanstrow Somset 7 N4
Wanswell Gloucs 15 M10
Wantage Oxon 16 D12
Wappenbury Warwks 23 S14
Wappenham Nhants 16 G2
Warbleton E Susx 10 H12
Warborough Oxon 16 F11
Warboys Cambs 25 R12
Warbreck Bpool 30 E1
Warbstow Cnwll 4 F12
Warburton Traffd 30 K9
Warcop Cumb 35 S4
Warden Nthumb 40 K7
Wardington Oxon 16 E2
Wardle Ches E 30 J15
Wardle Rochdl 31 N5
Wardley Gatesd 41 Q8
Wardley Rutlnd 24 J9
Wardlow Derbys 31 S12
Wardy Hill Cambs 26 E12
Ware Herts 17 S8
Wareham Dorset 7 R13
Warehorne Kent 11 N10
Warenford Nthumb 47 Q12
Wareside Herts 18 D11
Waresley Cambs 17 R1
Warfield Br For 16 K15
Warfleet Devon 3 Q8
Wargrave Wokham 16 J13
Warham All Saints Norfk 27 L2
Warham St Mary Norfk 27 L2
Wark Nthumb 40 J6
Wark Nthumb 47 L10
Warkleigh Devon 5 M7
Warkton Nhants 24 K12
Warkworth Nhants 16 E3
Warkworth Nthumb 47 S16
Warlaby N York 36 G8
Warleggan Cnwll 2 E5
Warley Town Calder 31 Q4
Warlingham Surrey 10 E5
Warmfield Wakefd 32 C4
Warmingham Ches E 30 K14
Warmington Nhants 25 M10
Warmington Warwks 16 D2
Warminster Wilts 7 Q3
Warmley S Glos 15 M14
Warmsworth Donc 32 E7
Warmwell Dorset 7 N13
Warnford Hants 8 K8
Warnham W Susx 9 T6
Warningcamp W Susx 9 R10
Warninglid W Susx 10 C11
Warren Ches E 31 N12
Warren Pembks 12 E10
Warrenhill S Lans 45 L10
Warren Row W & M 16 J13
Warren Street Kent 11 M6
Warrington M Keyn 17 L1
Warrington Warrtn 30 J10
Warriston C Edin 45 R4
Warsash Hants 8 H11
Warslow Staffs 31 R14
Warter E R Yk 37 Q15
Warthermaske N York 36 E10
Warthill N York 37 M14
Wartling E Susx 10 J13
Wartnaby Leics 24 G5
Warton Lancs 30 F3
Warton Lancs 35 N11
Warton Warwks 23 Q8
Warwick Warwks 23 Q14
Warwick Bridge Cumb 40 D9
Wasbister Ork 58 b2
Wasdale Head Cumb 34 J5
Washaway Cnwll 2 C4
Washbourne Devon 3 P7
Washbrook Suffk 19 P6
Washfield Devon 5 R8
Washford Somset 6 D4
Washford Pyne Devon 5 P9
Washingborough Lincs 33 M12
Washington Sundld 41 Q9
Washington W Susx 9 S9
Wasperton Warwks 23 Q15
Wass N York 36 K10
Watchet Somset 6 D4
Watchfield Oxon 16 A11
Watchgate Cumb 35 P7
Water Devon 5 P14
Waterbeach Cambs 26 E14
Waterbeach W Susx 9 P10
Waterbeck D & G 39 U6
Water End E R Yk 32 H1
Waterfall Staffs 31 R16
Waterfoot E Rens 44 F7
Waterford Herts 17 R8
Waterheads Border 45 R8
Waterhouses Staffs 31 R16
Wateringbury Kent 10 J6
Waterloo Highld 52 C11
Waterloo N Lans 44 J8
Waterloo P & K 50 G10
Waterloo Pembks 12 F9
Waterloo Sefton 30 E8
Waterlooville Hants 9 L10
Watermillock Cumb 35 M3
Water Newton Cambs 25 N9
Water Orton Warwks 23 P10
Waterperry Oxon 16 G9
Waterrow Somset 6 D6
Watersfield W Susx 9 R9
Waterside Bl w D 30 K4
Waterside E Ayrs 44 D15
Waterside E Ayrs 44 E9
Waterside E Duns 44 H5
Waterstein Highld 59 a8
Waterstock Oxon 16 G9
Waterston Pembks 12 E9
Water Stratford Bucks 16 G4
Waters Upton Wrekin 22 F6
Watford Herts 17 P11
Watford Nhants 24 F14
Wath N York 36 D12
Wath N York 36 G10
Wath upon Dearne Rothm 32 C7
Watlington Norfk 26 G7
Watlington Oxon 16 H11
Watten Highld 58 G5
Wattisfield Suffk 27 M13
Wattisham Suffk 19 M5
Watton Dorset 6 J12
Watton E R Yk 37 R15
Watton Norfk 27 L9
Watton-at-Stone Herts 17 R7
Wattston N Lans 44 J5
Wattsville Caerph 14 E11
Waulkmill Abers 55 N16
Waunarlwydd Swans 13 Q11
Waunfawr Cerdgn 20 E7
Waunfawr Gwynd 28 F8
Wavendon M Keyn 17 L4
Waverbridge Cumb 39 U10
Waverton Ches W 30 G14
Waverton Cumb 39 U11
Wawne E R Yk 33 N2
Waxham Norfk 27 T4
Wayford Somset 6 H10
Waytown Dorset 6 J11
Way Village Devon 5 Q9
Weacombe Somset 6 D4
Weald Oxon 16 B10
Wealdstone Gt Lon 17 P12
Weardley Leeds 36 F16
Weare Somset 6 J2
Weare Giffard Devon 4 K7
Wearhead Dur 40 J12
Wearne Somset 6 J6
Weasenham All Saints Norfk 26 K5
Weasenham St Peter Norfk 26 K5
Weaste Salfd 31 M8
Weaverham Ches W 30 J12
Weaverthorpe N York 37 R11
Webheath Worcs 23 M14
Wedderlairs Abers 55 R9
Weddington Warwks 23 R10
Wedhampton Wilts 7 T1
Wedmore Somset 6 J3
Wednesbury Sandw 23 L9
Wednesfield Wolves 23 L9
Weedon Bucks 16 J7
Weedon Nhants 24 F15
Weedon Lois Nhants 16 F2
Weeford Staffs 23 N8
Weeke Hants 8 H7
Weekley Nhants 24 K12
Week St Mary Cnwll 4 F11
Weel E R Yk 33 M1
Weeley Essex 19 P10
Weeley Heath Essex 19 P10
Weem P & K 50 D7
Weethley Warwks 23 M16
Weeting Norfk 26 J11
Weeton E R Yk 33 R4
Weeton Lancs 30 F2
Weeton N York 36 F15
Weetwood Leeds 31 T1
Weir Lancs 31 N3
Weir Quay Devon 2 J5
Weisdale Shet 59 q5
Welborne Norfk 27 N7
Welbourn Lincs 33 L15
Welburn N York 37 M12
Welbury N York 36 H6
Welby Lincs 25 L2
Welcombe Devon 4 F8
Welford Nhants 24 F12
Welford W Berk 16 D14
Welford-on-Avon Warwks 15 T1
Welham Leics 24 H10
Welham Notts 32 G11
Welham Green Herts 17 Q9
Well Hants 9 M4
Well Lincs 33 T12
Well N York 36 F10
Welland Worcs 15 N3
Wellbank Angus 51 N10
Wellesbourne Warwks 23 Q16
Well Head Herts 17 Q5
Welling Gt Lon 10 F2
Wellingborough Nhants 24 K14
Wellingham Norfk 26 K5
Wellingore Lincs 33 L15
Wellington Cumb 34 G6
Wellington Herefs 14 J2
Wellington Somset 6 E7
Wellington Wrekin 22 G7
Wellington Heath Herefs 15 M3
Wellow BaNES 7 N1
Wellow IoW 8 G14
Wellow Notts 32 G13
Wells Somset 6 K3
Wells-next-the-sea Norfk 27 L2
Wellstye Green Essex 18 G10
Welltree P & K 50 F12
Wellwood Fife 45 N2
Welney Norfk 26 E10
Welshampton Shrops 22 C3
Welsh Frankton Shrops 29 T13
Welsh Newton Herefs 14 J7
Welshpool Powys 21 N3
Welsh St Donats V Glam 14 C14
Welton Cumb 40 B11
Welton E R Yk 33 L3
Welton Lincs 33 L11
Welton Nhants 24 E14
Welton le Marsh Lincs 33 T13
Welton le Wold Lincs 33 Q10
Welwick E R Yk 33 R4
Welwyn Herts 17 Q7
Welwyn Garden City Herts 17 Q8
Wem Shrops 22 E4
Wembdon Somset 6 G4
Wembley Gt Lon 17 Q12
Wembury Devon 2 K8
Wembworthy Devon 5 M9
Wemyss Bay Inver 43 R5
Wendens Ambo Essex 18 E7
Wendlebury Oxon 16 F7
Wendling Norfk 27 L7
Wendover Bucks 16 K9
Wendron Cnwll 1 R13
Wendy Cambs 17 S2
Wenhaston Suffk 27 T13
Wennington Cambs 25 Q12
Wennington Gt Lon 10 G2
Wennington Lancs 35 Q12
Wensley Derbys 31 T14
Wensley N York 36 D8
Wentbridge Wakefd 32 D5
Wentnor Shrops 21 R5
Wentworth Cambs 26 E12
Wentworth Rothm 32 C8
Wenvoe V Glam 14 D14
Weobley Herefs 21 R12
Wepham W Susx 9 R10
Wereham Norfk 26 H8
Werrington C Pete 25 P8
Werrington Cnwll 4 H13
Wervin Ches W 30 F12
Wesham Lancs 30 F2
Wessington Derbys 32 B15
West Acre Norfk 26 J6
West Alvington Devon 3 N9
West Anstey Devon 5 Q6
West Ashby Lincs 33 Q12
West Ashling W Susx 9 N10
West Ashton Wilts 7 Q2
West Auckland Dur 41 N14
West Ayton N York 37 R9
West Bagborough Somset 6 E5
West Bank Halton 30 H10
West Barkwith Lincs 33 P11
West Barnby N York 37 P5
West Barns E Loth 46 J4
West Barsham Norfk 27 L3
West Bay Dorset 6 J12
West Beckham Norfk 27 P2
West Bedfont Surrey 17 N14
Westbere Kent 11 R5
West Bergholt Essex 19 L9
West Bexington Dorset 6 K13
West Bilney Norfk 26 H6
West Blatchington Br & H 10 C14
West Boldon S Tyne 41 R8
Westborough Lincs 24 J1
Westbourne Bmouth 7 T12
Westbourne W Susx 9 M10
West Bowling C Brad 31 S3
West Bradenham Norfk 27 L7
West Bradford Lancs 35 S16
West Bradley Somset 7 L5
West Bretton Wakefd 31 U5
West Bridgford Notts 24 E3
West Bromwich Sandw 23 L10
Westbrook Kent 11 T3
Westbrook W Berk 16 D14
West Buckland Devon 5 M5
West Buckland Somset 6 E7
West Burton N York 36 B9
Westbury Bucks 16 G4
Westbury Shrops 21 Q2
Westbury Wilts 7 Q2
Westbury Leigh Wilts 7 Q2
Westbury on Severn Gloucs 15 M8
Westbury-on-Trym Bristl 14 K14
Westbury-sub-Mendip Somset 6 K3
West Butterwick N Linc 32 J7
Westby Lancs 30 F2
West Byfleet Surrey 9 R1
West Cairngaan D & G 38 D13
West Caister Norfk 27 U7
West Calder W Loth 45 M6
West Camel Somset 7 L7
West Chaldon Dorset 7 P13
West Challow Oxon 16 C12
West Charleton Devon 3 P9
West Chiltington W Susx 9 S9
West Chinnock Somset 6 J8
West Clandon Surrey 9 R3
West Cliffe Kent 11 T8
Westcliff-on-Sea Sthend 18 K16
West Coker Somset 6 K8
Westcombe Somset 7 M4
West Compton Somset 7 L4
West Compton Abbas Dorset 7 L12
Westcote Gloucs 15 U7
Westcote Barton Oxon 16 D6
Westcott Bucks 16 H7
Westcott Devon 5 S10
Westcott Surrey 9 T4
West Cottingwith N York 37 M16
Westcourt Wilts 15 U16
West Cowick E R Yk 32 F4
West Cross Swans 13 Q12
West Curthwaite Cumb 40 A10
Westdean E Susx 10 G15
West Dean W Susx 9 P9
West Dean Wilts 8 E7
West Deeping Lincs 25 N7
West Derby Lpool 30 F9
West Dereham Norfk 26 G9
West Down Devon 4 K4
Westdowns Cnwll 4 D13
West Drayton Gt Lon 17 N13
West Drayton Notts 32 G12
West Dunnet Highld 58 G2
West Ella E R Yk 33 L3
West End Bed 17 M1
West End Hants 8 H9
West End N Som 14 J15
West End Norfk 27 U7
West End Surrey 9 Q2
West End Wilts 7 S7
West End Green Hants 9 L1
Westerdale Highld 58 E5
Westerdale N York 37 M6
Westerfield Suffk 19 Q5
Westergate W Susx 9 Q11
Westerham Kent 10 F6
Westerhope N u Ty 41 P7
Westerland Devon 3 Q6
Westerleigh S Glos 15 M13
Western Isles W Isls 56 d4
Wester Ochiltree W Loth 45 N4
Wester Pitkierie Fife 51 P15
Westerton of Rossie Angus 51 R7
Westerwick Shet 59 p6
West Farleigh Kent 10 J6
West Farndon Nhants 16 E1
West Felton Shrops 29 T14
Westfield BaNES 7 M2
Westfield Cumb 39 R14
Westfield E Susx 11 L12
Westfield Highld 58 D3
Westfield N Lans 44 H5
Westfield Norfk 27 M7
Westfield W Loth 45 L5
Westfields of Rattray P & K 50 J8
Westgate Dur 40 K12
Westgate N Linc 32 H6
Westgate on Sea Kent 11 T3
West Grafton Wilts 8 E2
West Green Hants 9 M2
West Grimstead Wilts 8 D7
West Grinstead W Susx 9 T8
West Haddlesey N York 32 E3
West Haddon Nhants 24 F13
West Hagbourne Oxon 16 E12
West Hagley Worcs 22 K12
Westhall Suffk 27 T12
West Hallam Derbys 23 S2
West Halton N Linc 32 K4
Westham Dorset 7 M14
Westham E Susx 10 H14
West Ham Gt Lon 18 D16
Westham Somset 6 H3
Westhampnett W Susx 9 P11
West Handley Derbys 32 C11
West Hanney Oxon 16 D11
West Hanningfield Essex 18 H13
West Harnham Wilts 8 C7
West Harptree BaNES 7 L1
West Harting W Susx 9 N8
West Hatch Somset 6 G7
West Hatch Wilts 7 R6
West Haven Angus 51 Q10
Westhay Somset 6 J4
West Heath Birm 23 M12
West Helmsdale Highld 58 D11
West Hendred Oxon 16 D12
West Heslerton N York 37 Q11
West Hewish N Som 14 H16
Westhide Herefs 14 K3
Westhill Abers 55 Q13
West Hill Devon 6 D12
West Hoathly W Susx 10 E10
West Holme Dorset 7 Q13
Westhope Herefs 21 S12
Westhope Shrops 21 S6
West Horndon Essex 18 G15
Westhorpe Lincs 25 P4
Westhorpe Suffk 27 N14
West Horrington Somset 7 L3
West Horsley Surrey 9 S3
West Hougham Kent 11 S8
Westhoughton Bolton 30 K7
Westhouse N York 35 R11
Westhouses Derbys 32 C15
West Howe Bmouth 7 T11
Westhumble Surrey 9 T3
West Huntingtower P & K 50 H12
West Huntspill Somset 6 G3
West Hythe Kent 11 Q9
West Ilsley W Berk 16 E13
West Itchenor W Susx 9 N11
West Kennett Wilts 15 T15
West Kilbride N Ayrs 43 R9
West Kingsdown Kent 10 G4
West Kington Wilts 15 P14
West Kirby Wirral 29 R4
West Knapton N York 37 Q11
West Knighton Dorset 7 N13
West Knoyle Wilts 7 Q5
Westlake Devon 3 M7
West Lambrook Somset 6 J8
West Langdon Kent 11 T7
West Lavington W Susx 9 P8
West Lavington Wilts 7 S2
West Layton N York 36 D5
West Leake Notts 24 E4
Westleigh Devon 4 K6
Westleigh Devon 6 D8
West Leigh Somset 6 E6
Westleton Suffk 27 T14
West Lexham Norfk 26 K6
Westley Suffk 18 K3
Westley Waterless Cambs 18 G4
West Lilling N York 37 L12
Westlington Bucks 16 J8
West Linton Border 45 P8
Westlinton Cumb 40 B8
West Littleton S Glos 15 N14
West Lockinge Oxon 16 D12
West Lulworth Dorset 7 P14
West Lutton N York 37 Q12
West Lydford Somset 7 L5
West Lyng Somset 6 G6
West Lynn Norfk 26 G5
West Malling Kent 10 J5
West Malvern Worcs 15 N2
West Marden W Susx 9 M9
West Markham Notts 32 G12
Westmarsh Kent 11 S5
West Marsh NE Lin 33 Q6
West Marton N York 35 U15
West Melbury Dorset 7 Q7
West Meon Hants 9 L8
West Mersea Essex 19 M11
Westmeston E Susx 10 D13
Westmill Herts 17 S5
West Milton Dorset 6 K11
Westminster Gt Lon 17 R13
West Minster Kent 11 M3
West Molesey Surrey 17 P15
West Monkton Somset 6 F6
West Moors Dorset 7 T10
West Morden Dorset 7 Q11
West Morriston Border 46 H10
West Mudford Somset 7 L7
Westmuir Angus 51 M7
West Ness N York 37 M10
Westnewton Cumb 39 T11
West Newton E R Yk 33 P1
West Newton Norfk 26 H4
West Newton Somset 6 G6
West Norwood Gt Lon 10 D3
Westoe S Tyne 41 R8
West Ogwell Devon 3 P4
Weston BaNES 15 M15
Weston Ches E 31 L15
Weston Devon 6 E11
Weston Devon 6 E12
Weston Hants 9 M8
Weston Herts 17 R5
Weston Lincs 25 Q5
Weston N York 36 E15
Weston Nhants 16 F2
Weston Notts 32 H13
Weston Shrops 22 F10
Weston Shrops 29 S14
Weston Staffs 23 L4
Weston W Berk 16 D14
Weston Beggard Herefs 14 K3
Westonbirt Gloucs 15 P12
Weston by Welland Nhants 24 H10
Weston Colville Cambs 18 G4
Weston Corbett Hants 9 L4
Weston Coyney C Stke 22 K2
Weston Favell Nhants 24 H15
Weston Green Cambs 18 G5
Weston Heath Shrops 22 H6
Westoning C Beds 17 N5
Weston-in-Gordano N Som 14 J14
Weston Jones Staffs 22 H5
Weston Longville Norfk 27 P6
Weston Lullingfields Shrops 22 C5
Weston-on-the-Green Oxon 16 F7
Weston Patrick Hants 9 L4
Weston Rhyn Shrops 29 S12
Weston-sub-Edge Gloucs 15 T3
Weston-super-Mare N Som 14 G16
Weston Turville Bucks 16 K8
Weston-under-Lizard Staffs 22 J7
Weston under Penyard Herefs 15 L6
Weston-under-Redcastle Shrops 22 E4
Weston under Wetherley Warwks 23 S14
Weston Underwood Derbys 23 Q2
Weston Underwood M Keyn 16 K2
Weston-upon-Trent Derbys 23 S4
Westonzoyland Somset 6 H5
West Orchard Dorset 7 P8
West Overton Wilts 15 T15
Westow N York 37 N12
West Park Abers 55 Q15
West Parley Dorset 7 T11
West Peckham Kent 10 J6
West Pelton Dur 41 P10
West Pennard Somset 6 K4
West Pentire Cnwll 1 S8
West Perry Cambs 25 N14
West Porlock Somset 5 Q3
Westport Somset 6 H7
West Putford Devon 4 H8
West Quantoxhead Somset 6 D4
Westquarter Falk 45 L4
West Rainton Dur 41 Q11
West Rasen Lincs 33 M9
Westray Airport Ork 58 c1
West Raynham Norfk 26 K5
Westrigg W Loth 45 L6
Westrop Swindn 15 U11
West Rounton N York 36 H6
West Row Suffk 26 H13
West Rudham Norfk 26 K4
West Runton Norfk 27 Q2
Westruther Border 46 H8
Westry Cambs 25 S9
West Saltoun E Loth 46 F6
West Sandford Devon 5 P10
West Sandwick Shet 59 q3
West Scrafton N York 36 C9
West Stafford Dorset 7 N12
West Stockwith Notts 32 H8
West Stoke W Susx 9 N10
West Stour Dorset 7 P7
West Stourmouth Kent 11 S5
West Stow Suffk 26 J13
West Stowell Wilts 15 T16
West Street Suffk 27 M13
West Tanfield N York 36 F10
West Taphouse Cnwll 2 E5
West Tarbert Ag & B 43 L5
West Tarring W Susx 9 S11
West Thirston Nthumb 41 N2
West Thorney W Susx 9 M11
West Thorpe Notts 24 F5
West Thurrock Thurr 10 H2
West Tilbury Thurr 10 J2
West Tisted Hants 9 L7
West Torrington Lincs 33 N11
West Town Hants 9 M12
West Town N Som 14 J15
West Tytherley Hants 8 E7
West Walton Norfk 26 E6
West Walton Highway Norfk 26 E7
Westward Cumb 39 V11
Westward Ho! Devon 4 J6
Westwell Kent 11 N7
Westwell Oxon 15 U8
Westwell Leacon Kent 11 N7
West Wellow Hants 8 F8
West Wembury Devon 2 K8
West Wemyss Fife 45 S1
Westwick Cambs 26 D14
West Wickham Cambs 18 G5
West Wickham Gt Lon 10 E4
West Williamston Pembks 12 G9
West Winch Norfk 26 G6
West Winterslow Wilts 8 E6
West Wittering W Susx 9 N12
West Witton N York 36 C9
Westwood Devon 5 S11
Westwood Kent 11 U4
Westwood Wilts 7 P1
West Woodburn Nthumb 40 J4
West Woodhay W Berk 8 G1
Westwoodside N Linc 32 H8
West Worldham Hants 9 M6
West Worthing W Susx 9 S11
West Wratting Cambs 18 G5
Wetheral Cumb 40 C9
Wetherby Leeds 36 H15
Wetherden Suffk 19 M3
Wetheringsett Suffk 27 P14
Wethersfield Essex 18 H8
Wetherup Street Suffk 19 P3
Wetley Rocks Staffs 31 P16
Wettenhall Ches E 30 J14
Wetton Staffs 31 R15
Wetwang E R Yk 37 Q13
Wetwood Staffs 22 H3
Wexcombe Wilts 8 E2
Weybourne Norfk 27 P2
Weybourne Surrey 9 N4
Weybread Suffk 27 Q12
Weybread Street Suffk 27 R12
Weybridge Surrey 17 N16
Weycroft Devon 6 G11
Weydale Highld 58 F3
Weyhill Hants 8 F4
Weymouth Dorset 7 M14
Whaddon Bucks 16 J4
Whaddon Cambs 17 S2
Whaddon Gloucs 15 P8
Whaddon Wilts 8 D7
Whaddon Wilts 15 Q16
Whaley Derbys 32 D12
Whaley Bridge Derbys 31 Q11
Whaley Thorns Derbys 32 E12
Whaligoe Highld 58 H7
Whalley Lancs 31 L2
Whalton Nthumb 41 N5
Whaplode Lincs 25 R5
Whaplode Drove Lincs 25 R6
Wharf Warwks 16 D1
Wharfe N York 35 S12
Wharles Lancs 30 G2
Wharley End C Beds 17 L3
Wharncliffe Side Sheff 31 U8
Wharram-le-Street N York 37 P12
Wharton Herefs 22 D16
Whashton N York 36 D6
Whasset Cumb 35 N10
Whatcote Warwks 16 B3
Whateley Warwks 23 Q9
Whatfield Suffk 19 M6
Whatley Somset 6 H9
Whatley Somset 7 N3
Whatlington E Susx 10 K12
Whatton Notts 24 H2
Whauphill D & G 38 H10
Wheatacre Norfk 27 U10
Wheathampstead Herts 17 Q8
Wheatley Hants 9 N5
Wheatley Oxon 16 F9
Wheatley Hill Dur 41 R12
Wheatley Hills Donc 32 F7
Wheaton Aston Staffs 22 J7
Wheddon Cross Somset 5 R4
Wheelock Ches E 31 L14
Wheelton Lancs 30 J4
Wheldrake C York 37 M16
Whelford Gloucs 15 U10
Whelpley Hill Bucks 17 M9
Whempstead Herts 17 S6
Whenby N York 37 L12
Whepstead Suffk 18 K4
Wherstead Suffk 19 P7
Wherwell Hants 8 G5
Wheston Derbys 31 R11
Whetsted Kent 10 J7
Whetstone Leics 24 E9
Whicham Cumb 34 H10
Whichford Warwks 16 B4
Whickham Gatesd 41 P8
Whiddon Down Devon 5 N12
Whigstreet Angus 51 N8
Whilton Nhants 24 F14
Whimple Devon 6 C11
Whimpwell Green Norfk 27 S4
Whinburgh Norfk 27 M7
Whinnie Liggate D & G 39 M10
Whinnyfold Abers 55 U9
Whippingham IoW 8 J13
Whipsnade C Beds 17 M7
Whipton Devon 5 R12
Whisby Lincs 32 K13
Whissendine Rutlnd 24 J6
Whissonsett Norfk 27 L5
Whistlefield Ag & B 43 R1
Whistlefield Inn Ag & B 43 Q1
Whistley Green Wokham 16 J14
Whiston Knows 30 G9
Whiston Nhants 24 J15
Whiston Rothm 32 D9
Whiston Staffs 22 K6
Whiston Staffs 23 M1
Whitbeck Cumb 34 H9
Whitbourne Herefs 22 H16
Whitburn S Tyne 41 S8
Whitburn W Loth 45 L6
Whitby N York 37 Q5
Whitchester Border 46 K7
Whitchurch BaNES 15 L15
Whitchurch Bucks 16 J7
Whitchurch Cardif 14 D13
Whitchurch Devon 2 K4
Whitchurch Hants 8 H4
Whitchurch Herefs 14 K7
Whitchurch Oxon 16 G14
Whitchurch Pembks 12 C6
Whitchurch Shrops 22 E2
Whitchurch Canonicorum Dorset 6 H11
Whitchurch Hill Oxon 16 G13
Whitcombe Dorset 7 N13
Whitcot Shrops 21 R5
Whitcott Keysett Shrops 21 P7
Whiteacre Heath Warwks 23 P10
White Ball Somset 6 D8
Whitebridge Highld 53 P12
Whitebrook Mons 14 K9
Whitecairns Abers 55 S12
Whitechapel Gt Lon 17 S13
White Chapel Lancs 30 H1
Whitecliffe Gloucs 14 K8
White Colne Essex 18 K8
Whitecraig E Loth 46 D5
Whitecrook D & G 38 D9
White Cross Cnwll 1 R14
Whitecross Falk 45 M4
Whiteface Highld 57 R15
Whitefarland N Ayrs 43 L10
Whitefaulds S Ayrs 43 S15
Whitefield Bury 31 M7
Whitefield Somset 6 D6
Whiteford Abers 55 P10
Whitegate Ches W 30 J13
Whitehall Ork 58 d3
Whitehaven Cumb 34 F4
Whitehill and Bordon Hants 9 N6
Whitehills Abers 55 N4
Whitehouse Abers 55 M12
Whitehouse Ag & B 43 L6
Whitekirk E Loth 46 H3
White Lackington Dorset 7 N11
Whitelackington Somset 6 H8
White Ladies Aston Worcs 15 Q1
Whiteleaf Bucks 16 K9
Whiteley Hants 8 J10
Whiteley Bank IoW 8 J15
Whitemire Moray 54 C6
Whitemoor C Nott 24 E2
Whitemoor Cnwll 2 C6
Whiteness Shet 59 q6
White Notley Essex 18 J10
Whiteparish Wilts 8 E8
White Pit Lincs 33 S11
Whiterashes Abers 55 R11
White Roding Essex 18 F11
Whiterow Highld 58 J6
Whiterow Moray 54 D5
Whiteshill Gloucs 15 P9
Whitesmith E Susx 10 G13
Whitestaunton Somset 6 G9
Whitestone Cross Devon 5 Q12
White Waltham W & M 16 K14
Whitewell Lancs 35 Q15
Whitfield C Dund 51 N10
Whitfield Kent 11 T7
Whitfield Nhants 16 G3
Whitfield Nthumb 40 H9
Whitfield S Glos 15 M11
Whitford Devon 6 F11
Whitford Flints 29 Q5
Whitgift E R Yk 32 J4
Whitgreave Staffs 22 K4
Whithorn D & G 38 H12
Whiting Bay N Ayrs 43 P12
Whitkirk Leeds 32 B2
Whitland Carmth 12 J7
Whitlaw Border 46 G15
Whitletts S Ayrs 44 C13
Whitley N York 32 E4
Whitley Readg 16 H15
Whitley Sheff 32 B8
Whitley Wilts 15 Q15
Whitley Bay N Tyne 41 R7
Whitley Chapel Nthumb 40 K9
Whitley Lower Kirk 31 T5
Whitminster Gloucs 15 N9
Whitmore Staffs 22 J2
Whitnage Devon 5 S8
Whitnash Warwks 23 R15
Whitney-on-Wye Herefs 21 P12
Whitsbury Hants 8 C8
Whitsome Border 47 M8
Whitson Newpt 14 H13
Whitstable Kent 11 Q4
Whitstone Cnwll 4 G11
Whittingham Nthumb 47 P15
Whittingslow Shrops 21 R6
Whittington Derbys 32 C12
Whittington Gloucs 15 R6
Whittington Lancs 35 Q11
Whittington Norfk 26 H9
Whittington Shrops 29 T13
Whittington Staffs 22 J12
Whittington Staffs 23 P7
Whittington Warwks 23 R9
Whittington Worcs 15 Q1
Whittlebury Nhants 16 H3
Whittle-le-Woods Lancs 30 J4
Whittlesey Cambs 25 Q9
Whittlesford Cambs 18 E5
Whitton N Linc 32 K4
Whitton Nthumb 41 M2
Whitton Powys 21 P9
Whitton S on T 36 H3
Whitton Shrops 22 E13
Whittonstall Nthumb 41 M9
Whitway Hants 8 H2
Whitwell Derbys 32 E11
Whitwell Herts 17 Q7
Whitwell IoW 8 J15
Whitwell N York 36 F7
Whitwell Rutlnd 24 K7
Whitwell-on-the-Hill N York 37 M12
Whitwell Street Norfk 27 P5
Whitwick Leics 23 T6
Whitworth Lancs 31 N5
Whixall Shrops 22 E3
Whixley N York 36 H14
Whorlton Dur 36 D4
Whyle Herefs 22 E15
Whyteleafe Surrey 10 D5
Wibsey C Brad 31 S3
Wibtoft Warwks 24 D11
Wichenford Worcs 22 H15
Wichling Kent 11 M6
Wick Bmouth 8 D13
Wick Highld 58 J5
Wick S Glos 15 M14
Wick V Glam 13 U15
Wick W Susx 9 R11
Wick Worcs 15 R2
Wicken Cambs 26 F14
Wicken Nhants 16 H3
Wicken Bonhunt Essex 18 E8
Wickenby Lincs 33 N11
Wicken Green Village Norfk 26 K3
Wickersley Rothm 32 D9
Wicker Street Green Suffk 19 M6
Wickford Essex 18 J14
Wickham Hants 8 K10
Wickham W Berk 16 D15
Wickham Bishops Essex 18 K11
Wickhambreaux Kent 11 S5
Wickhambrook Suffk 18 J4
Wickhamford Worcs 15 S3
Wickham Green Suffk 27 N14
Wickham Market Suffk 19 R4
Wickhampton Norfk 27 T8
Wickham St Paul Essex 18 K7
Wickham Skeith Suffk 27 N14
Wickham Street Suffk 27 N14
Wick John o' Groats Airport Highld 58 J5
Wicklewood Norfk 27 N8
Wickmere Norfk 27 P3
Wick St Lawrence N Som 14 G16
Wickwar S Glos 15 M12
Widdington Essex 18 F8
Widdrington Nthumb 41 P3
Widdrington Station Nthumb 41 P3
Widecombe in the Moor Devon 3 N3
Widegates Cnwll 2 G6
Widemouth Bay Cnwll 4 F10
Wide Open N Tyne 41 P6
Widford Essex 18 H12
Widford Herts 18 D11
Widmer End Bucks 16 K11
Widmerpool Notts 24 F4
Widmore Gt Lon 10 E4
Widnes Halton 30 H10
Widworthy Devon 6 F11
Wigan Wigan 30 J7
Wigborough Somset 6 J8
Wiggaton Devon 6 D12
Wiggenhall St Germans Norfk 26 F6
Wiggenhall St Mary Magdalen Norfk 26 F7
Wiggenhall St Mary the Virgin Norfk 26 F6
Wigginton C York 37 L14
Wigginton Herts 17 L8
Wigginton Oxon 16 D4
Wigginton Staffs 23 P8
Wigglesworth N York 35 S14
Wiggonby Cumb 40 A10
Wighill N York 36 J15
Wighton Norfk 27 L2
Wightwick Wolves 22 J9
Wigley Hants 8 F9
Wigmore Herefs 21 R9
Wigmore Medway 11 L4
Wigsley Notts 32 J12
Wigsthorpe Nhants 25 M12
Wigston Leics 24 F9
Wigston Parva Leics 24 D10
Wigthorpe Notts 32 F10
Wigtoft Lincs 25 Q3
Wigton Cumb 39 U10
Wigtown D & G 38 H9
Wike Leeds 36 G16
Wilbarston Nhants 24 J11
Wilberfoss E R Yk 37 N15
Wilburton Cambs 26 E13
Wilby Nhants 24 J14
Wilby Norfk 27 N10
Wilby Suffk 27 Q13
Wilcot Wilts 15 T16
Wilcott Shrops 22 C6
Wildboarclough Ches E 31 P13
Wilden Bed 25 N16
Wilden Worcs 22 J13
Wildmanbridge S Lans 44 K8
Wildmoor Worcs 23 L13
Wildsworth Lincs 32 J8
Wilkesley Ches E 22 F2
Wilkhaven Highld 58 C16
Wilkieston W Loth 45 P5
Willand Devon 5 S9
Willaston Ches E 30 K15
Willaston Ches W 30 E11
Willen M Keyn 16 K3
Willenhall Covtry 23 R13
Willenhall Wsall 23 L9
Willerby E R Yk 33 M3
Willerby N York 37 R10
Willersey Gloucs 15 T3
Willersley Herefs 21 Q12
Willesborough Kent 11 P8
Willesborough Lees Kent 11 P8
Willesden Gt Lon 17 Q12
Willesley Wilts 15 P12
Willett Somset 6 D5
Willey Shrops 22 G9
Willey Warwks 24 D11
Willey Green Surrey 9 Q3
Williamscot Oxon 16 E2
Willian Herts 17 Q5
Willingale Essex 18 F12
Willingdon E Susx 10 H14
Willingham Cambs 25 S14
Willingham by Stow Lincs 32 K10
Willington Bed 17 P2
Willington Derbys 23 R4
Willington Dur 41 P13
Willington Kent 10 K6
Willington Warwks 16 B4
Willington Quay N Tyne 41 Q7
Willitoft E R Yk 32 H2
Williton Somset 6 D4
Willoughby Lincs 33 T12
Willoughby Warwks 24 E14
Willoughby-on-the-Wolds Notts 24 F5
Willoughby Waterleys Leics 24 E10
Willoughton Lincs 32 K9
Willows Green Essex 18 H10
Willtown Somset 6 H7
Wilmcote Warwks 23 P16
Wilmington Devon 6 F11
Wilmington E Susx 10 G14
Wilmington Kent 10 G3
Wilmslow Ches E 31 M11
Wilpshire Lancs 30 K2
Wilsden C Brad 31 R2
Wilsford Lincs 25 L2
Wilsford Wilts 8 C2
Wilsford Wilts 8 C5
Wilshaw Kirk 31 R6
Wilsill N York 36 E13
Wilson Leics 23 S5
Wilsontown S Lans 45 L8
Wilstead Bed 17 N3
Wilsthorpe Lincs 25 N6
Wilstone Herts 17 L8
Wilton Herefs 14 K6
Wilton N York 37 P10
Wilton R & Cl 36 K3
Wilton Wilts 8 C6
Wilton Wilts 8 E1
Wilton Dean Border 46 F14
Wimbish Green Essex 18 G7
Wimbledon Gt Lon 10 C3
Wimblington Cambs 25 S10
Wimboldsley Ches W 30 K14
Wimborne Minster Dorset 7 S11
Wimborne St Giles Dorset 7 S9
Wimbotsham Norfk 26 G8
Wimpole Cambs 17 S2
Wimpstone Warwks 15 U2
Wincanton Somset 7 N6
Winchburgh W Loth 45 N4
Winchcombe Gloucs 15 S5
Winchelsea E Susx 11 M12
Winchester Hants 8 H7
Winchet Hill Kent 10 K8
Winchfield Hants 9 M3
Winchmore Hill Bucks 17 L11
Winchmore Hill Gt Lon 17 R11
Wincle Ches E 31 P13
Wincobank Sheff 32 C9
Windermere Cumb 35 M7
Winderton Warwks 16 C3
Windhill Highld 53 Q7
Windlesham Surrey 17 L16
Windmill Cnwll 1 U5
Windmill Hill E Susx 10 J13
Windmill Hill Somset 6 G8
Windrush Gloucs 15 U8
Windsole Abers 55 M5
Windsor W & M 17 L14
Windsoredge Gloucs 15 P10
Windsor Green Suffk 19 L4
Windy Arbour Warwks 23 R13
Windygates Fife 51 L16
Wineham W Susx 10 C12
Winestead E R Yk 33 Q4
Winfarthing Norfk 27 P11
Winford IoW 8 J14
Winford N Som 14 K16
Winforton Herefs 21 P12
Winfrith Newburgh Dorset 7 P13
Wing Bucks 16 K6
Wing Rutlnd 24 K8
Wingate Dur 41 R12
Wingerworth Derbys 32 C13
Wingfield C Beds 17 M6
Wingfield Suffk 27 Q12
Wingfield Wilts 7 P1
Wingham Kent 11 S5
Wingrave Bucks 16 K7
Winkburn Notts 32 G14
Winkfield Br For 17 L15
Winkfield Row Br For 17 L15
Winkhill Staffs 31 Q16
Winkleigh Devon 5 M9
Winksley N York 36 F11
Winlaton Gatesd 41 N8
Winless Highld 58 H5
Winmarleigh Lancs 35 N15
Winnall Hants 8 H7
Winnersh Wokham 16 J15
Winnington Ches W 30 K12
Winscombe N Som 6 J1
Winsford Ches W 30 K13
Winsford Somset 5 R5
Winsham Somset 6 H10
Winshill Staffs 23 Q5
Winshwen Swans 13 R11
Winskill Cumb 40 E13
Winsley Wilts 15 N16
Winslow Bucks 16 J5
Winson Gloucs 15 T9
Winsor Hants 8 F9
Winster Cumb 35 M8
Winster Derbys 31 T14
Winston Dur 36 D4
Winston Suffk 19 Q3
Winstone Gloucs 15 R8
Winswell Devon 4 K8
Winterborne Came Dorset 7 N13
Winterborne Clenston Dorset 7 Q10
Winterborne Houghton Dorset 7 P10
Winterborne Kingston Dorset 7 Q11
Winterborne Monkton Dorset 7 M13
Winterborne Stickland Dorset 7 Q10
Winterborne Whitechurch Dorset 7 Q11
Winterborne Zelston Dorset 7 Q11
Winterbourne S Glos 15 L13
Winterbourne W Berk 16 D14
Winterbourne Abbas Dorset 7 L12
Winterbourne Bassett Wilts 15 T14
Winterbourne Dauntsey Wilts 8 D6
Winterbourne Earls Wilts 8 D6

EXCLUSIVE AA ALL–WEATHER CAR KIT
Half-price offer with this atlas

(Kit includes: Warning Triangle, High Visibility Vest, Tow Rope, Booster Cables, Snow & Ice Grips, Emergency Foil Blanket, Pack of 4 Ponchos, 3–Piece Torch Set, Picnic Blanket, Sunblinds, Canvas Carry Bag)

Only £45.00* (£90.00 RRP) Includes FREE P&P**

How To Purchase:
Visit **theAA.com/shop/AllWeather** add the kit to your shopping basket, then enter the promotional code: **ALLWEATHER** to receive your discount.

RRP: £9.99

RRP: £7.99

RRP: £9.99

RRP: £16.99

RRP: £6.99

RRP: £1.99

RRP: £4.99

RRP: £12.99

RRP: £2.99

Note: 3–Piece Headtorch Set not shown, RRP: £19.99

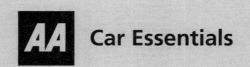
AA Car Essentials